SOUL EATER 15

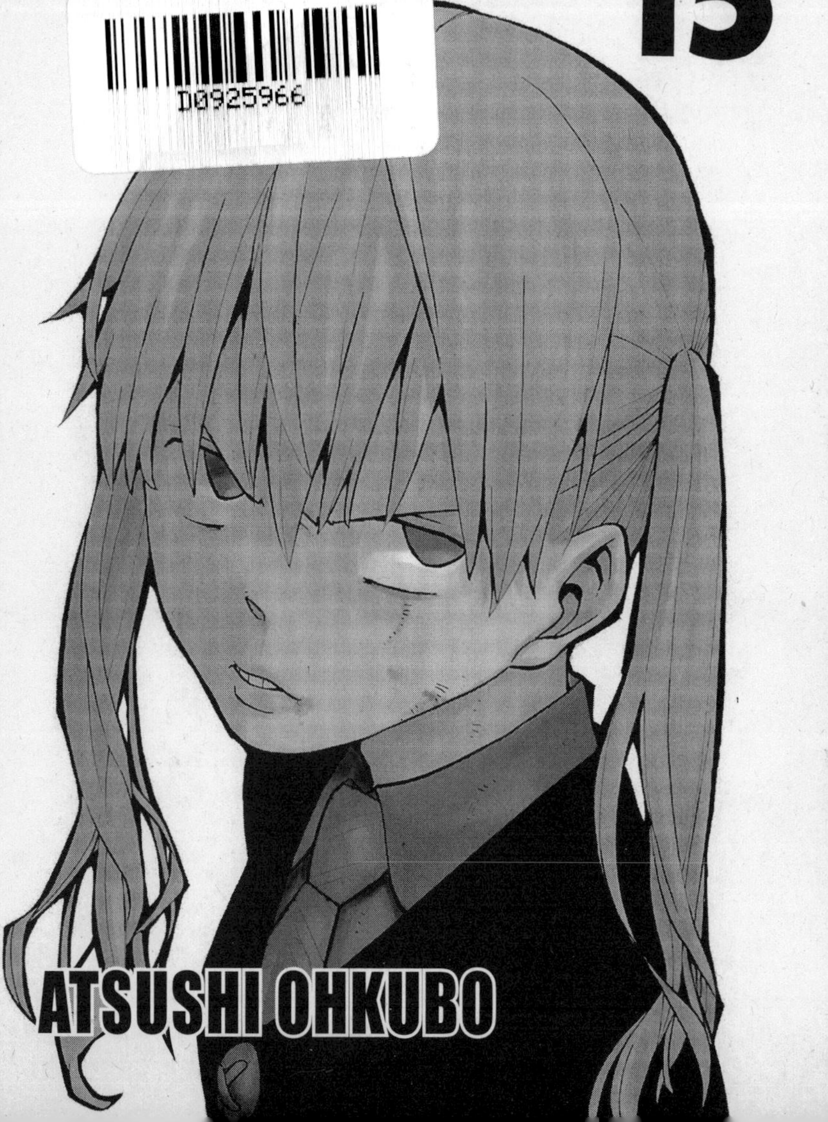

ATSUSHI OHKUBO

SOUL EATER

vol. 15
by ATSUSHI OHKUBO

I will get your SOUL

SOUL EATER 15

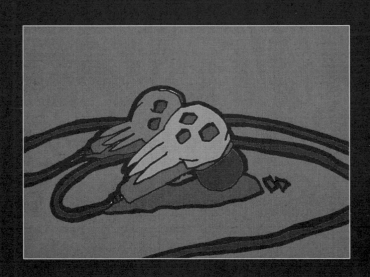

CONTENTS

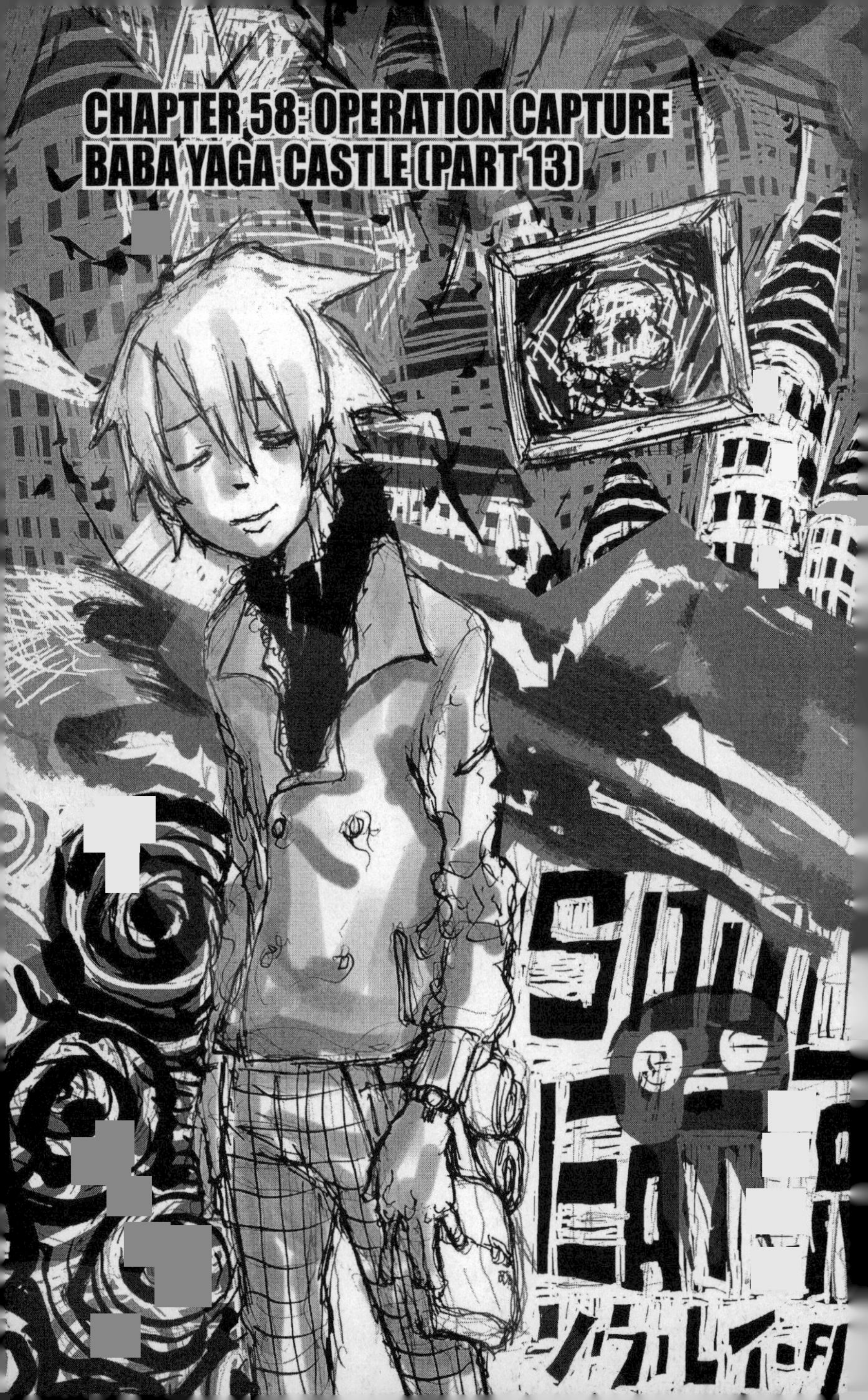
CHAPTER 58: OPERATION CAPTURE
BABA YAGA CASTLE (PART 13)

SOUL EATER

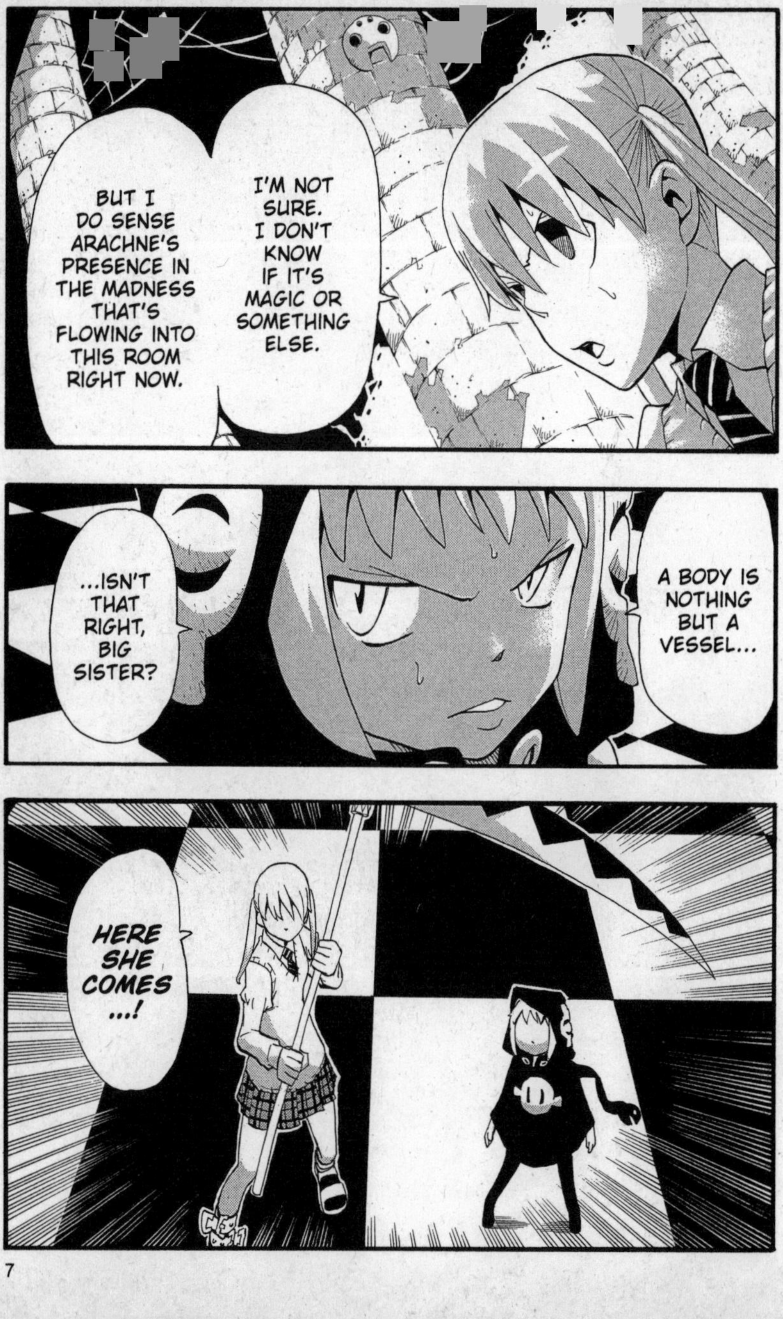
I'M NOT SURE. I DON'T KNOW IF IT'S MAGIC OR SOMETHING ELSE.
BUT I DO SENSE ARACHNE'S PRESENCE IN THE MADNESS THAT'S FLOWING INTO THIS ROOM RIGHT NOW.
A BODY IS NOTHING BUT A VESSEL...
...ISN'T THAT RIGHT, BIG SISTER?
HERE SHE COMES ...!

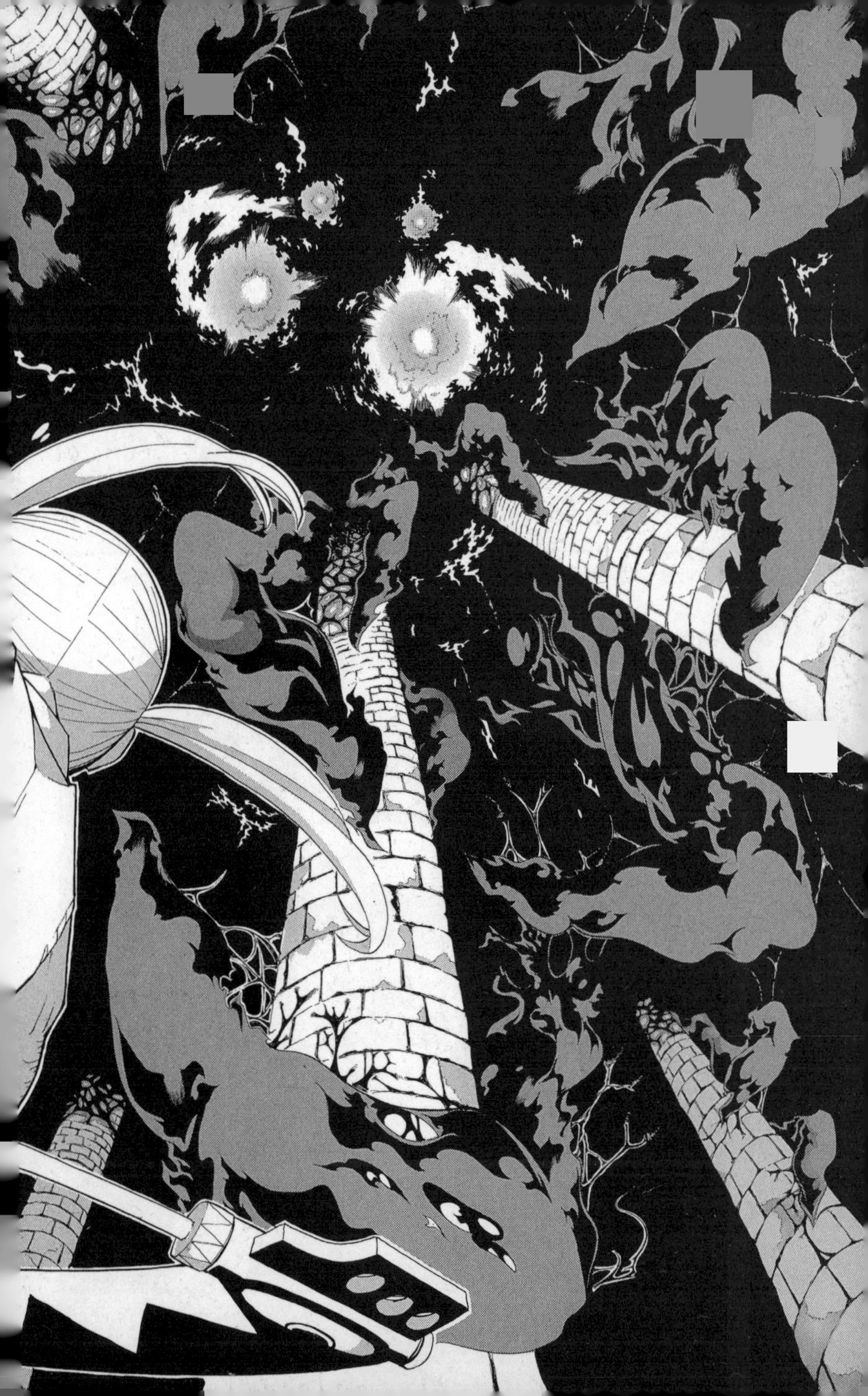

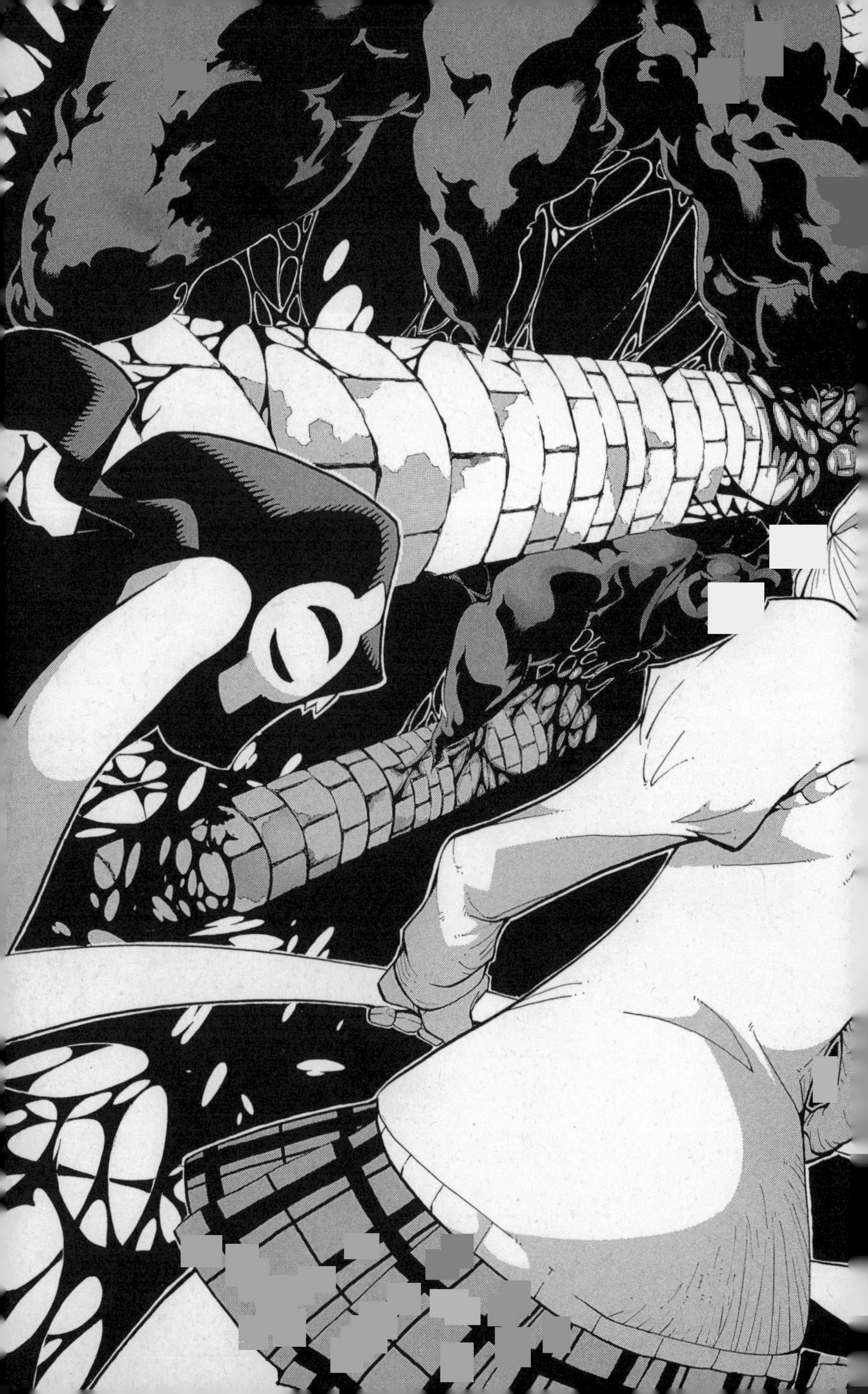

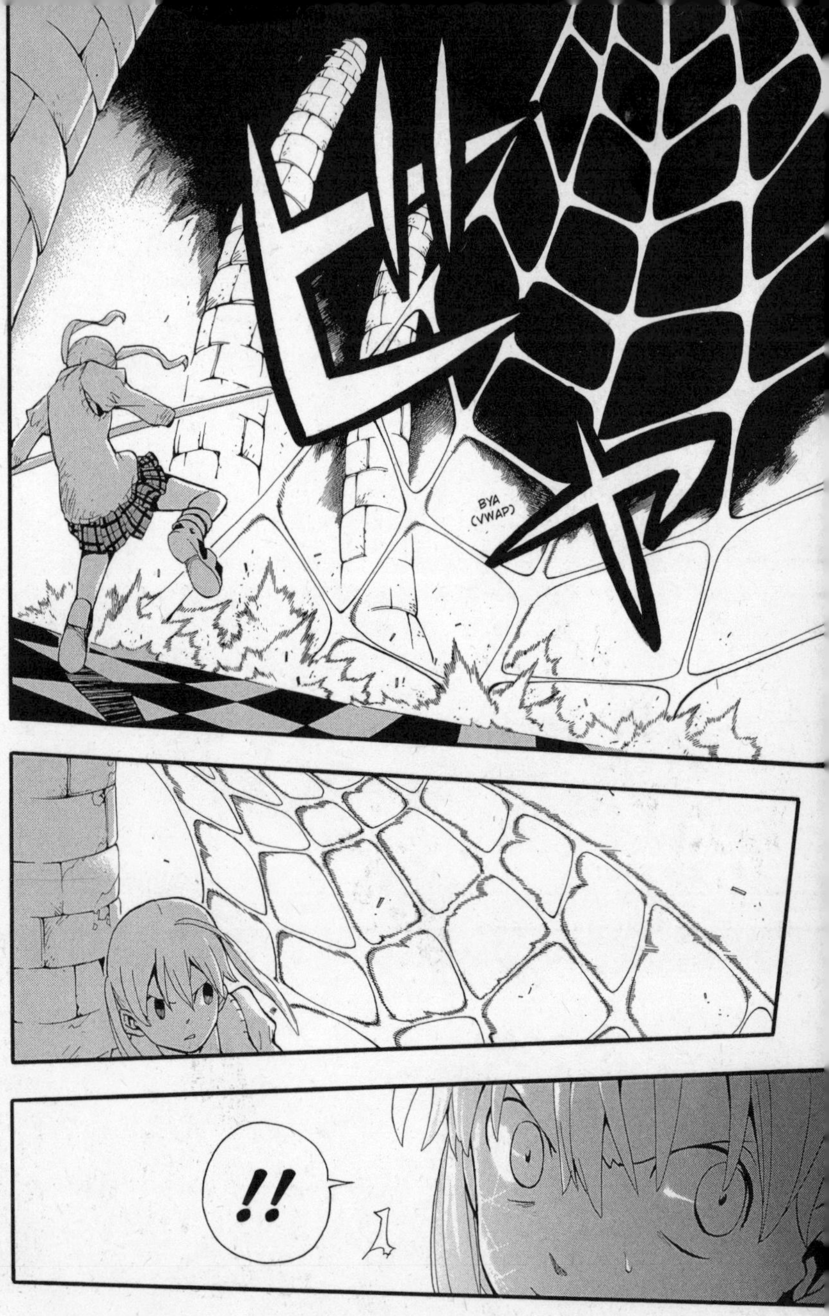
BYA
(VWAP)
!!

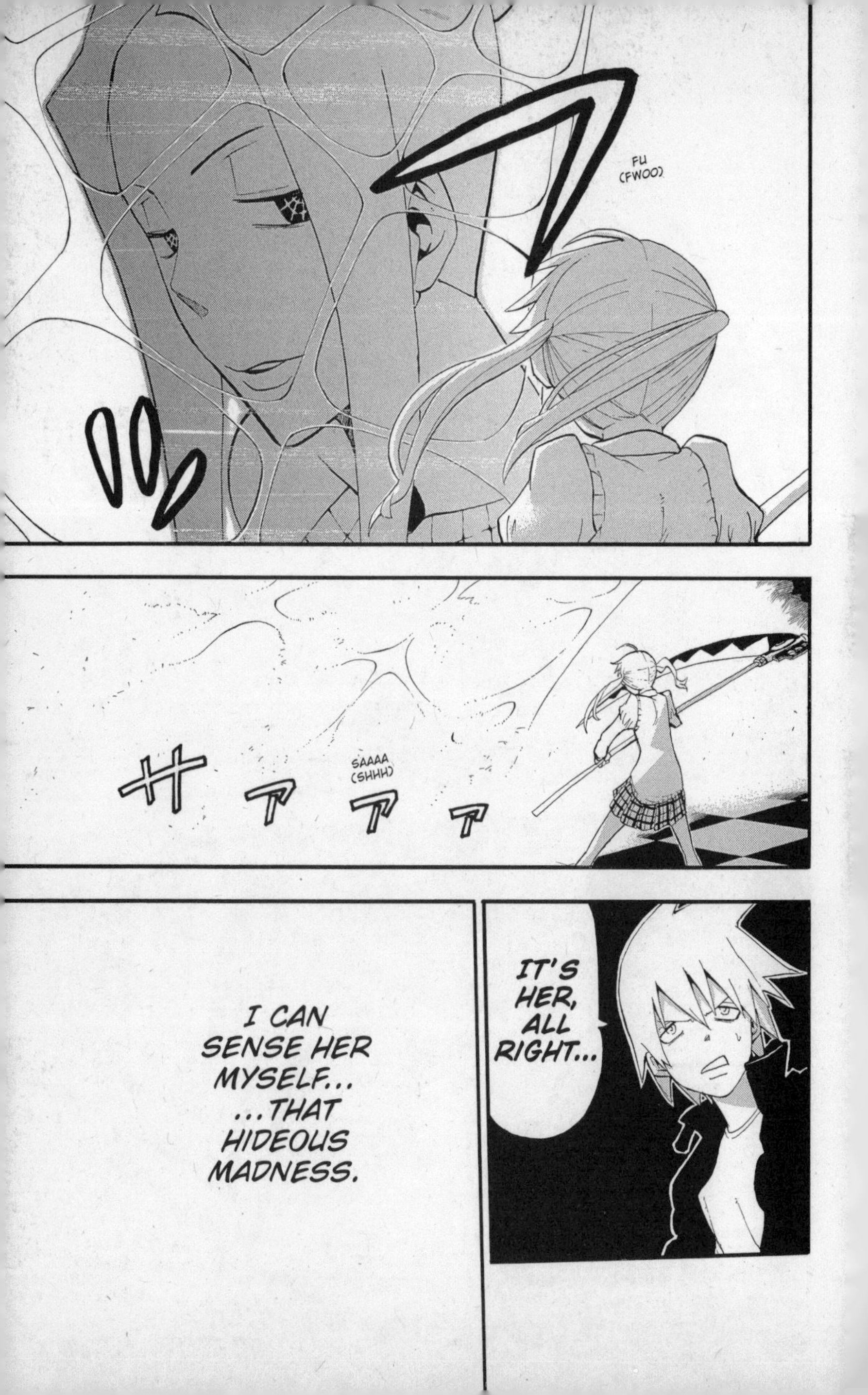
FU (FWOO)
SAAAA (SHHH)
IT'S HER, ALL RIGHT...
I CAN SENSE HER MYSELF... ...THAT HIDEOUS MADNESS.

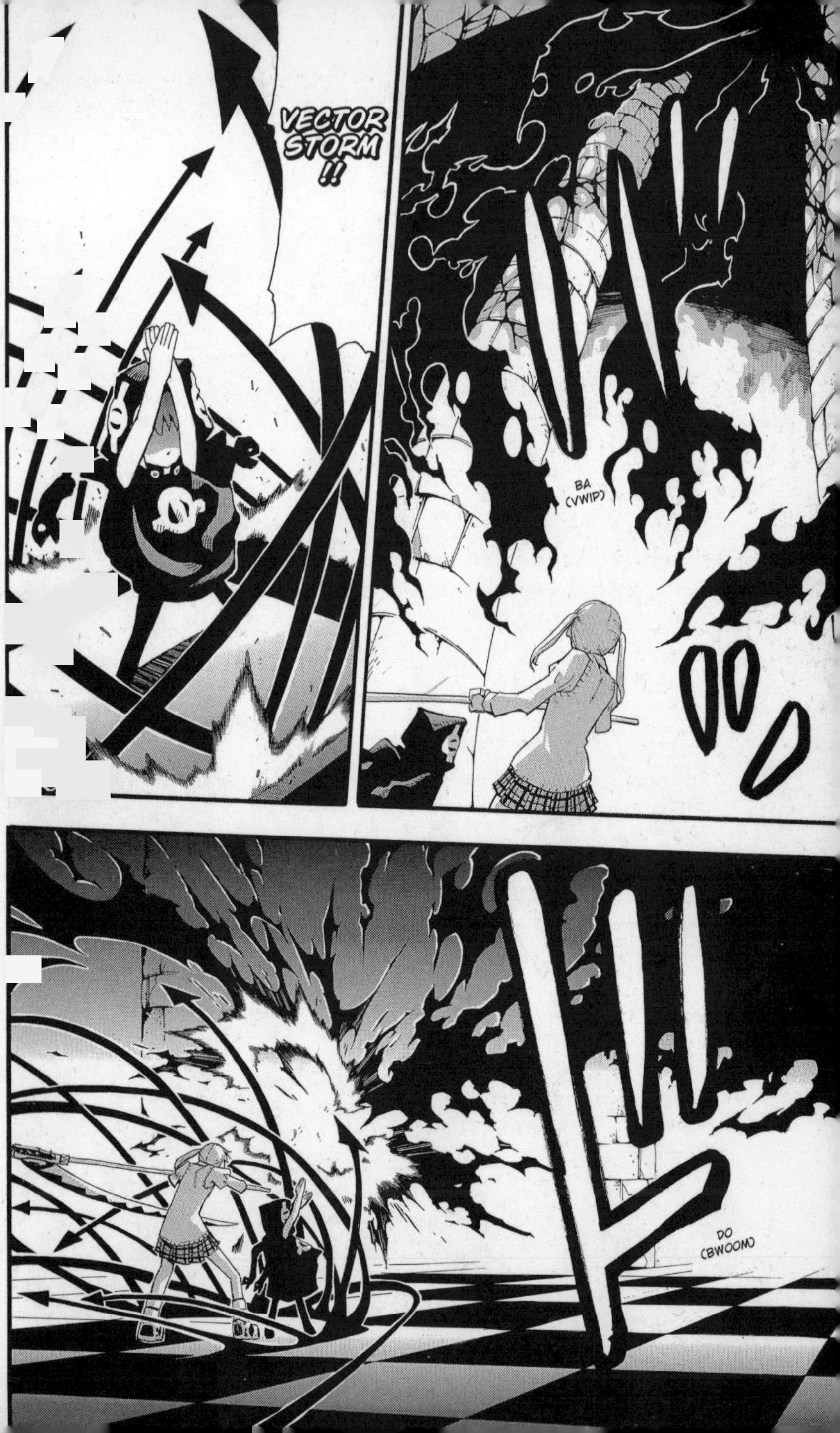
BA
(VWIP)
VECTOR STORM!!
DO
(BWOOM)

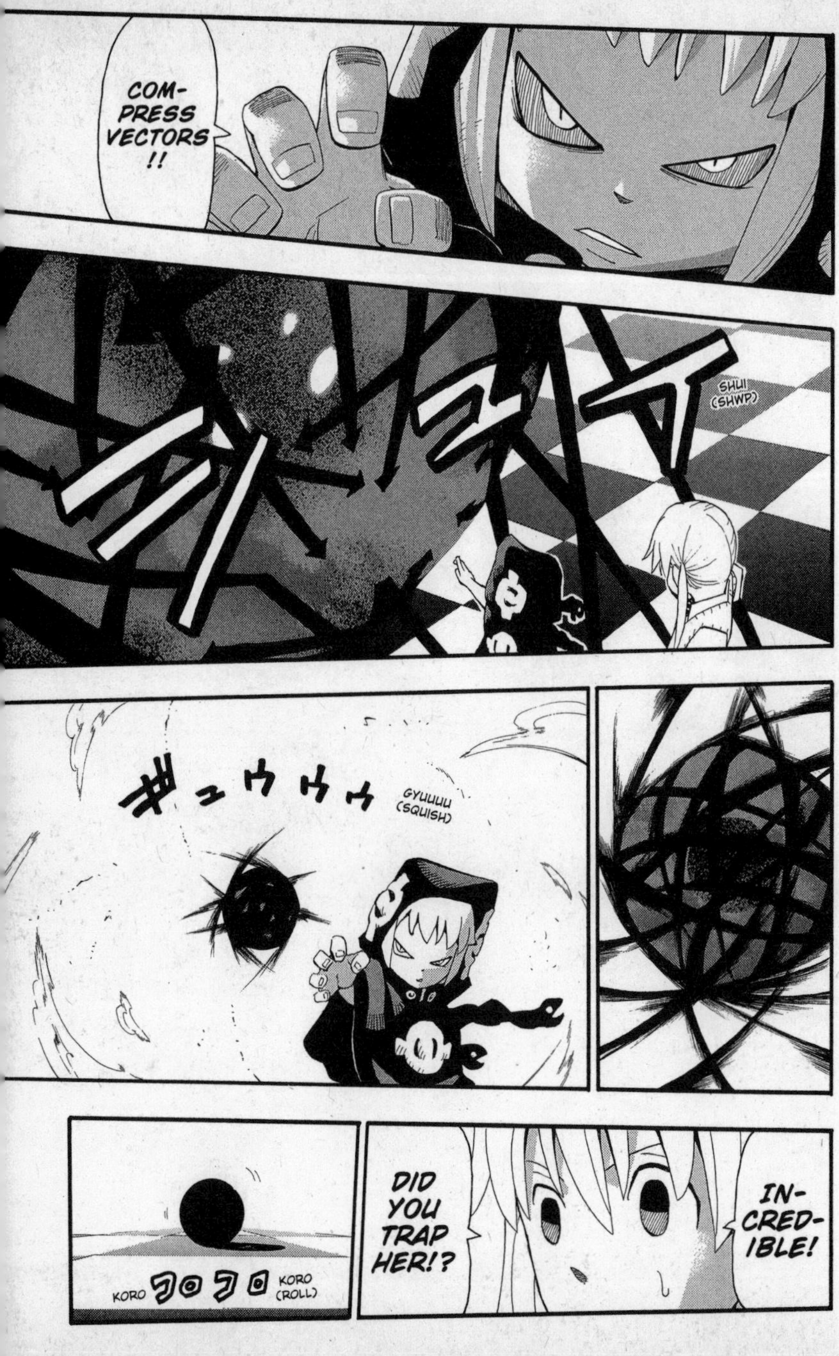
COM-PRESS VECTORS!!
SHUI (SHWP)
ギュウウウ
GYUUUU (SQUISH)
IN-CRED-IBLE!
DID YOU TRAP HER!?
コロコロ
KORO KORO (ROLL)

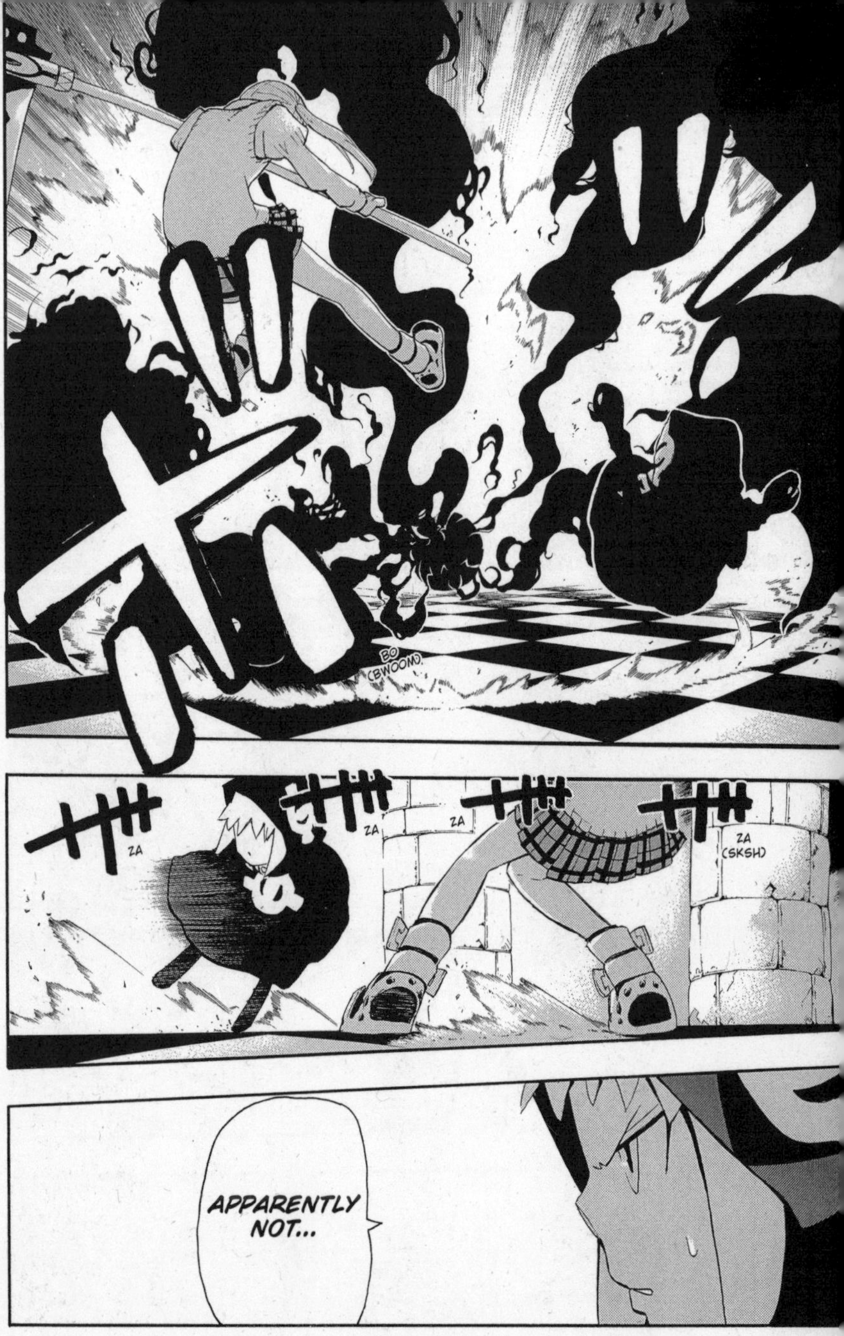
BO
(BWOOM)
ZA
(SKSH)
ZA
ZA
ZA
APPARENTLY NOT...

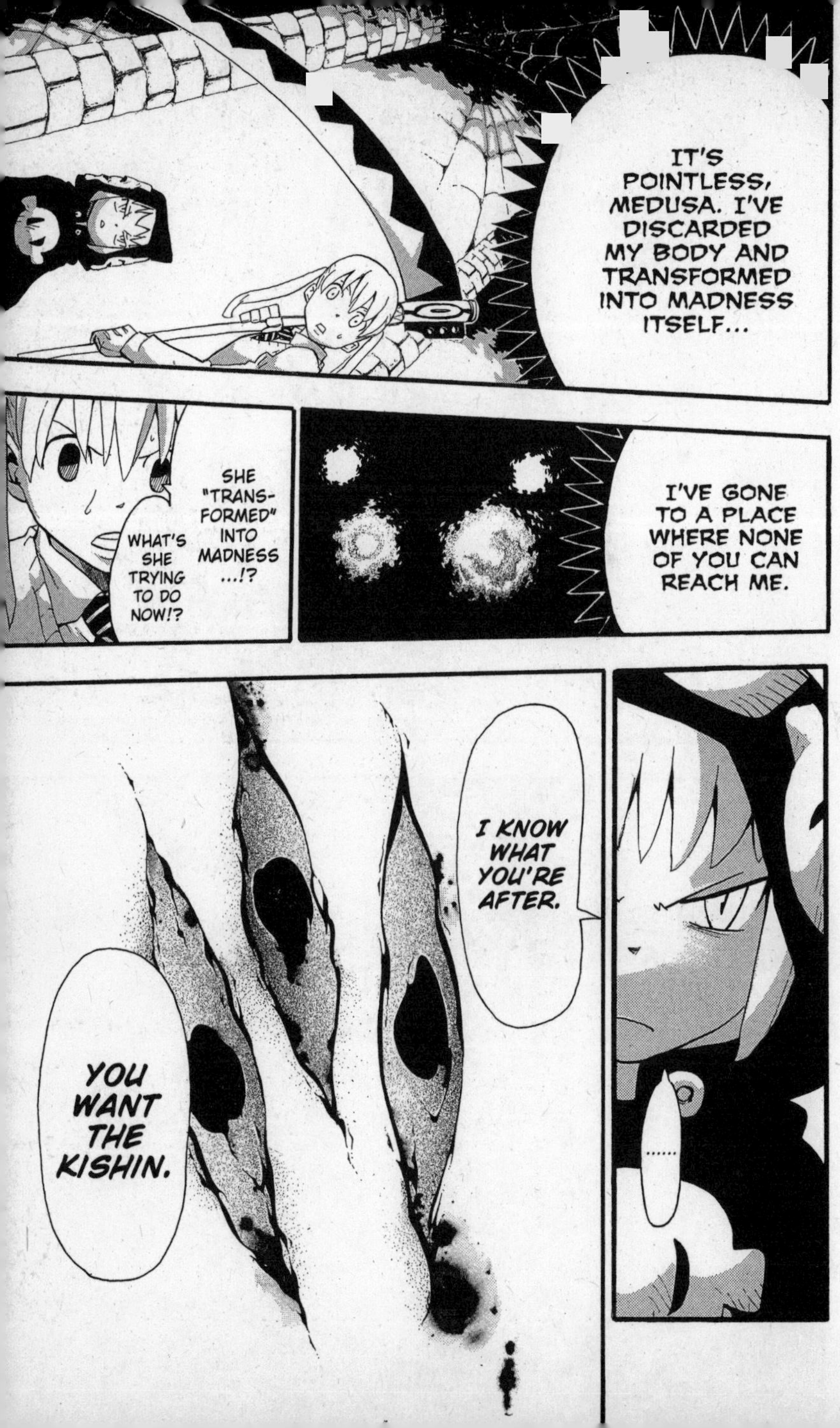
IT'S POINTLESS, MEDUSA. I'VE DISCARDED MY BODY AND TRANSFORMED INTO MADNESS ITSELF...
I'VE GONE TO A PLACE WHERE NONE OF YOU CAN REACH ME.
SHE "TRANS-FORMED" INTO MADNESS ...!?
WHAT'S SHE TRYING TO DO NOW!?
......
I KNOW WHAT YOU'RE AFTER.
YOU WANT THE KISHIN.

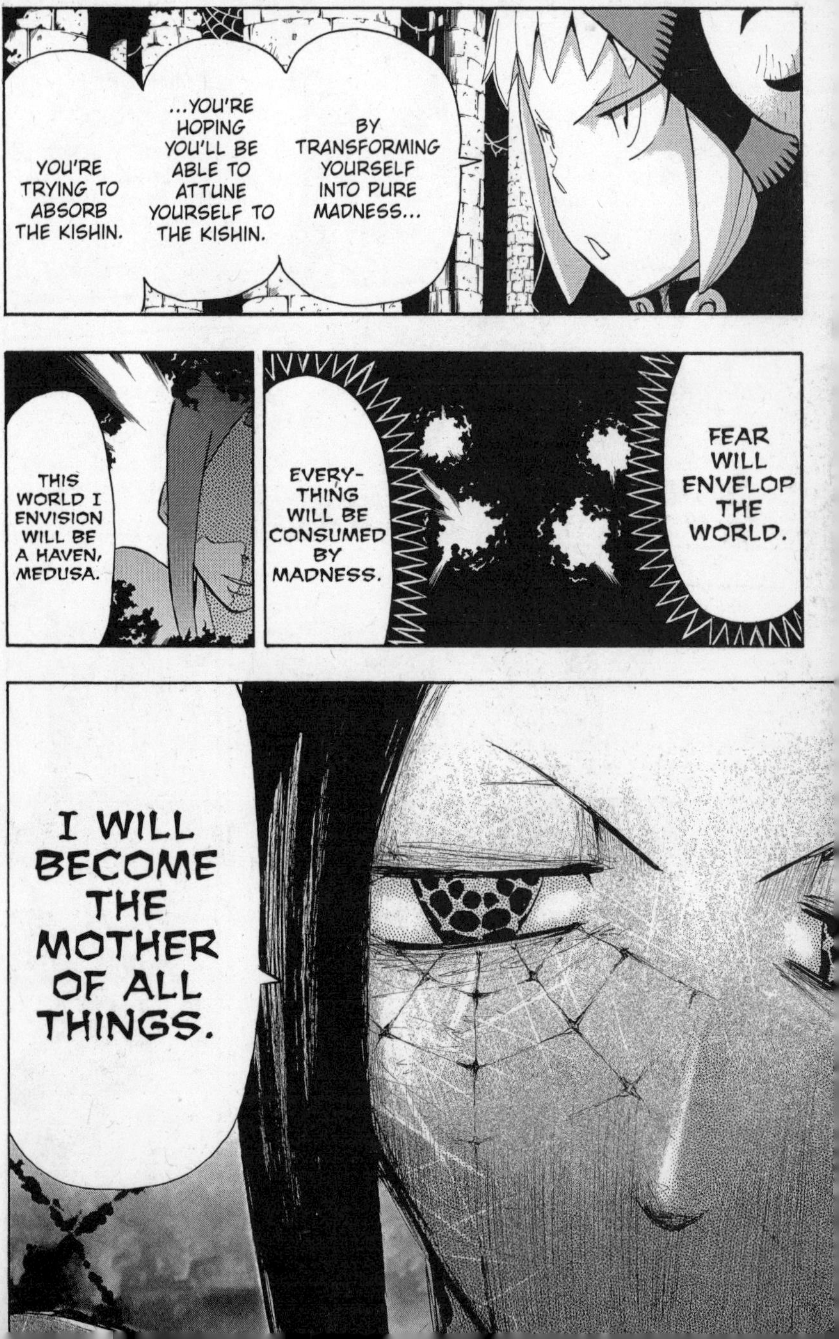
BY TRANSFORMING YOURSELF INTO PURE MADNESS...
...YOU'RE HOPING YOU'LL BE ABLE TO ATTUNE YOURSELF TO THE KISHIN.
YOU'RE TRYING TO ABSORB THE KISHIN.
FEAR WILL ENVELOP THE WORLD.
EVERY-THING WILL BE CONSUMED BY MADNESS.
THIS WORLD I ENVISION WILL BE A HAVEN, MEDUSA.
I WILL BECOME THE MOTHER OF ALL THINGS.

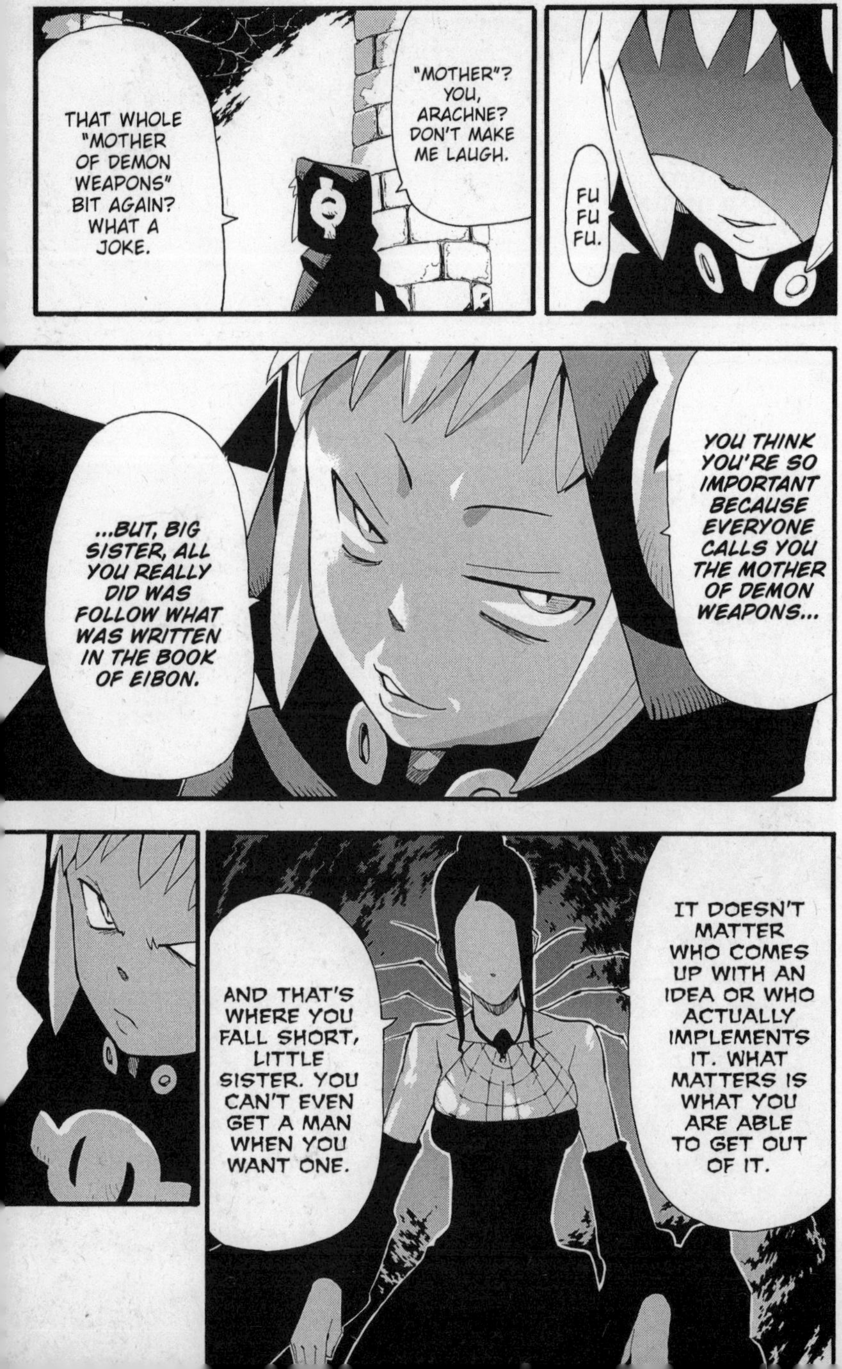
FU FU FU.
"MOTHER"? YOU, ARACHNE? DON'T MAKE ME LAUGH.
THAT WHOLE "MOTHER OF DEMON WEAPONS" BIT AGAIN? WHAT A JOKE.
YOU THINK YOU'RE SO IMPORTANT BECAUSE EVERYONE CALLS YOU THE MOTHER OF DEMON WEAPONS...
...BUT, BIG SISTER, ALL YOU REALLY DID WAS FOLLOW WHAT WAS WRITTEN IN THE BOOK OF EIBON.
IT DOESN'T MATTER WHO COMES UP WITH AN IDEA OR WHO ACTUALLY IMPLEMENTS IT. WHAT MATTERS IS WHAT YOU ARE ABLE TO GET OUT OF IT.
AND THAT'S WHERE YOU FALL SHORT, LITTLE SISTER. YOU CAN'T EVEN GET A MAN WHEN YOU WANT ONE.

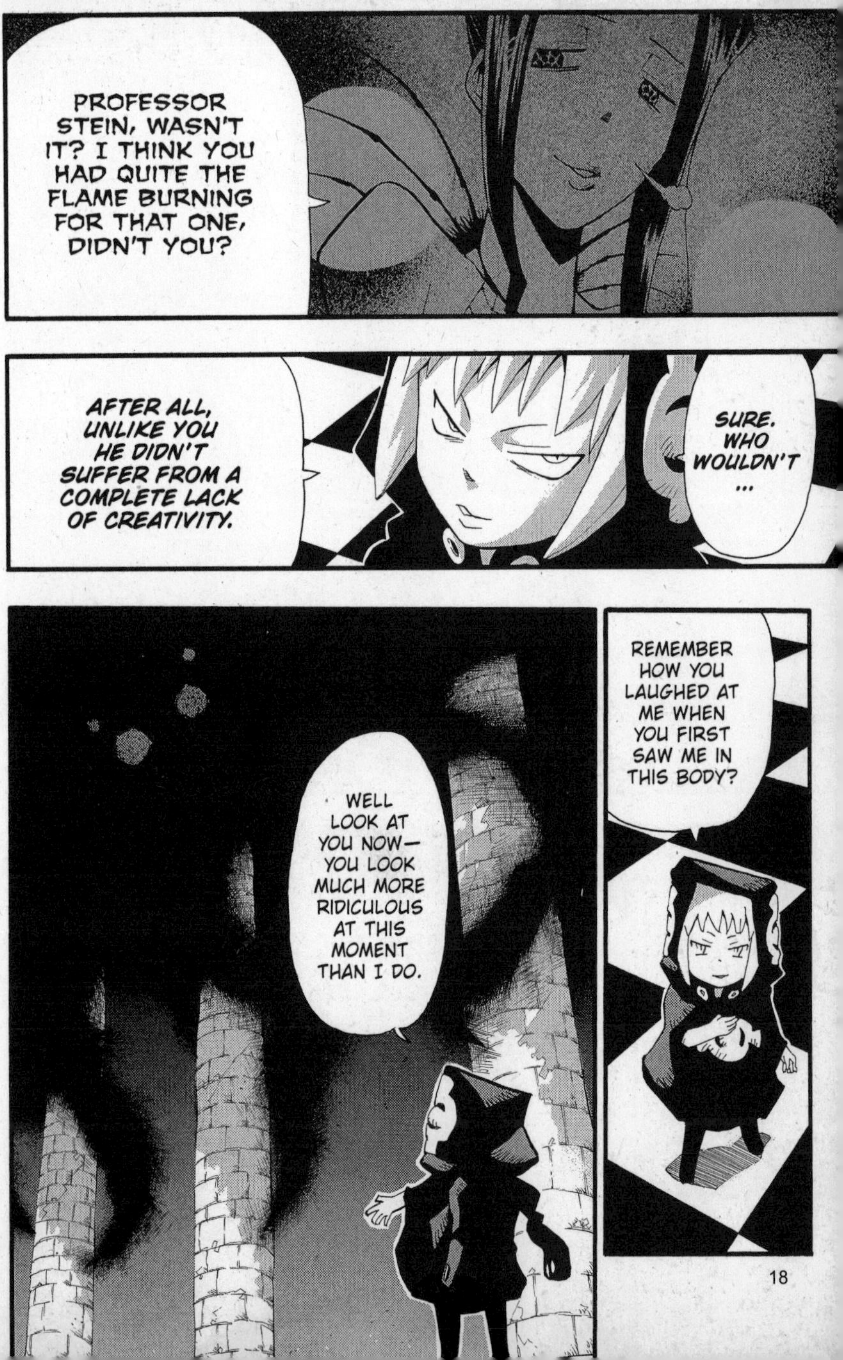
PROFESSOR STEIN, WASN'T IT? I THINK YOU HAD QUITE THE FLAME BURNING FOR THAT ONE, DIDN'T YOU?
SURE. WHO WOULDN'T ...
AFTER ALL, UNLIKE YOU HE DIDN'T SUFFER FROM A COMPLETE LACK OF CREATIVITY.
REMEMBER HOW YOU LAUGHED AT ME WHEN YOU FIRST SAW ME IN THIS BODY?
WELL LOOK AT YOU NOW— YOU LOOK MUCH MORE RIDICULOUS AT THIS MOMENT THAN I DO.

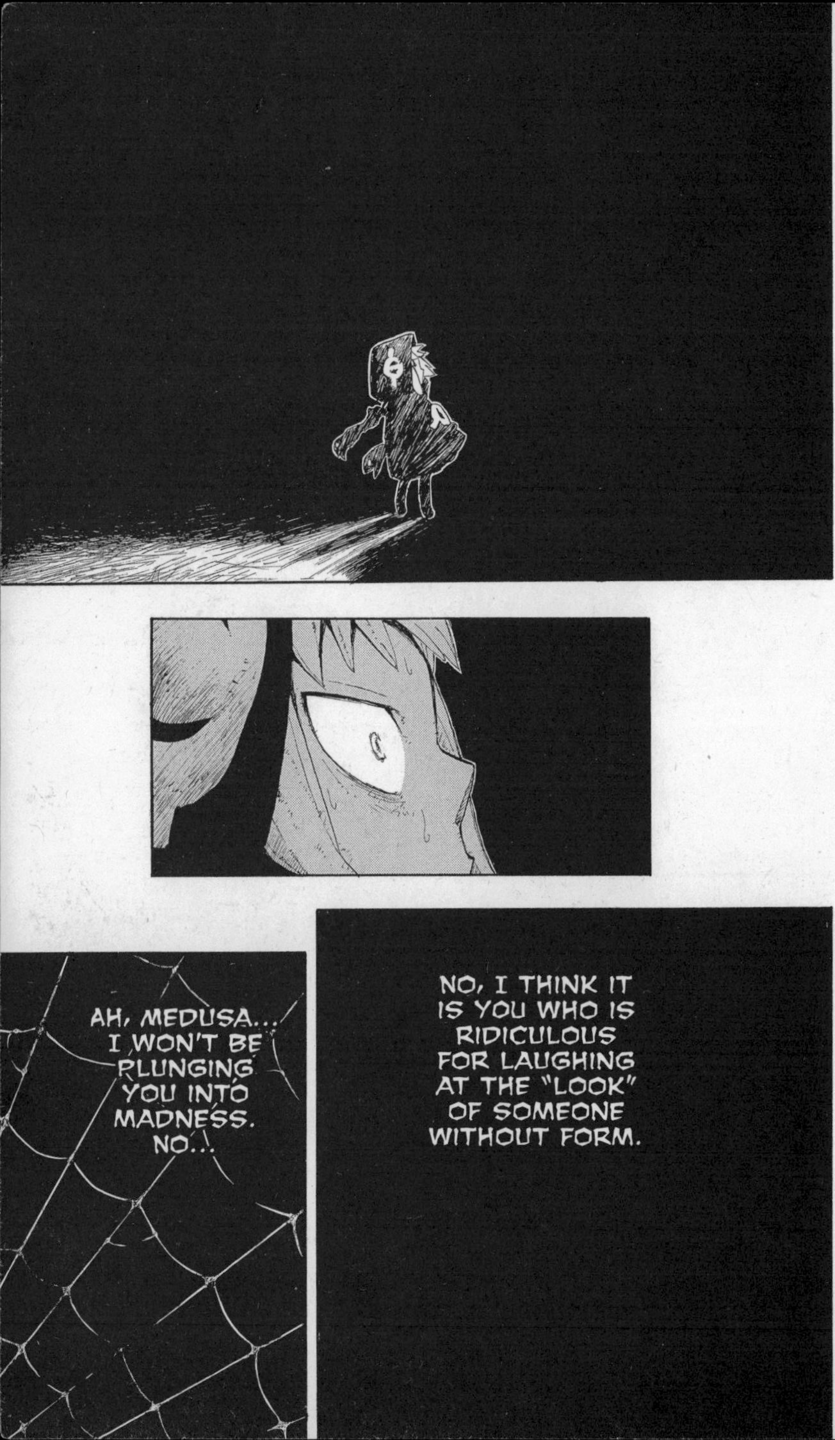
NO, I THINK IT IS YOU WHO IS RIDICULOUS FOR LAUGHING AT THE "LOOK" OF SOMEONE WITHOUT FORM.
AH, MEDUSA... I WON'T BE PLUNGING YOU INTO MADNESS. NO...

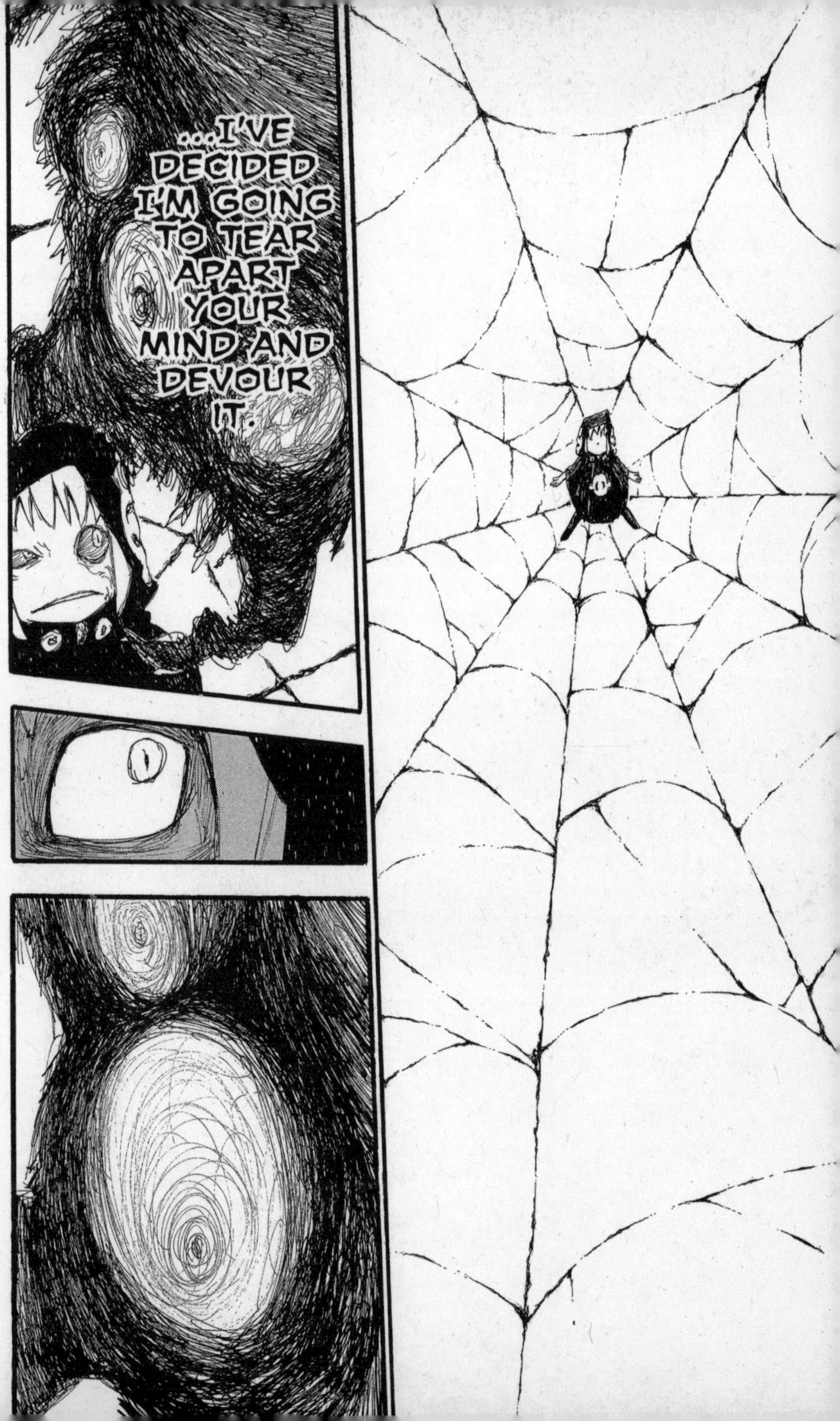
...I'VE DECIDED I'M GOING TO TEAR APART YOUR MIND AND DEVOUR IT.

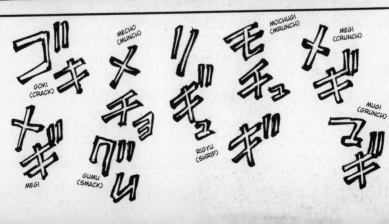

GOKI
(CRACK)

MECHO
(MUNCH)

MOCHUGI
(MRUNCH)

MEGI
(CRUNCH)

MUGI
(GRUNCH)

MEGI

RIGYU
(SHRIP)

GUMU
(SMACK)

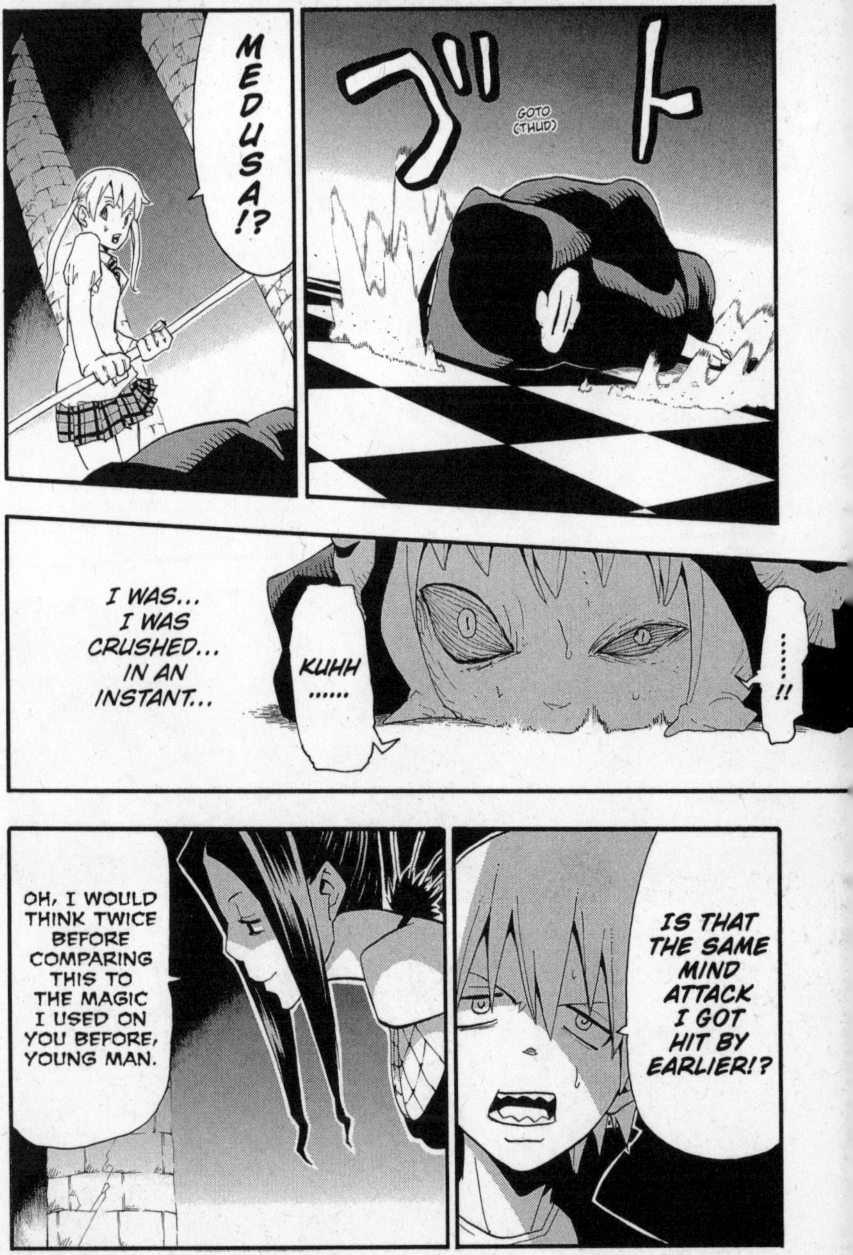
ゴト
GOTO (THUD)
MEDUSA!?
......!!
KUHH ......
I WAS... I WAS CRUSHED... IN AN INSTANT...
IS THAT THE SAME MIND ATTACK I GOT HIT BY EARLIER!?
OH, I WOULD THINK TWICE BEFORE COMPARING THIS TO THE MAGIC I USED ON YOU BEFORE, YOUNG MAN.

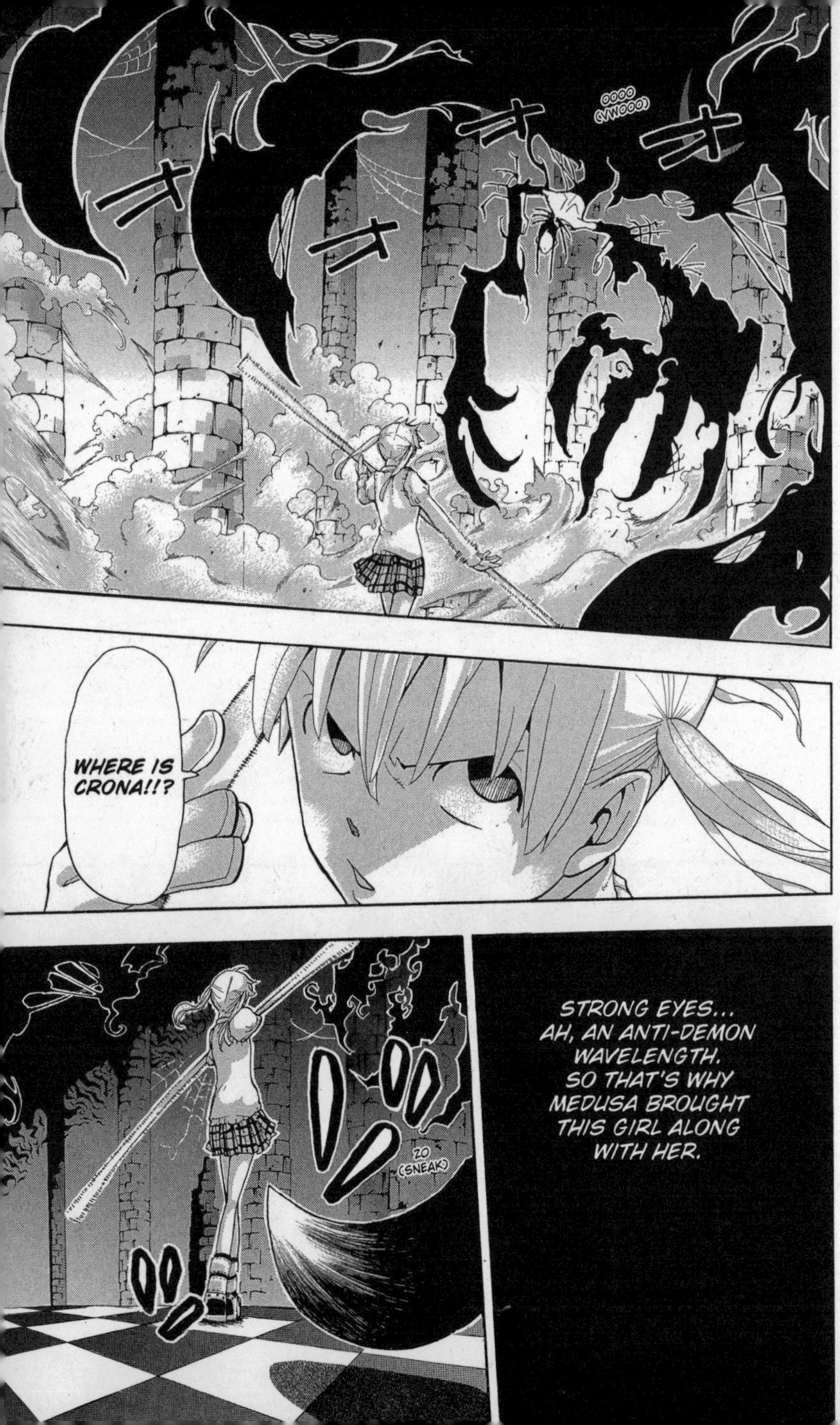
OOOO
(VWOOO)
WHERE IS CRONA!!?
STRONG EYES... AH, AN ANTI-DEMON WAVELENGTH. SO THAT'S WHY MEDUSA BROUGHT THIS GIRL ALONG WITH HER.
ZO
(SNEAK)

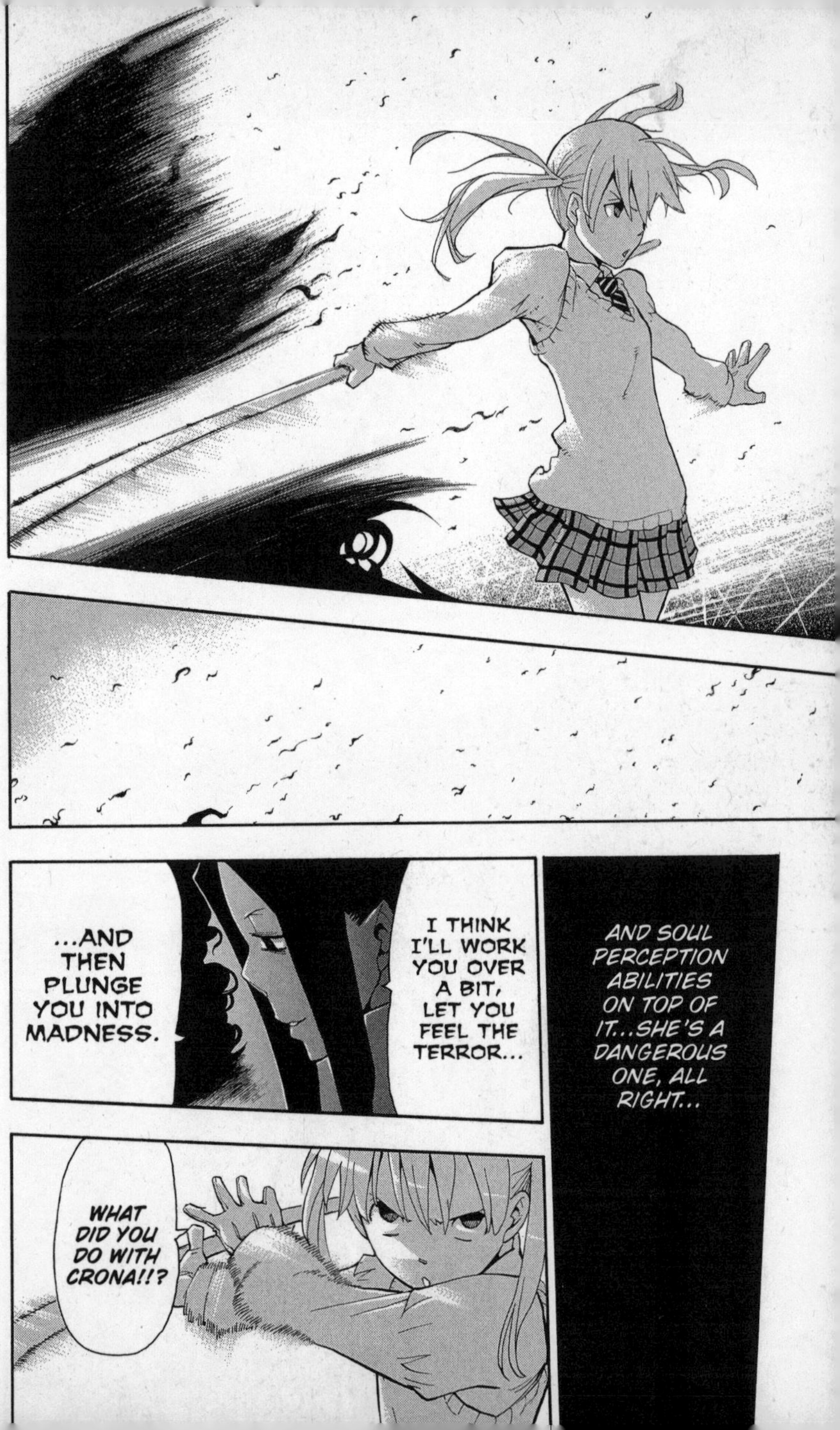
AND SOUL PERCEPTION ABILITIES ON TOP OF IT...SHE'S A DANGEROUS ONE, ALL RIGHT...
I THINK I'LL WORK YOU OVER A BIT, LET YOU FEEL THE TERROR...
...AND THEN PLUNGE YOU INTO MADNESS.
WHAT DID YOU DO WITH CRONA!!?

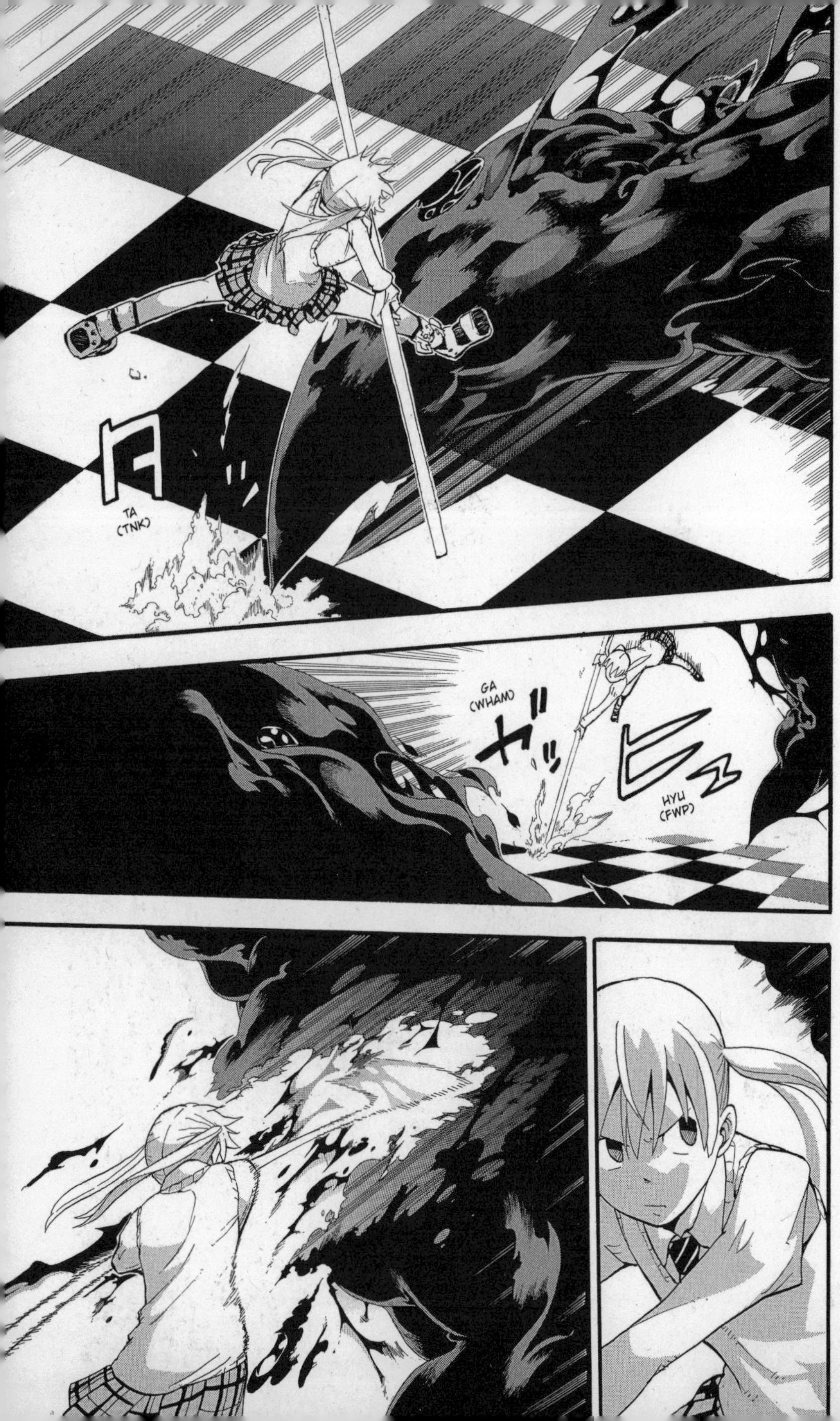

TA
(TNK)
HYU
(FWP)
GA
(WHAM)

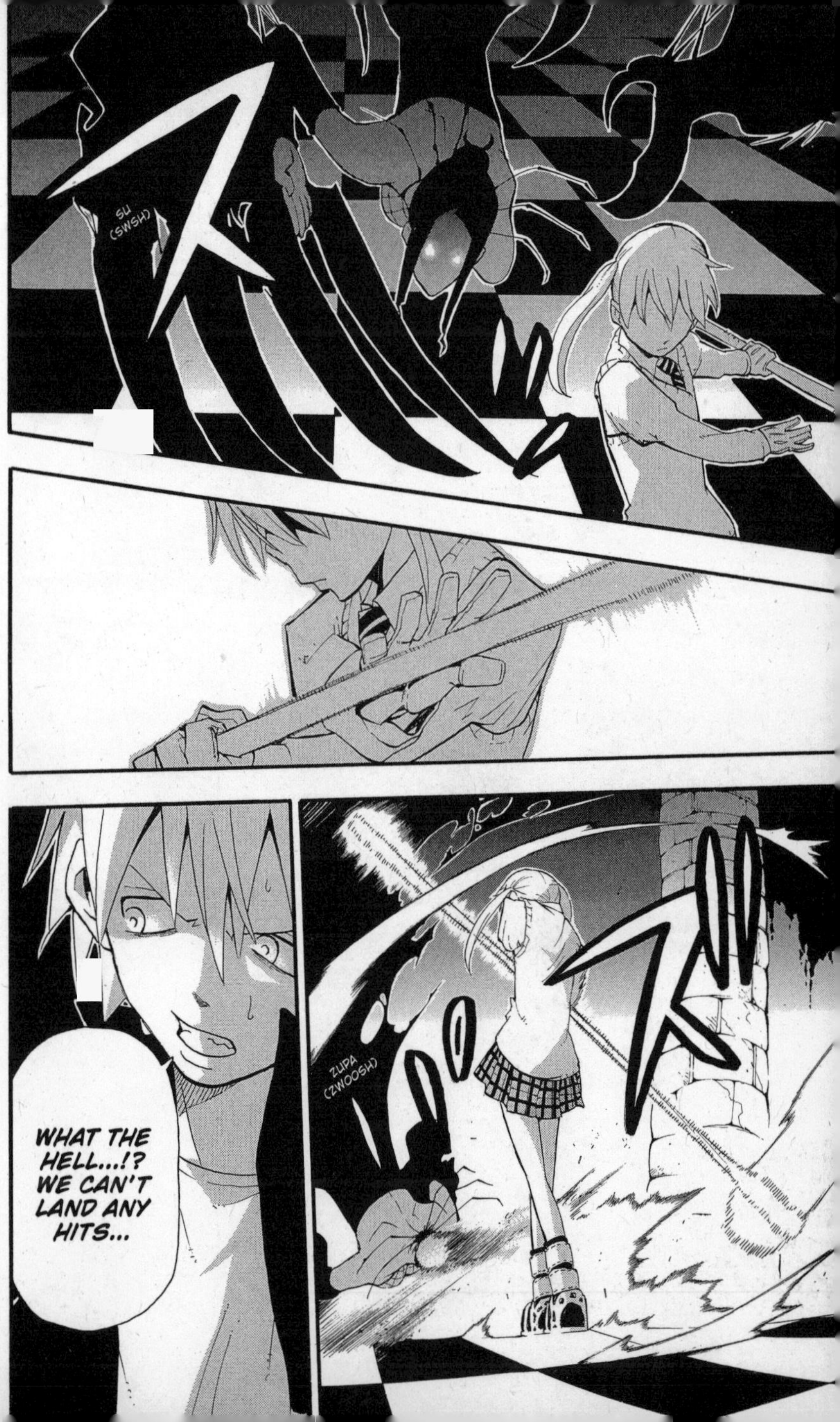
SU
(SWSH)
ZUPA
(ZWOOSH)
WHAT THE HELL...!? WE CAN'T LAND ANY HITS...

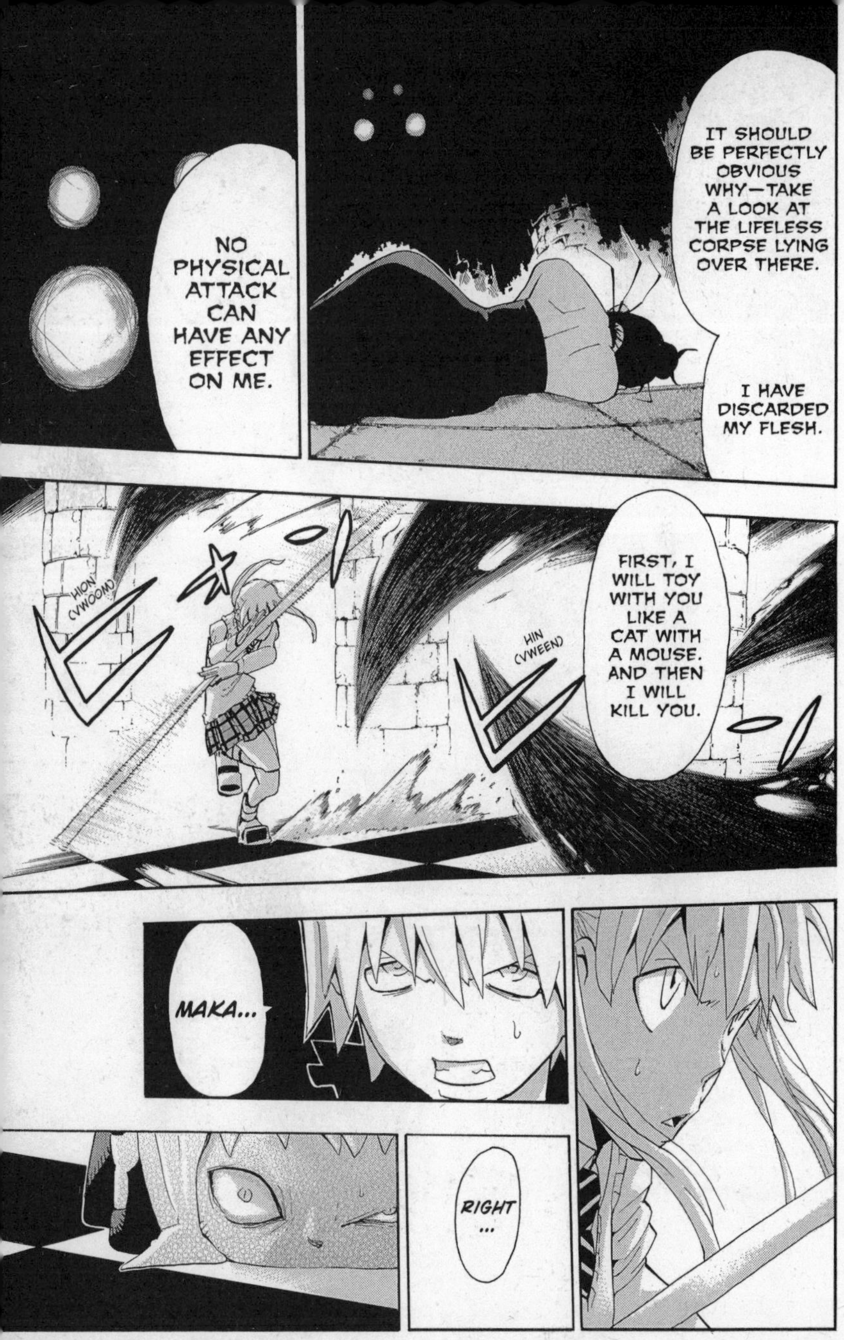
IT SHOULD BE PERFECTLY OBVIOUS WHY—TAKE A LOOK AT THE LIFELESS CORPSE LYING OVER THERE.
I HAVE DISCARDED MY FLESH.
NO PHYSICAL ATTACK CAN HAVE ANY EFFECT ON ME.
FIRST, I WILL TOY WITH YOU LIKE A CAT WITH A MOUSE. AND THEN I WILL KILL YOU.
HIN (VWEEN)
HION (VWOOM)
MAKA...
RIGHT ...

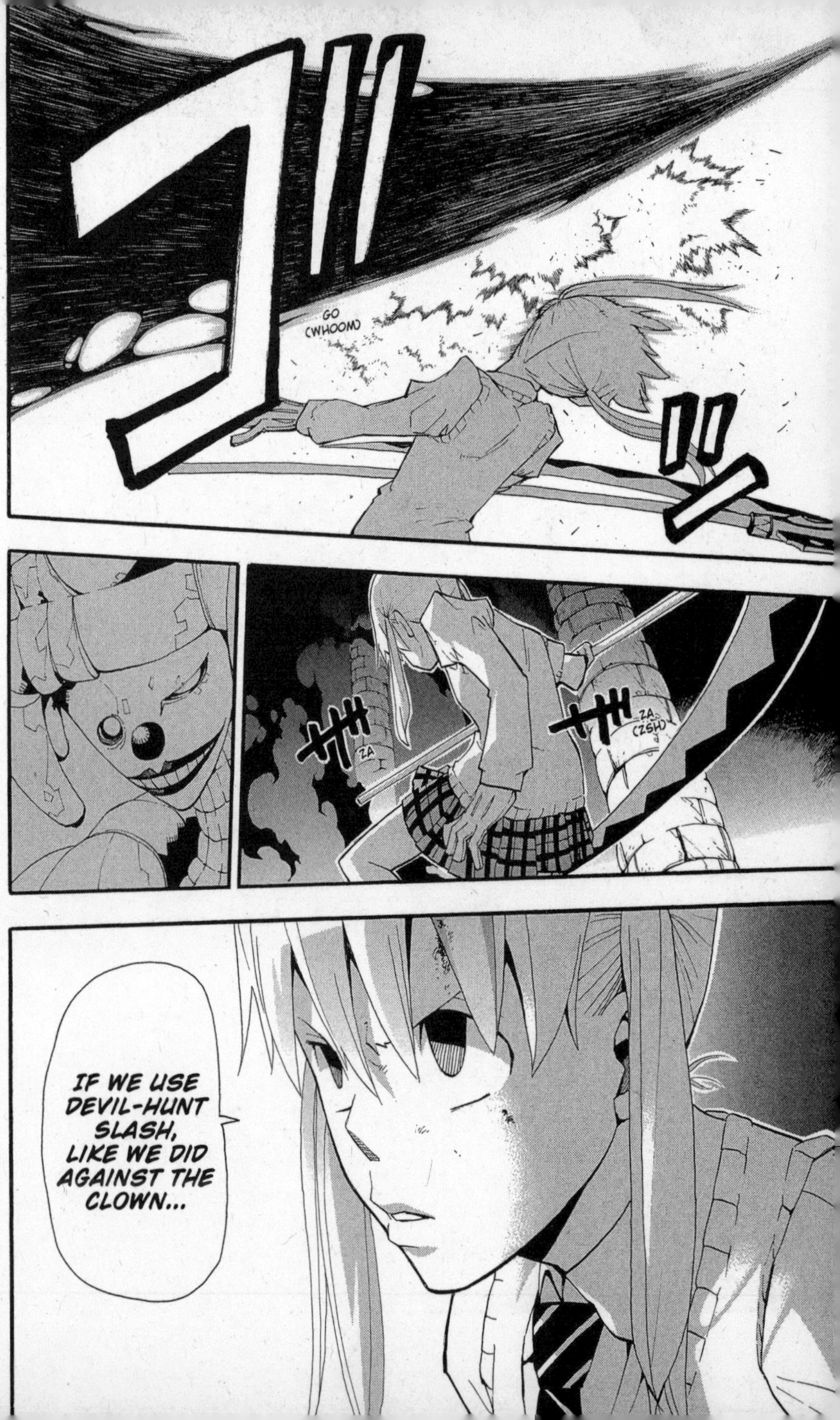
GO
(WHOOM)
ZA
(ZSH)
ZA
IF WE USE DEVIL-HUNT SLASH, LIKE WE DID AGAINST THE CLOWN...

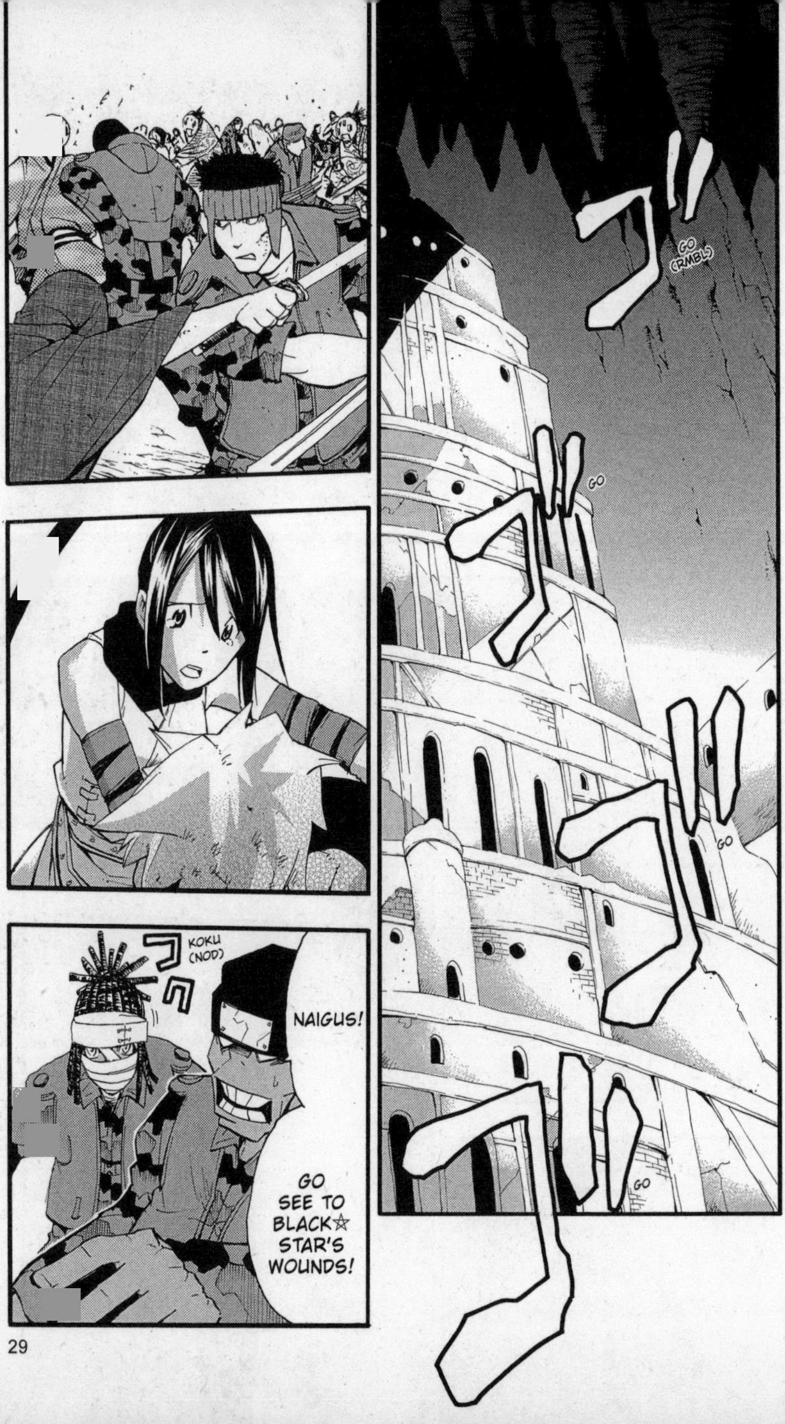
GO (RMBL)
GO
GO
GO
KOKU (NOD)
NAIGUS!
GO SEE TO BLACK☆STAR'S WOUNDS!

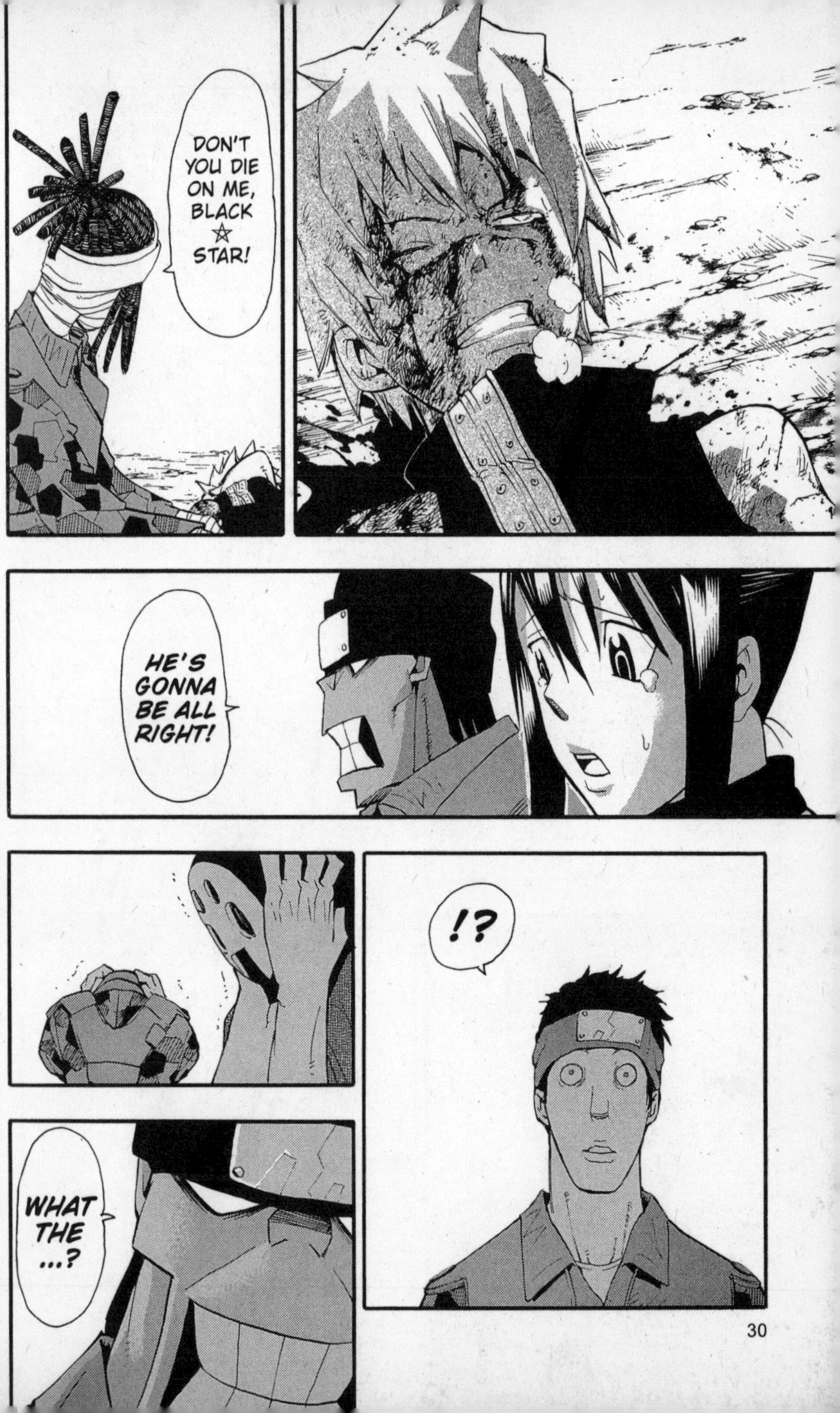
DON'T YOU DIE ON ME, BLACK ☆ STAR!
HE'S GONNA BE ALL RIGHT!
!?
WHAT THE ...?

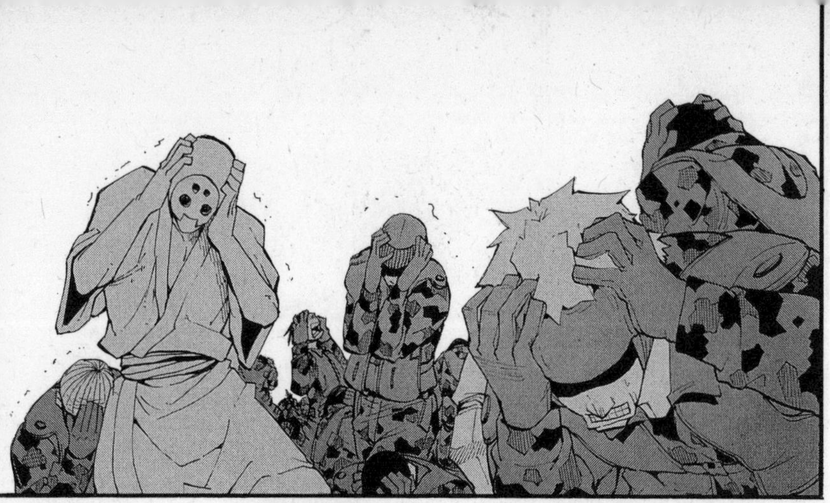

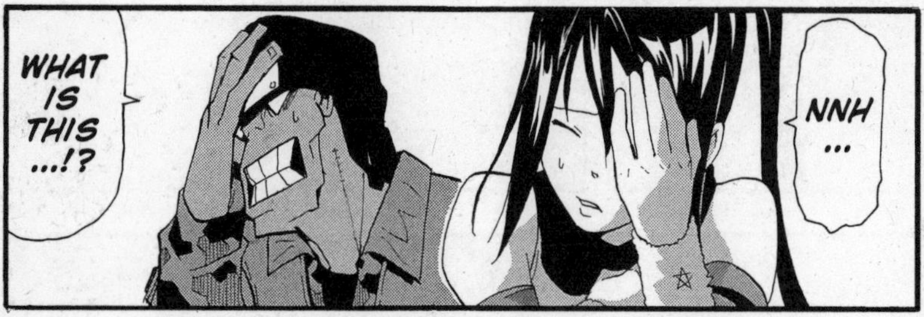
NNH ...
WHAT IS THIS ...!?

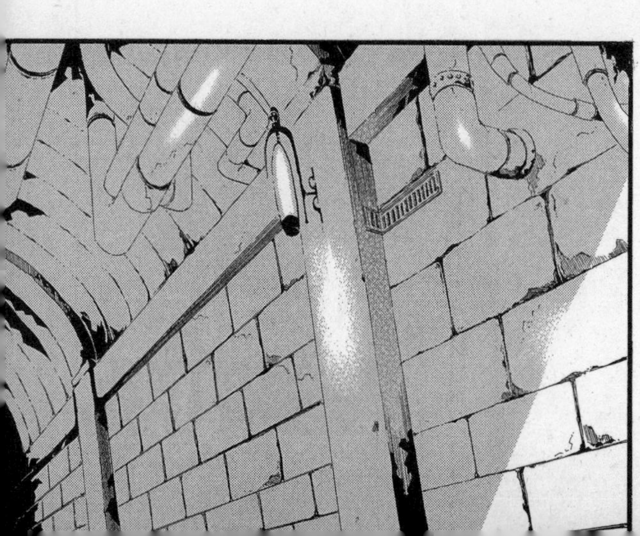

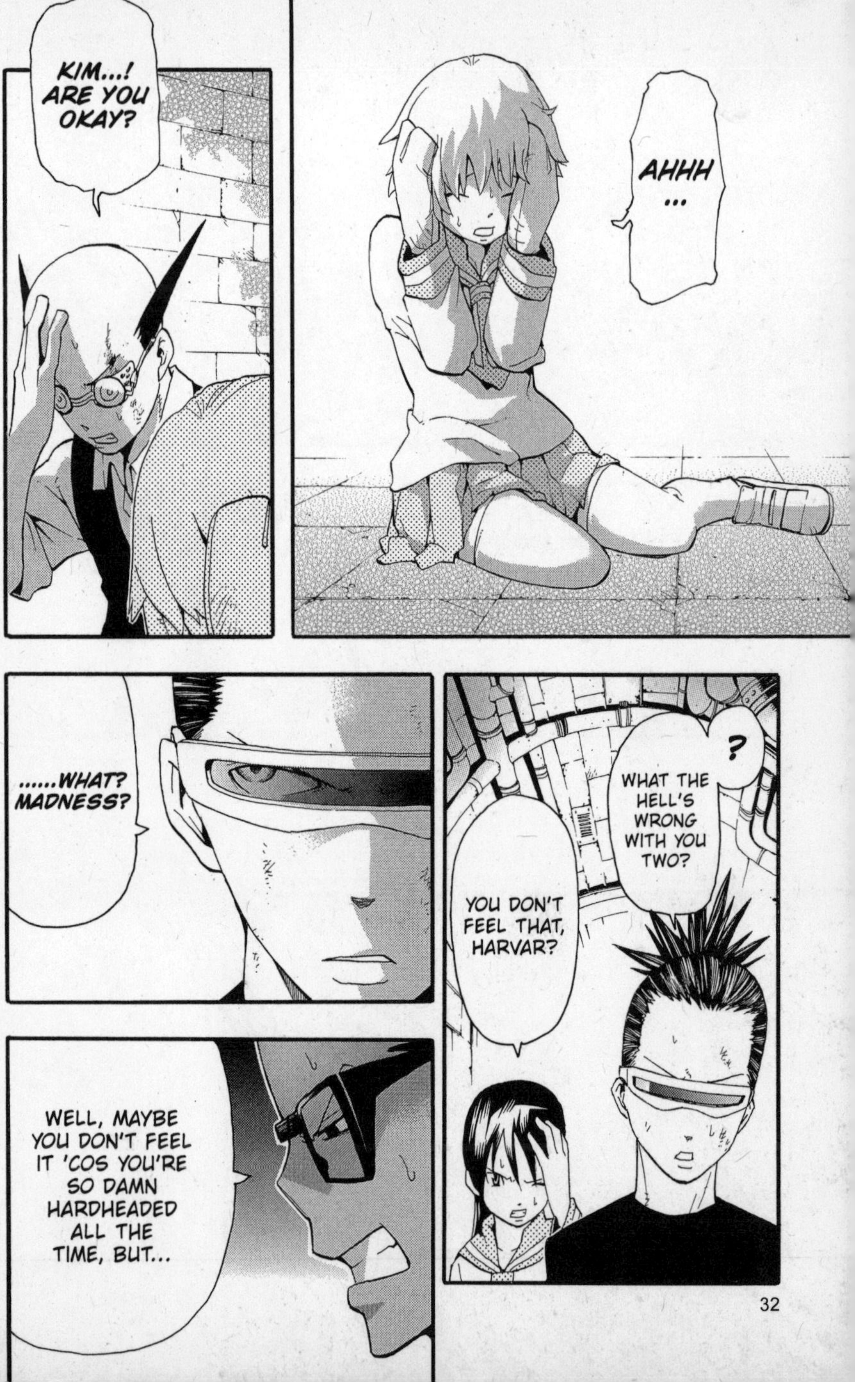
AHHH ...
KIM...! ARE YOU OKAY?
?
WHAT THE HELL'S WRONG WITH YOU TWO?
YOU DON'T FEEL THAT, HARVAR?
......WHAT? MADNESS?
WELL, MAYBE YOU DON'T FEEL IT 'COS YOU'RE SO DAMN HARDHEADED ALL THE TIME, BUT...

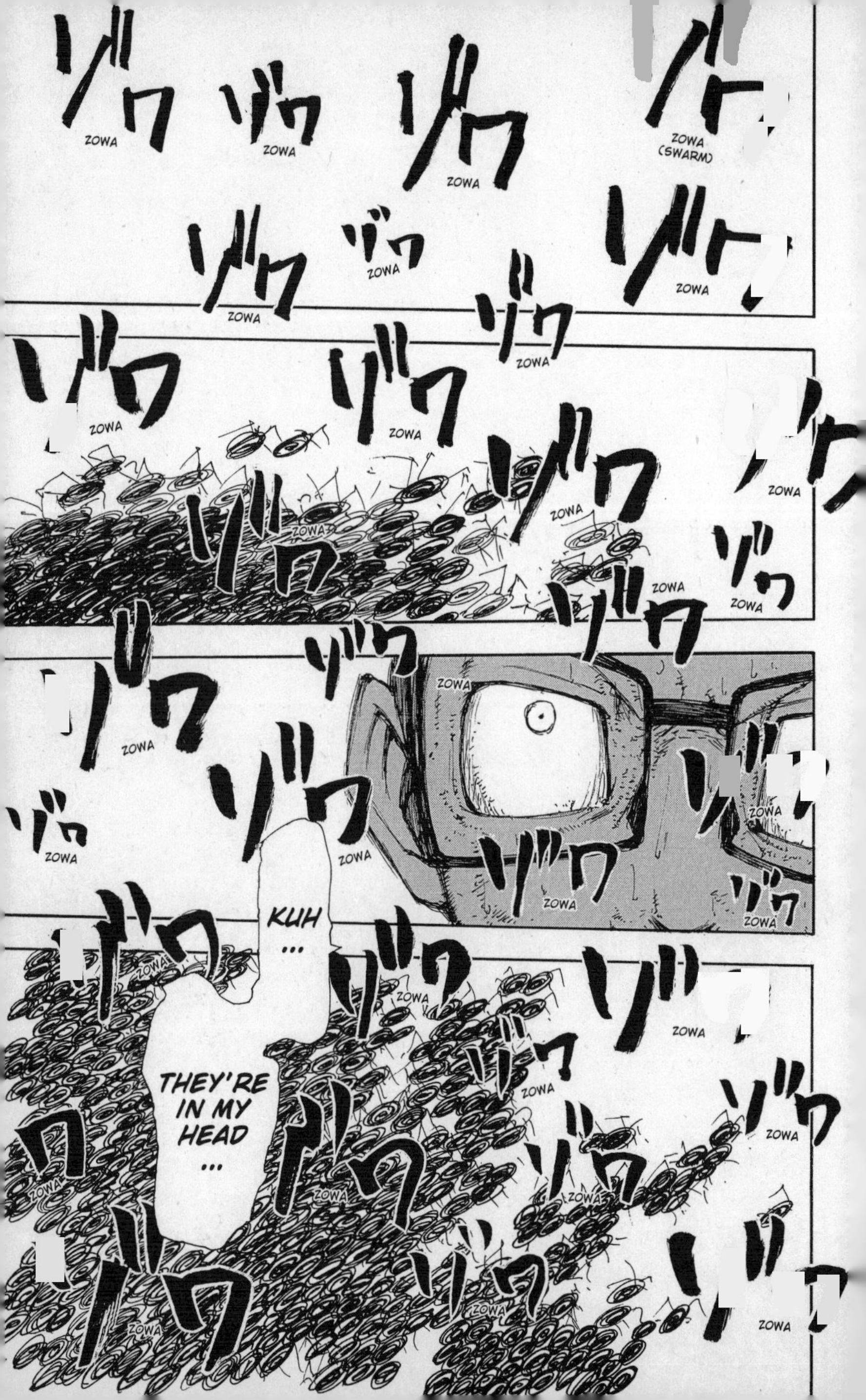
ゾワ
ZOWA (SWARM)
ゾワ
ZOWA
ゾワ
ZOWA
ゾワ
ZOWA
ゾワ
ZOWA
ゾワ
ZOWA
ゾワ
ZOWA
ゾワ
ZOWA
ゾワ
ZOWA
ゾワ
ZOWA
ゾワ
ZOWA
ゾワ
ZOWA
ゾワ
ZOWA
ゾワ
ZOWA
ゾワ
ZOWA
ゾワ
ZOWA
ゾワ
ZOWA
ゾワ
ZOWA
ゾワ
ZOWA
ゾワ
ZOWA
ゾワ
ZOWA
ゾワ
ZOWA
ゾワ
ZOWA
ゾワ
ZOWA
ゾワ
ZOWA
ゾワ
ZOWA
KUH...
THEY'RE IN MY HEAD...
ゾワ
ZOWA
ゾワ
ZOWA
ゾワ
ZOWA
ゾワ
ZOWA
ゾワ
ZOWA
ゾワ
ZOWA
ゾワ
ZOWA
ゾワ
ZOWA
ゾワ
ZOWA
ゾワ
ZOWA

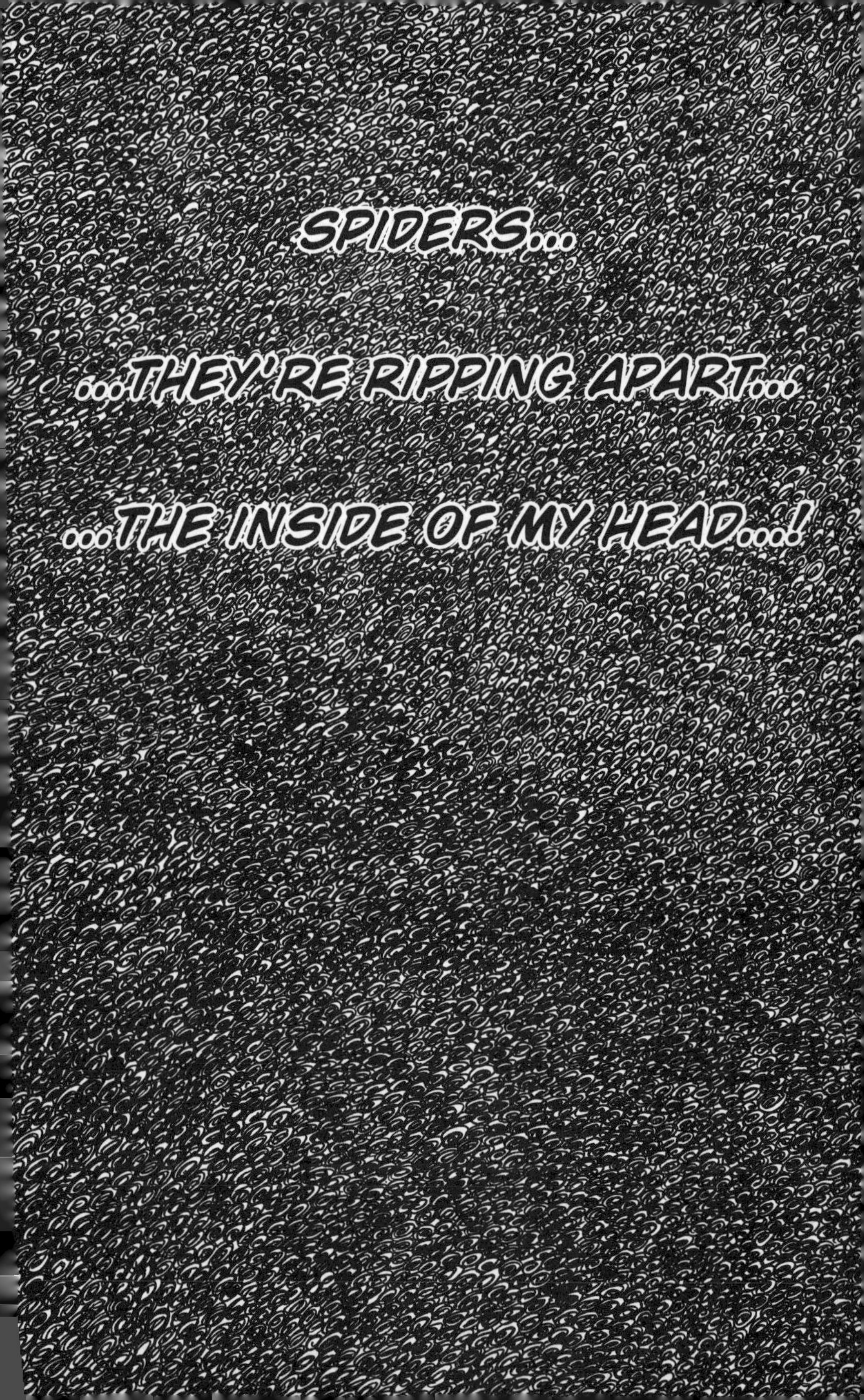
SPIDERS...
...THEY'RE RIPPING APART...
...THE INSIDE OF MY HEAD...!

SOUL EATER

YAGA CASTLE (PART 14)

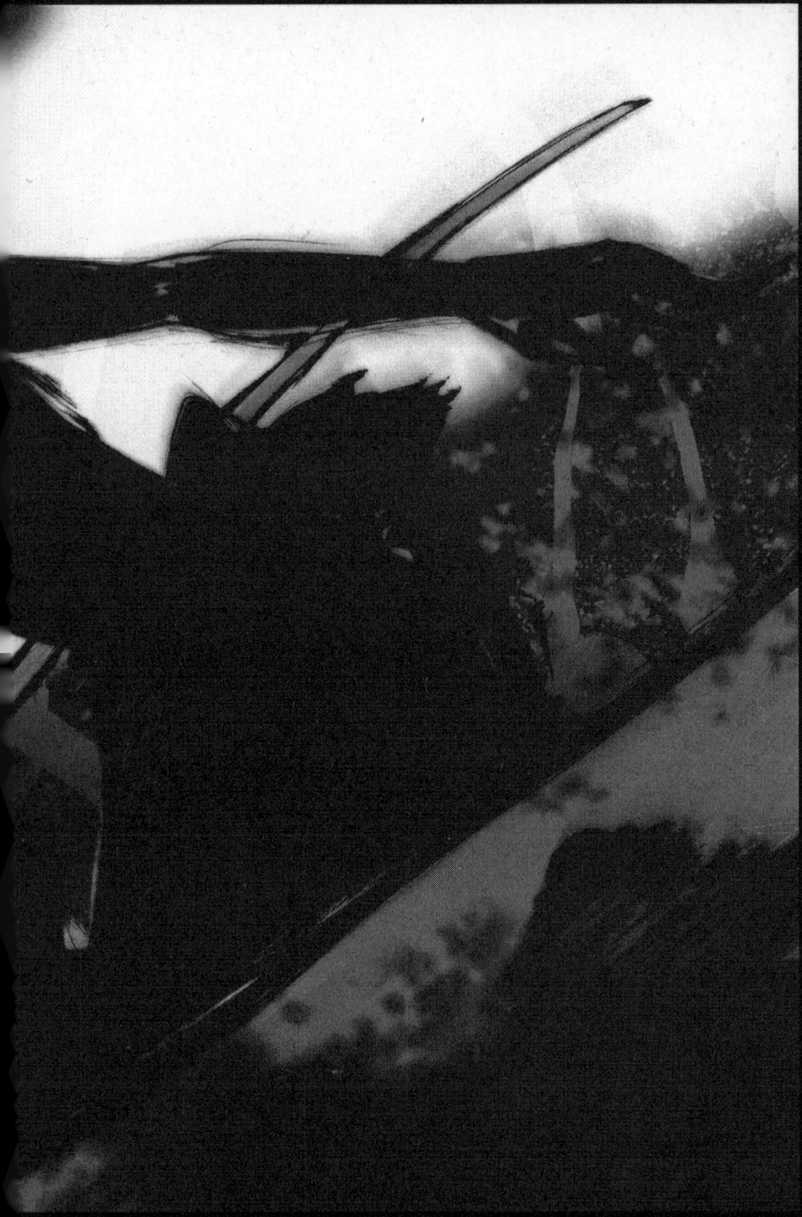

CHAPTER 59: OPERATION CAPTURE BABA

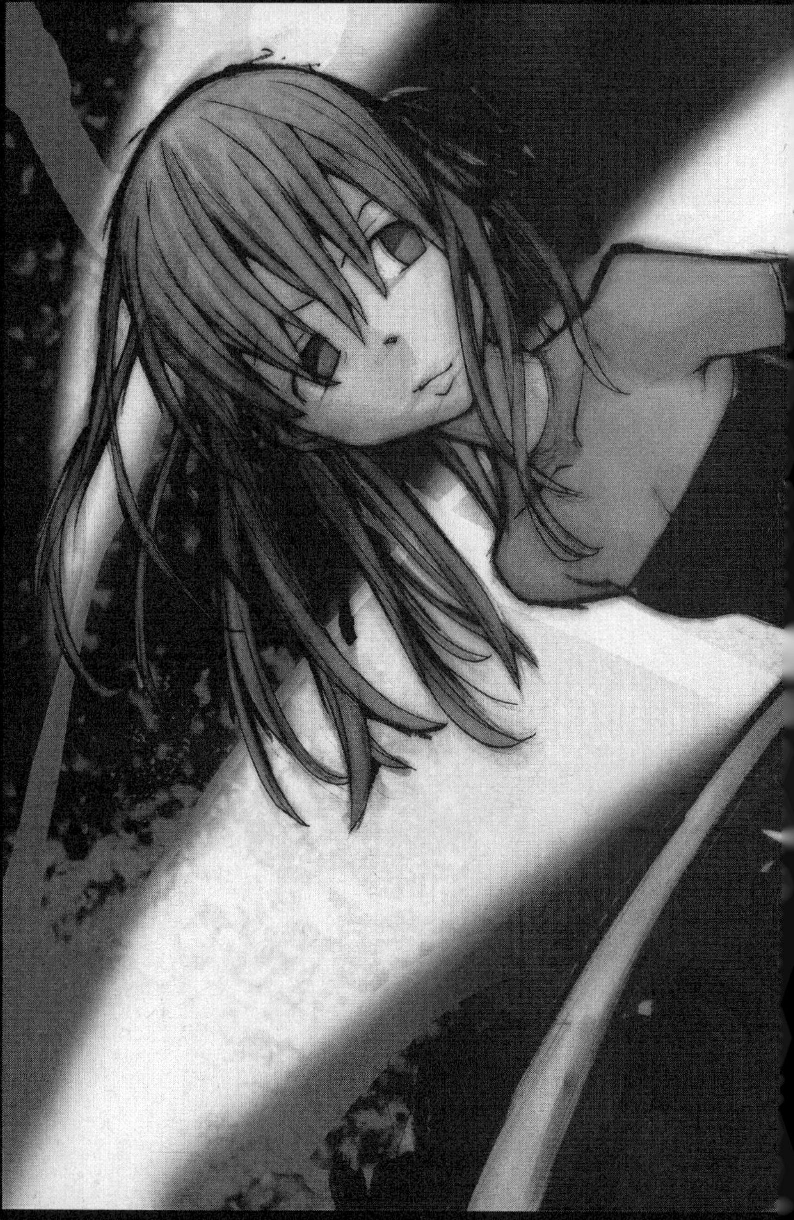

SOUL EATER

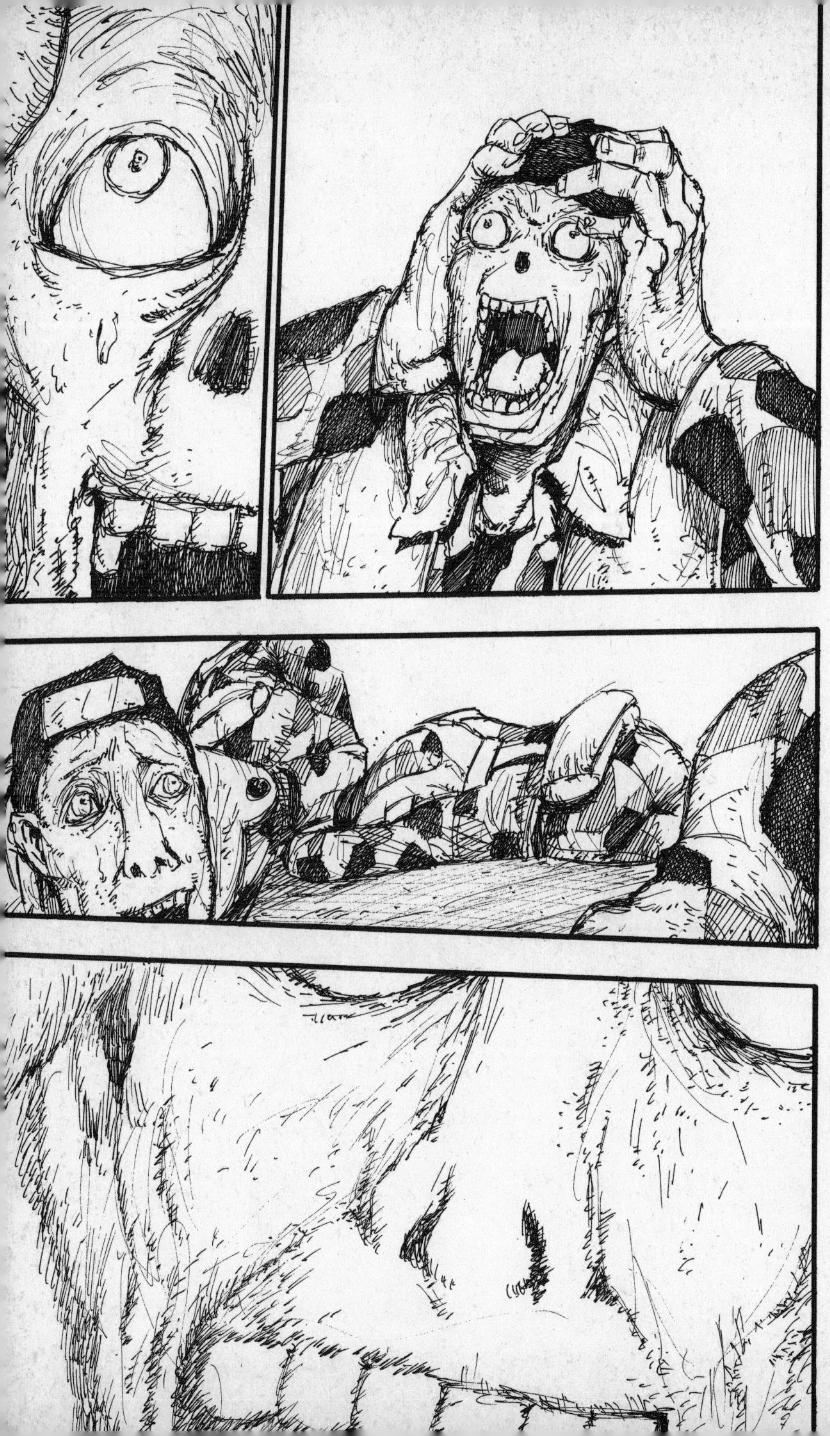

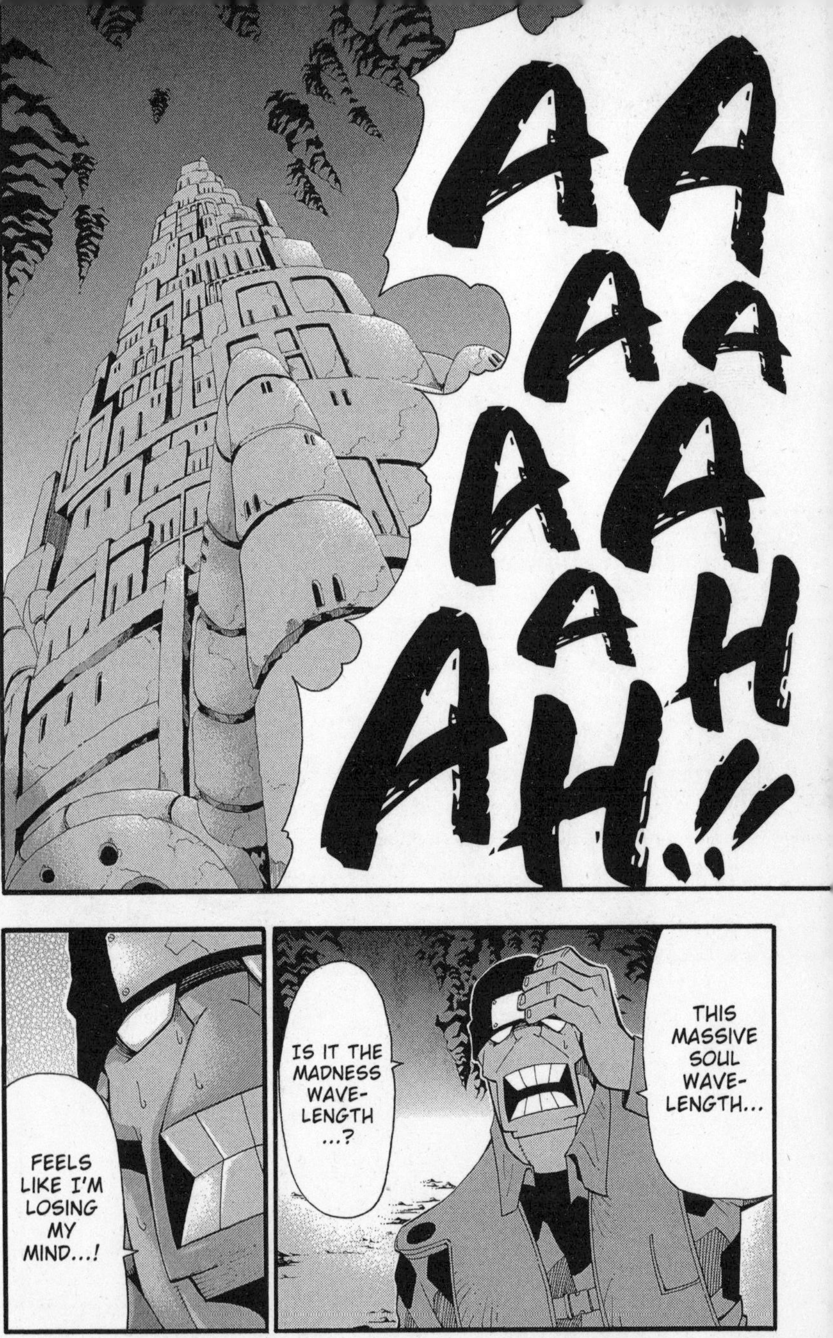
AAAAAAAAAH!!
THIS MASSIVE SOUL WAVE-LENGTH...
IS IT THE MADNESS WAVE-LENGTH...?
FEELS LIKE I'M LOSING MY MIND...!

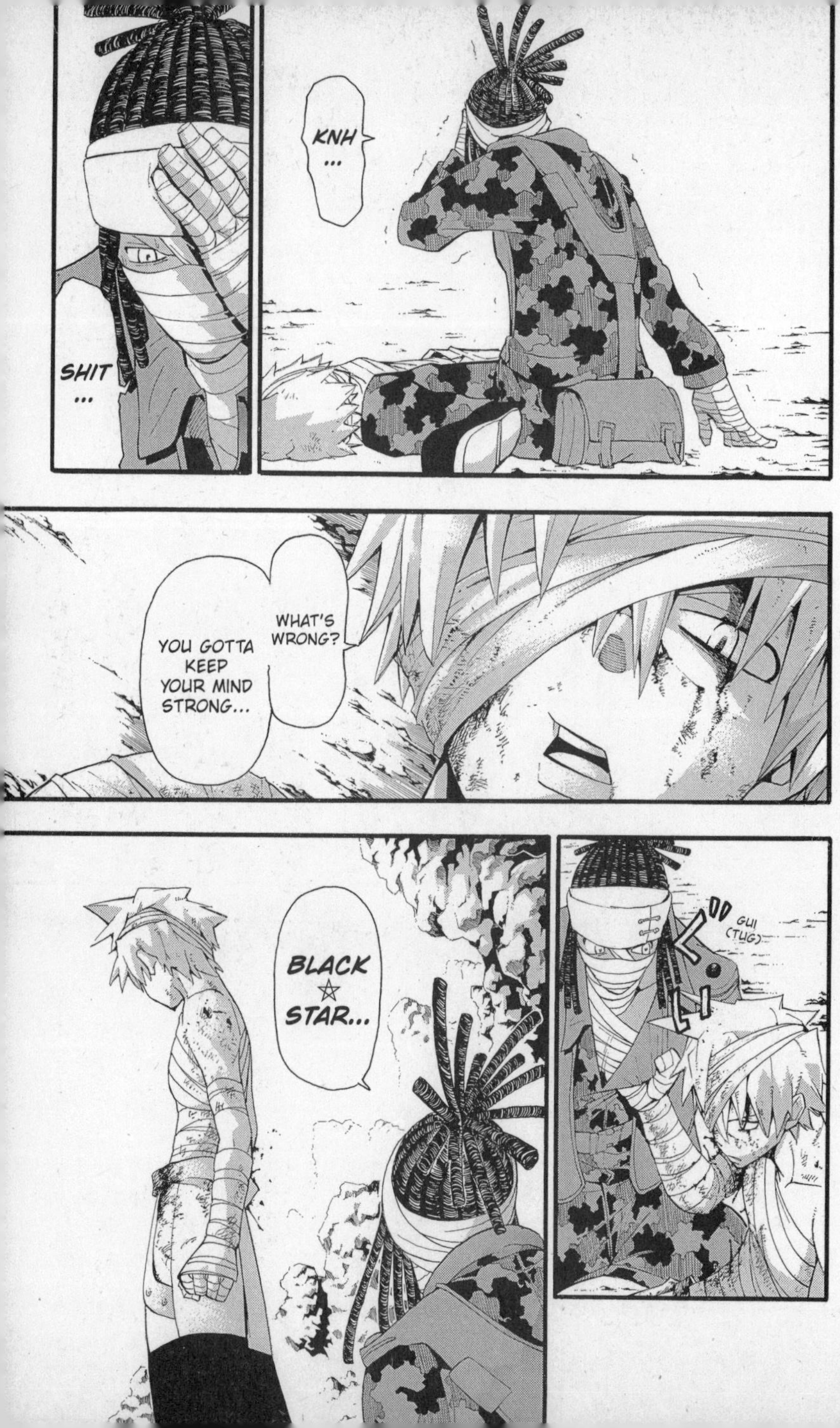
KNH ...
SHIT ...
WHAT'S WRONG?
YOU GOTTA KEEP YOUR MIND STRONG...
GUI (TUG)
BLACK ☆ STAR...

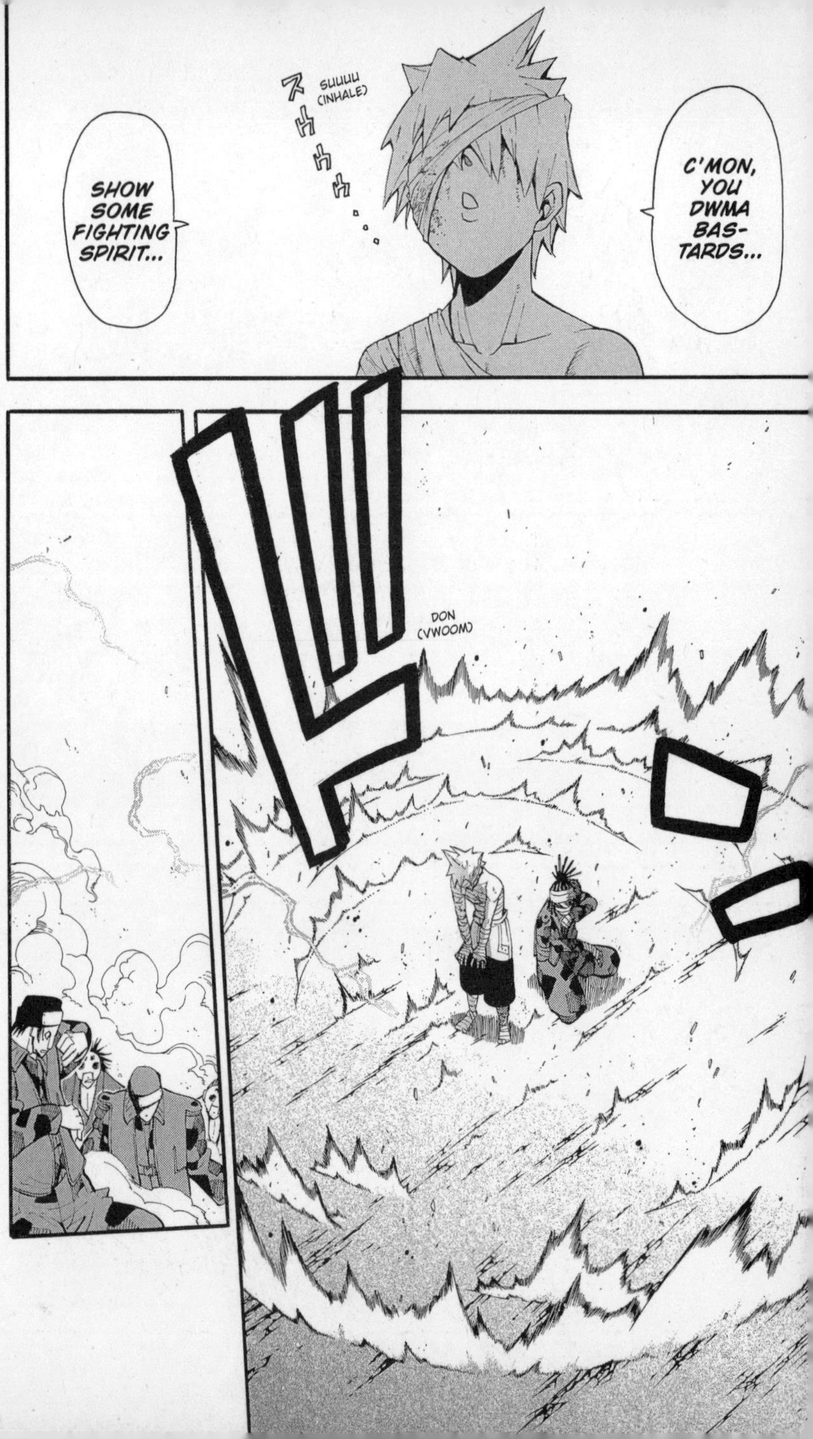
C'MON, YOU DWMA BAS-TARDS...
SUUUU (INHALE)
SHOW SOME FIGHTING SPIRIT...
DON (VWOOM)

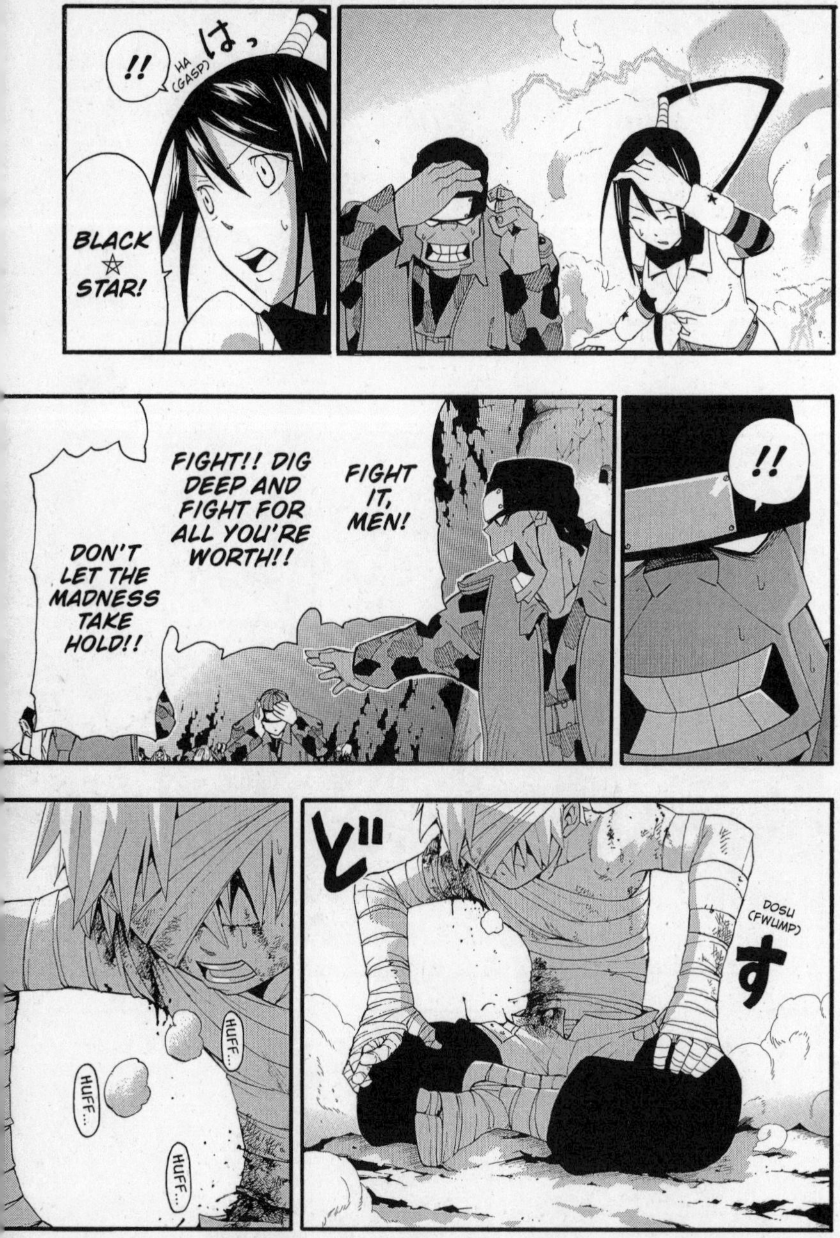
はっ
HA (GASP)
!!
BLACK ☆ STAR!
!!
FIGHT IT, MEN!
FIGHT!! DIG DEEP AND FIGHT FOR ALL YOU'RE WORTH!!
DON'T LET THE MADNESS TAKE HOLD!!
どす
DOSU (FWUMP)
HUFF...
HUFF...
HUFF...

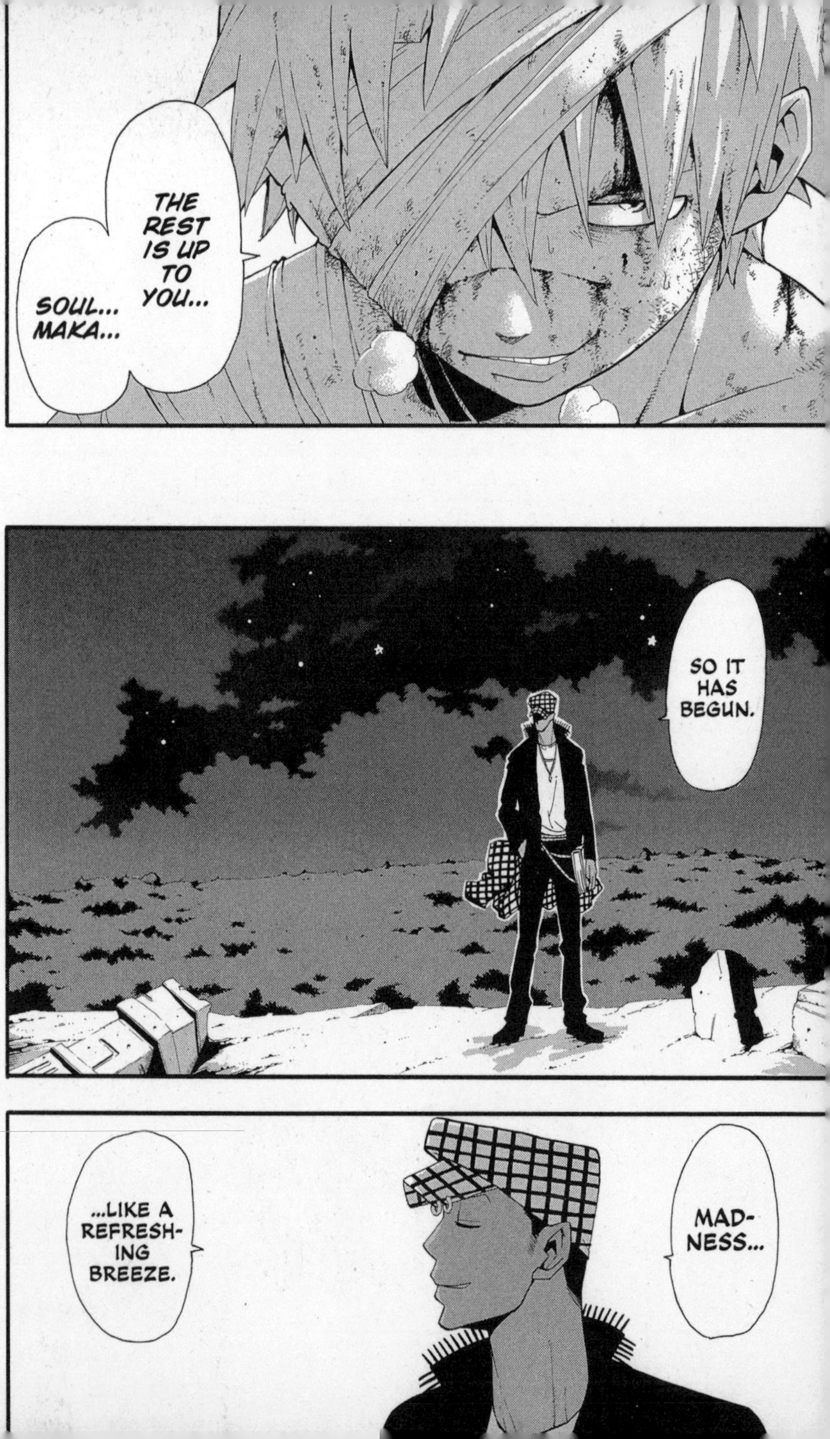
THE REST IS UP TO YOU...
SOUL... MAKA...
SO IT HAS BEGUN.
MAD-NESS...
...LIKE A REFRESH-ING BREEZE.

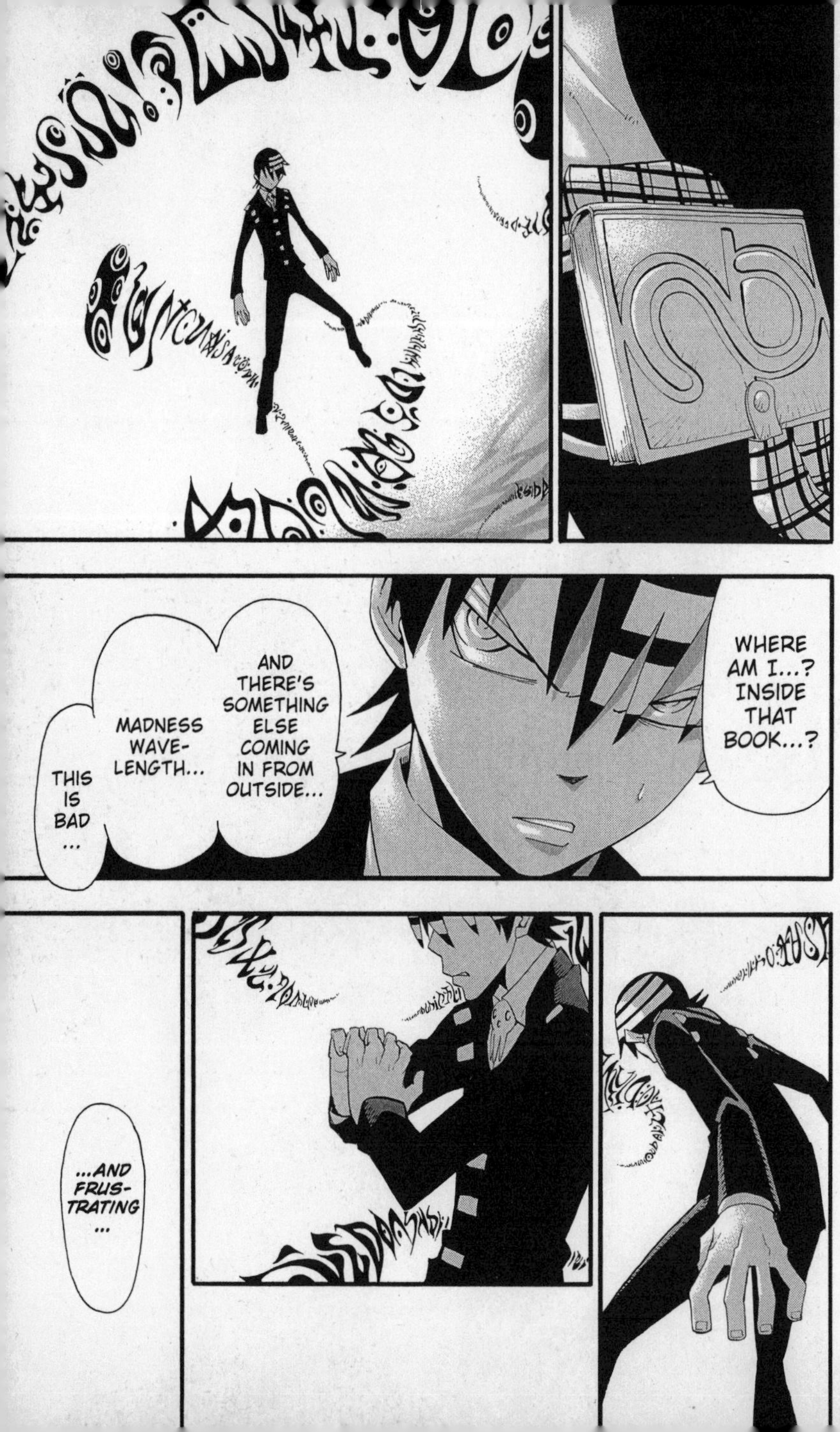
WHERE AM I...? INSIDE THAT BOOK...?
AND THERE'S SOMETHING ELSE COMING IN FROM OUTSIDE...
MADNESS WAVE-LENGTH...
THIS IS BAD ...
...AND FRUS-TRATING ...

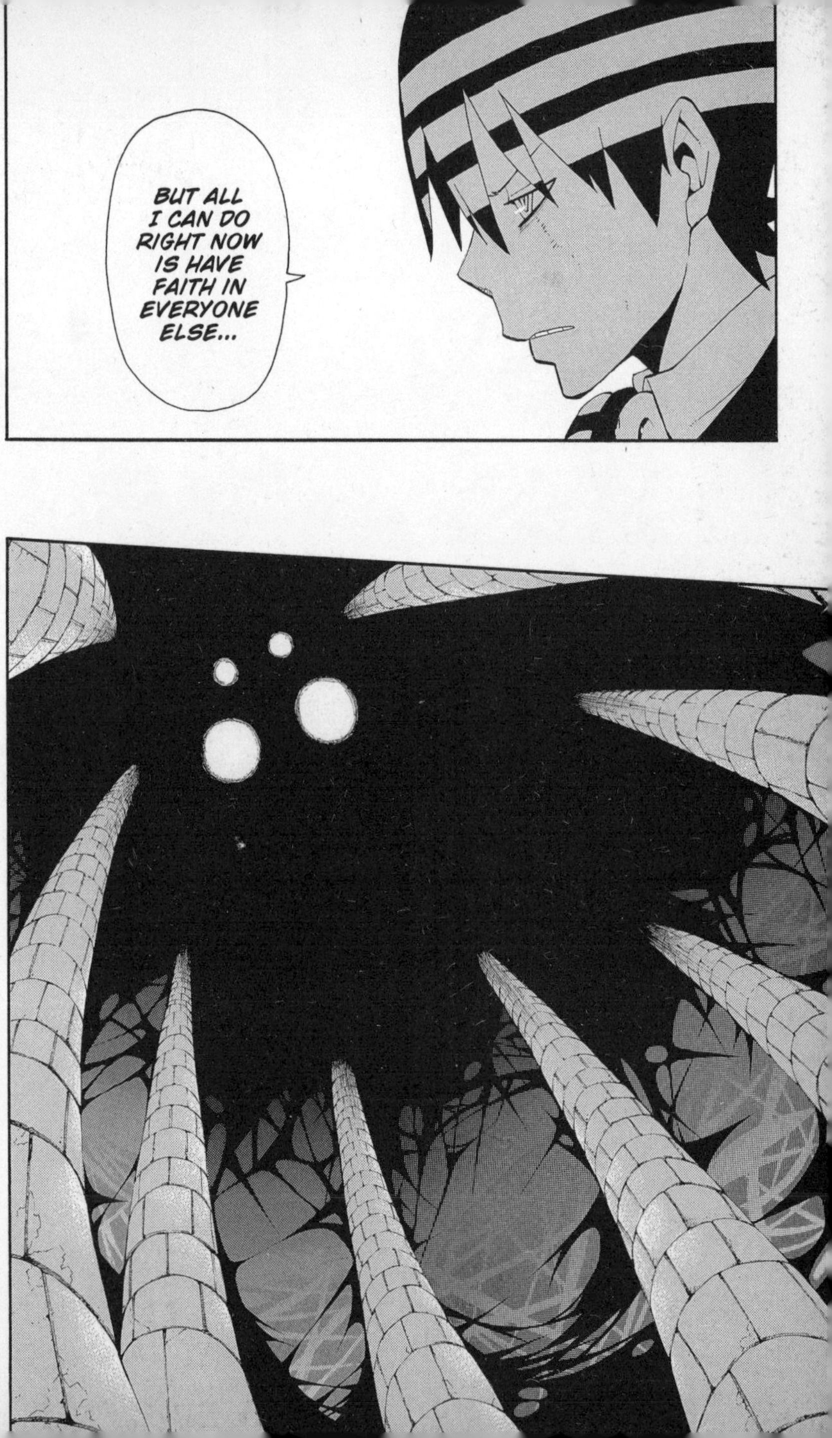
BUT ALL I CAN DO RIGHT NOW IS HAVE FAITH IN EVERYONE ELSE...

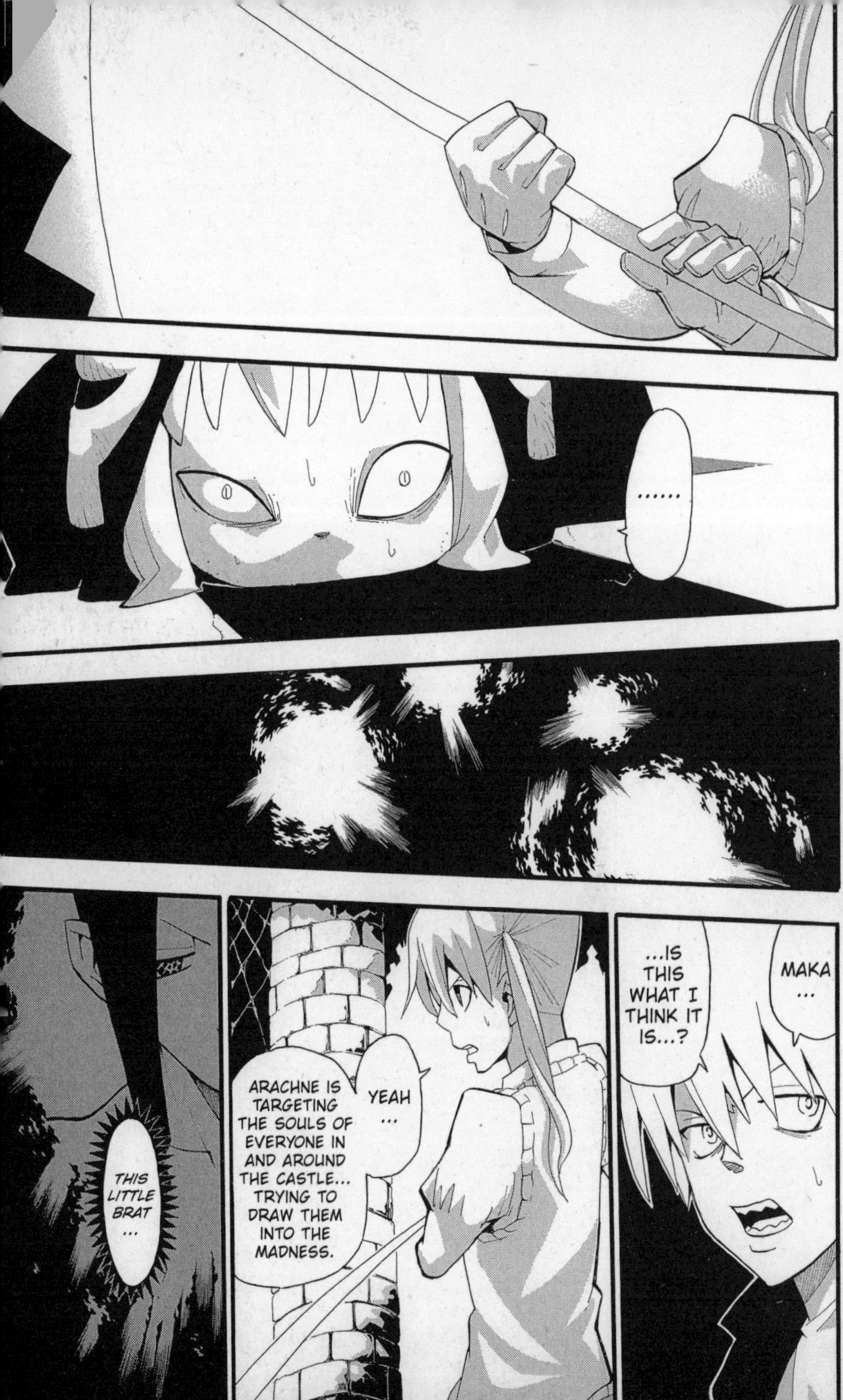
……
MAKA …
…IS THIS WHAT I THINK IT IS…?
YEAH …
ARACHNE IS TARGETING THE SOULS OF EVERYONE IN AND AROUND THE CASTLE… TRYING TO DRAW THEM INTO THE MADNESS.
THIS LITTLE BRAT …

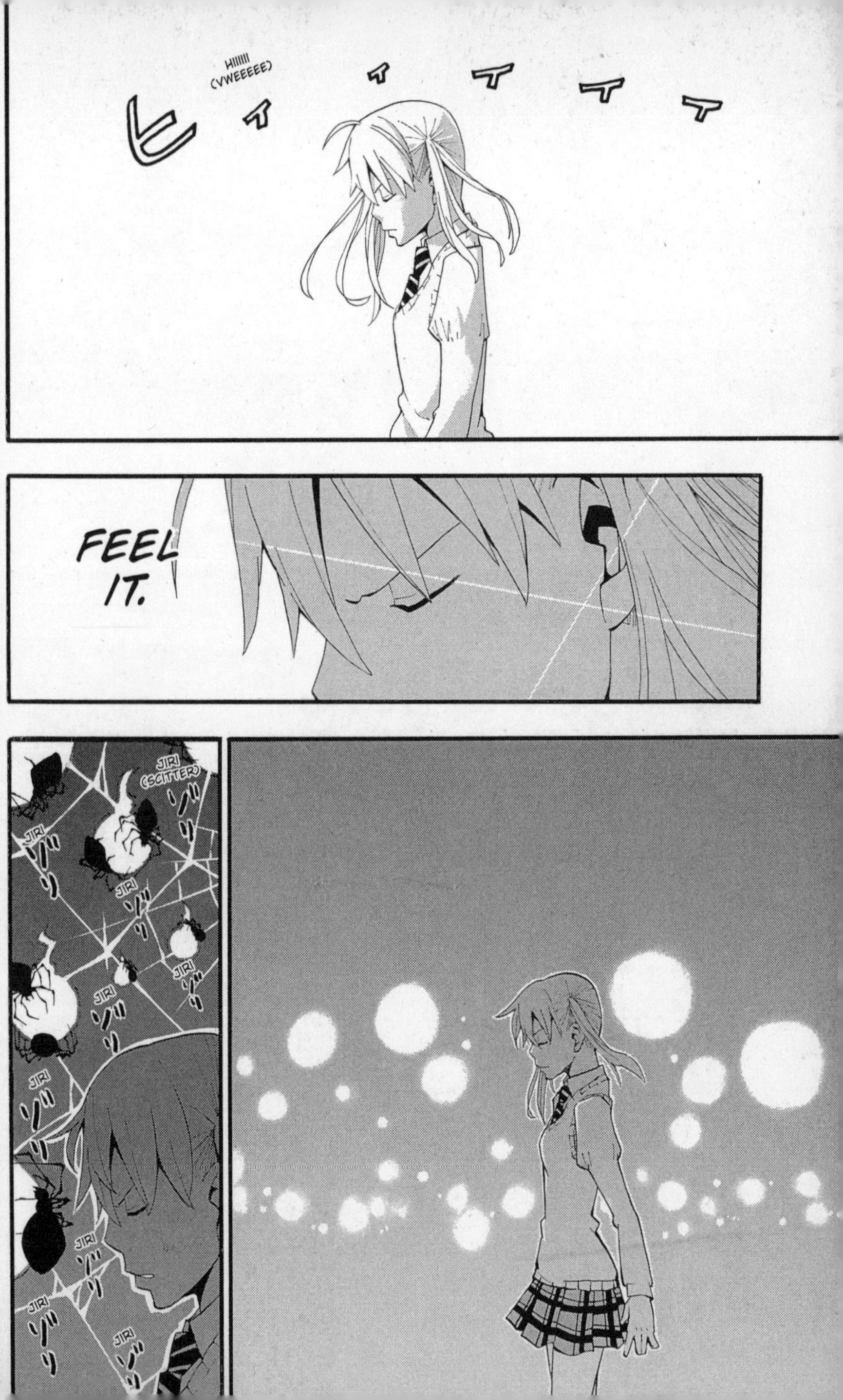

HIIIIII (VWEEEEE)
ヒィィィィィ
FEEL IT.
JIRI (SCITTER)
JIRI
JIRI
JIRI
JIRI
JIRI
JIRI
JIRI
JIRI

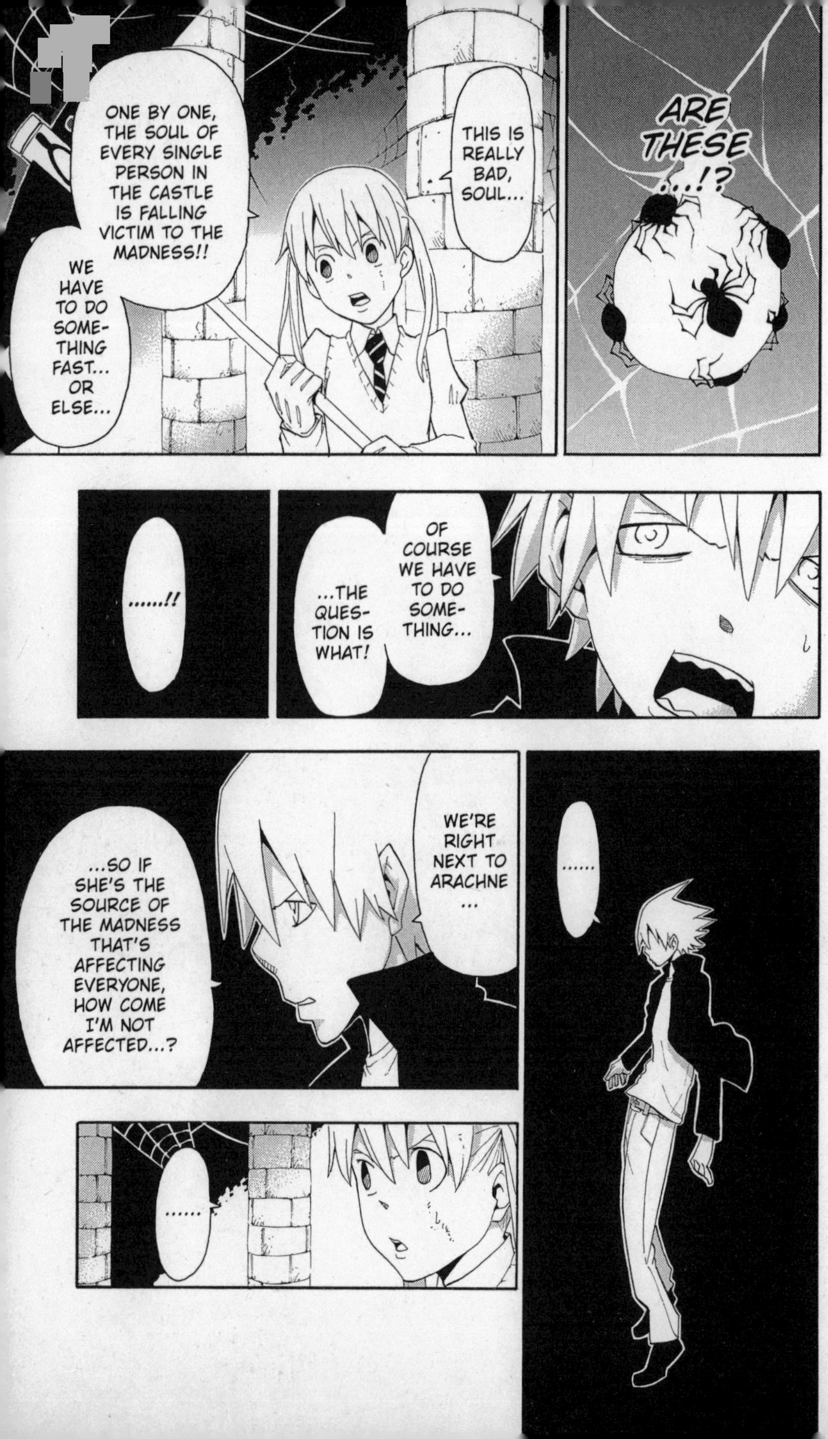
ARE THESE ...!?
THIS IS REALLY BAD, SOUL...
ONE BY ONE, THE SOUL OF EVERY SINGLE PERSON IN THE CASTLE IS FALLING VICTIM TO THE MADNESS!!
WE HAVE TO DO SOMETHING FAST... OR ELSE...
OF COURSE WE HAVE TO DO SOMETHING...
...THE QUESTION IS WHAT!
......!!
......
WE'RE RIGHT NEXT TO ARACHNE...
...SO IF SHE'S THE SOURCE OF THE MADNESS THAT'S AFFECTING EVERYONE, HOW COME I'M NOT AFFECTED...?
......

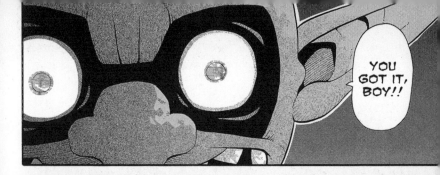

YOU GOT IT, BOY!!

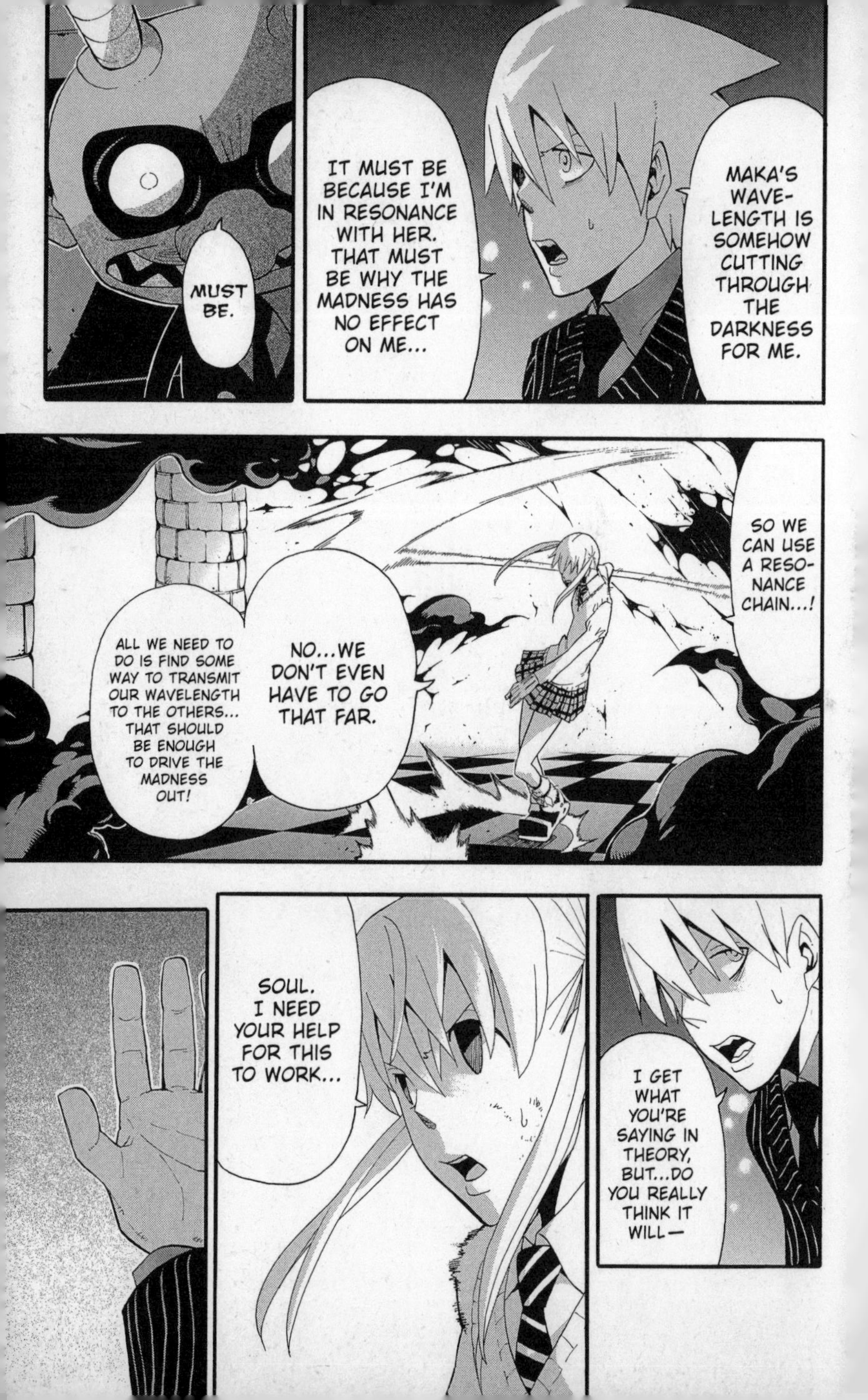
MAKA'S WAVE-LENGTH IS SOMEHOW CUTTING THROUGH THE DARKNESS FOR ME.
IT MUST BE BECAUSE I'M IN RESONANCE WITH HER. THAT MUST BE WHY THE MADNESS HAS NO EFFECT ON ME...
MUST BE.
SO WE CAN USE A RESO-NANCE CHAIN...!
NO...WE DON'T EVEN HAVE TO GO THAT FAR.
ALL WE NEED TO DO IS FIND SOME WAY TO TRANSMIT OUR WAVELENGTH TO THE OTHERS... THAT SHOULD BE ENOUGH TO DRIVE THE MADNESS OUT!
I GET WHAT YOU'RE SAYING IN THEORY, BUT...DO YOU REALLY THINK IT WILL—
SOUL. I NEED YOUR HELP FOR THIS TO WORK...

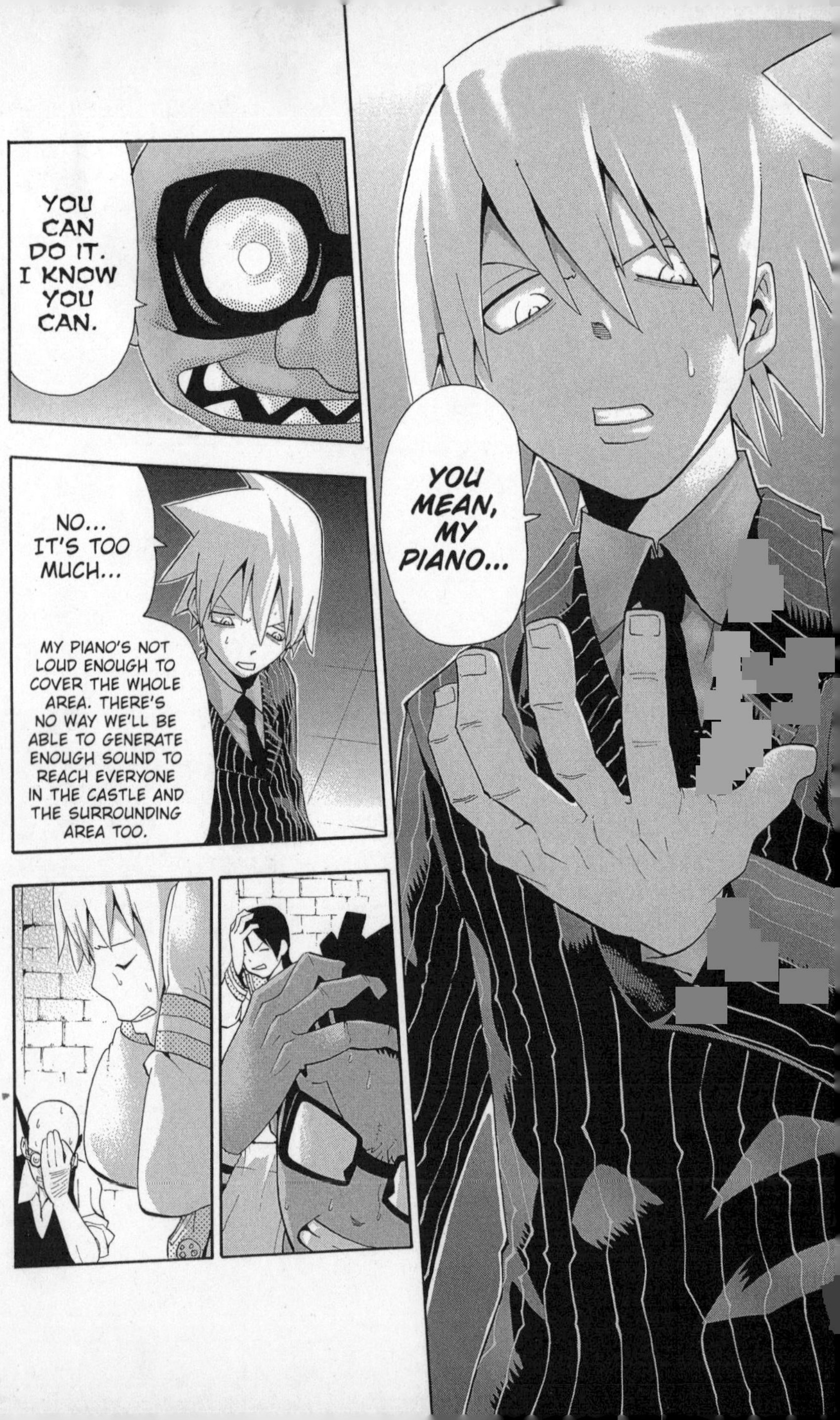
YOU MEAN, MY PIANO...
YOU CAN DO IT. I KNOW YOU CAN.
NO... IT'S TOO MUCH...
MY PIANO'S NOT LOUD ENOUGH TO COVER THE WHOLE AREA. THERE'S NO WAY WE'LL BE ABLE TO GENERATE ENOUGH SOUND TO REACH EVERYONE IN THE CASTLE AND THE SURROUNDING AREA TOO.

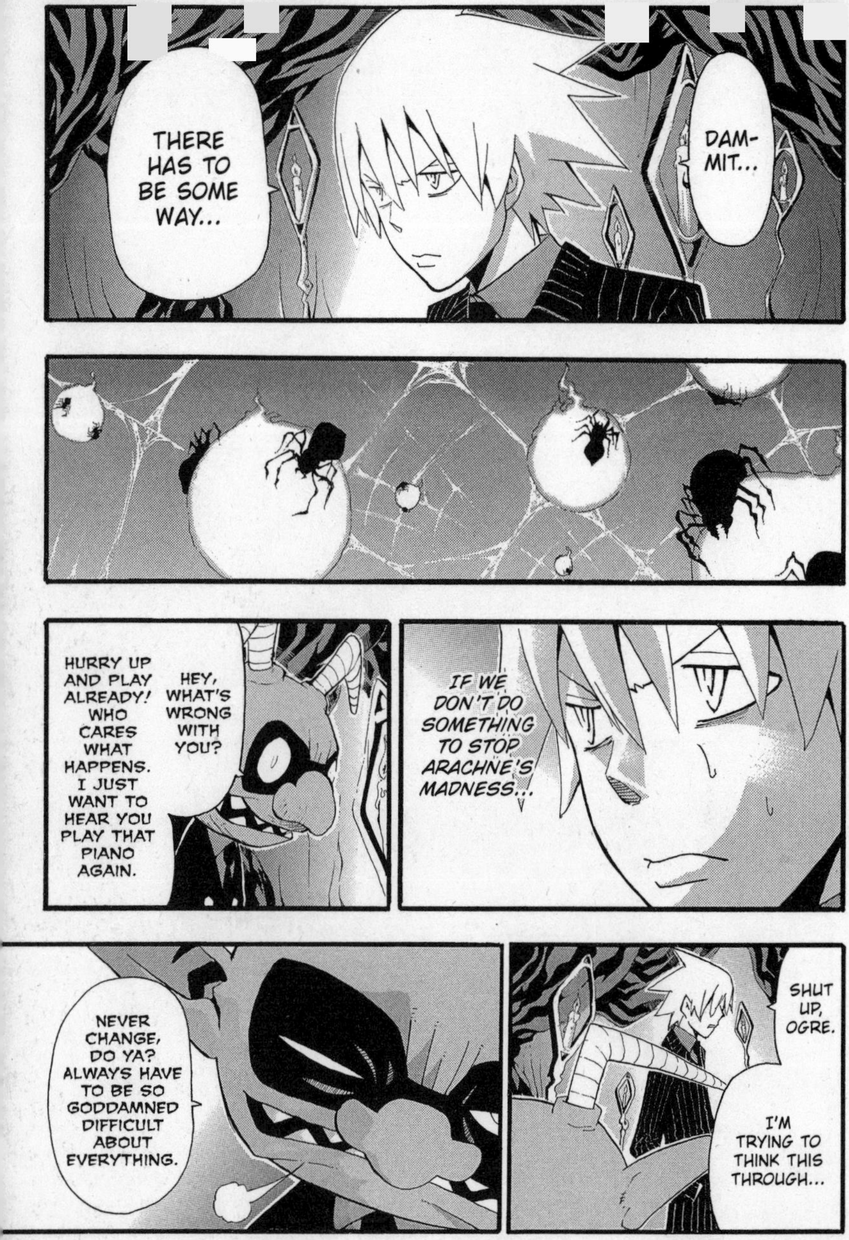
DAM-MIT...
THERE HAS TO BE SOME WAY...
IF WE DON'T DO SOMETHING TO STOP ARACHNE'S MADNESS...
HEY, WHAT'S WRONG WITH YOU?
HURRY UP AND PLAY ALREADY! WHO CARES WHAT HAPPENS. I JUST WANT TO HEAR YOU PLAY THAT PIANO AGAIN.
SHUT UP, OGRE.
I'M TRYING TO THINK THIS THROUGH...
NEVER CHANGE, DO YA? ALWAYS HAVE TO BE SO GODDAMNED DIFFICULT ABOUT EVERYTHING.

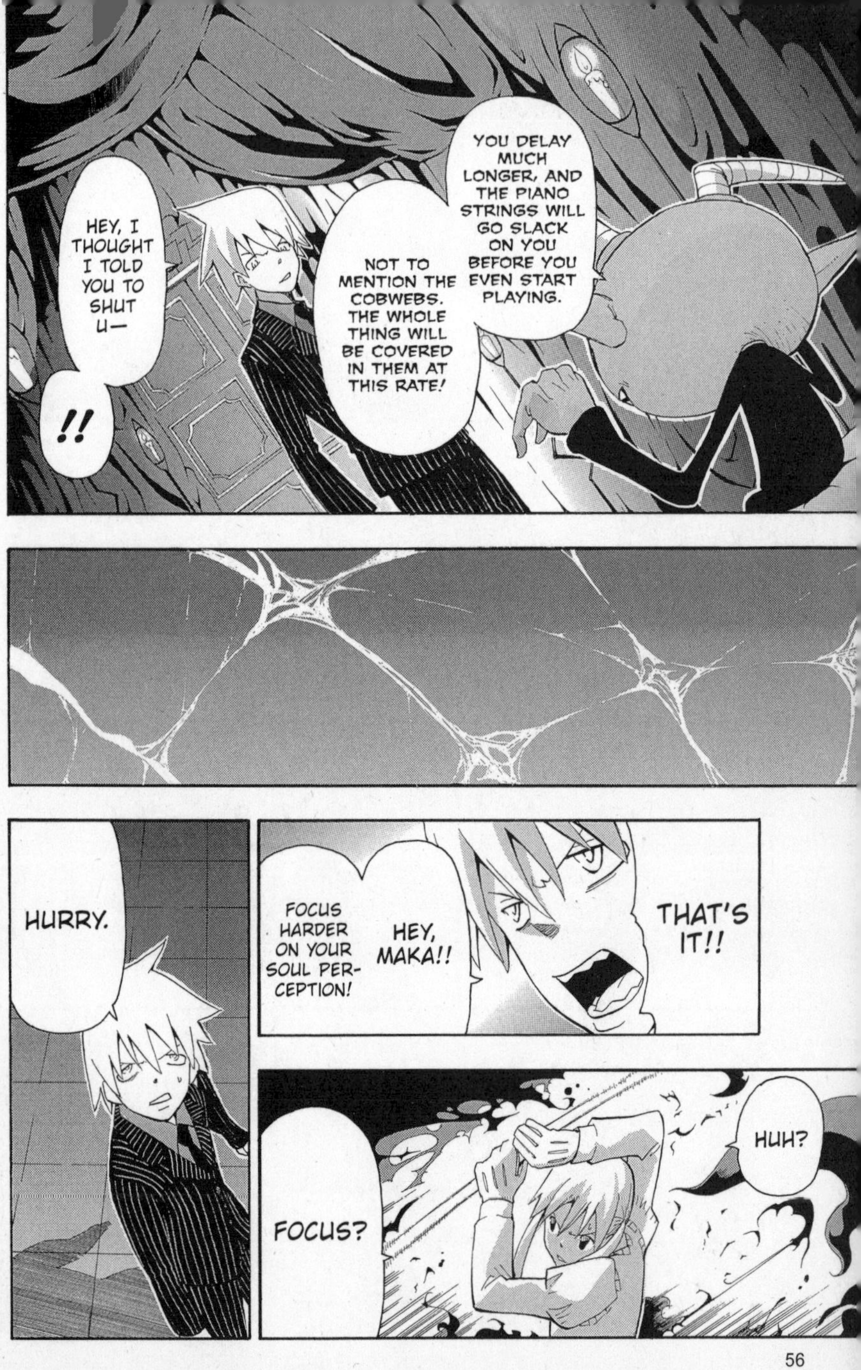
YOU DELAY MUCH LONGER, AND THE PIANO STRINGS WILL GO SLACK ON YOU BEFORE YOU EVEN START PLAYING.
NOT TO MENTION THE COBWEBS. THE WHOLE THING WILL BE COVERED IN THEM AT THIS RATE!
HEY, I THOUGHT I TOLD YOU TO SHUT U—
!!
THAT'S IT!!
HEY, MAKA!!
FOCUS HARDER ON YOUR SOUL PER-CEPTION!
HUH?
FOCUS?
HURRY.

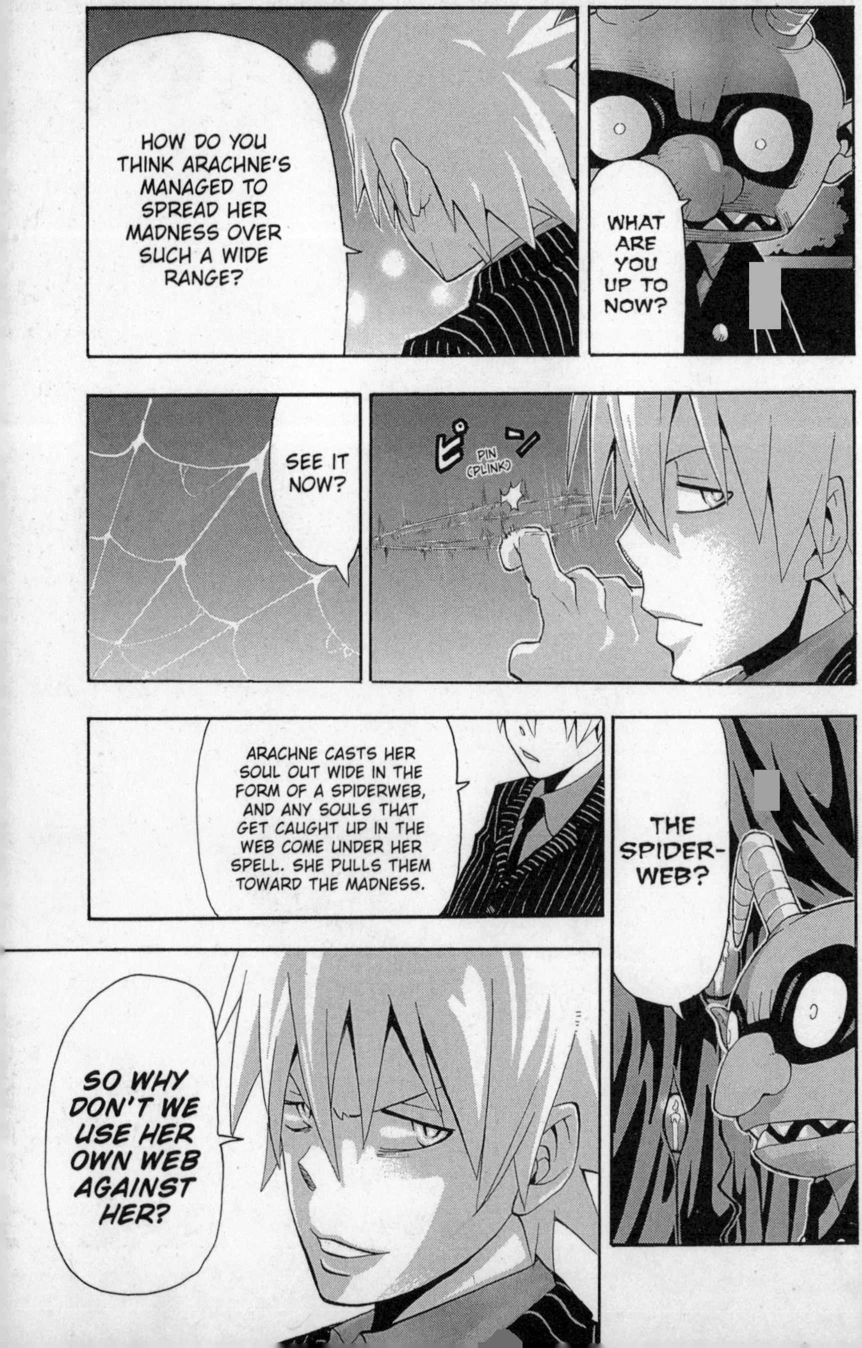
WHAT ARE YOU UP TO NOW?
HOW DO YOU THINK ARACHNE'S MANAGED TO SPREAD HER MADNESS OVER SUCH A WIDE RANGE?
ピン
PIN (PLINK)
SEE IT NOW?
THE SPIDER-WEB?
ARACHNE CASTS HER SOUL OUT WIDE IN THE FORM OF A SPIDERWEB, AND ANY SOULS THAT GET CAUGHT UP IN THE WEB COME UNDER HER SPELL. SHE PULLS THEM TOWARD THE MADNESS.
SO WHY DON'T WE USE HER OWN WEB AGAINST HER?

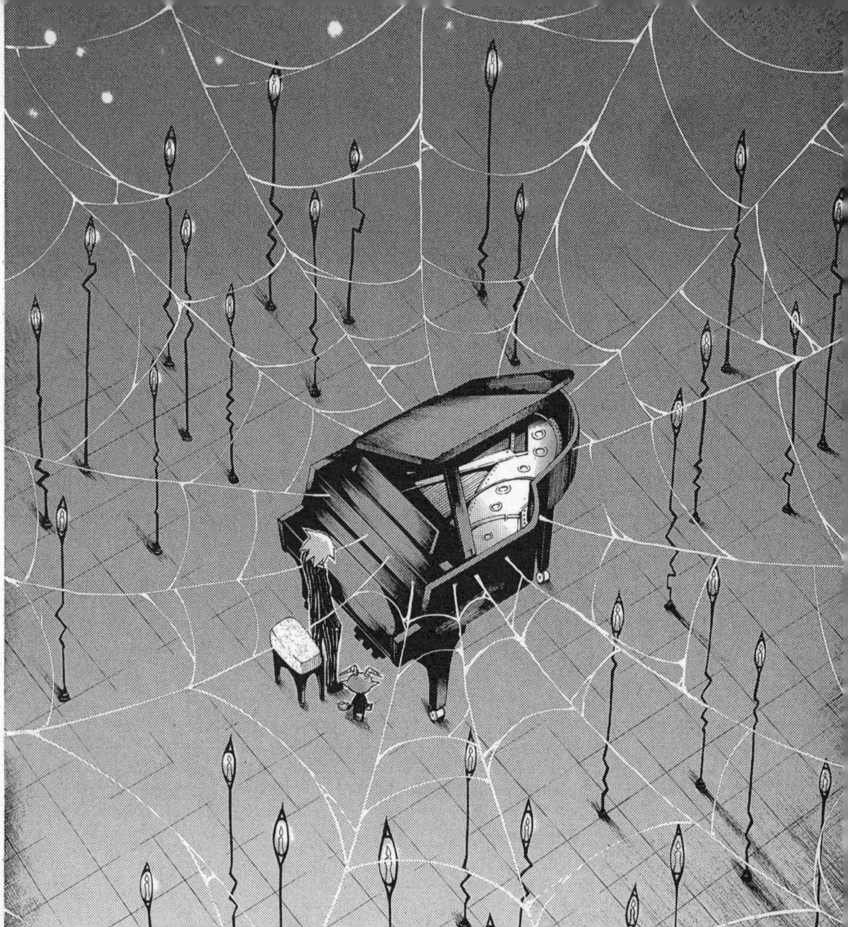
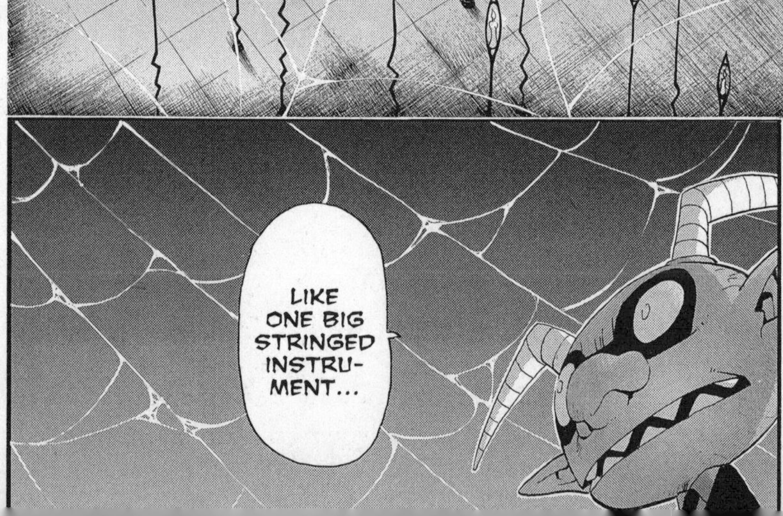
LIKE ONE BIG STRINGED INSTRU- MENT...

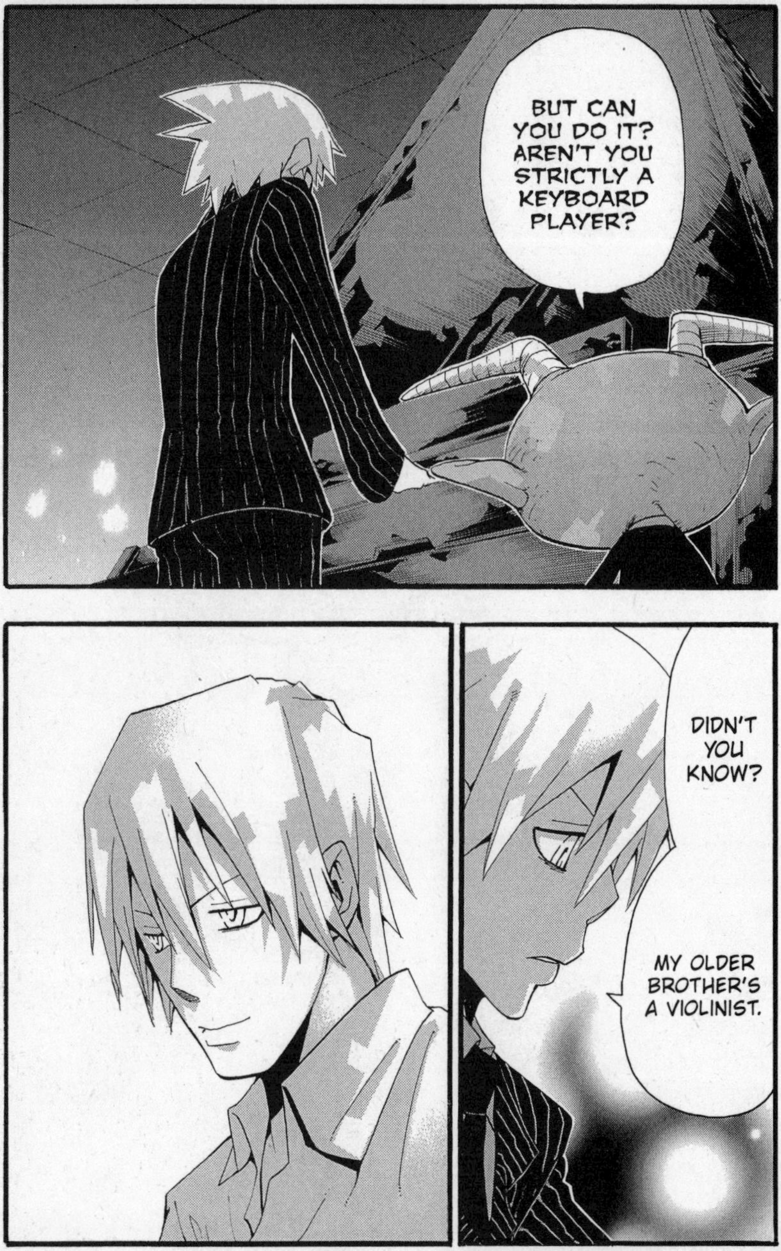
BUT CAN YOU DO IT? AREN'T YOU STRICTLY A KEYBOARD PLAYER?
DIDN'T YOU KNOW?
MY OLDER BROTHER'S A VIOLINIST.

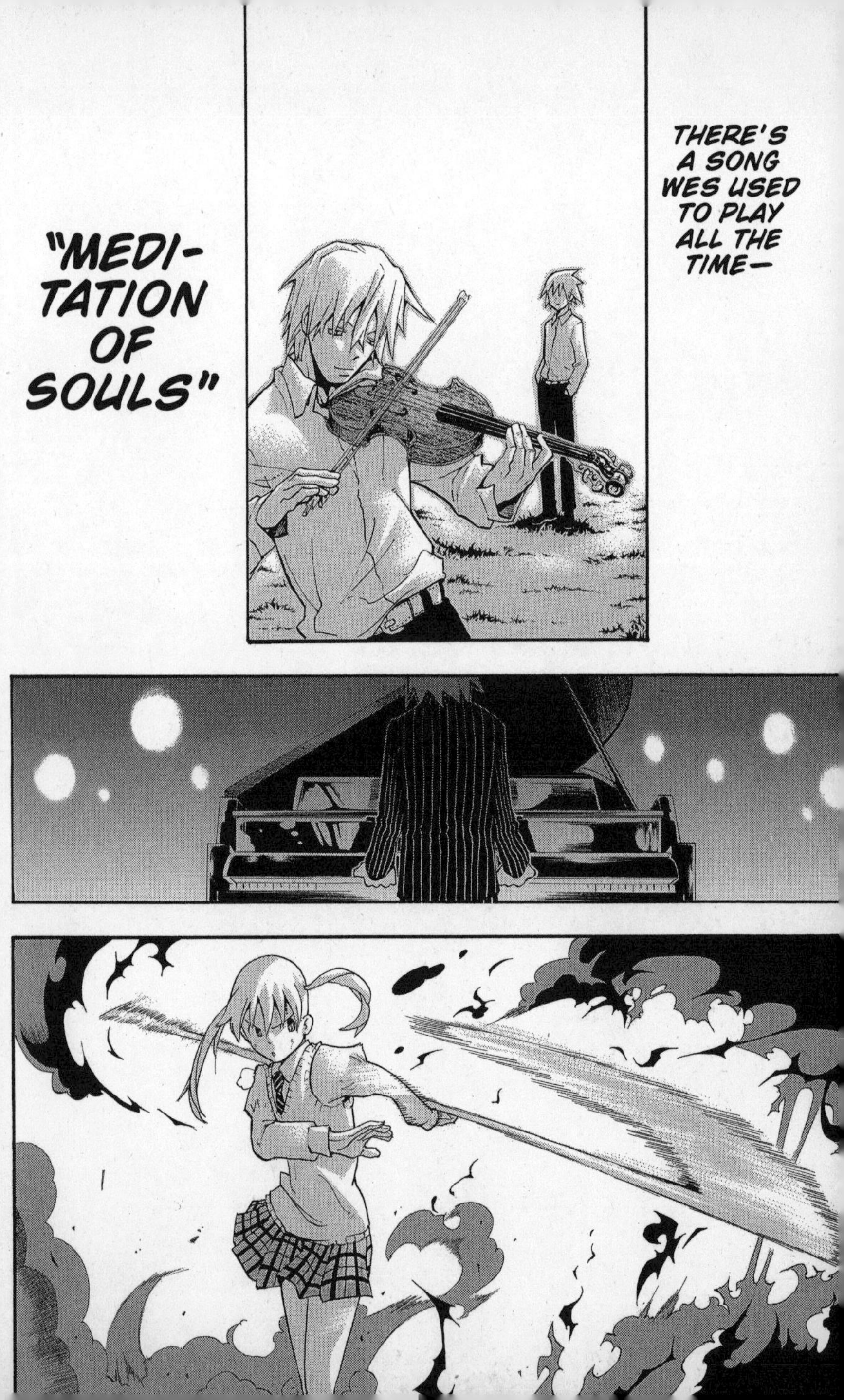
THERE'S A SONG WES USED TO PLAY ALL THE TIME—
"MEDI-TATION OF SOULS"

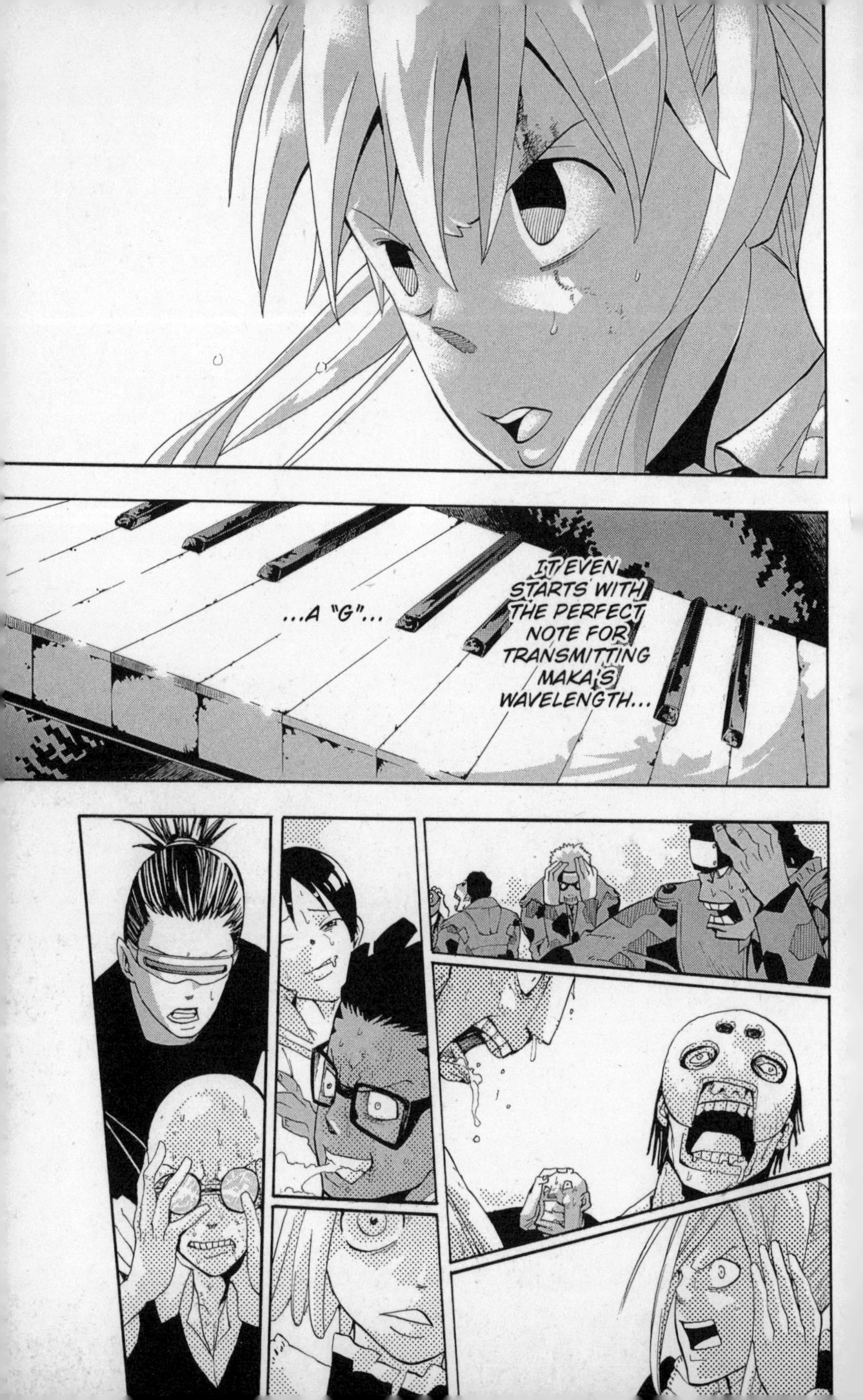
IT EVEN STARTS WITH THE PERFECT NOTE FOR TRANSMITTING MAKA'S WAVELENGTH...
...A "G"...

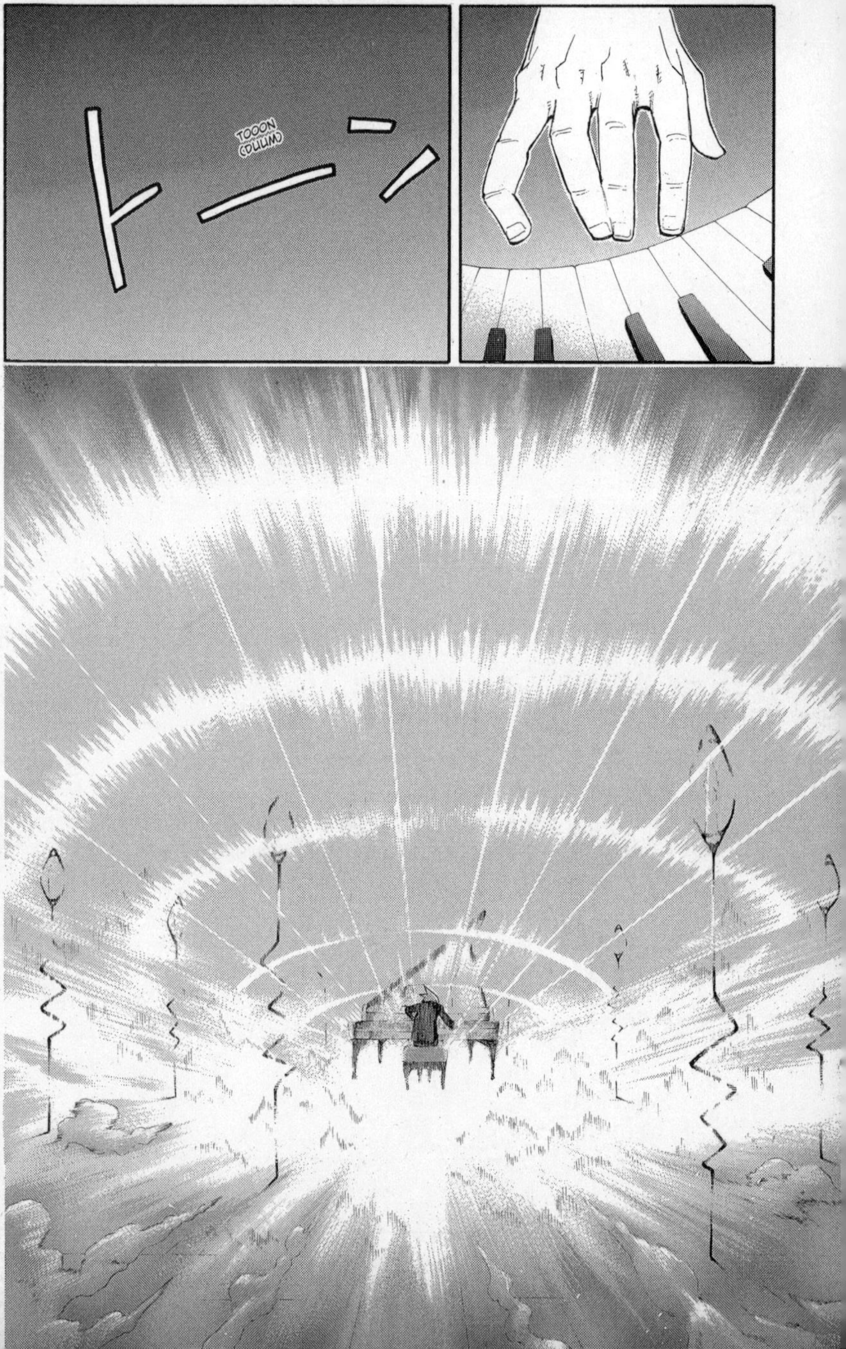
TOOON
(DUUM)

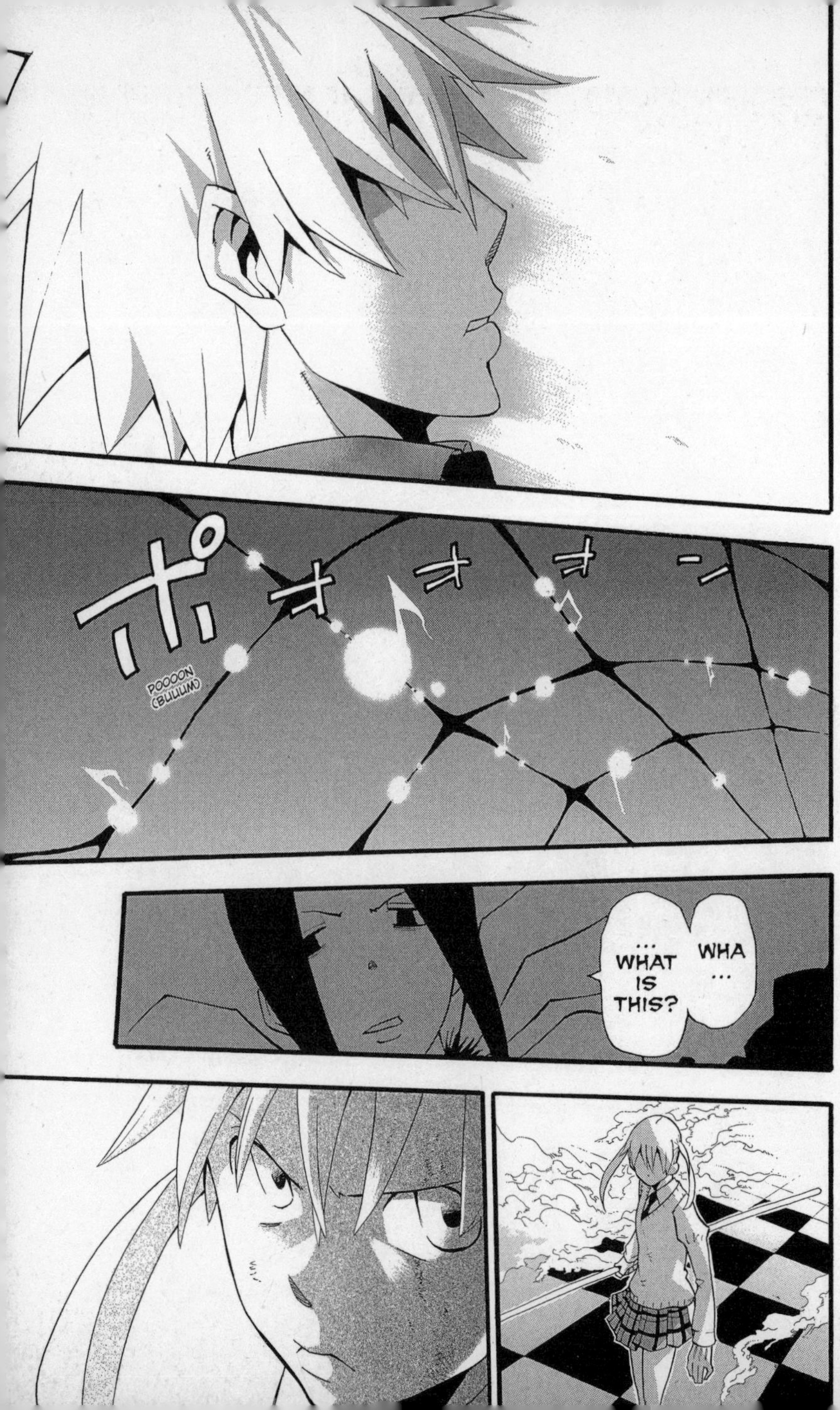
ポオオオー
POOOON (BUUUM)
WHA ...
... WHAT IS THIS?

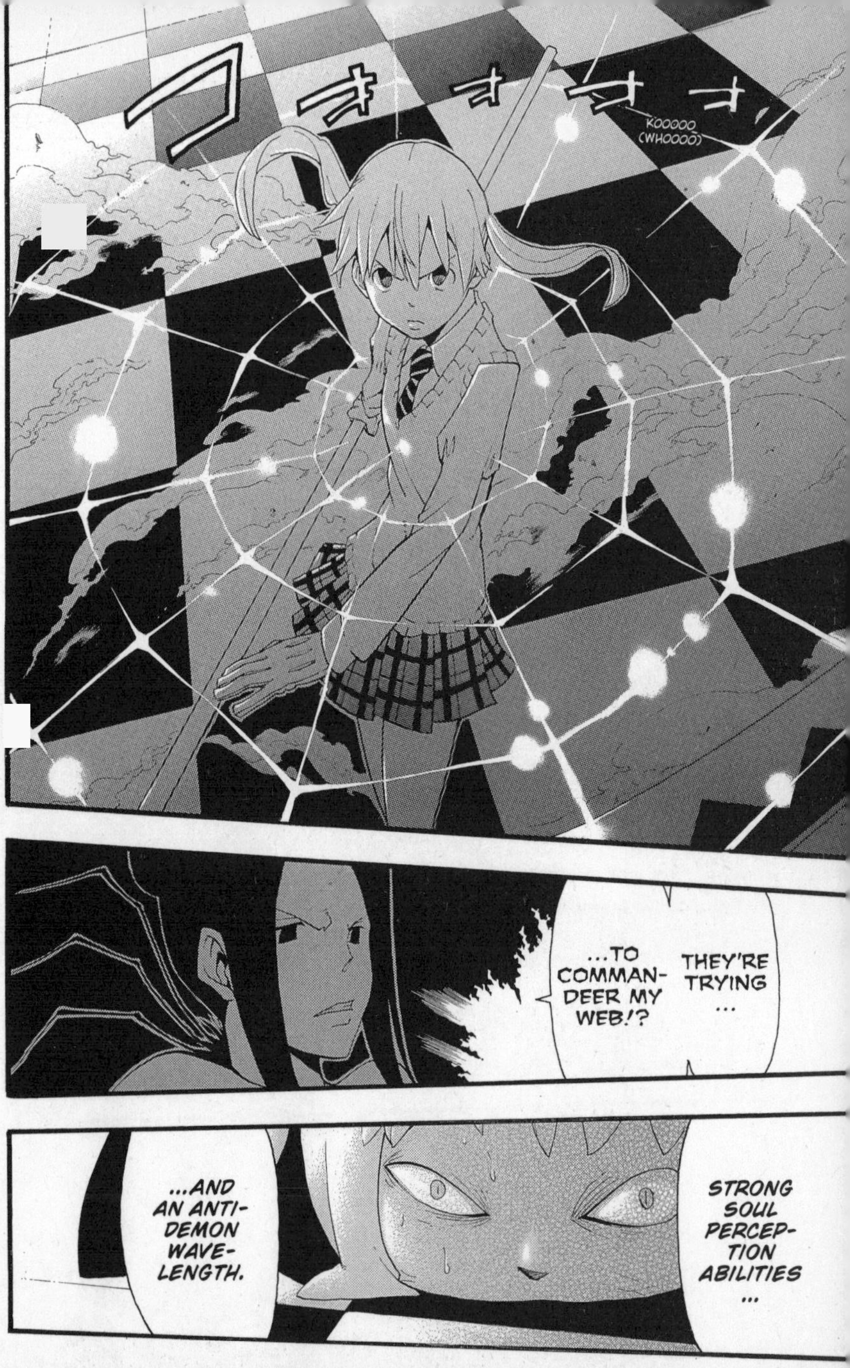
KOOOOO (WHOOOO)
THEY'RE TRYING ...
...TO COMMANDEER MY WEB!?
STRONG SOUL PERCEPTION ABILITIES ...
...AND AN ANTI-DEMON WAVELENGTH.

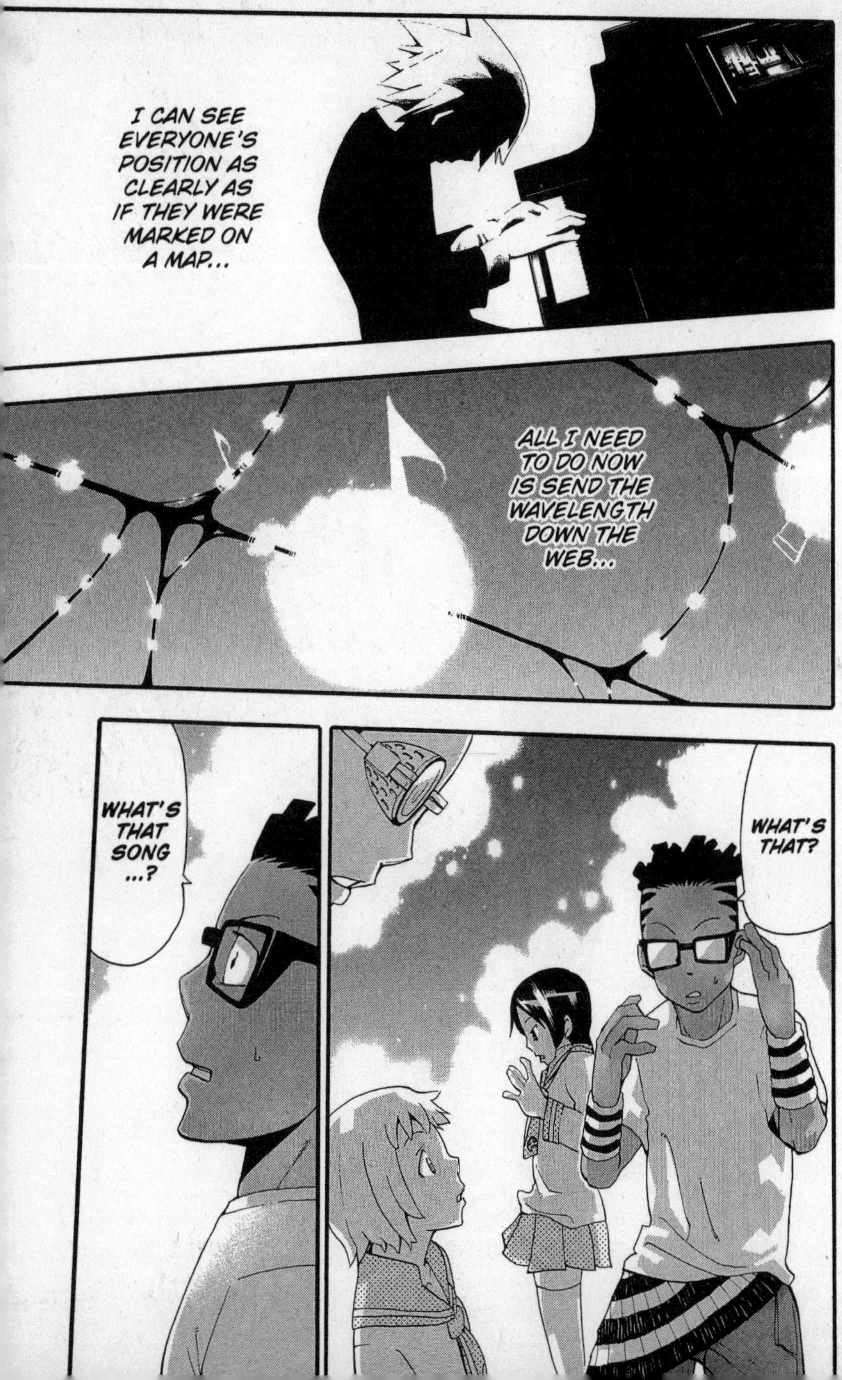
I CAN SEE EVERYONE'S POSITION AS CLEARLY AS IF THEY WERE MARKED ON A MAP...
ALL I NEED TO DO NOW IS SEND THE WAVELENGTH DOWN THE WEB...
WHAT'S THAT?
WHAT'S THAT SONG ...?

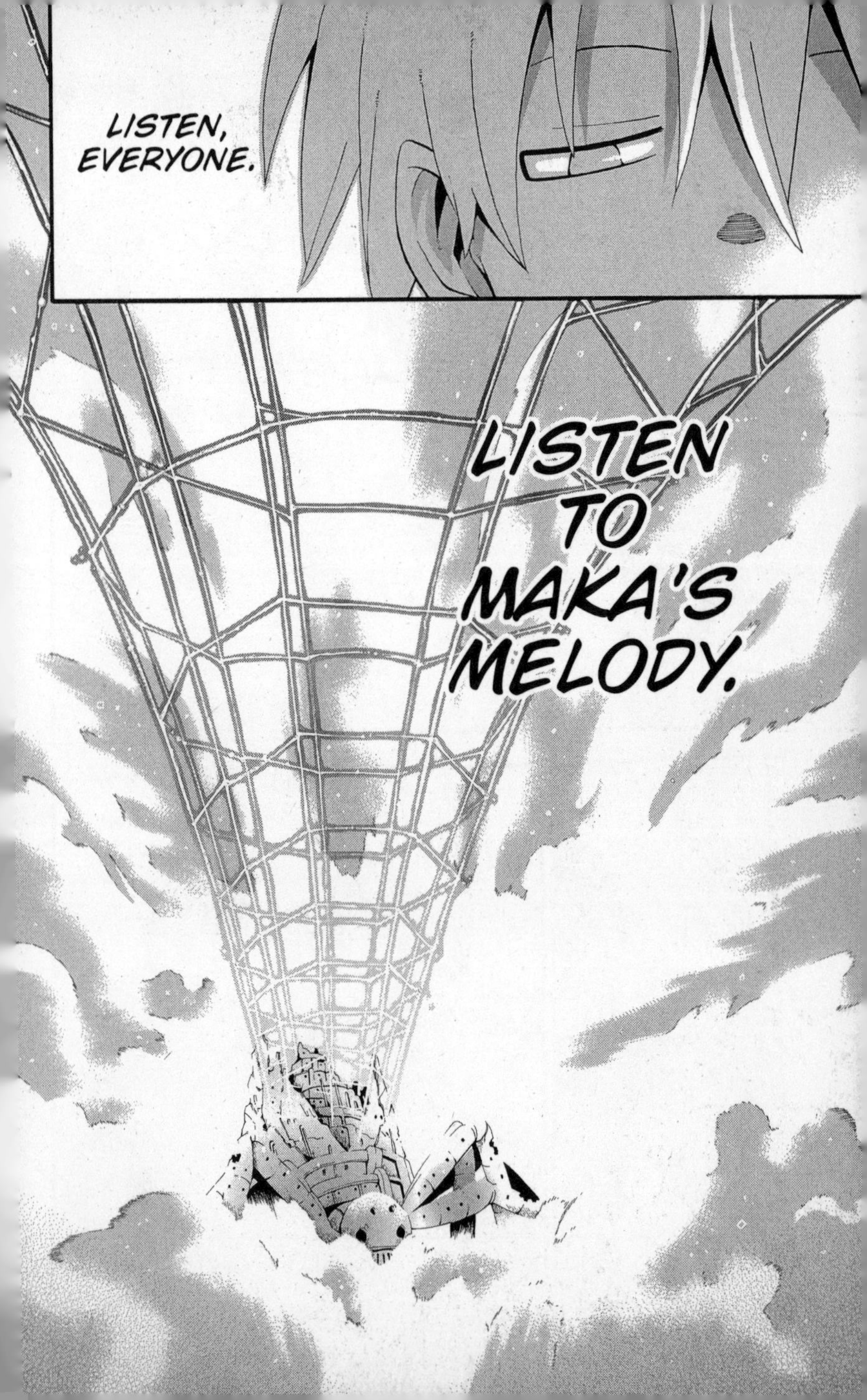
LISTEN, EVERYONE.
LISTEN TO MAKA'S MELODY.

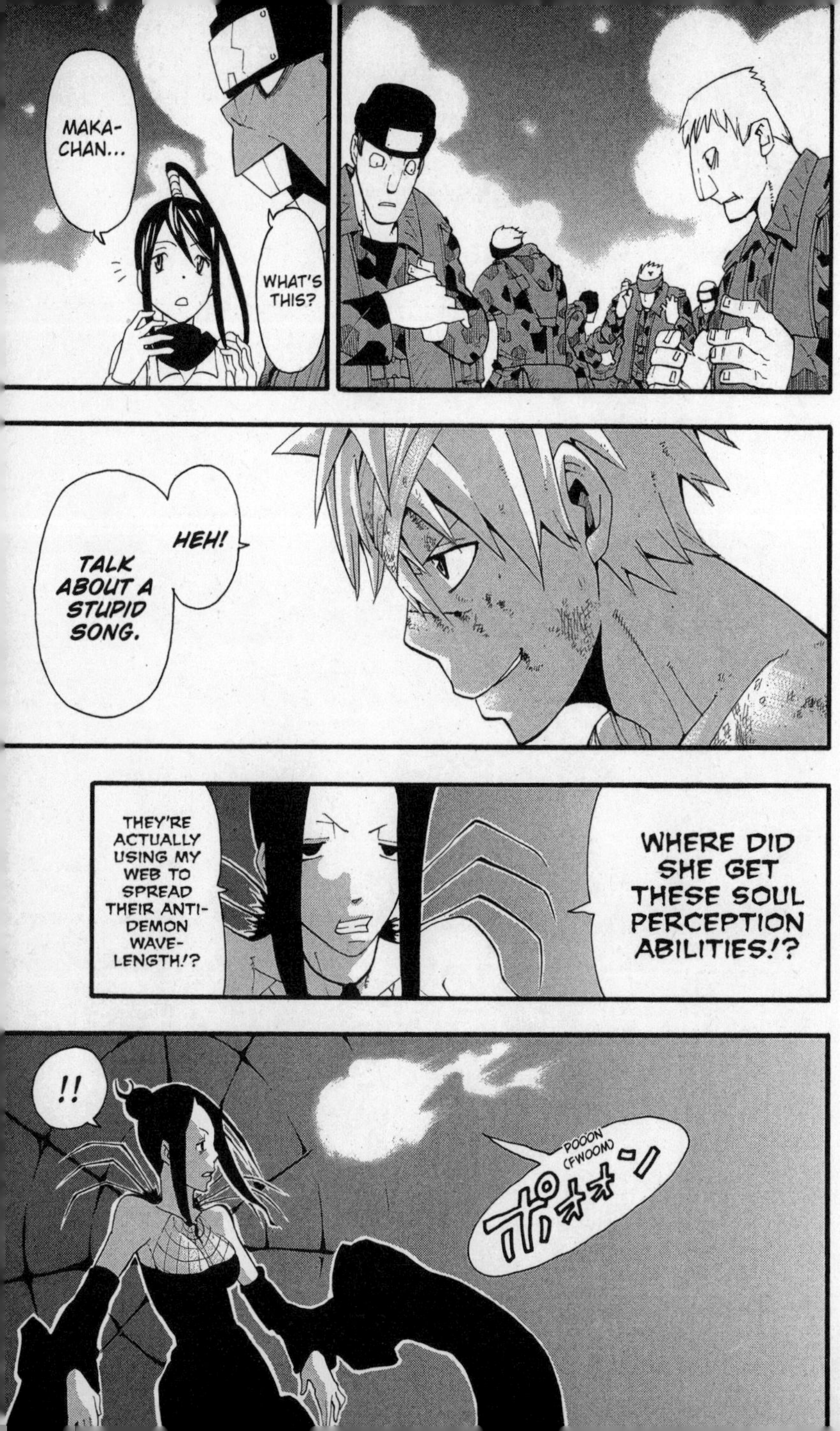
MAKA-CHAN...
WHAT'S THIS?
HEH!
TALK ABOUT A STUPID SONG.
WHERE DID SHE GET THESE SOUL PERCEPTION ABILITIES!?
THEY'RE ACTUALLY USING MY WEB TO SPREAD THEIR ANTI-DEMON WAVELENGTH!?
ポォォーン
POOON (FWOOM)
!!

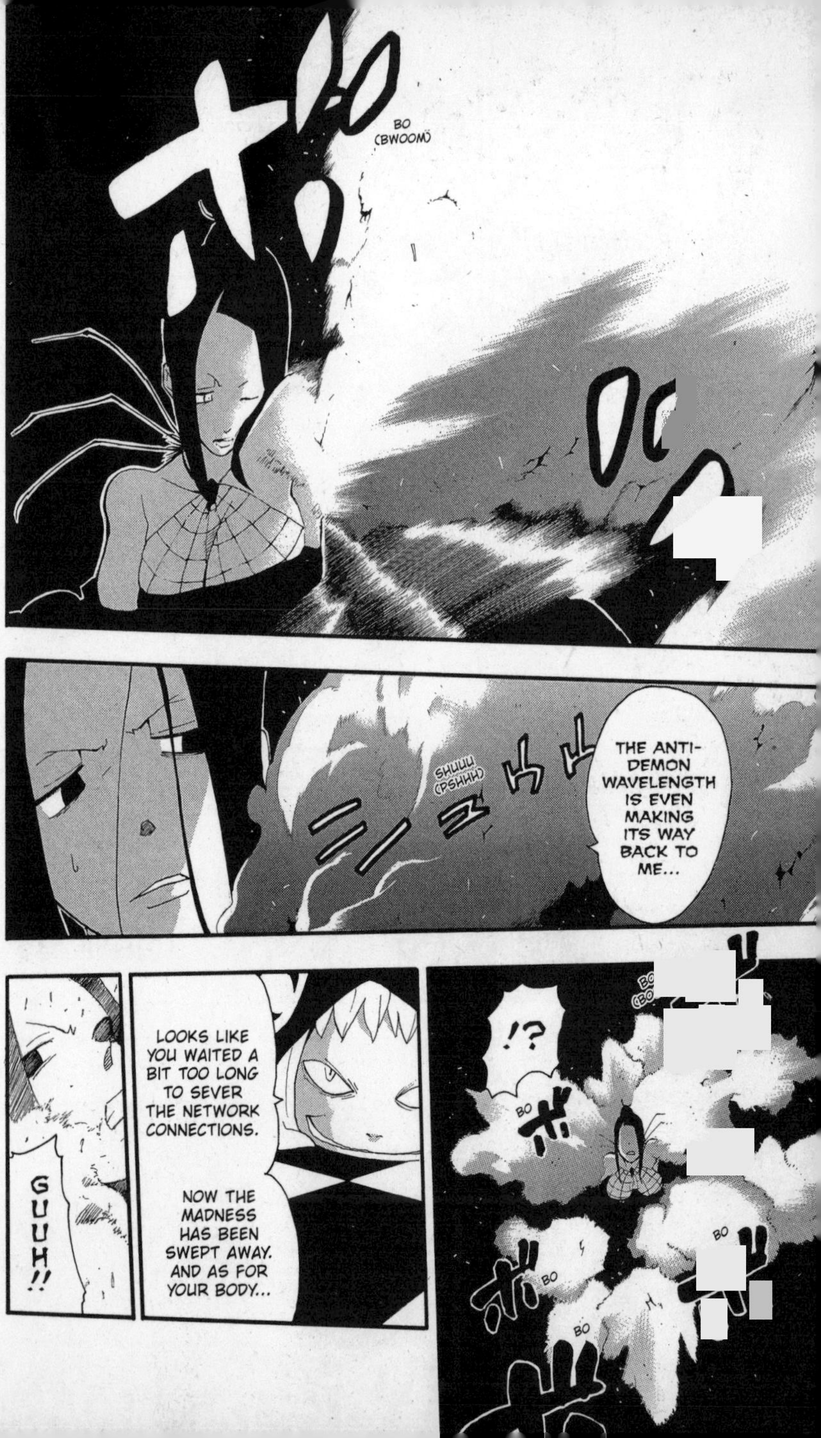
BO
(BWOOM)
THE ANTI-DEMON WAVELENGTH IS EVEN MAKING ITS WAY BACK TO ME...
SHUUU
(PSHHH)
BO
!?
BO
BO
BO
BO
LOOKS LIKE YOU WAITED A BIT TOO LONG TO SEVER THE NETWORK CONNECTIONS.
NOW THE MADNESS HAS BEEN SWEPT AWAY. AND AS FOR YOUR BODY...
GUUH!!

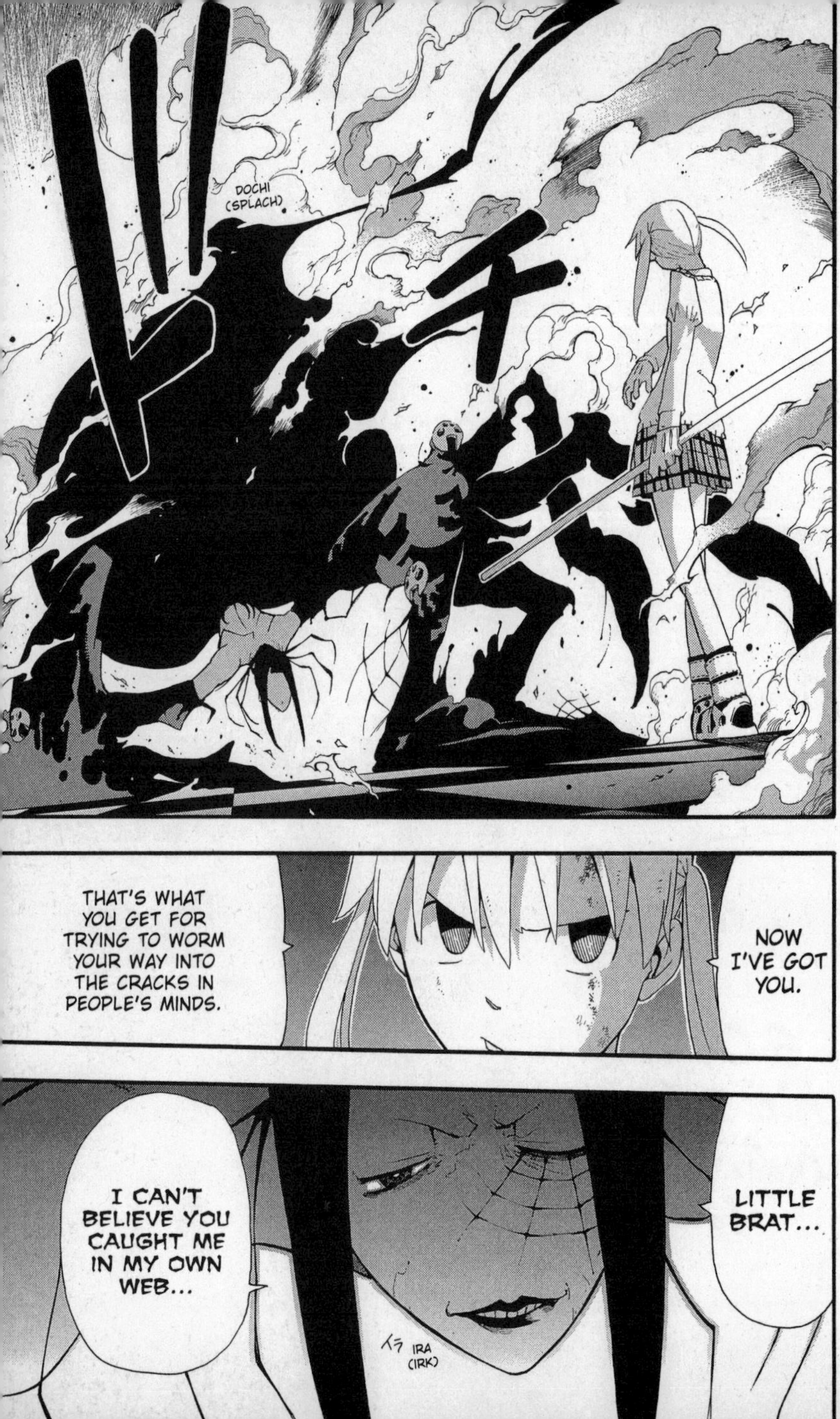
DOCHI (SPLACH)
NOW I'VE GOT YOU.
THAT'S WHAT YOU GET FOR TRYING TO WORM YOUR WAY INTO THE CRACKS IN PEOPLE'S MINDS.
LITTLE BRAT...
イラ IRA (IRK)
I CAN'T BELIEVE YOU CAUGHT ME IN MY OWN WEB...

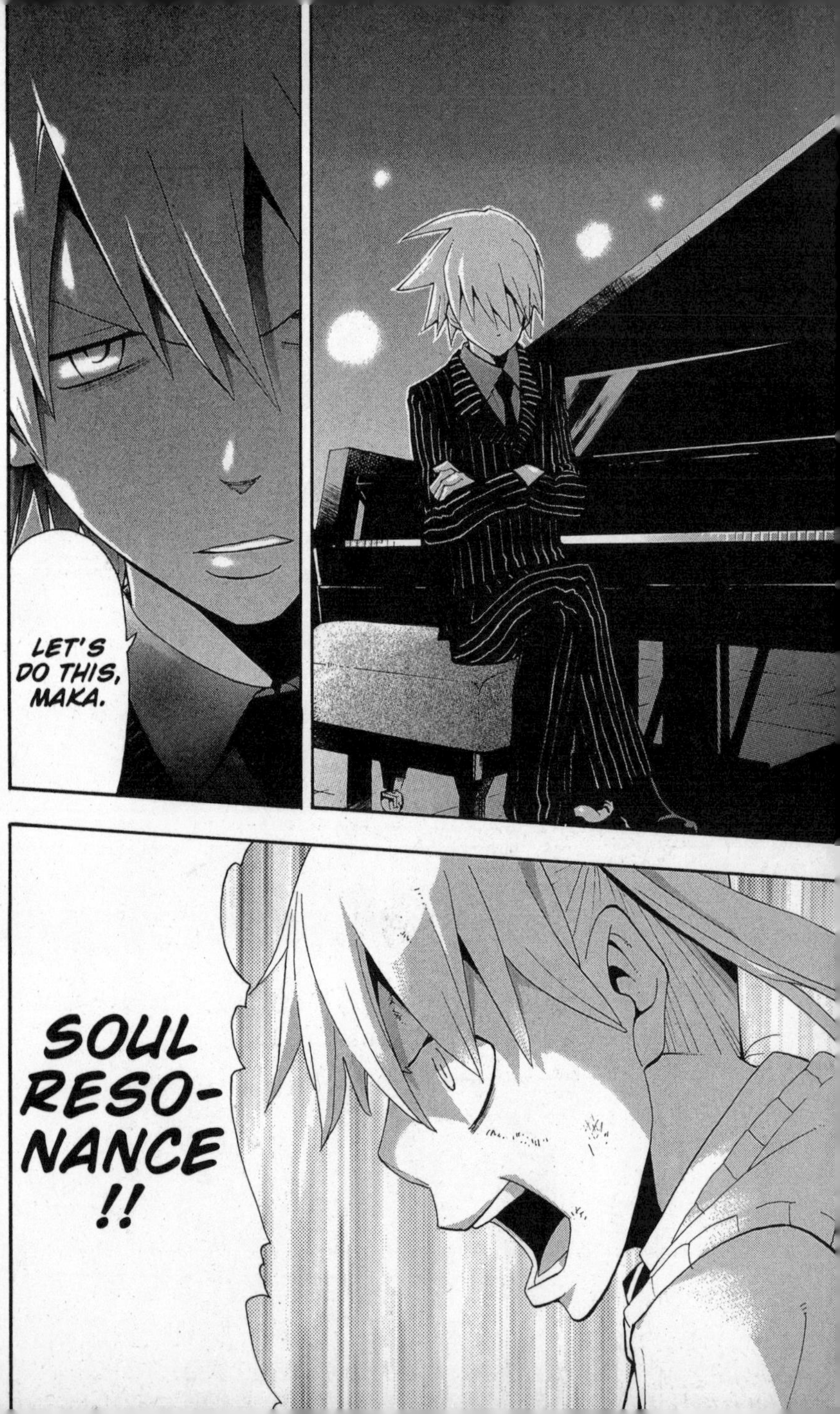
LET'S DO THIS, MAKA.
SOUL RESONANCE!!

HYA
AAA
AAA
AAH!

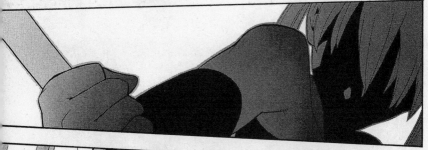

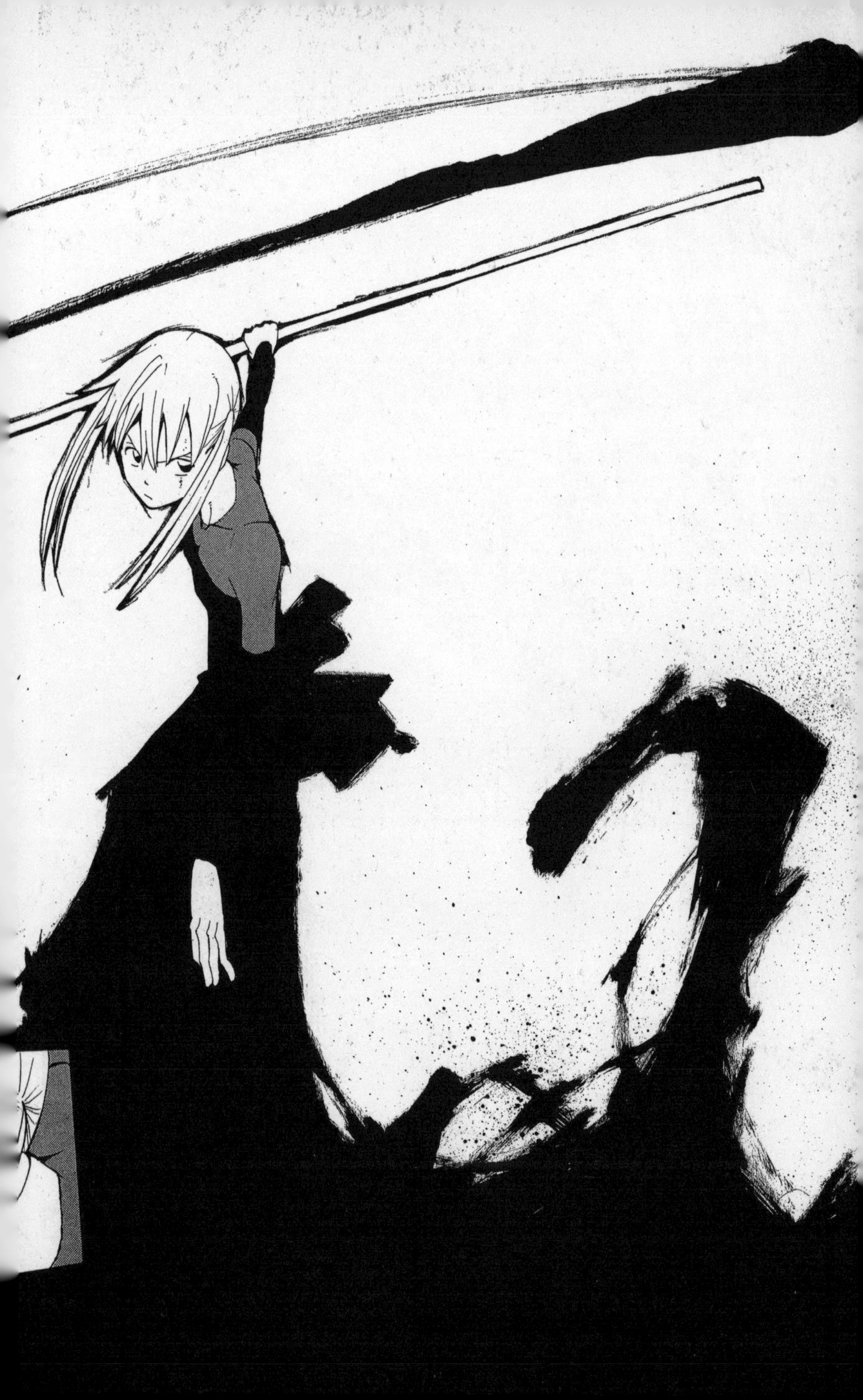

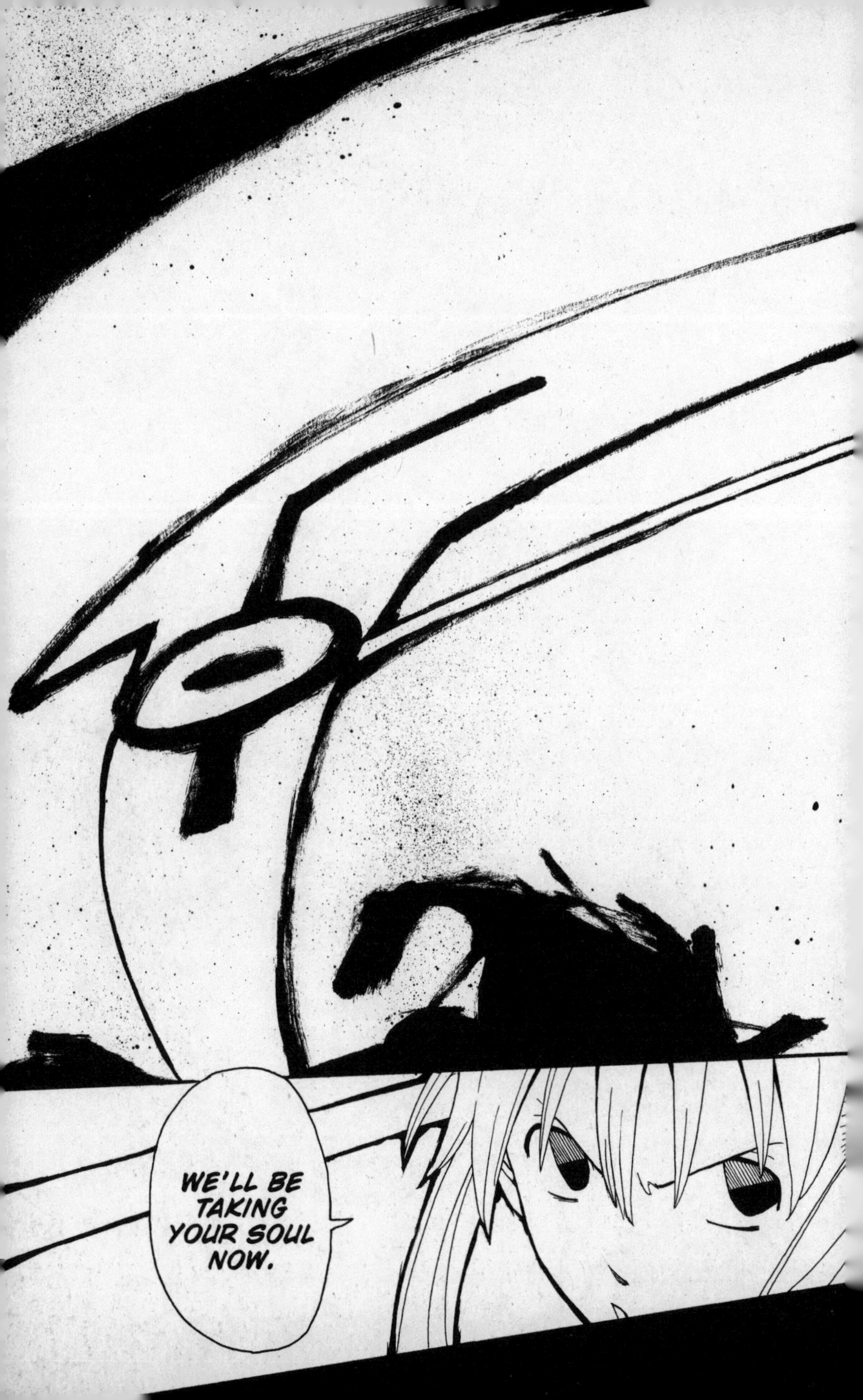
WE'LL BE TAKING YOUR SOUL NOW.

SOUL EATER

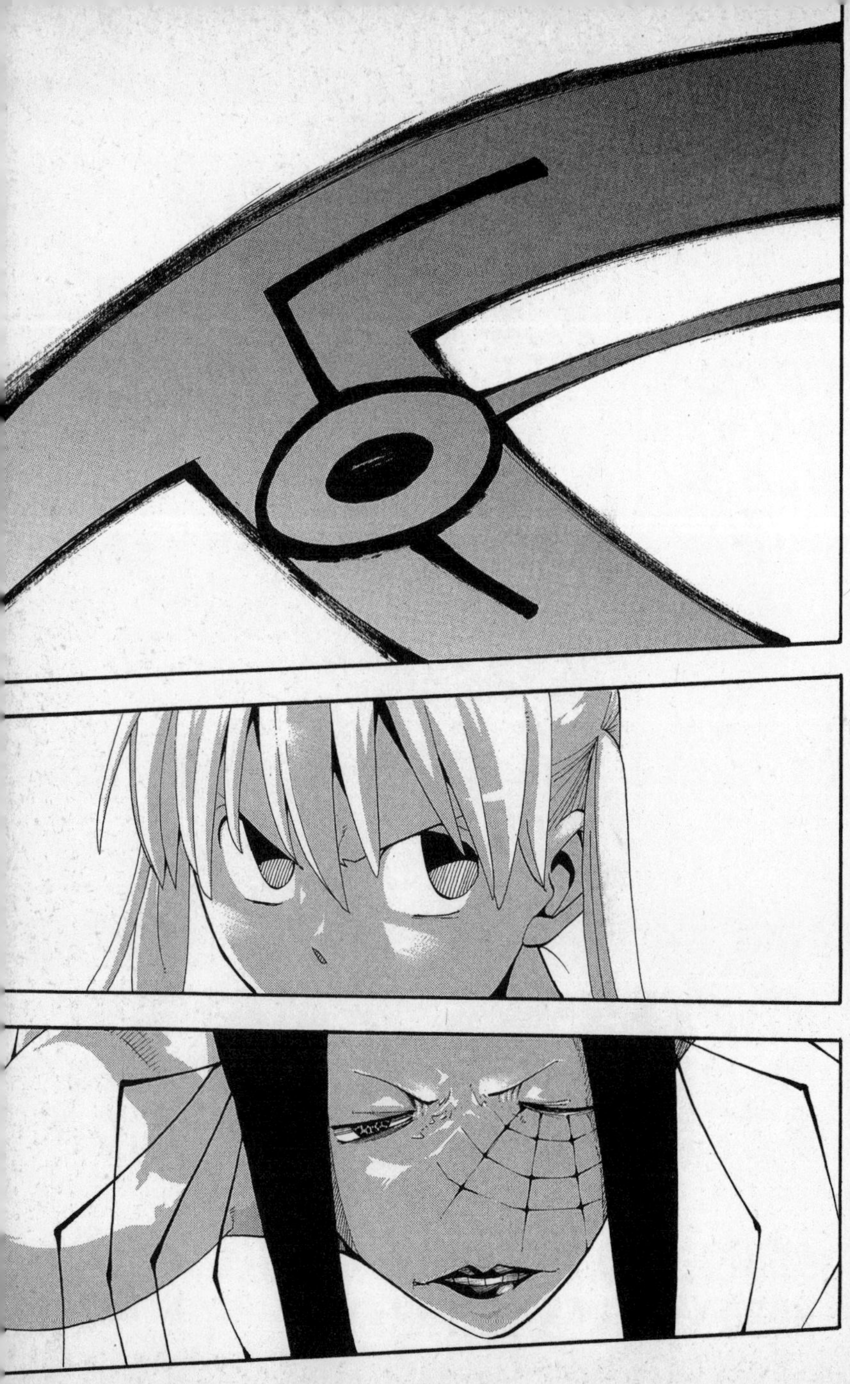

DEVIL-
HUNT
SLASH
!!!

SOUL EATER

CHAPTER 60: OPERATION CAPTURE BABA YAGA CASTLE (PART 15)

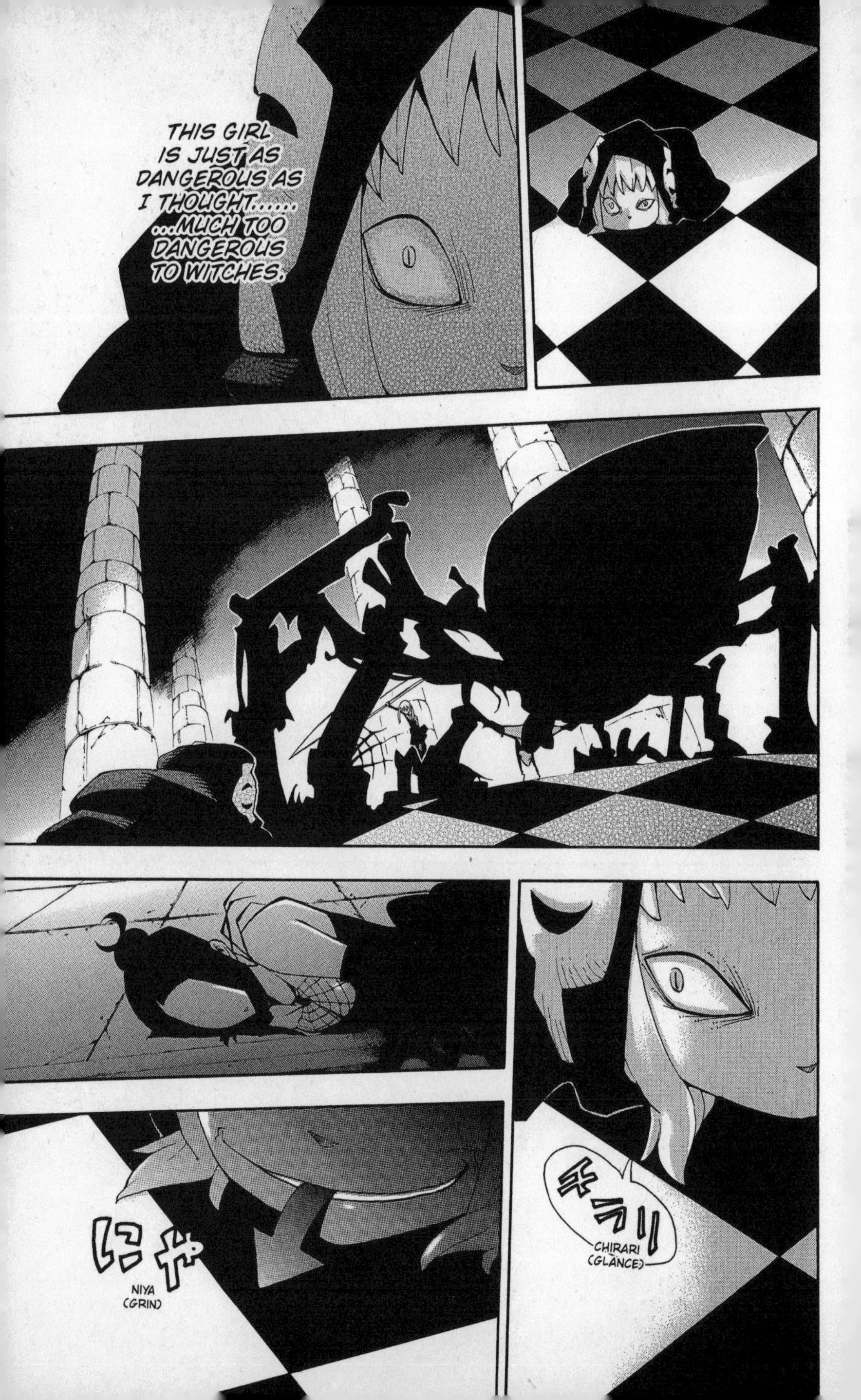

THIS GIRL IS JUST AS DANGEROUS AS I THOUGHT......
...MUCH TOO DANGEROUS TO WITCHES.
CHIRARI (GLANCE)
NIYA (GRIN)

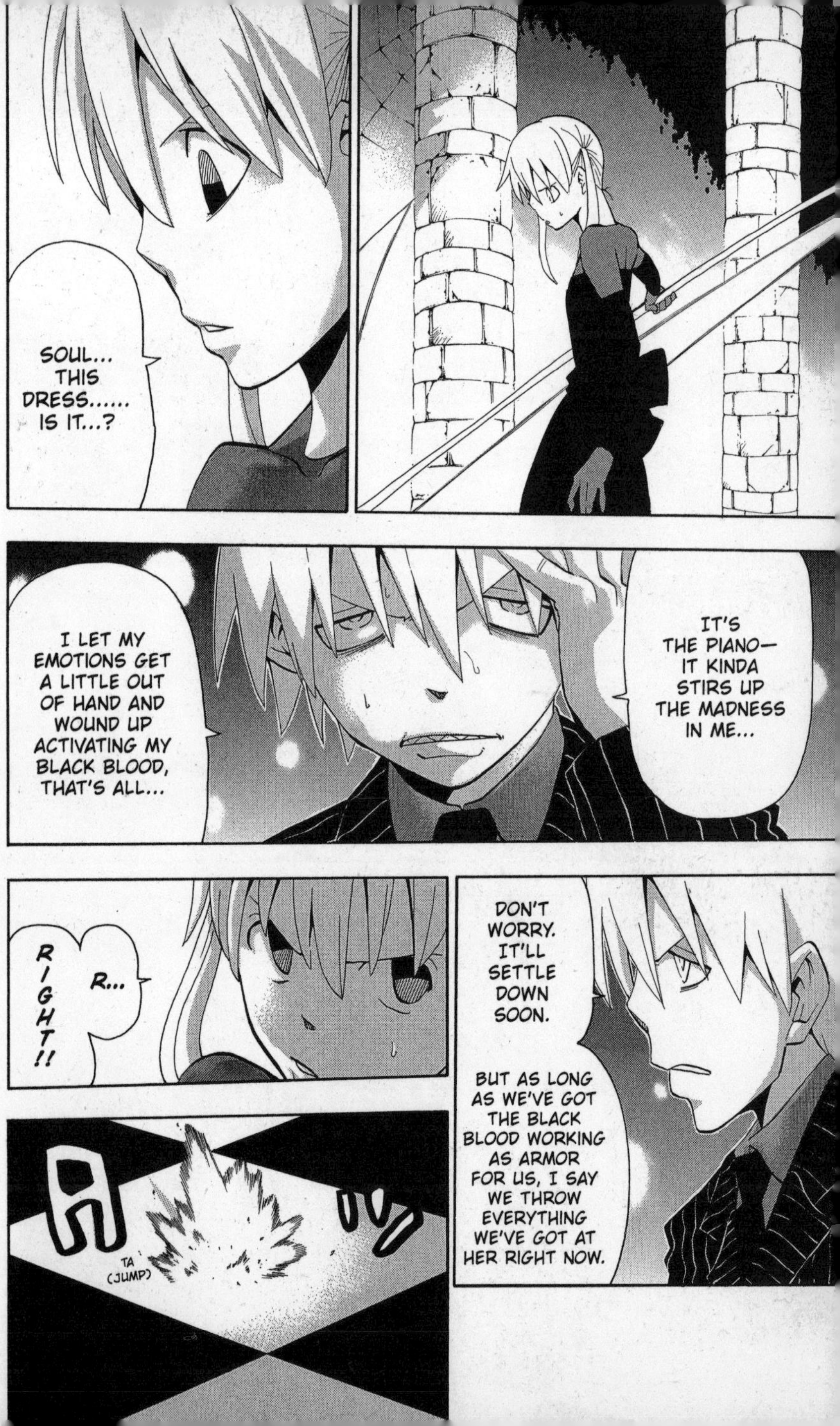
SOUL... THIS DRESS...... IS IT...?
IT'S THE PIANO— IT KINDA STIRS UP THE MADNESS IN ME...
I LET MY EMOTIONS GET A LITTLE OUT OF HAND AND WOUND UP ACTIVATING MY BLACK BLOOD, THAT'S ALL...
DON'T WORRY. IT'LL SETTLE DOWN SOON.
BUT AS LONG AS WE'VE GOT THE BLACK BLOOD WORKING AS ARMOR FOR US, I SAY WE THROW EVERYTHING WE'VE GOT AT HER RIGHT NOW.
R...
RIGHT!!
TA (JUMP)

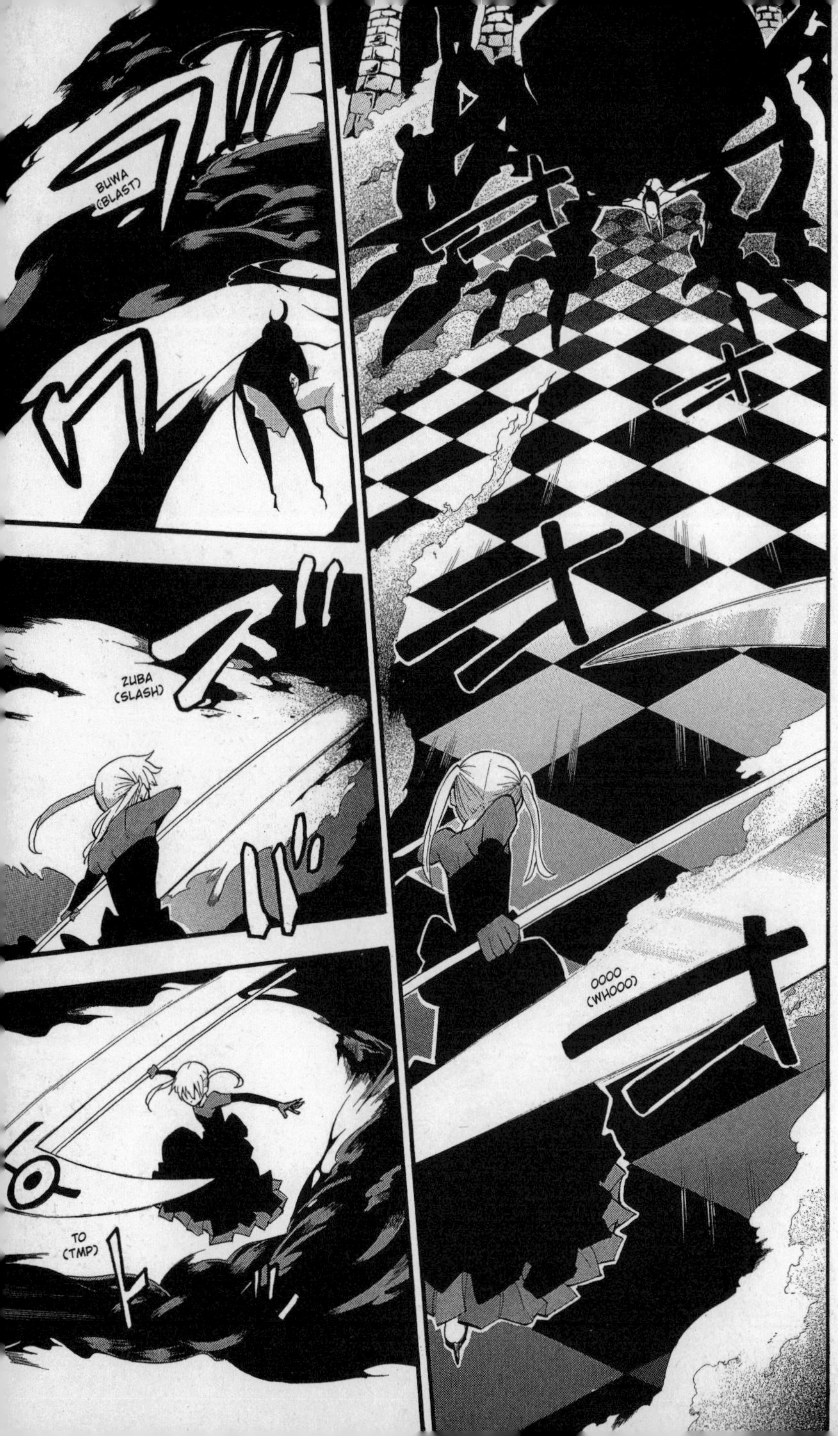
OOOO (WHOOO)
BUWA (BLAST)
ZUBA (SLASH)
TO (TMP)

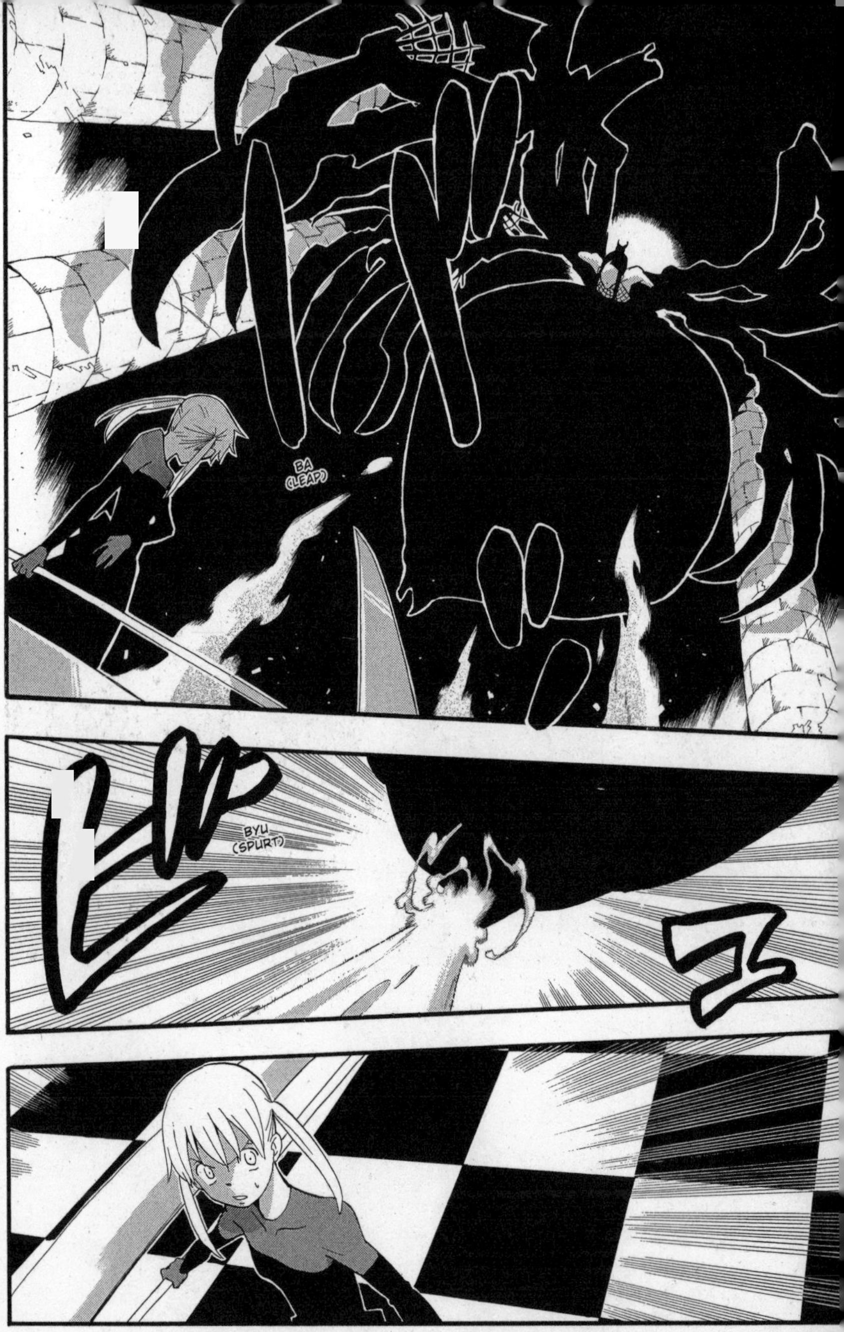
BA (LEAP)
BYU (SPURT)

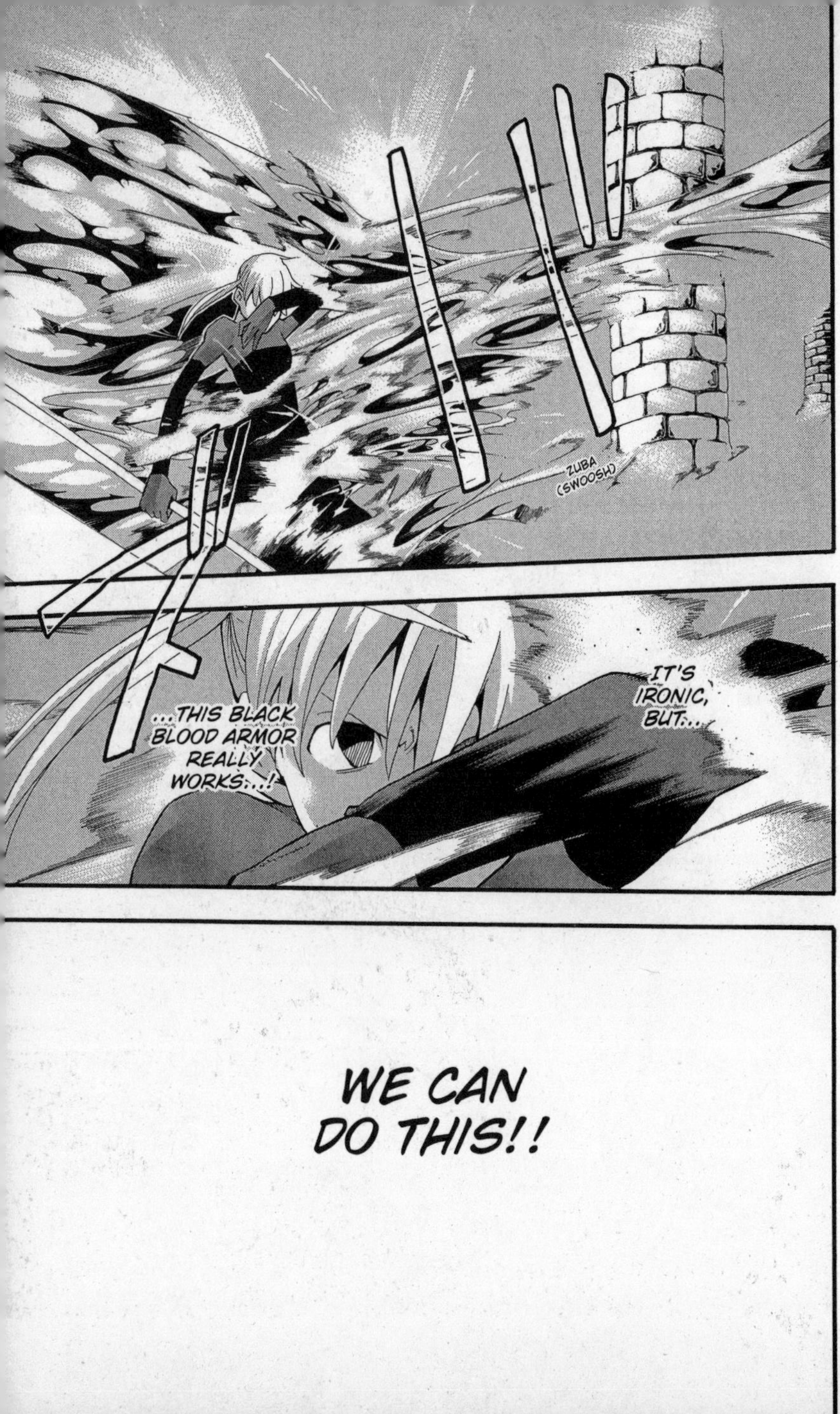
ZUBA (SWOOSH)
IT'S IRONIC, BUT...
...THIS BLACK BLOOD ARMOR REALLY WORKS...!
WE CAN DO THIS!!

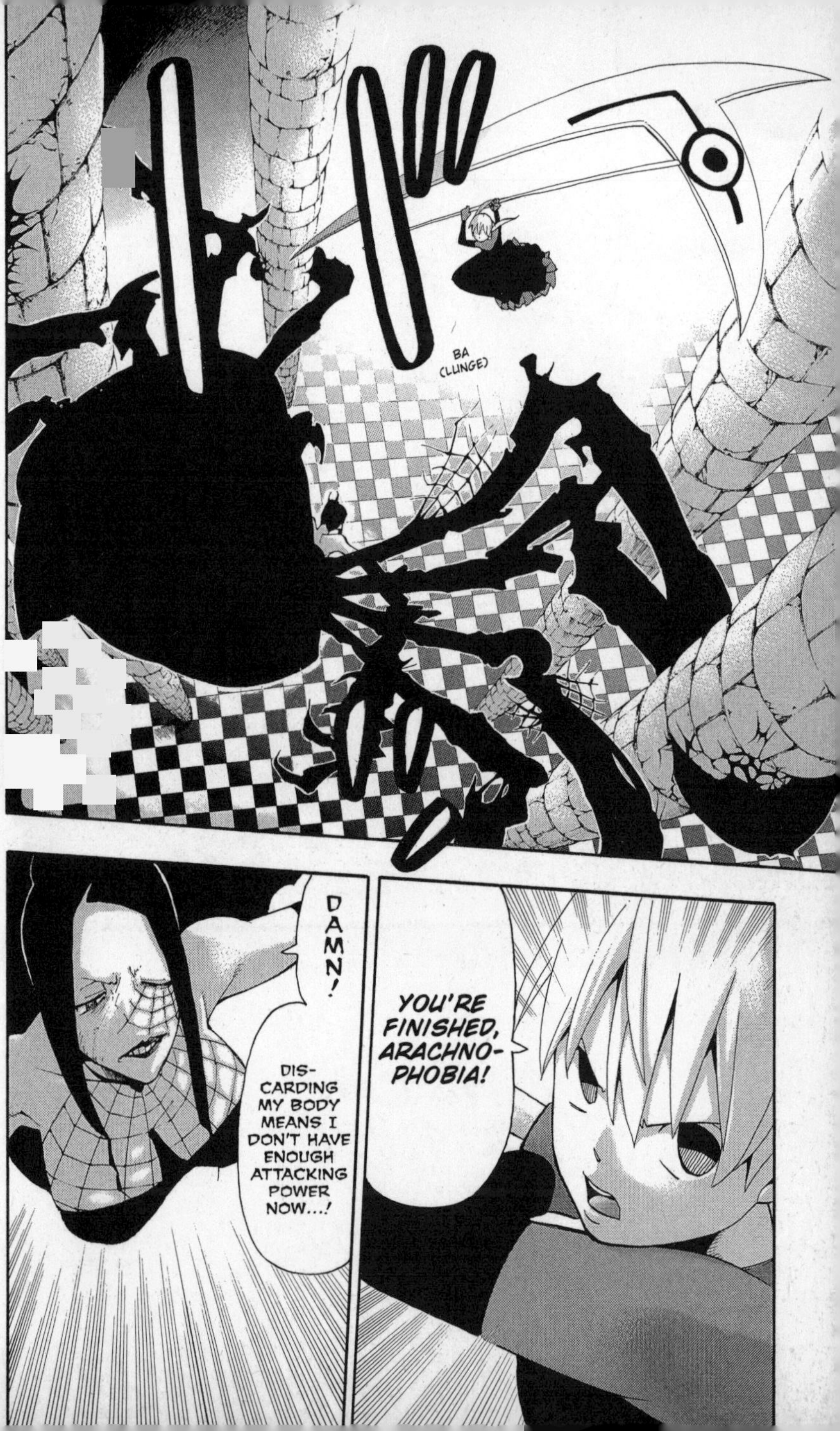
BA (LUNGE)
YOU'RE FINISHED, ARACHNO-PHOBIA!
DAMN!
DIS-CARDING MY BODY MEANS I DON'T HAVE ENOUGH ATTACKING POWER NOW...!

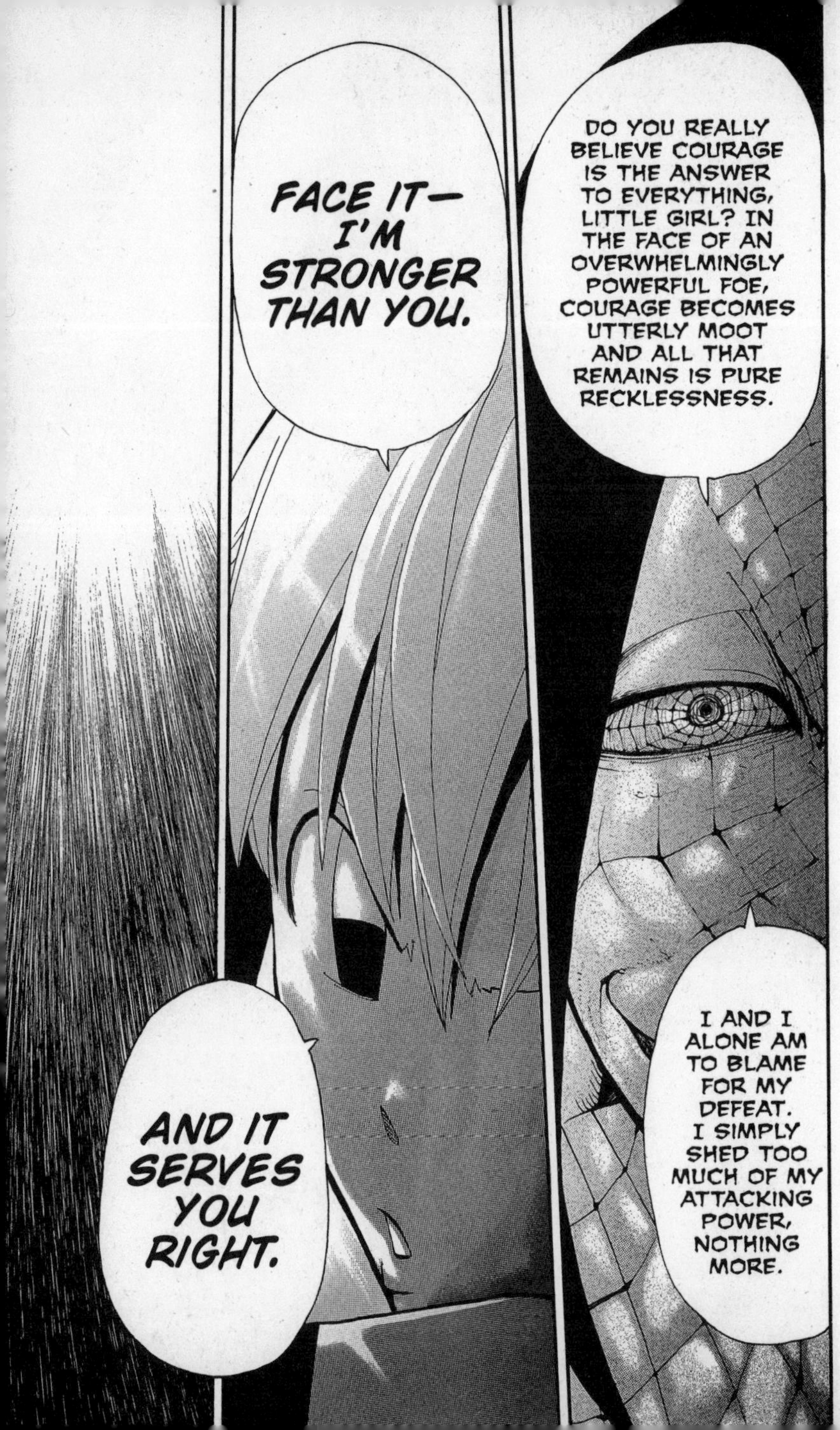
DO YOU REALLY BELIEVE COURAGE IS THE ANSWER TO EVERYTHING, LITTLE GIRL? IN THE FACE OF AN OVERWHELMINGLY POWERFUL FOE, COURAGE BECOMES UTTERLY MOOT AND ALL THAT REMAINS IS PURE RECKLESSNESS.
I AND I ALONE AM TO BLAME FOR MY DEFEAT. I SIMPLY SHED TOO MUCH OF MY ATTACKING POWER, NOTHING MORE.
FACE IT— I'M STRONGER THAN YOU.
AND IT SERVES YOU RIGHT.

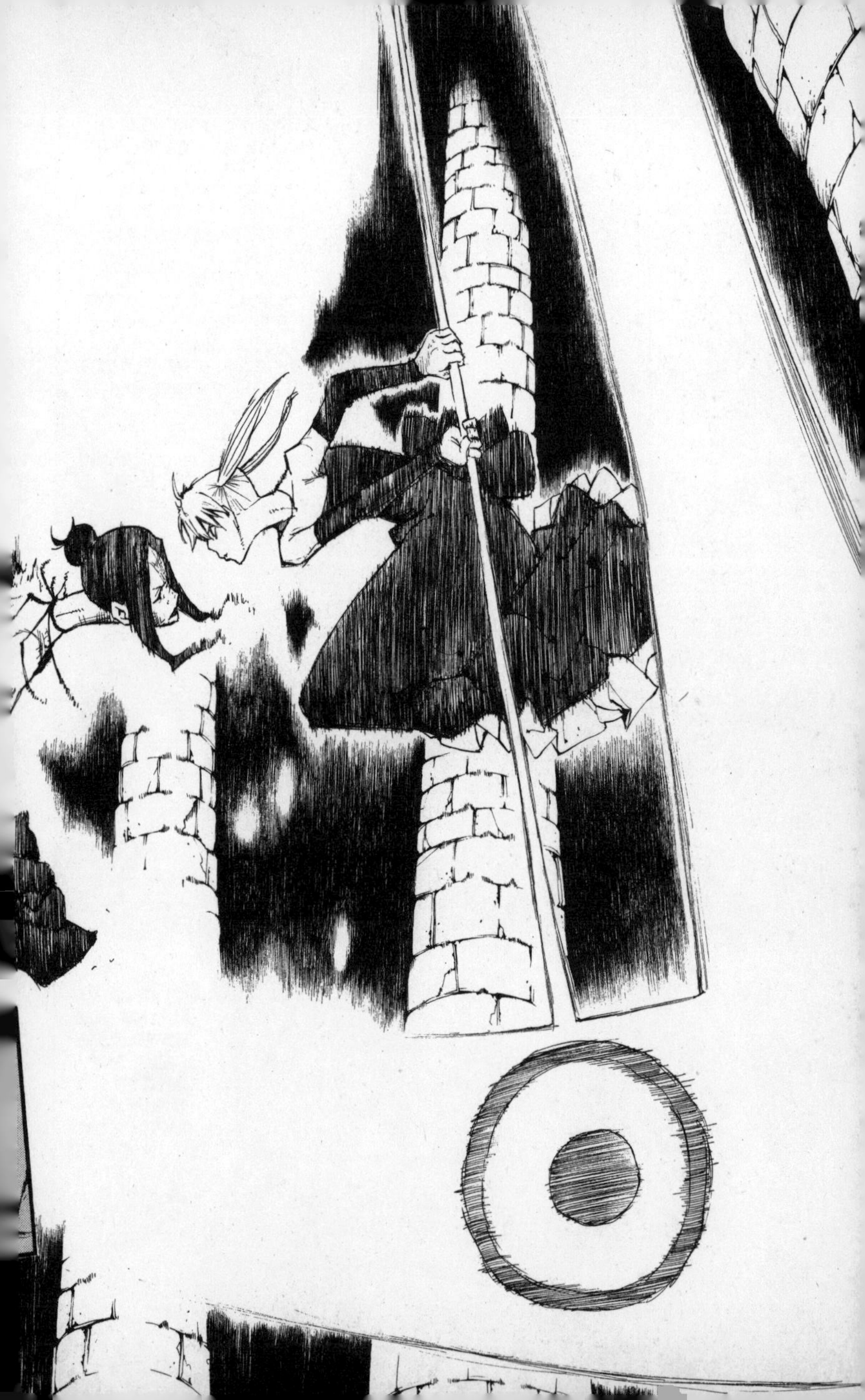

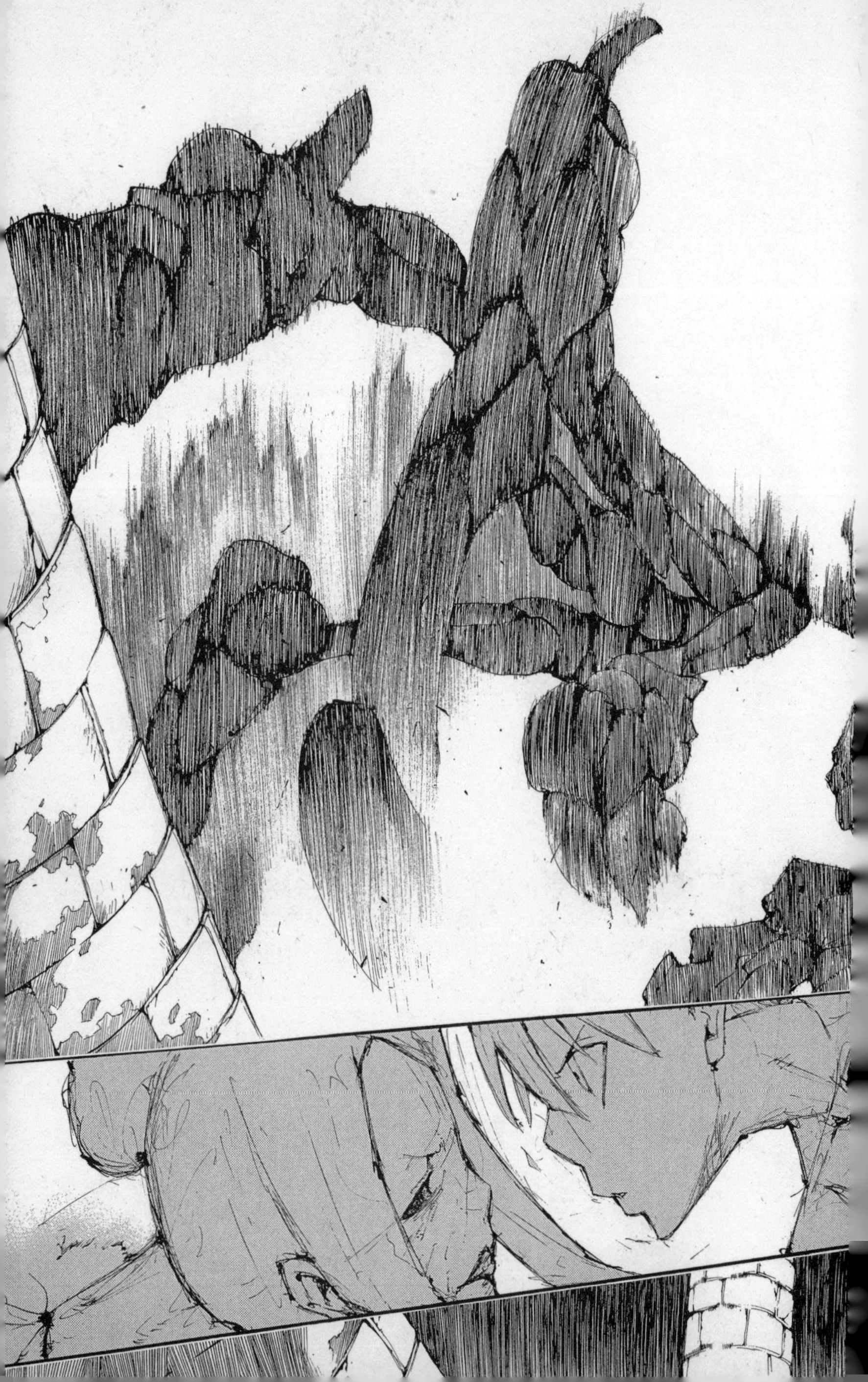

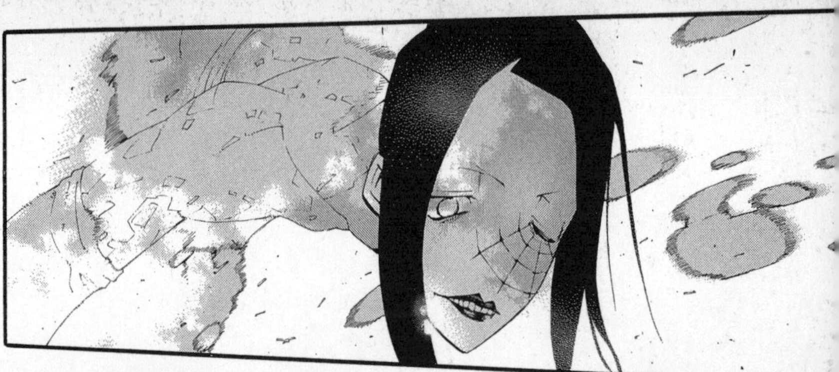

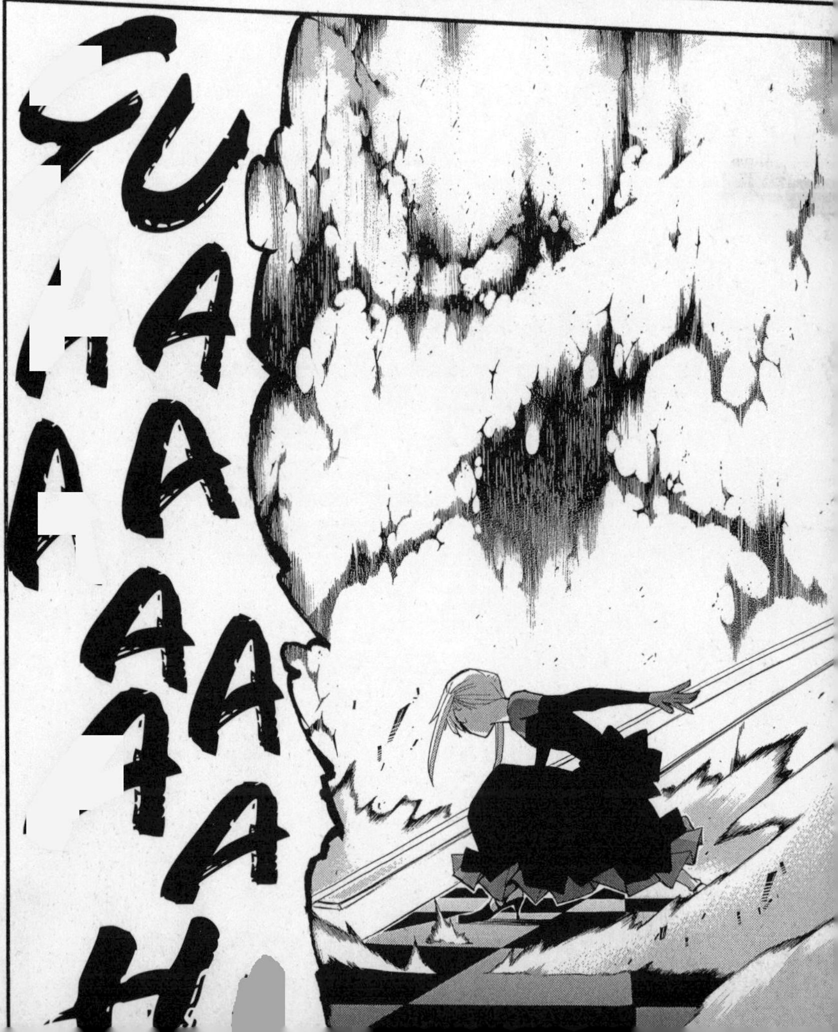
UAAAAAAH

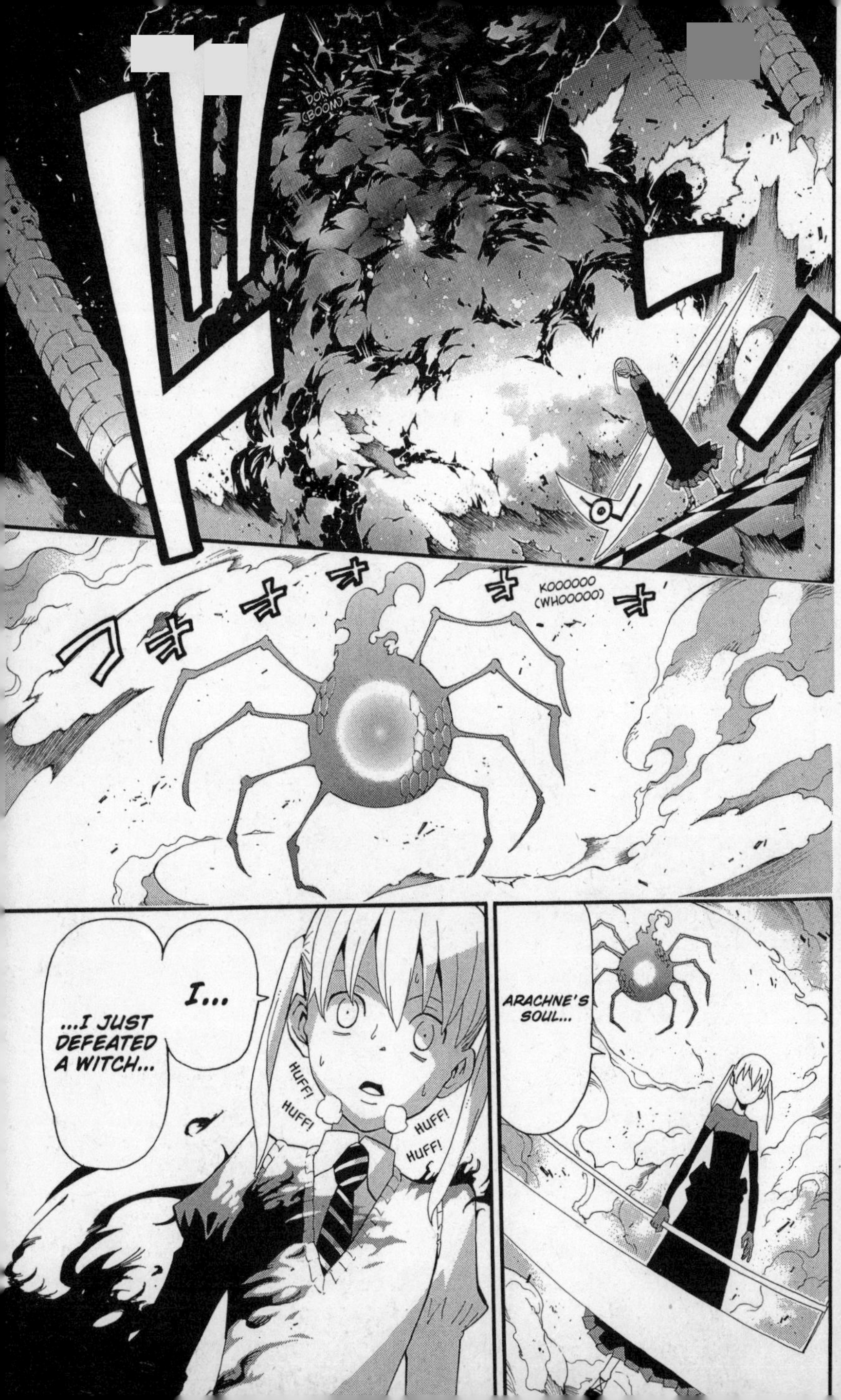
DON (BOOM)
KOOOOOO (WHOOOOO)
ARACHNE'S SOUL...
I...
...I JUST DEFEATED A WITCH...
HUFF! HUFF!
HUFF! HUFF!

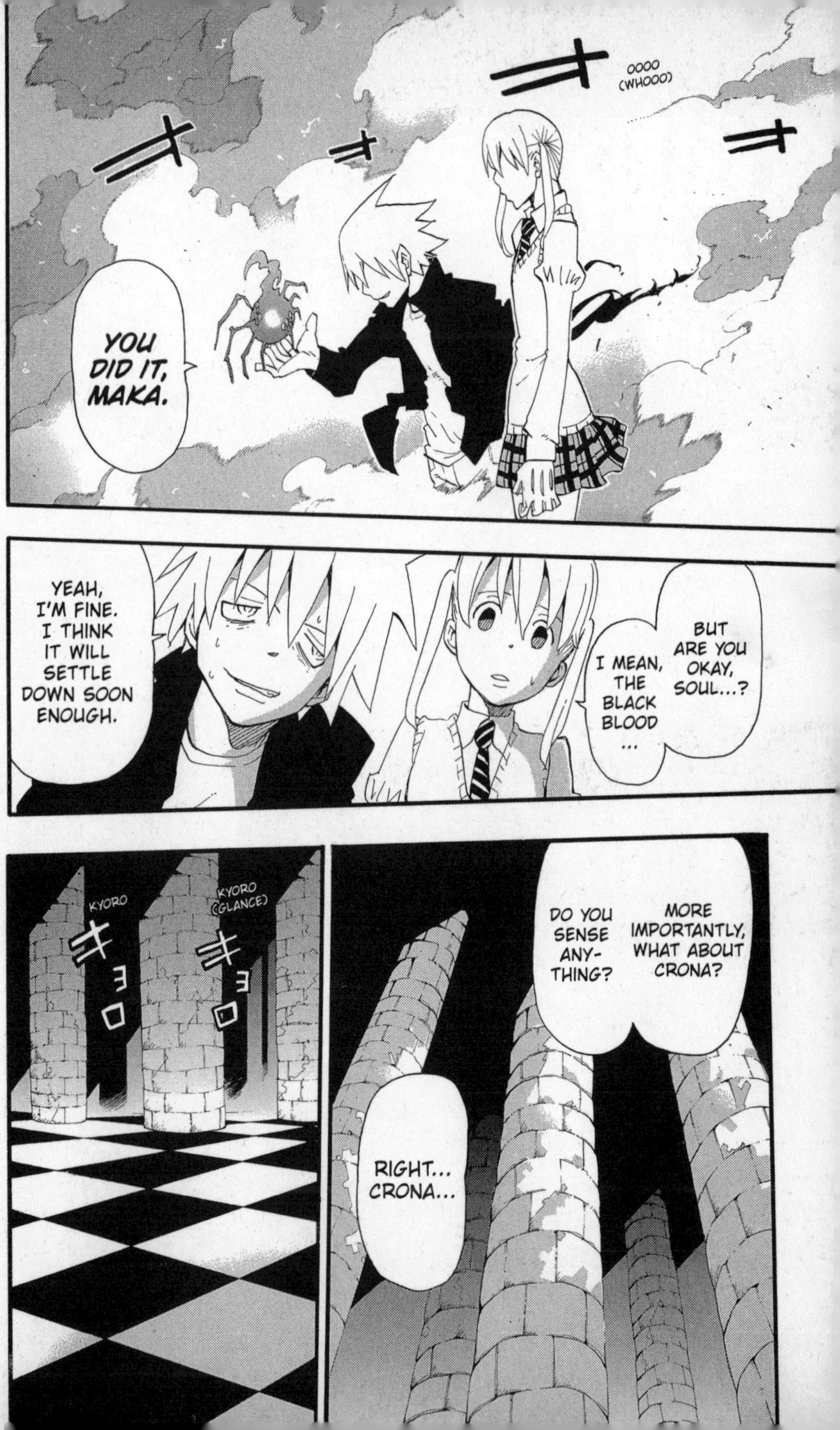
OOOO (WHOOO)
YOU DID IT, MAKA.
BUT ARE YOU OKAY, SOUL...?
I MEAN, THE BLACK BLOOD ...
YEAH, I'M FINE. I THINK IT WILL SETTLE DOWN SOON ENOUGH.
MORE IMPORTANTLY, WHAT ABOUT CRONA?
DO YOU SENSE ANY-THING?
RIGHT... CRONA...
KYORO (GLANCE)
KYORO

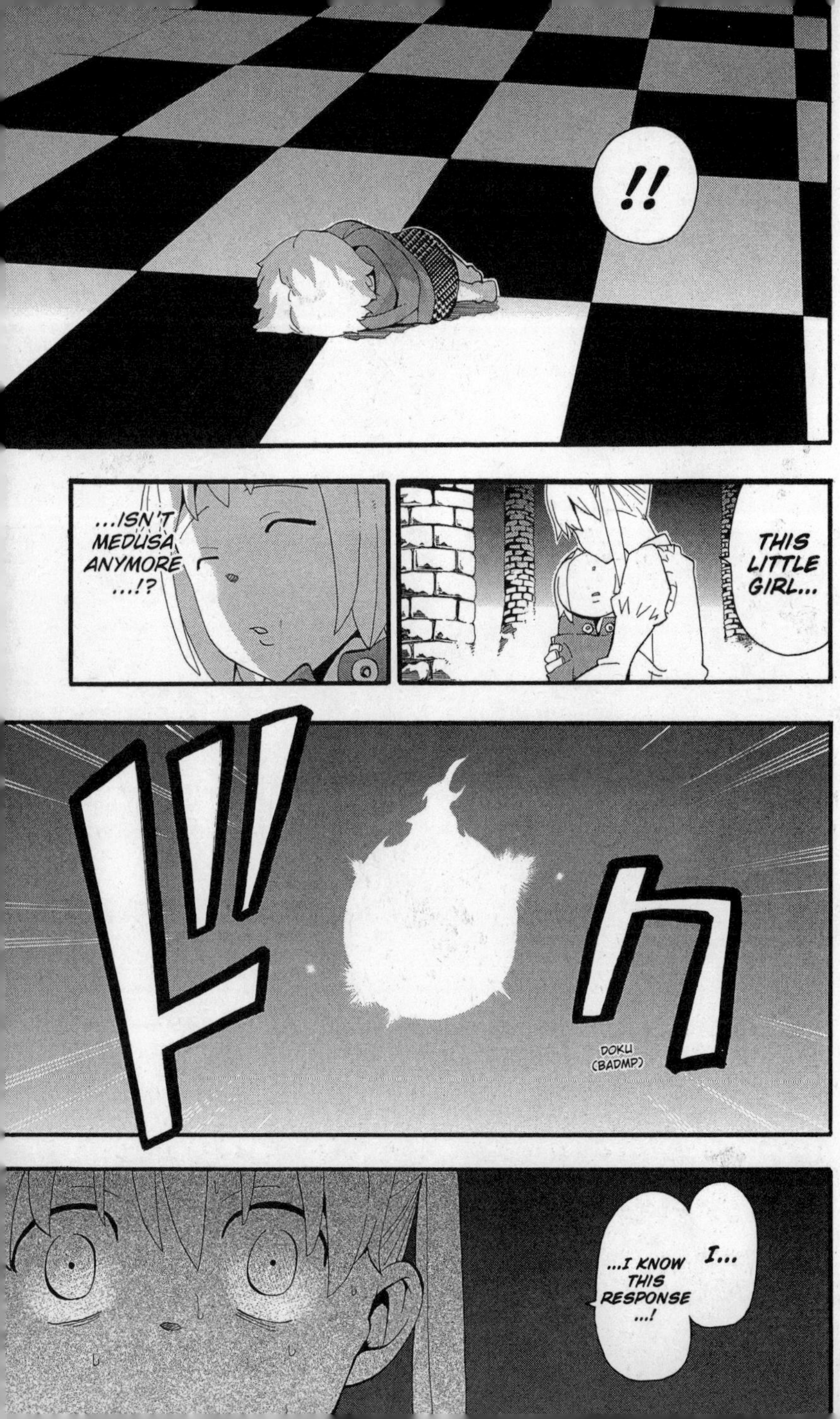
!!
THIS LITTLE GIRL...
...ISN'T MEDUSA ANYMORE ...!?
ドクン
DOKU (BADMP)
I...
...I KNOW THIS RESPONSE ...!

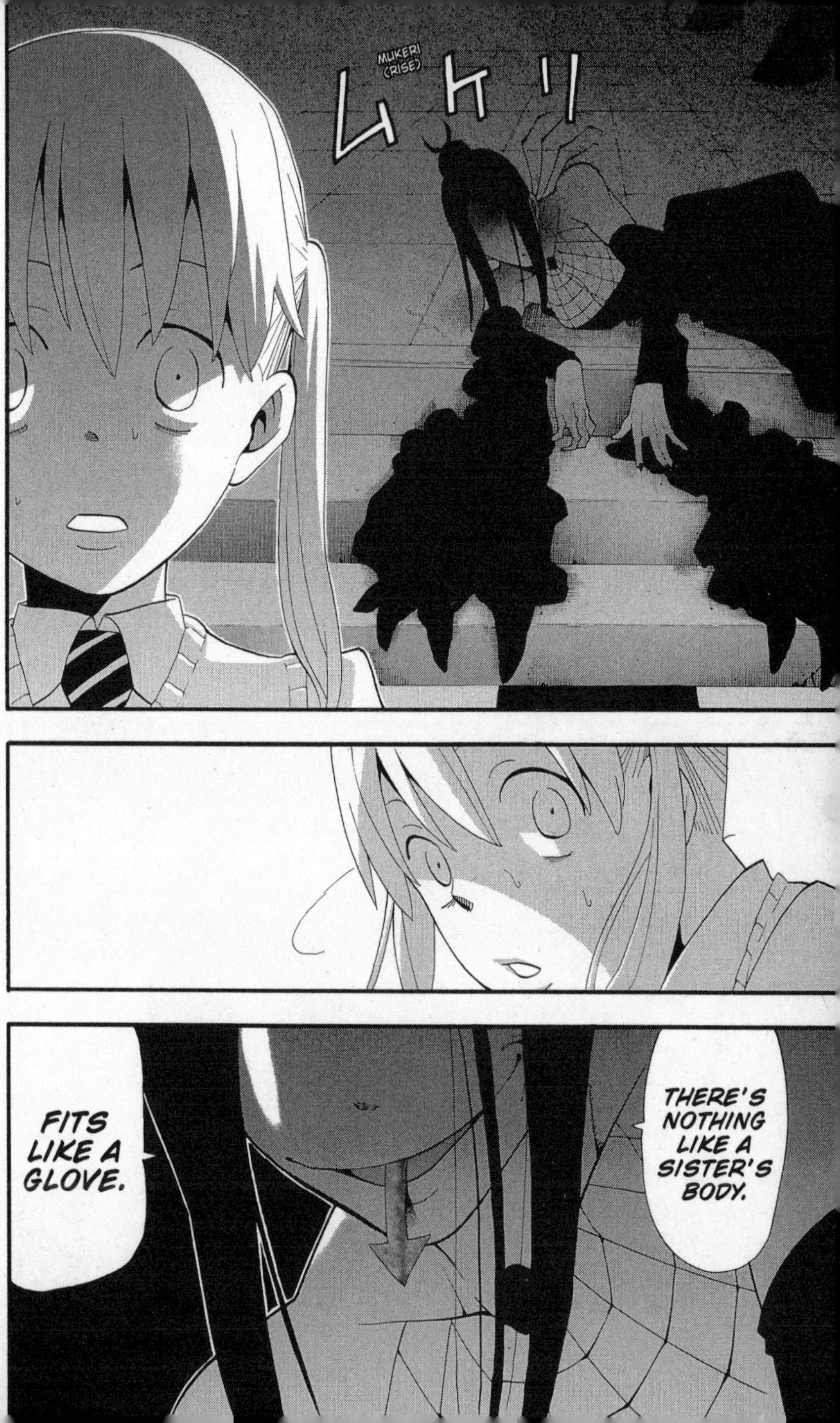
MUKERI (RISE)
THERE'S NOTHING LIKE A SISTER'S BODY.
FITS LIKE A GLOVE.

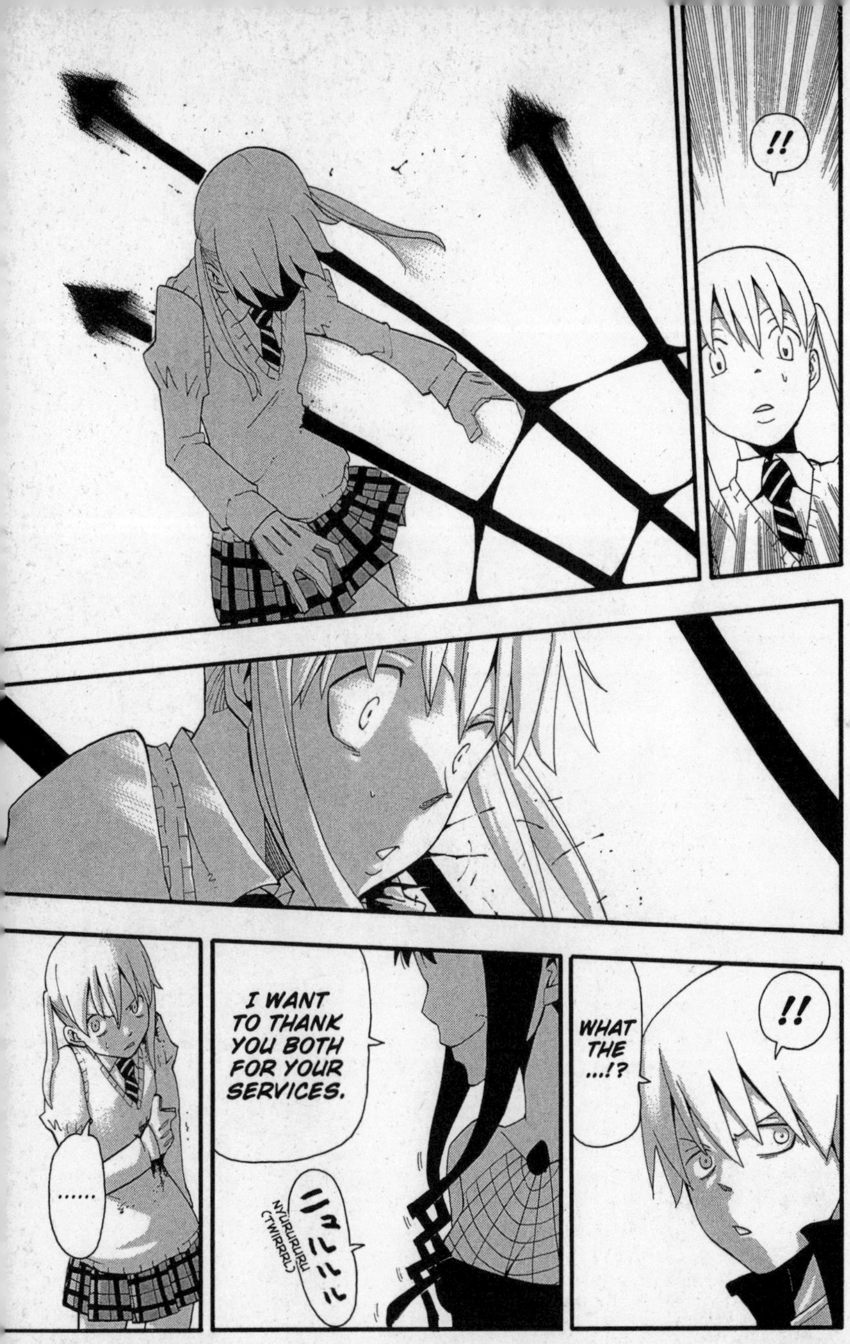
!!
!!
WHAT THE ...!?
I WANT TO THANK YOU BOTH FOR YOUR SERVICES.
ニュルルル
NYURURURU (TWIRRL)
......

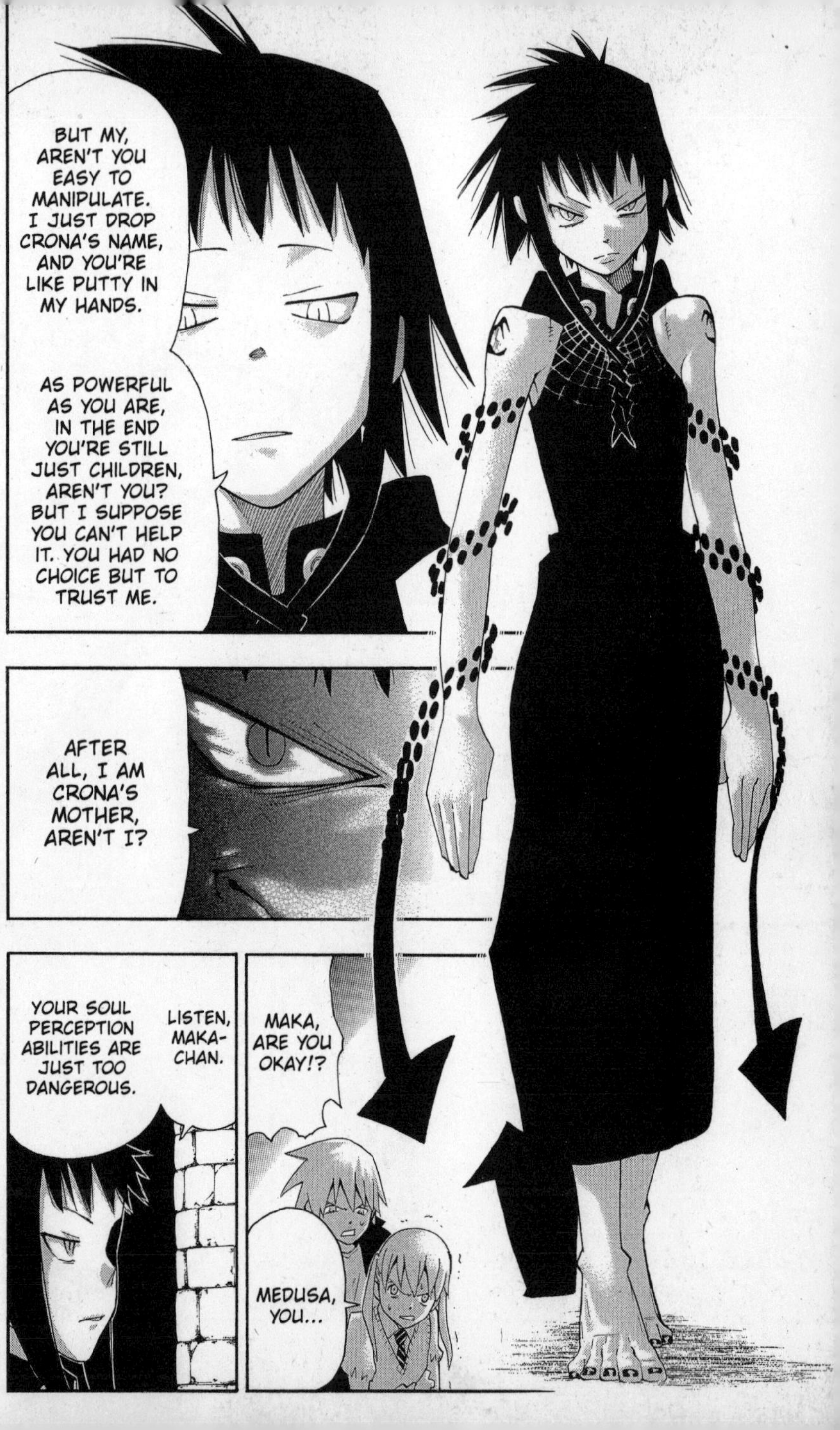
BUT MY, AREN'T YOU EASY TO MANIPULATE. I JUST DROP CRONA'S NAME, AND YOU'RE LIKE PUTTY IN MY HANDS.
AS POWERFUL AS YOU ARE, IN THE END YOU'RE STILL JUST CHILDREN, AREN'T YOU? BUT I SUPPOSE YOU CAN'T HELP IT. YOU HAD NO CHOICE BUT TO TRUST ME.
AFTER ALL, I AM CRONA'S MOTHER, AREN'T I?
MAKA, ARE YOU OKAY!?
MEDUSA, YOU...
LISTEN, MAKA-CHAN.
YOUR SOUL PERCEPTION ABILITIES ARE JUST TOO DANGEROUS.

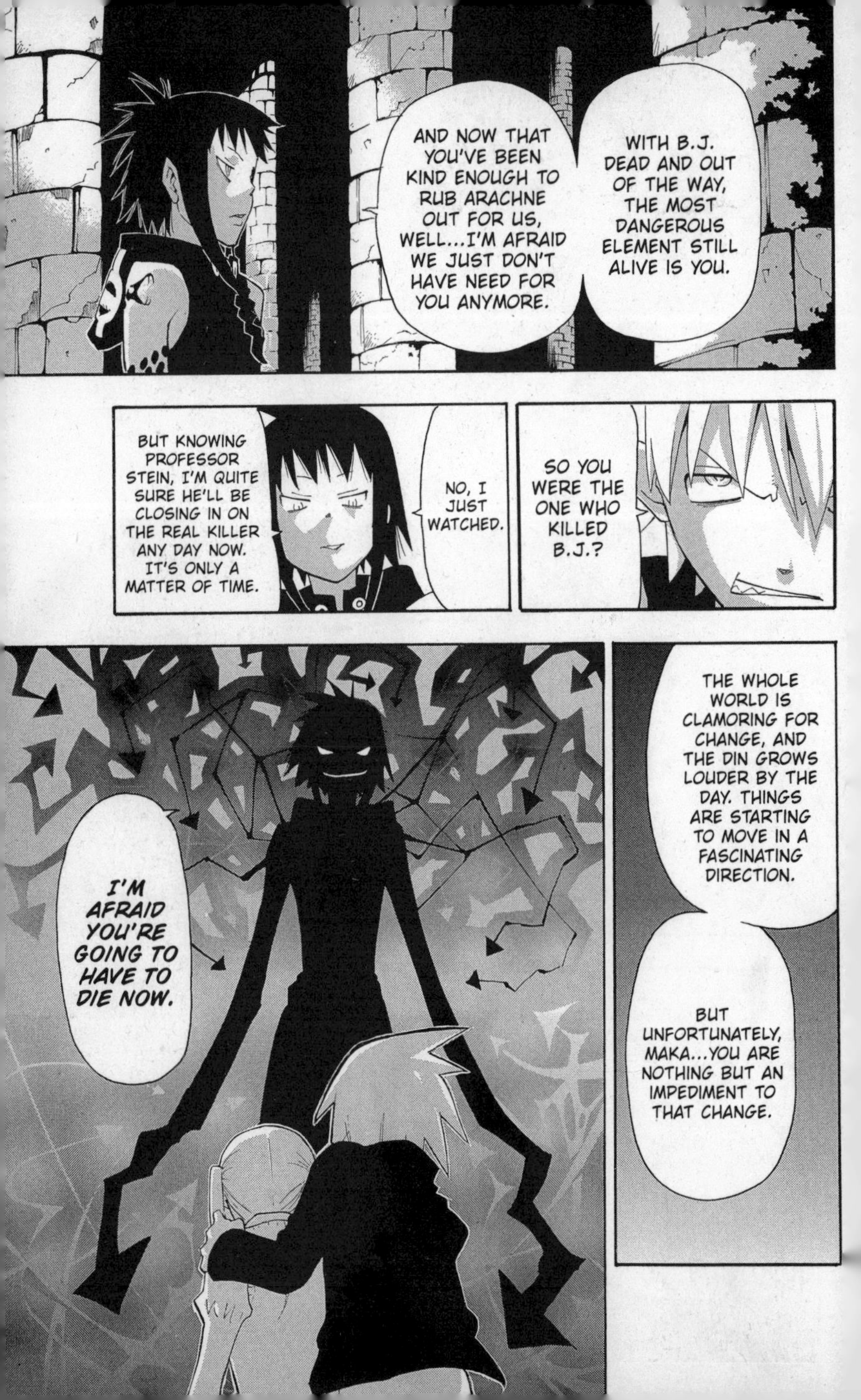
WITH B.J. DEAD AND OUT OF THE WAY, THE MOST DANGEROUS ELEMENT STILL ALIVE IS YOU.
AND NOW THAT YOU'VE BEEN KIND ENOUGH TO RUB ARACHNE OUT FOR US, WELL...I'M AFRAID WE JUST DON'T HAVE NEED FOR YOU ANYMORE.
SO YOU WERE THE ONE WHO KILLED B.J.?
NO, I JUST WATCHED.
BUT KNOWING PROFESSOR STEIN, I'M QUITE SURE HE'LL BE CLOSING IN ON THE REAL KILLER ANY DAY NOW. IT'S ONLY A MATTER OF TIME.
THE WHOLE WORLD IS CLAMORING FOR CHANGE, AND THE DIN GROWS LOUDER BY THE DAY. THINGS ARE STARTING TO MOVE IN A FASCINATING DIRECTION.
BUT UNFORTUNATELY, MAKA...YOU ARE NOTHING BUT AN IMPEDIMENT TO THAT CHANGE.
I'M AFRAID YOU'RE GOING TO HAVE TO DIE NOW.

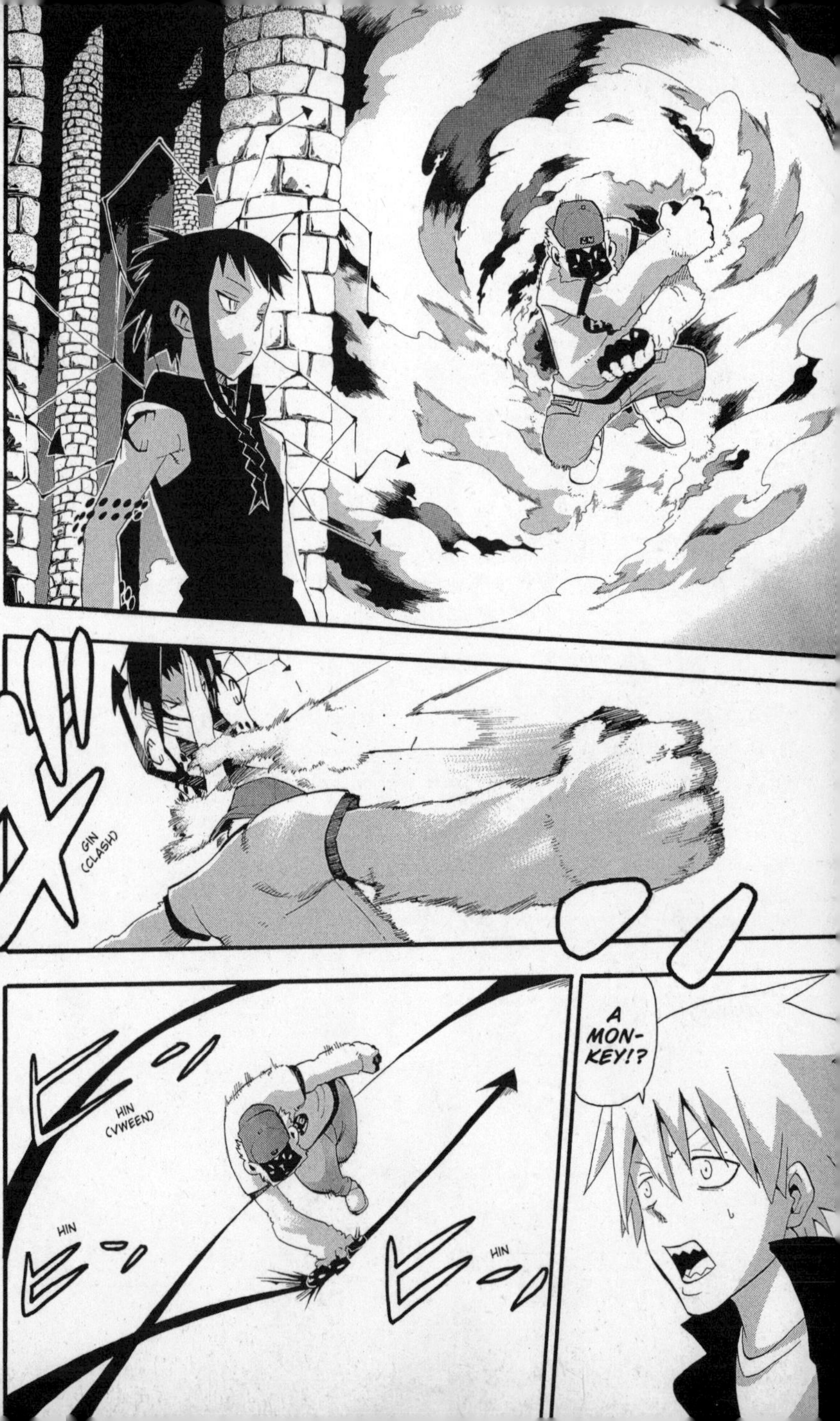
GIN (CLASH)
A MON-KEY!?
HIN (VWEEN)
HIN
HIN

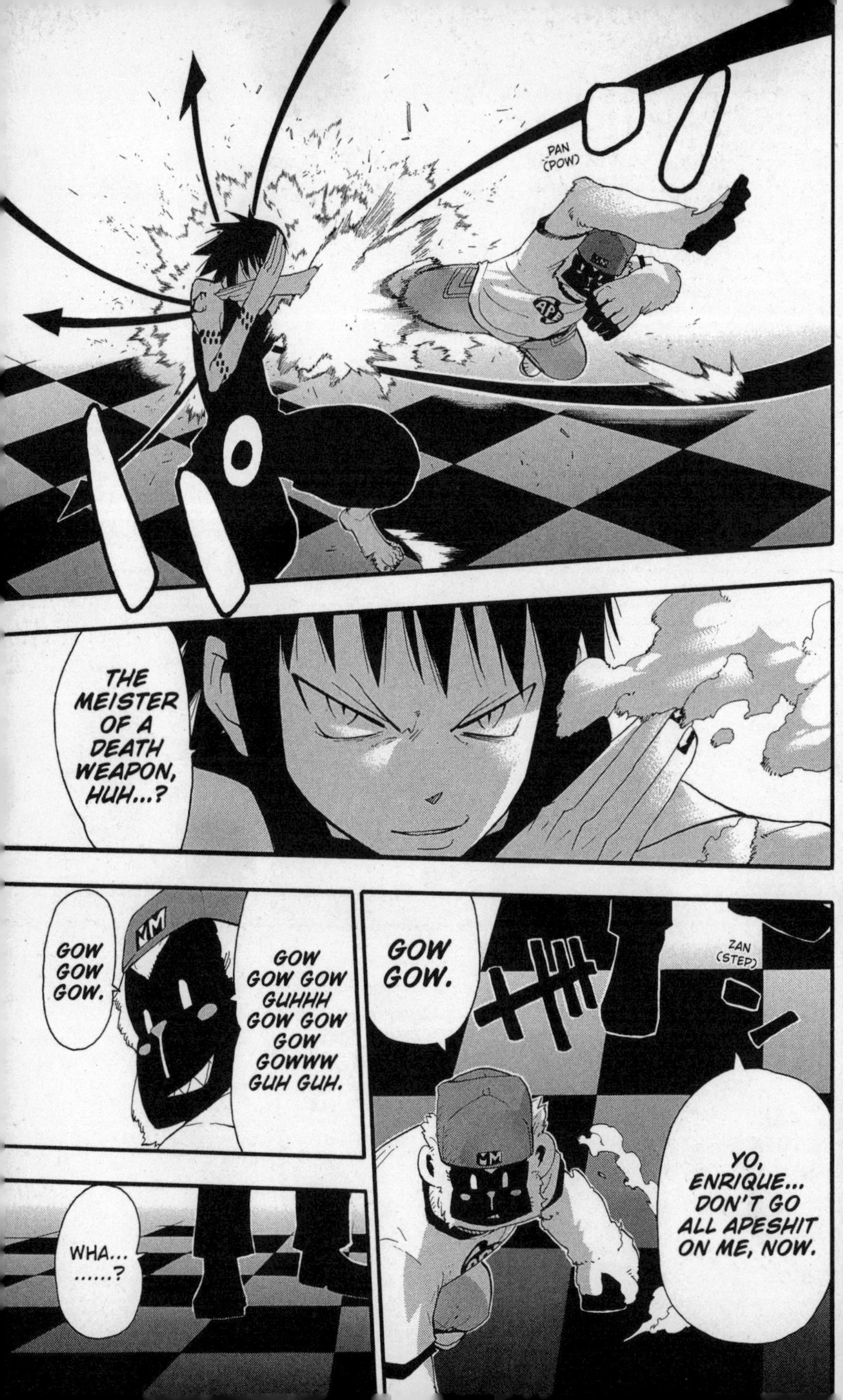
PAN (POW)
THE MEISTER OF A DEATH WEAPON, HUH...?
ZAN (STEP)
GOW GOW.
YO, ENRIQUE... DON'T GO ALL APESHIT ON ME, NOW.
GOW GOW GOW GUHHH GOW GOW GOW GOWWW GUH GUH.
GOW GOW GOW.
WHA... ......?

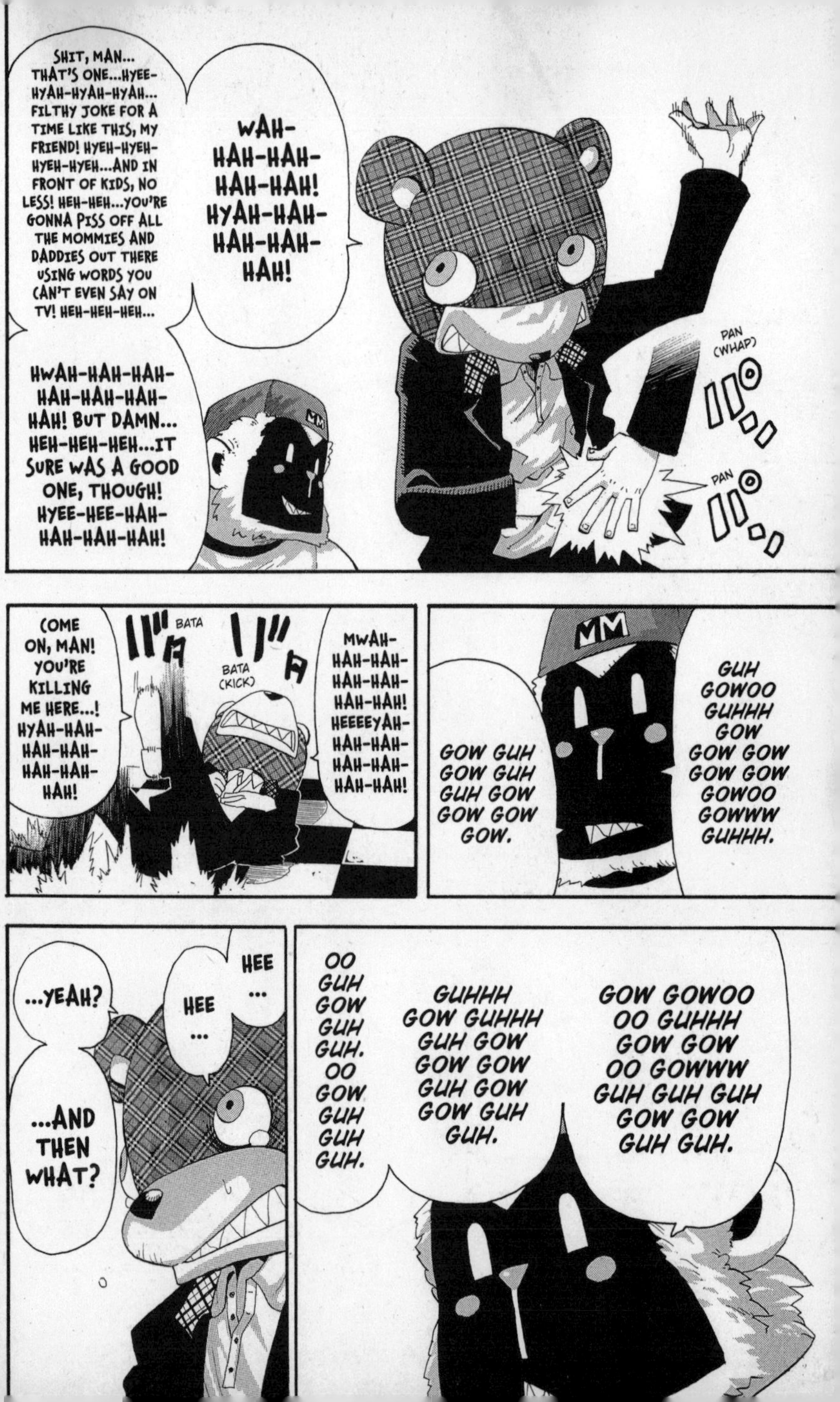

PAN (WHAP)
PAN
WAH-HAH-HAH-HAH-HAH! HYAH-HAH-HAH-HAH-HAH!
SHIT, MAN... THAT'S ONE...HYEE-HYAH-HYAH-HYAH... FILTHY JOKE FOR A TIME LIKE THIS, MY FRIEND! HYEH-HYEH-HYEH-HYEH...AND IN FRONT OF KIDS, NO LESS! HEH-HEH...YOU'RE GONNA PISS OFF ALL THE MOMMIES AND DADDIES OUT THERE USING WORDS YOU CAN'T EVEN SAY ON TV! HEH-HEH-HEH...
HWAH-HAH-HAH-HAH-HAH-HAH-HAH! BUT DAMN... HEH-HEH-HEH...IT SURE WAS A GOOD ONE, THOUGH! HYEE-HEE-HAH-HAH-HAH-HAH!
GUH GOWOO GUHHH GOW GOW GOW GOW GOW GOWOO GOWWW GUHHH.
GOW GUH GOW GUH GUH GOW GOW GOW GOW.
MWAH-HAH-HAH-HAH-HAH-HAH-HAH! HEEEEYAH-HAH-HAH-HAH-HAH-HAH-HAH!
BATA (KICK)
BATA
COME ON, MAN! YOU'RE KILLING ME HERE...! HYAH-HAH-HAH-HAH-HAH-HAH-HAH!
GOW GOWOO OO GUHHH GOW GOW OO GOWWW GUH GUH GUH GOW GOW GUH GUH.
GUHHH GOW GUHHH GUH GOW GOW GOW GUH GOW GOW GUH GUH.
OO GUH GOW GUH GUH. OO GOW GUH GUH GUH.
HEE ...
HEE ...
...YEAH?
...AND THEN WHAT?

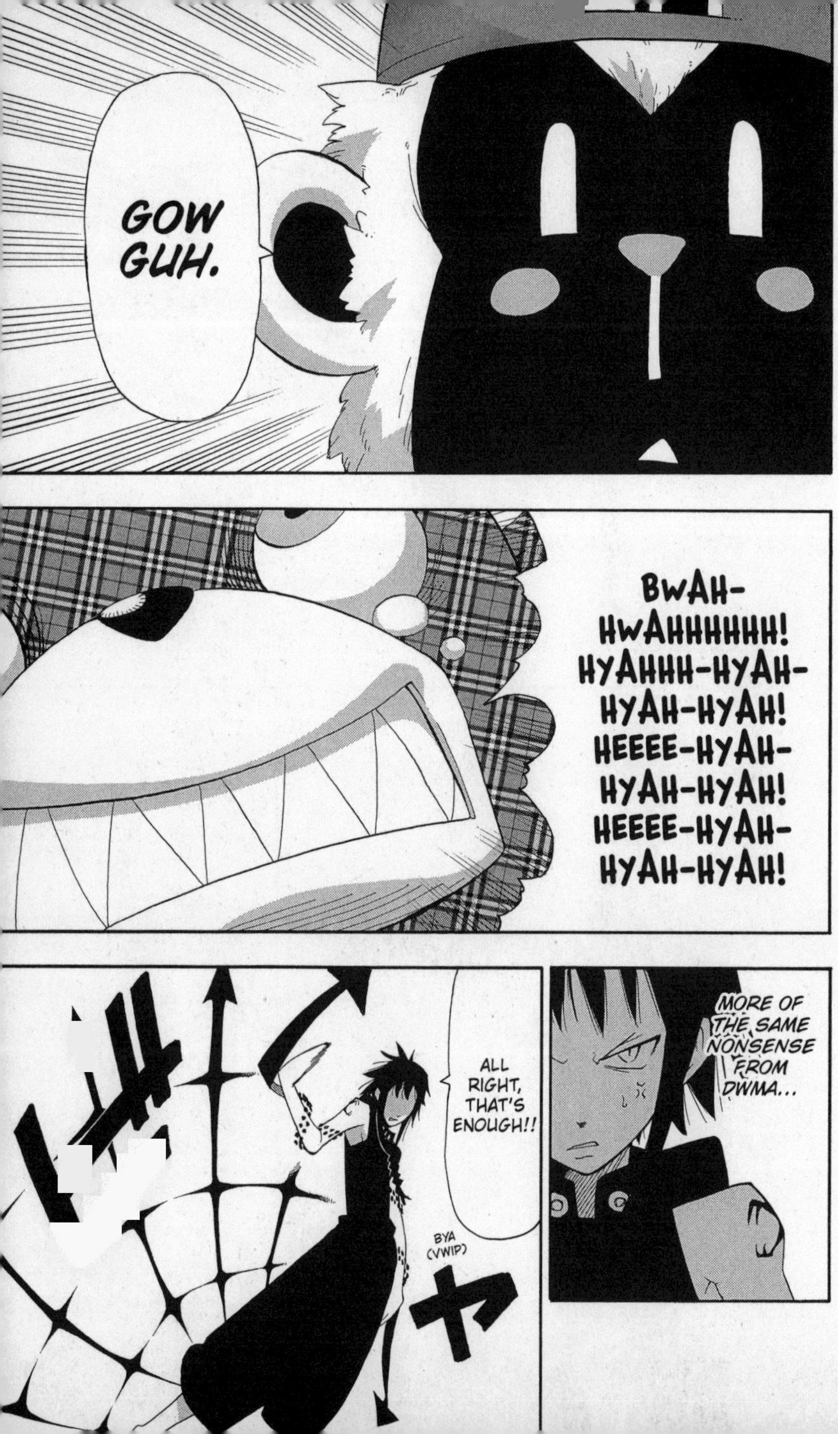
GOW GUH.
BWAH-HWAHHHHHH! HYAHHH-HYAH-HYAH-HYAH! HEEEE-HYAH-HYAH-HYAH! HEEEE-HYAH-HYAH-HYAH!
MORE OF THE SAME NONSENSE FROM DWMA...
ALL RIGHT, THAT'S ENOUGH!!
BYA (VWIP)

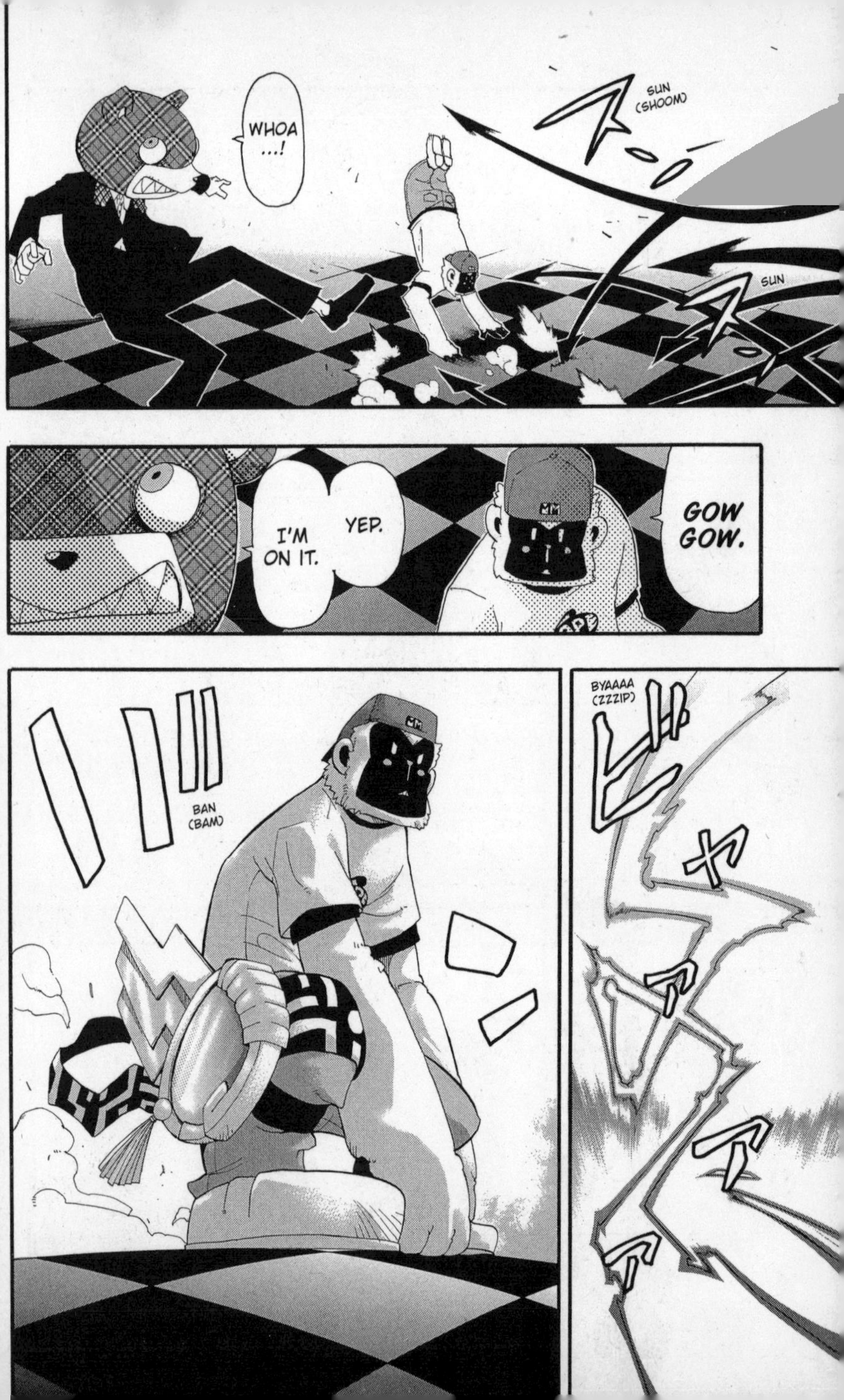
SUN (SHOOM)
WHOA ...!
SUN
GOW GOW.
YEP.
I'M ON IT.
BYAAAA (ZZZIP)
BAN (BAM)

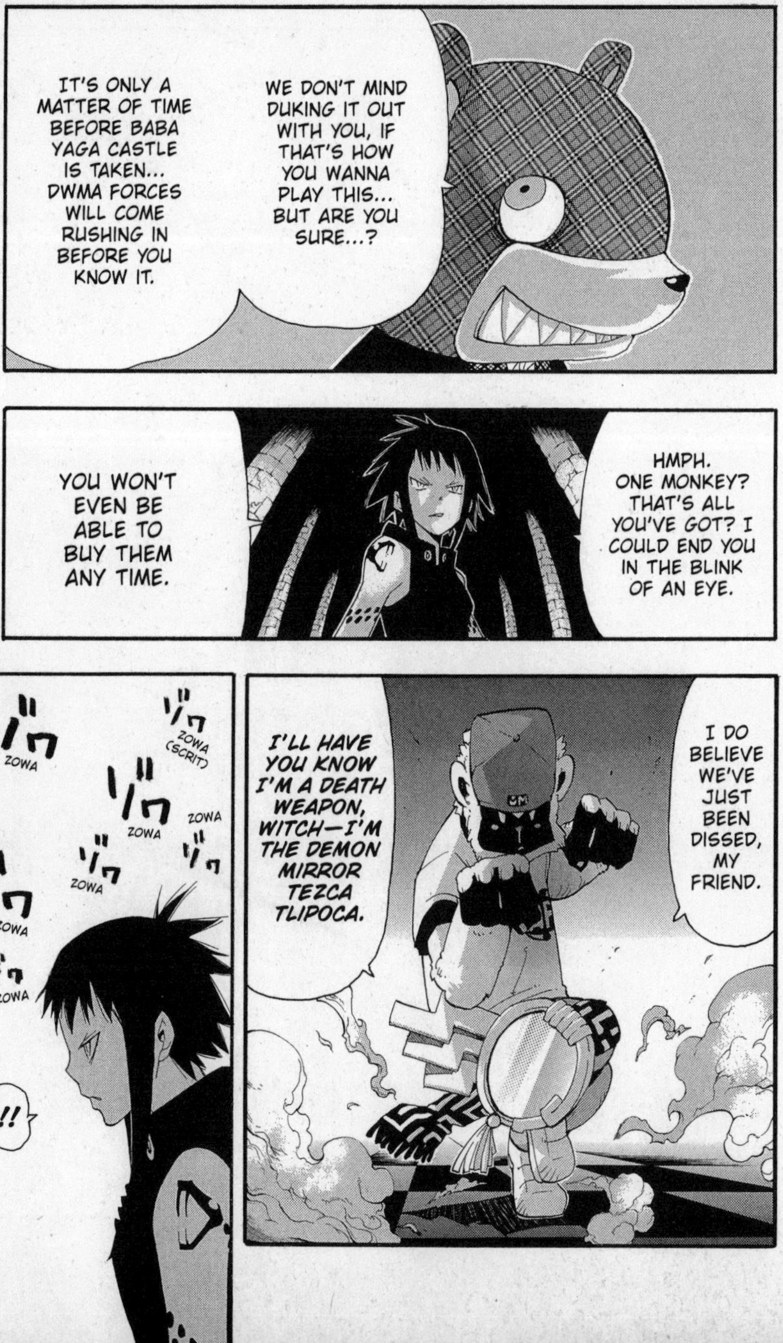
WE DON'T MIND DUKING IT OUT WITH YOU, IF THAT'S HOW YOU WANNA PLAY THIS... BUT ARE YOU SURE...?
IT'S ONLY A MATTER OF TIME BEFORE BABA YAGA CASTLE IS TAKEN... DWMA FORCES WILL COME RUSHING IN BEFORE YOU KNOW IT.
HMPH. ONE MONKEY? THAT'S ALL YOU'VE GOT? I COULD END YOU IN THE BLINK OF AN EYE.
YOU WON'T EVEN BE ABLE TO BUY THEM ANY TIME.
I DO BELIEVE WE'VE JUST BEEN DISSED, MY FRIEND.
I'LL HAVE YOU KNOW I'M A DEATH WEAPON, WITCH—I'M THE DEMON MIRROR TEZCA TLIPOCA.
ゾワ ZOWA (SCRIT)
ゾワ ZOWA
ゾワ ZOWA
ゾワ ZOWA
ゾワ ZOWA
ゾワ ZOWA
ゾワ ZOWA
!!

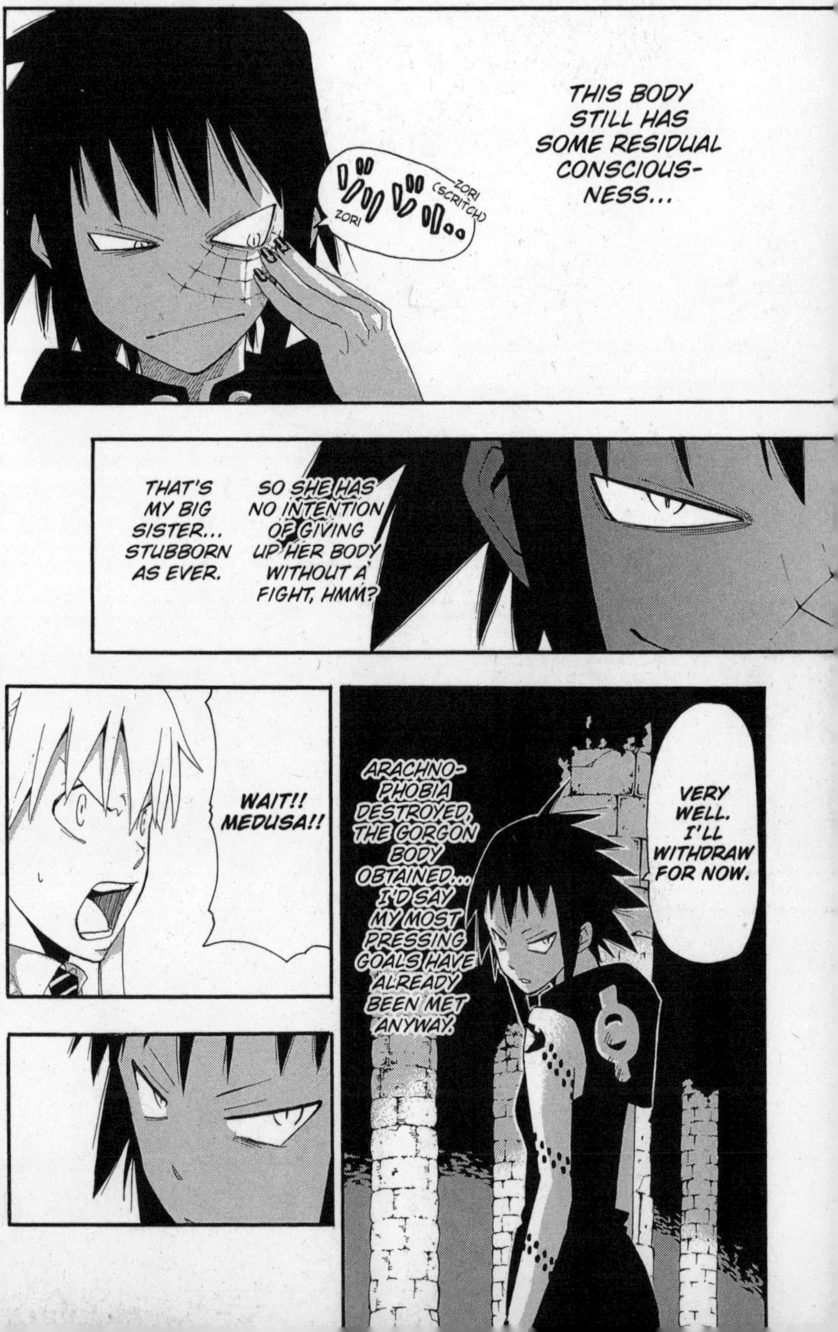
THIS BODY STILL HAS SOME RESIDUAL CONSCIOUS-NESS...
ZORI (SCRITCH) ZORI
SO SHE HAS NO INTENTION OF GIVING UP HER BODY WITHOUT A FIGHT, HMM?
THAT'S MY BIG SISTER... STUBBORN AS EVER.
VERY WELL. I'LL WITHDRAW FOR NOW.
ARACHNO-PHOBIA DESTROYED, THE GORGON BODY OBTAINED... I'D SAY MY MOST PRESSING GOALS HAVE ALREADY BEEN MET ANYWAY.
WAIT!! MEDUSA!!

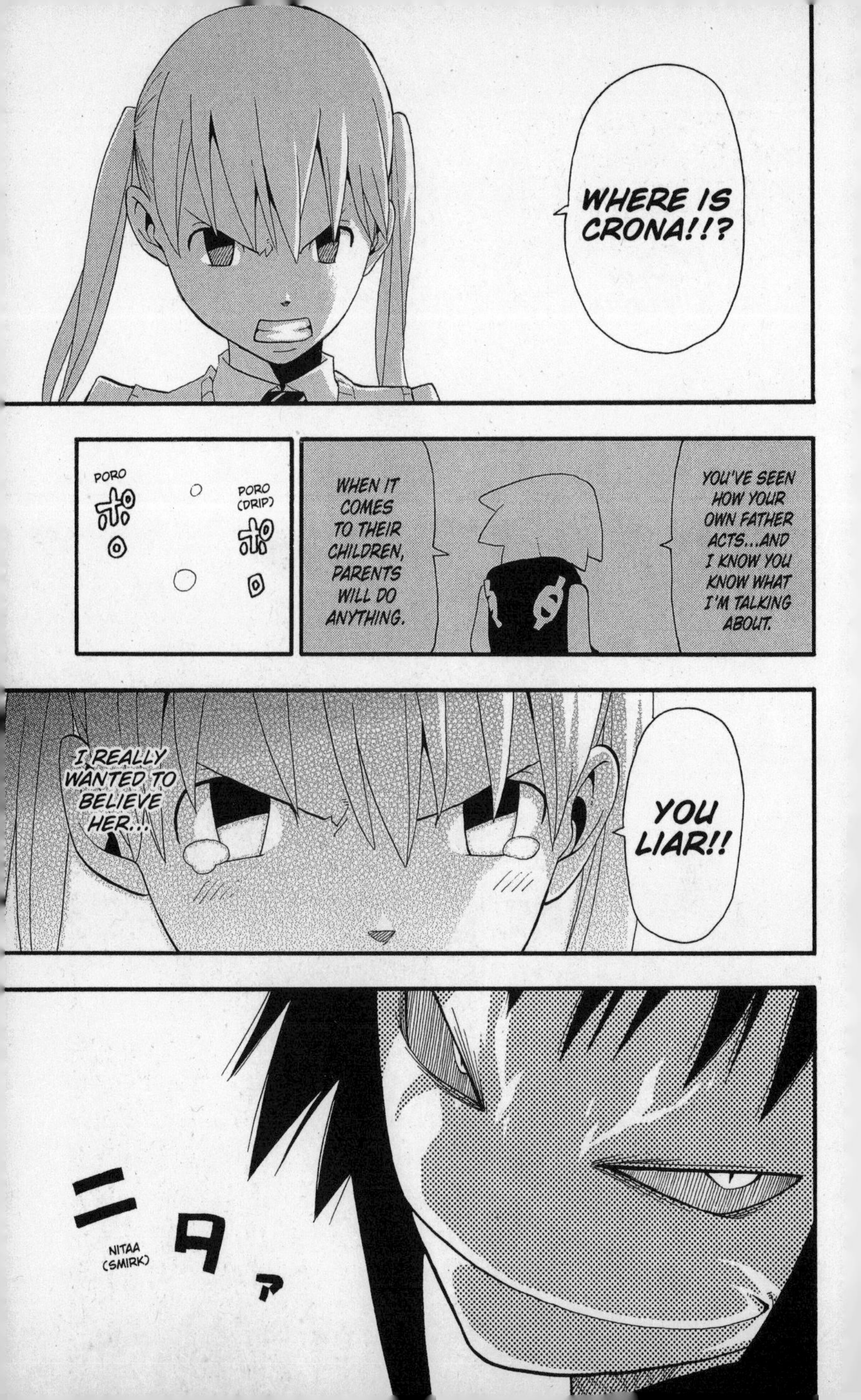
WHERE IS CRONA!!?
YOU'VE SEEN HOW YOUR OWN FATHER ACTS...AND I KNOW YOU KNOW WHAT I'M TALKING ABOUT.
WHEN IT COMES TO THEIR CHILDREN, PARENTS WILL DO ANYTHING.
PORO (DRIP)
PORO
YOU LIAR!!
I REALLY WANTED TO BELIEVE HER...
ニタァ
NITAA (SMIRK)

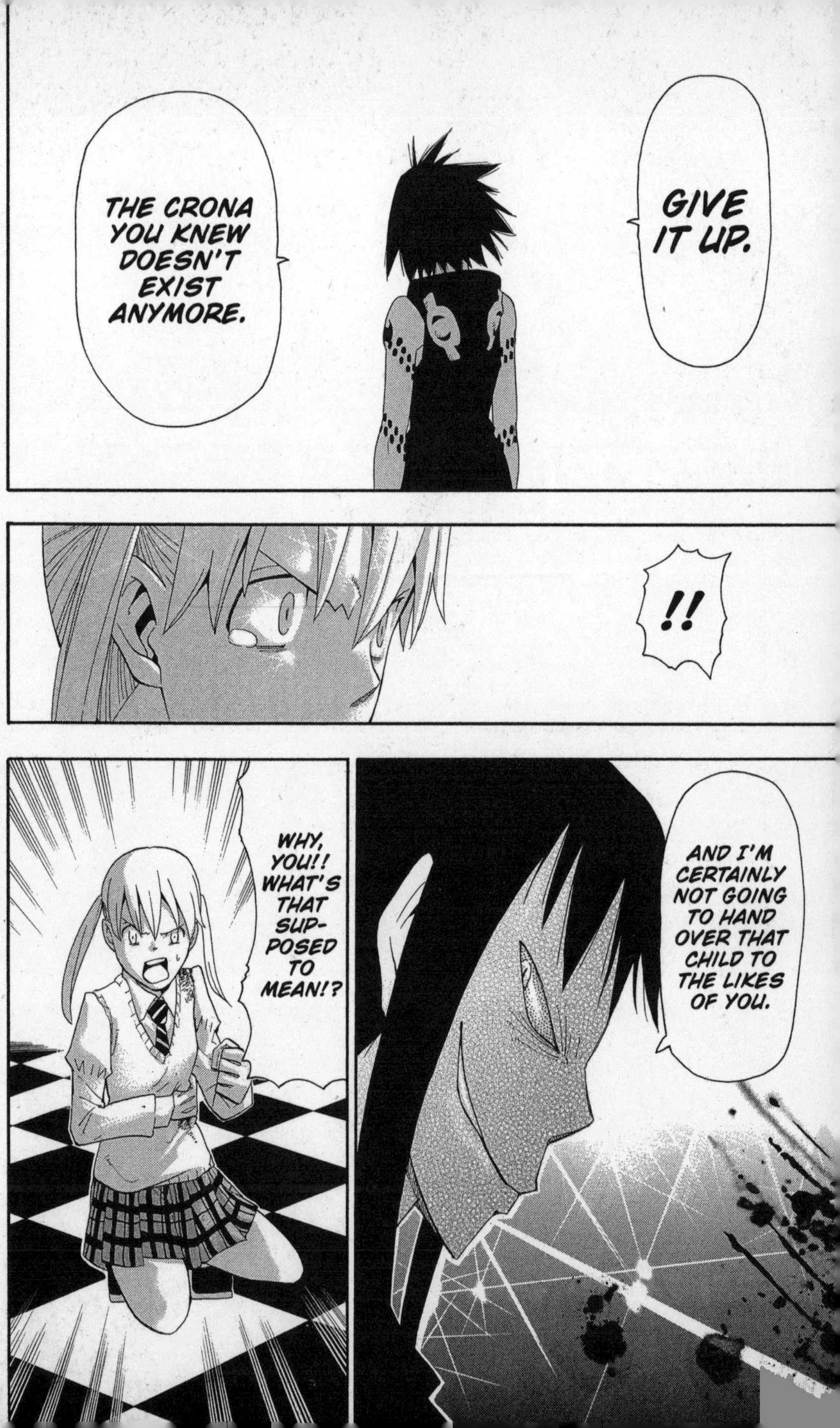
GIVE IT UP.
THE CRONA YOU KNEW DOESN'T EXIST ANYMORE.
!!
AND I'M CERTAINLY NOT GOING TO HAND OVER THAT CHILD TO THE LIKES OF YOU.
WHY, YOU!! WHAT'S THAT SUP-POSED TO MEAN!?

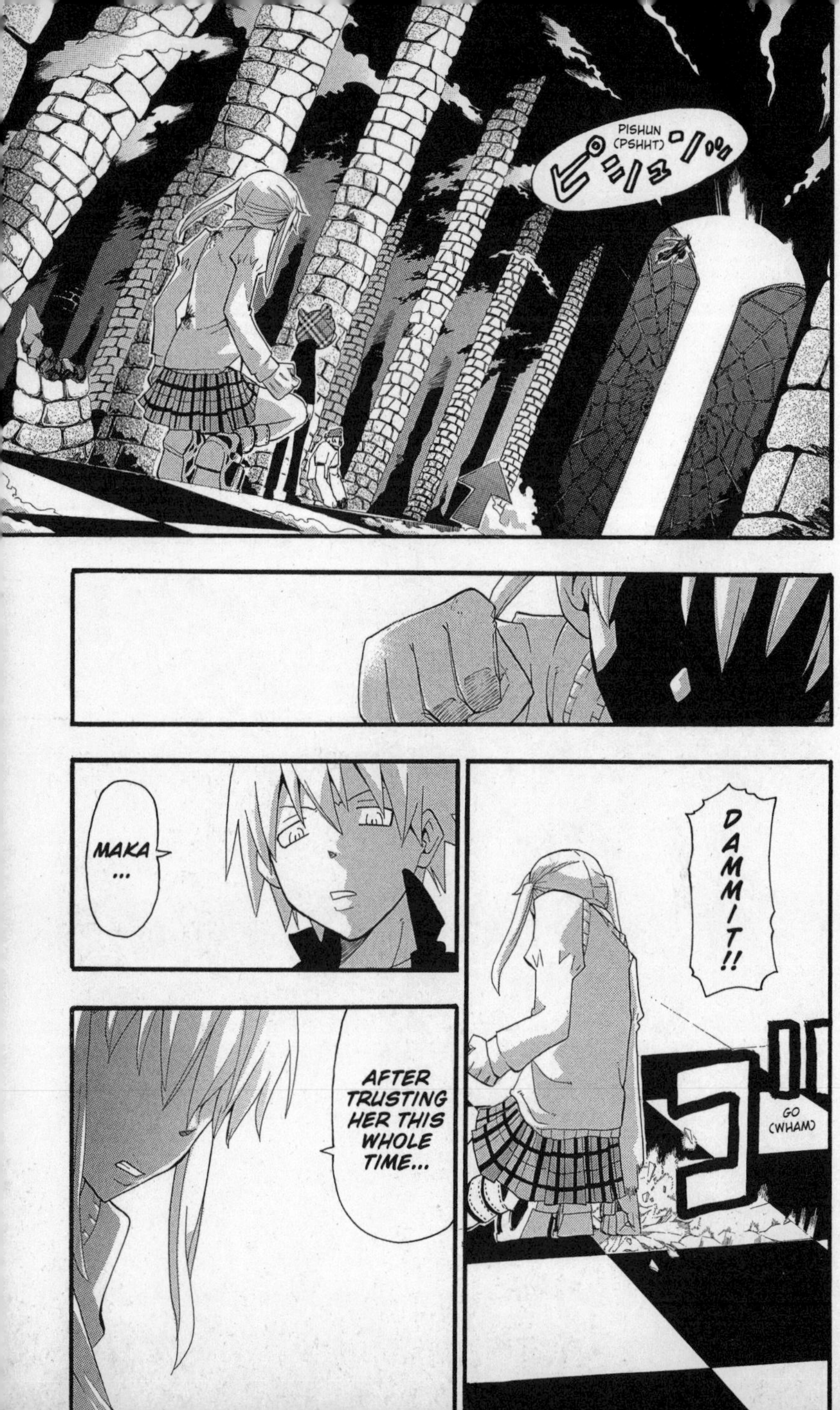
PISHUN
(PSHHT)
DAMMIT!!
GO
(WHAM)
MAKA
...
AFTER TRUSTING HER THIS WHOLE TIME...

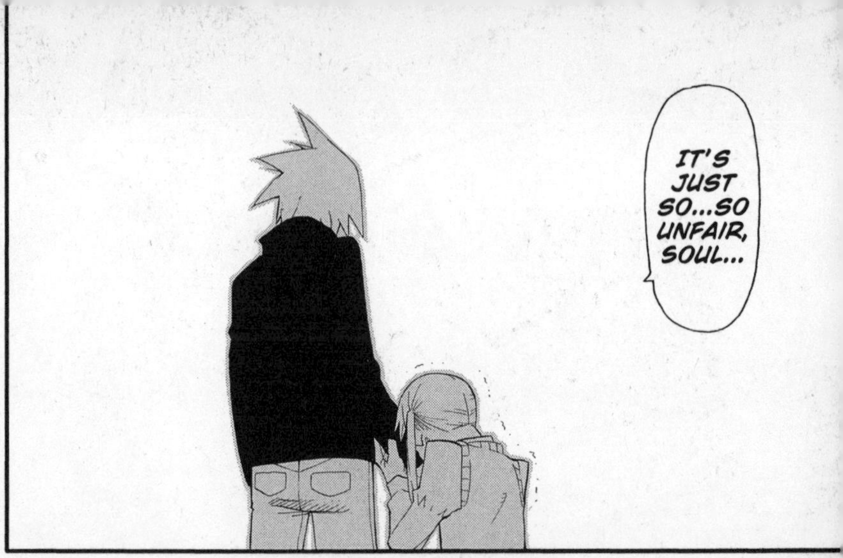
IT'S JUST SO...SO UNFAIR, SOUL...
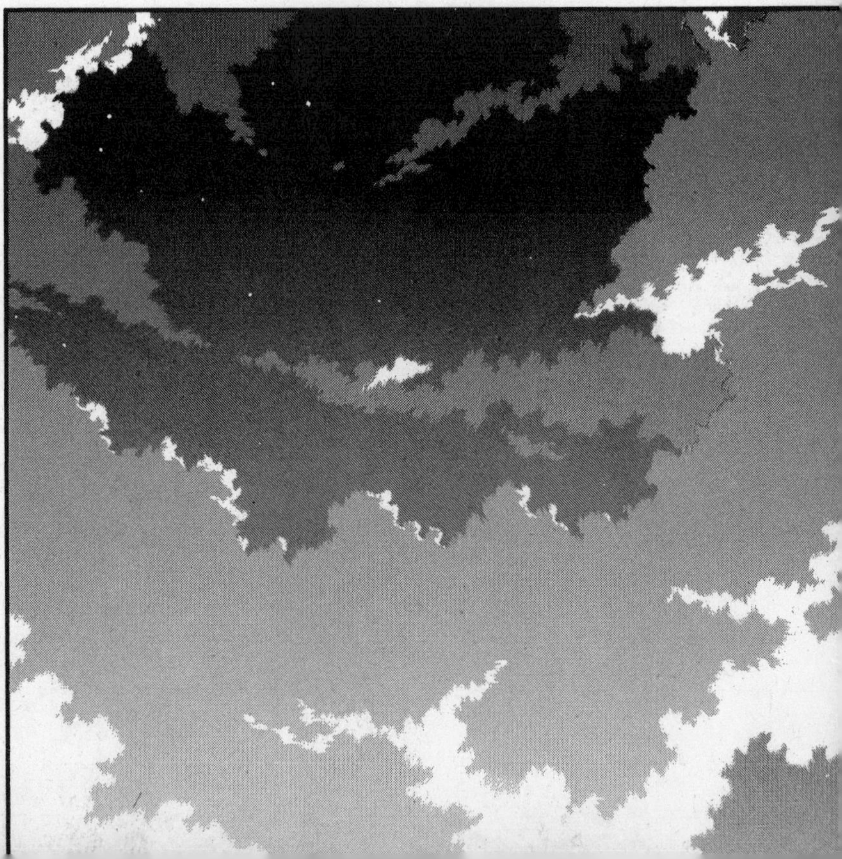

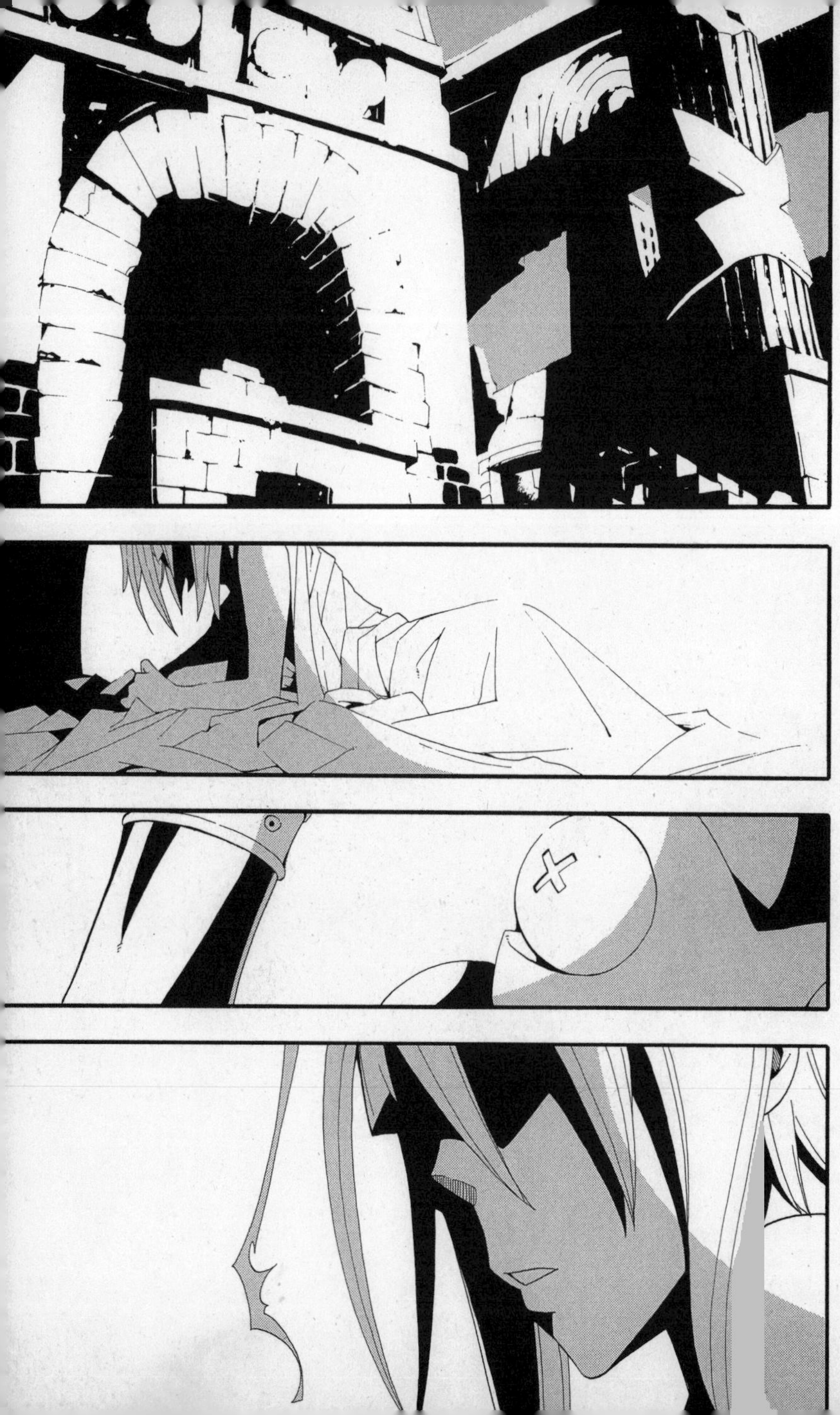

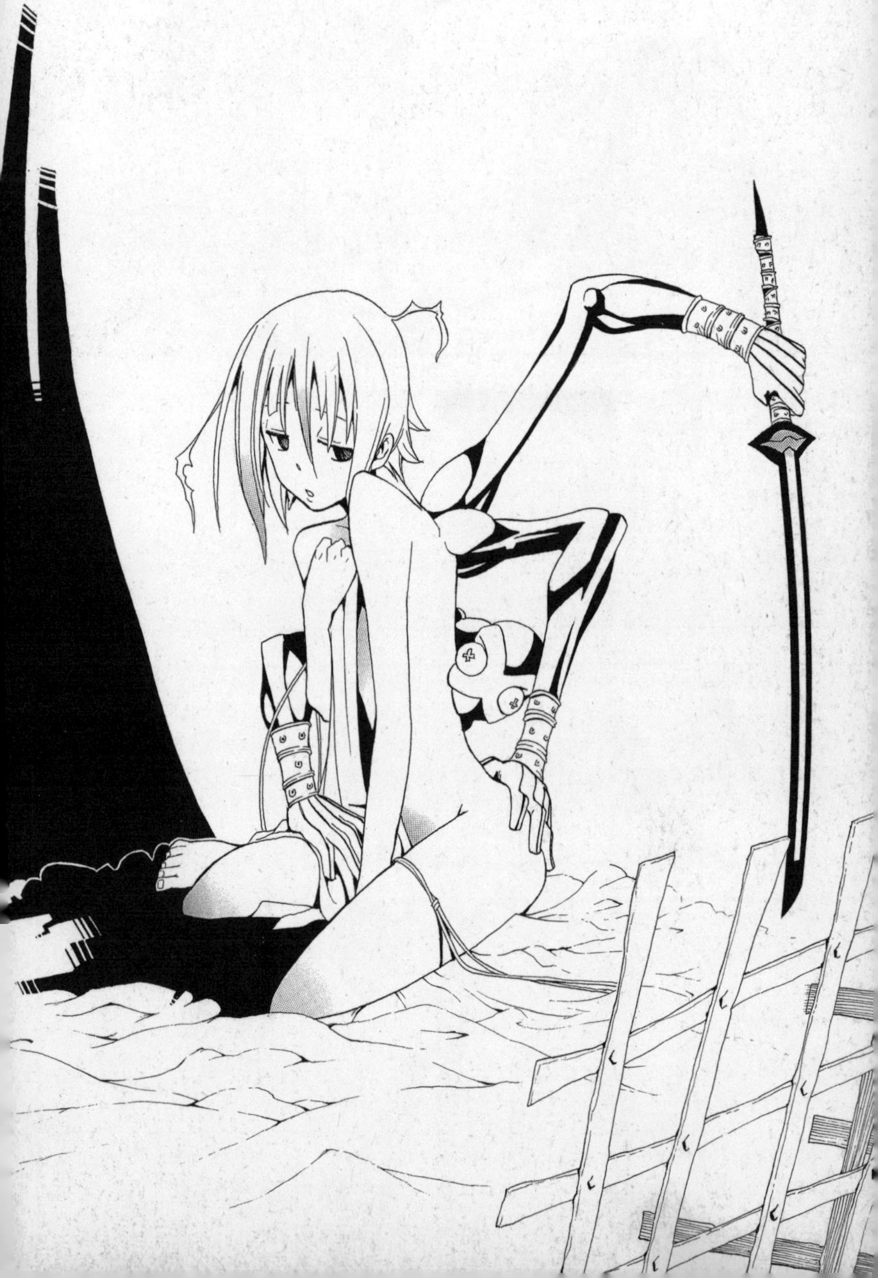

SOUL EATER

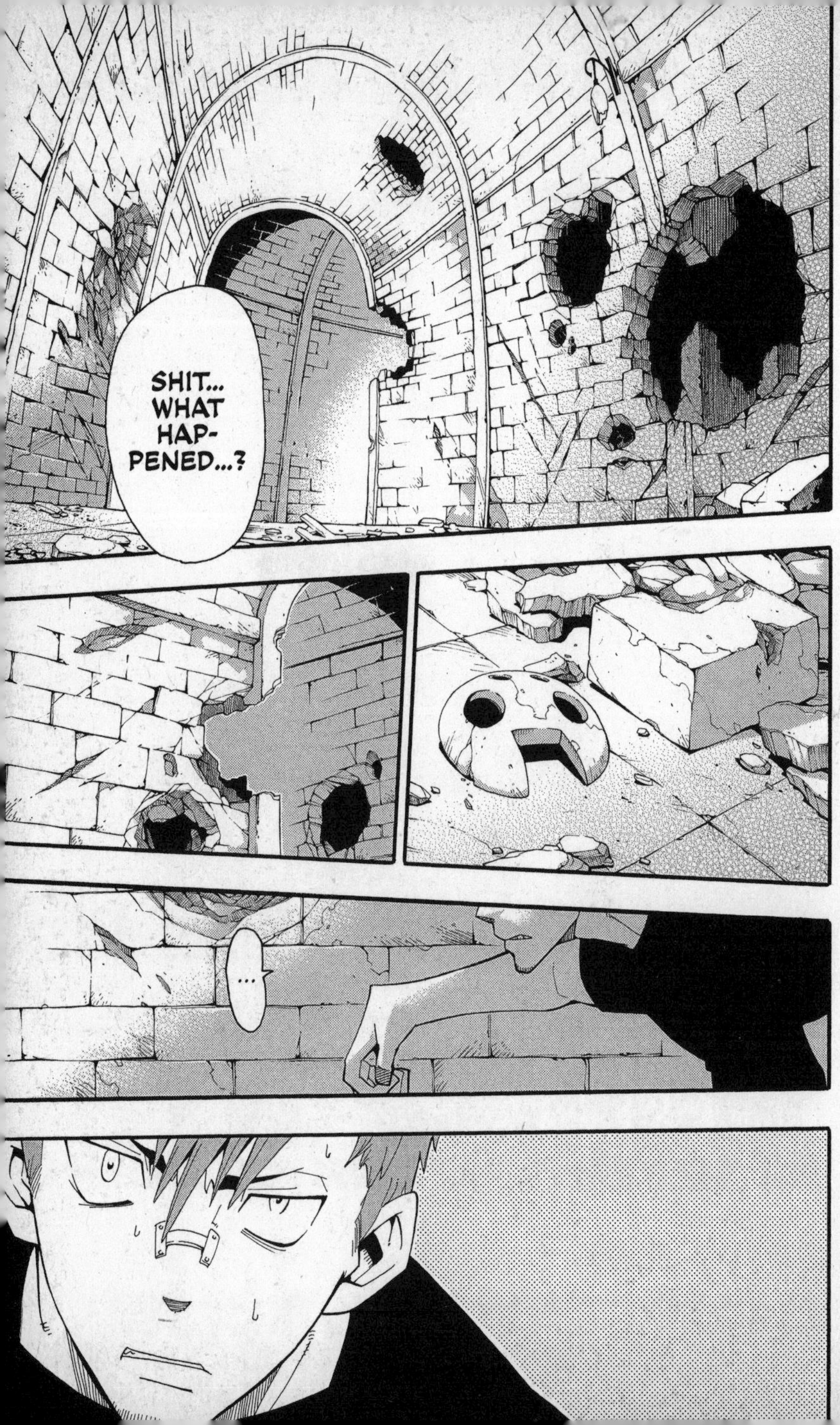
SHIT... WHAT HAP-PENED...?
...

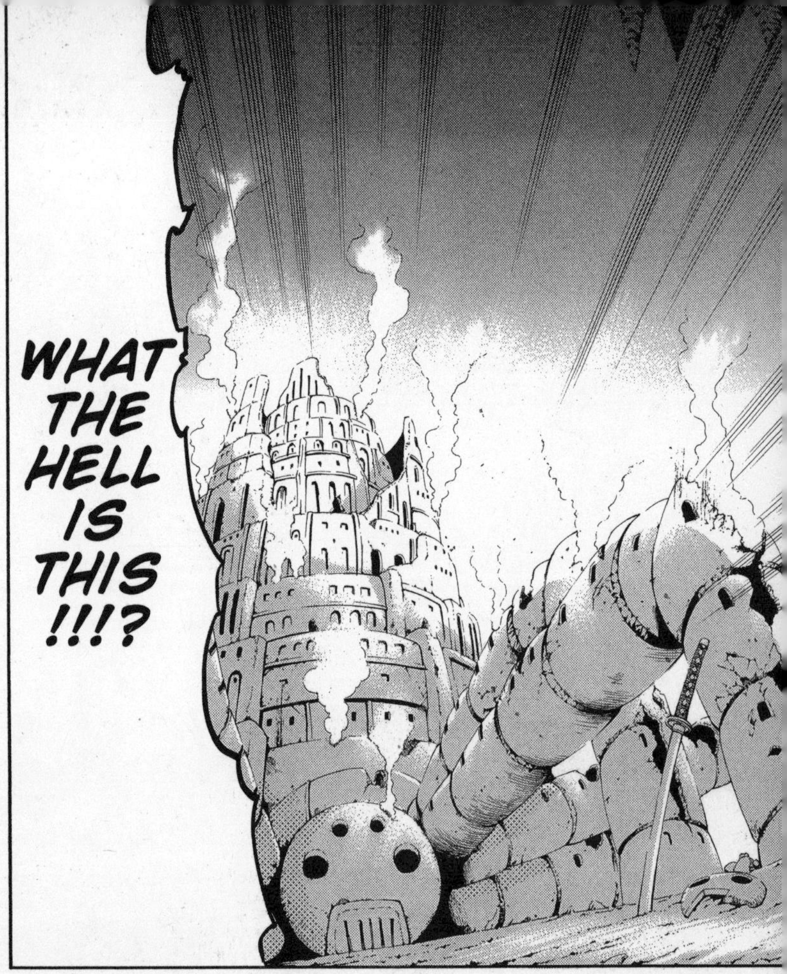
WHAT THE HELL IS THIS !!!?

SOUL EATER

CHAPTER 61: BEGINNING BY WRAPPING THINGS UP

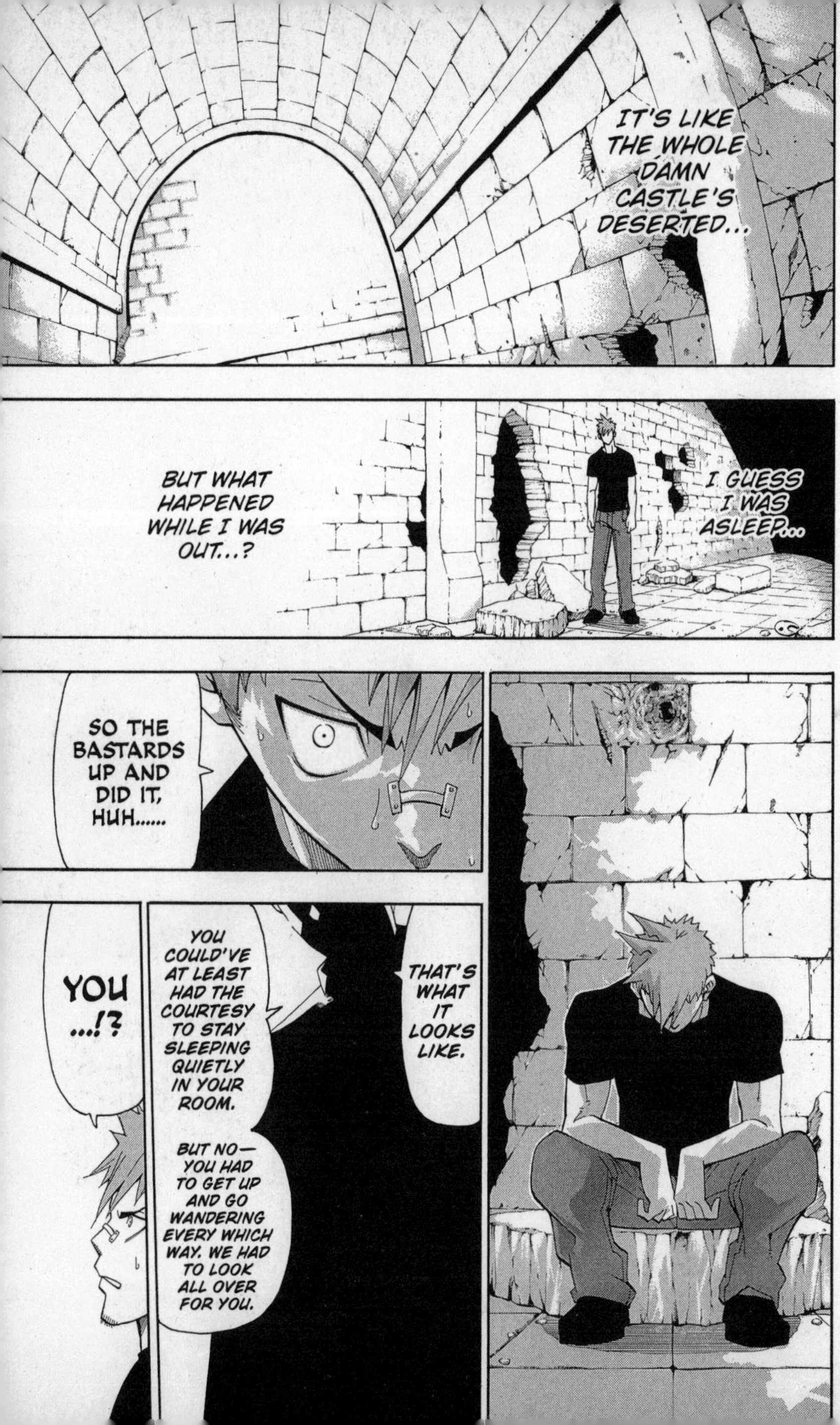
IT'S LIKE THE WHOLE DAMN CASTLE'S DESERTED...
I GUESS I WAS ASLEEP...
BUT WHAT HAPPENED WHILE I WAS OUT...?
SO THE BASTARDS UP AND DID IT, HUH......
THAT'S WHAT IT LOOKS LIKE.
YOU COULD'VE AT LEAST HAD THE COURTESY TO STAY SLEEPING QUIETLY IN YOUR ROOM.
BUT NO— YOU HAD TO GET UP AND GO WANDERING EVERY WHICH WAY. WE HAD TO LOOK ALL OVER FOR YOU.
YOU ...!?

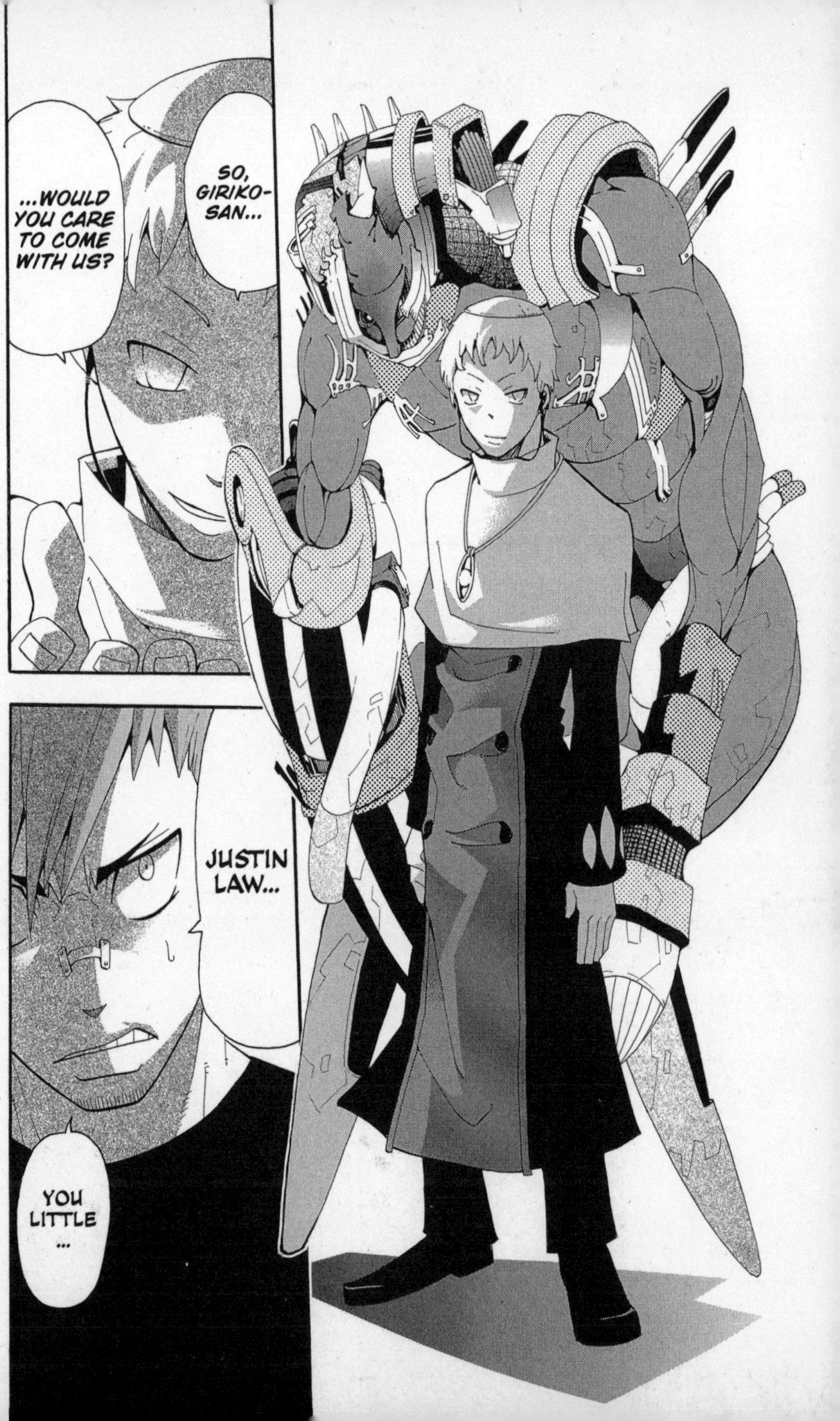
SO, GIRIKO-SAN...
...WOULD YOU CARE TO COME WITH US?
JUSTIN LAW...
YOU LITTLE ...

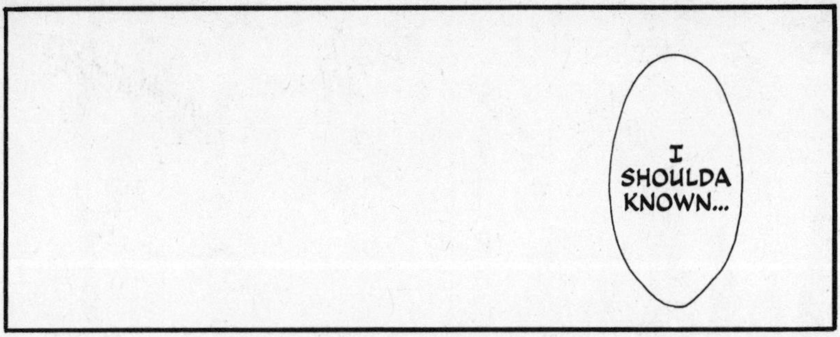
I SHOULDA KNOWN...
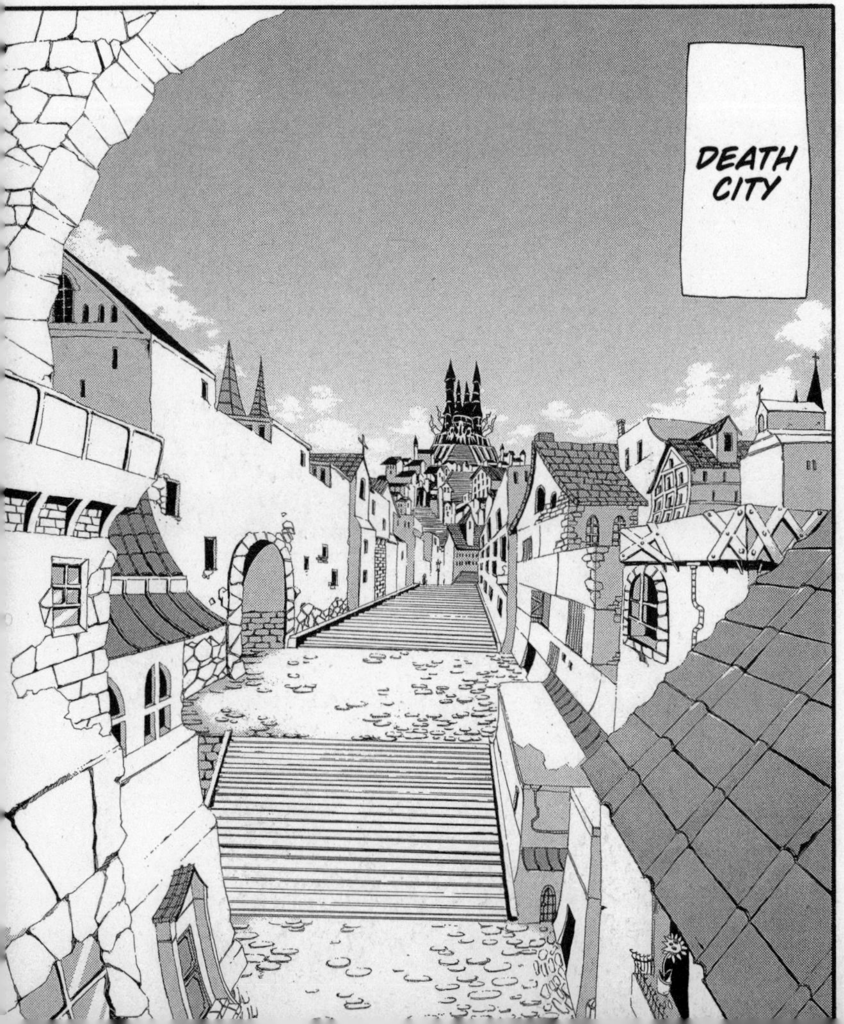
DEATH CITY

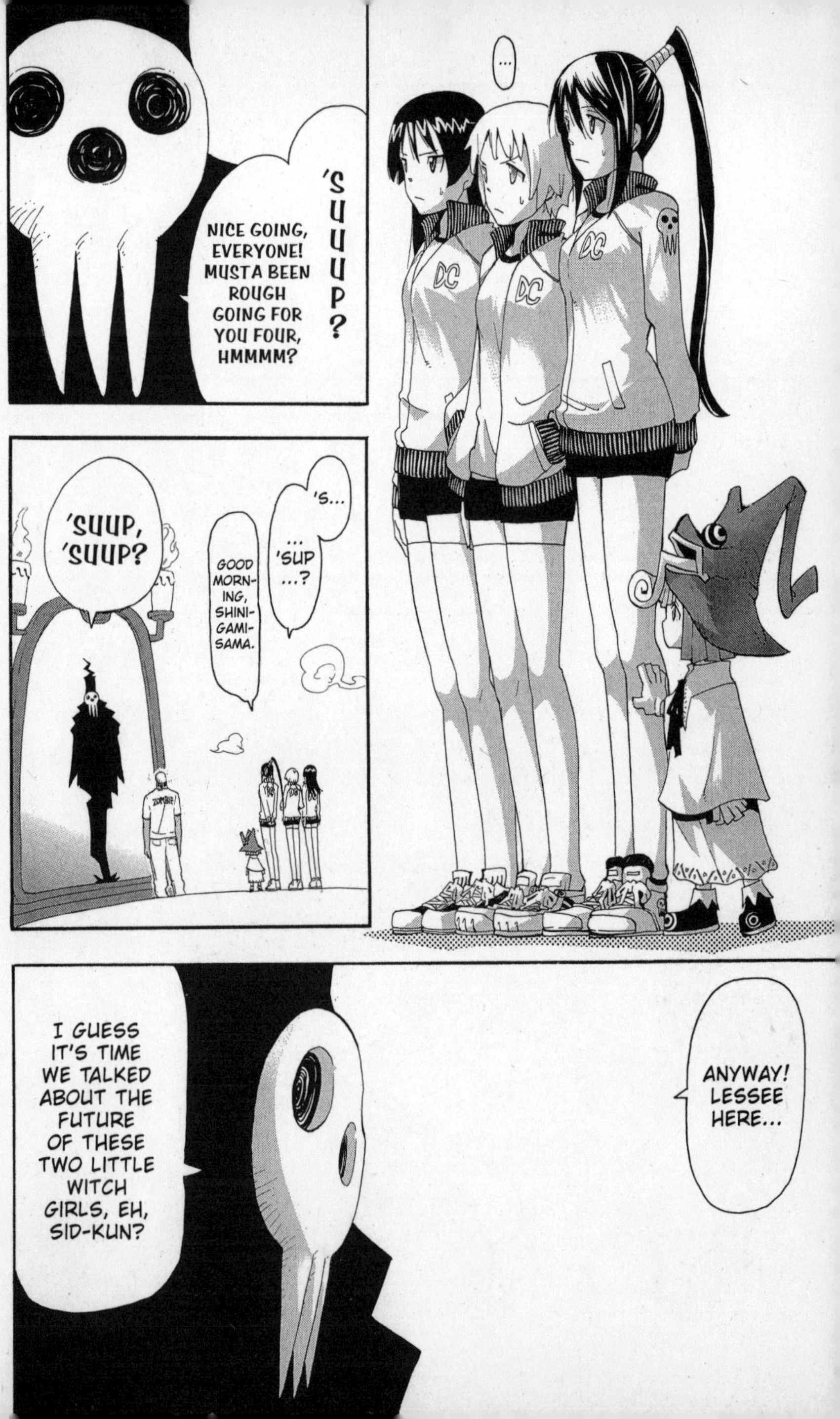
…
'SUUUP?
NICE GOING, EVERYONE! MUSTA BEEN ROUGH GOING FOR YOU FOUR, HMMMM?
'S…
… 'SUP …?
GOOD MORNING, SHINIGAMI-SAMA.
'SUUP, 'SUUP?
ZOMBIE!
ANYWAY! LESSEE HERE…
I GUESS IT'S TIME WE TALKED ABOUT THE FUTURE OF THESE TWO LITTLE WITCH GIRLS, EH, SID-KUN?

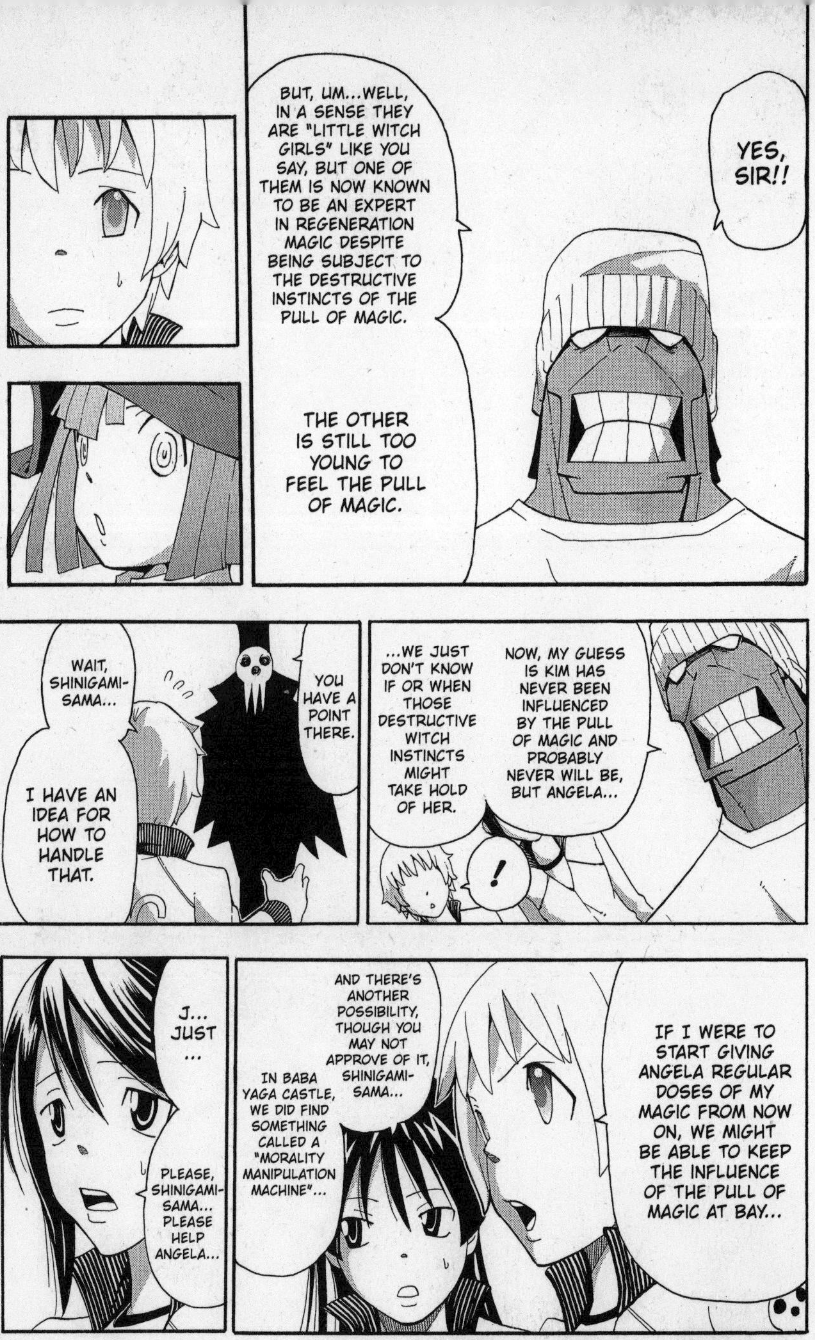
YES, SIR!!
BUT, UM...WELL, IN A SENSE THEY ARE "LITTLE WITCH GIRLS" LIKE YOU SAY, BUT ONE OF THEM IS NOW KNOWN TO BE AN EXPERT IN REGENERATION MAGIC DESPITE BEING SUBJECT TO THE DESTRUCTIVE INSTINCTS OF THE PULL OF MAGIC.
THE OTHER IS STILL TOO YOUNG TO FEEL THE PULL OF MAGIC.
NOW, MY GUESS IS KIM HAS NEVER BEEN INFLUENCED BY THE PULL OF MAGIC AND PROBABLY NEVER WILL BE, BUT ANGELA...
...WE JUST DON'T KNOW IF OR WHEN THOSE DESTRUCTIVE WITCH INSTINCTS MIGHT TAKE HOLD OF HER.
!
YOU HAVE A POINT THERE.
WAIT, SHINIGAMI-SAMA...
I HAVE AN IDEA FOR HOW TO HANDLE THAT.
IF I WERE TO START GIVING ANGELA REGULAR DOSES OF MY MAGIC FROM NOW ON, WE MIGHT BE ABLE TO KEEP THE INFLUENCE OF THE PULL OF MAGIC AT BAY...
AND THERE'S ANOTHER POSSIBILITY, THOUGH YOU MAY NOT APPROVE OF IT, SHINIGAMI-SAMA...
IN BABA YAGA CASTLE, WE DID FIND SOMETHING CALLED A "MORALITY MANIPULATION MACHINE"...
J... JUST ...
PLEASE, SHINIGAMI-SAMA... PLEASE HELP ANGELA...

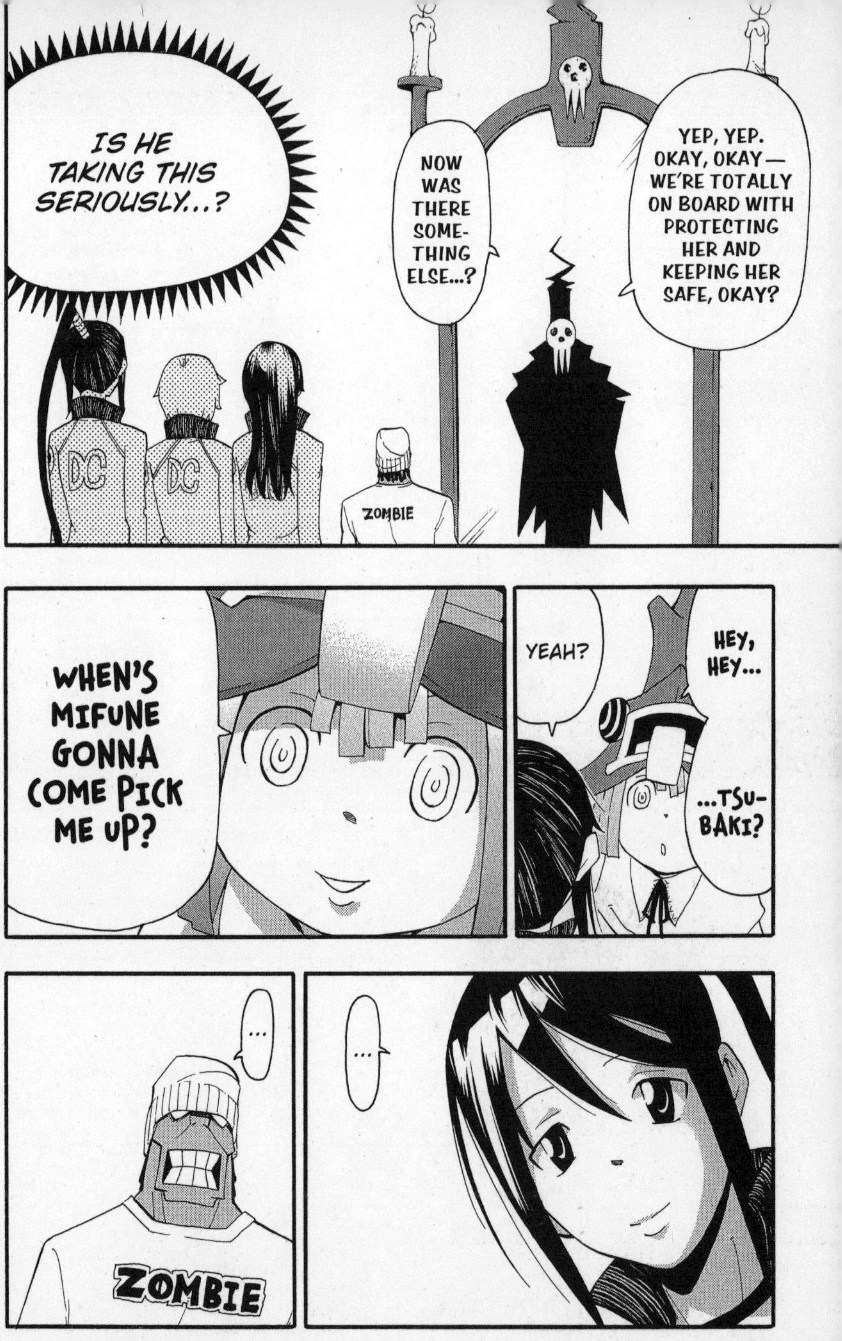
YEP, YEP. OKAY, OKAY— WE'RE TOTALLY ON BOARD WITH PROTECTING HER AND KEEPING HER SAFE, OKAY?
NOW WAS THERE SOME-THING ELSE...?
IS HE TAKING THIS SERIOUSLY...?
ZOMBIE
DC
DC
HEY, HEY... ...TSU-BAKI?
YEAH?
WHEN'S MIFUNE GONNA COME PICK ME UP?
...
...
ZOMBIE

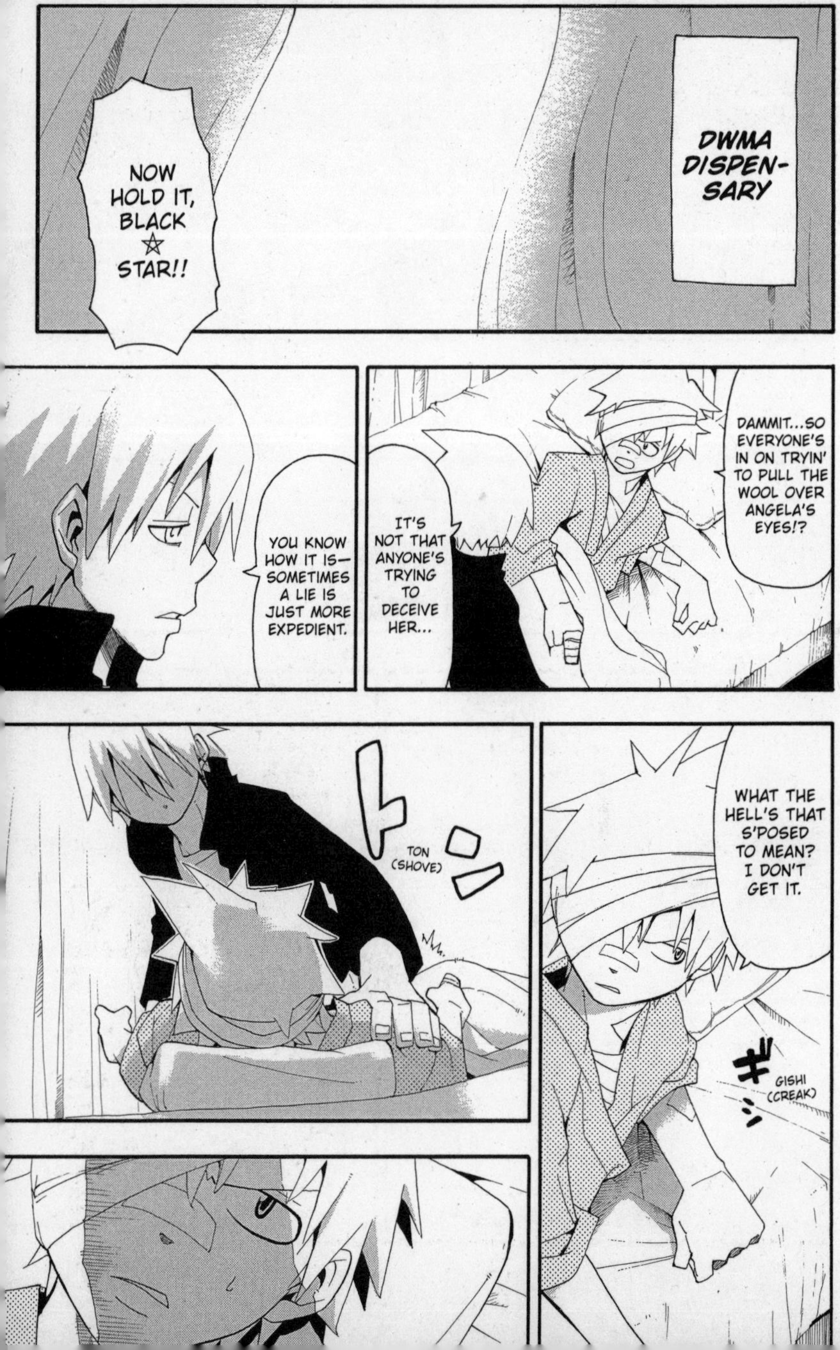
DWMA DISPENSARY
NOW HOLD IT, BLACK☆STAR!!
DAMMIT...SO EVERYONE'S IN ON TRYIN' TO PULL THE WOOL OVER ANGELA'S EYES!?
IT'S NOT THAT ANYONE'S TRYING TO DECEIVE HER...
YOU KNOW HOW IT IS—SOMETIMES A LIE IS JUST MORE EXPEDIENT.
WHAT THE HELL'S THAT S'POSED TO MEAN? I DON'T GET IT.
GISHI (CREAK)
TON (SHOVE)

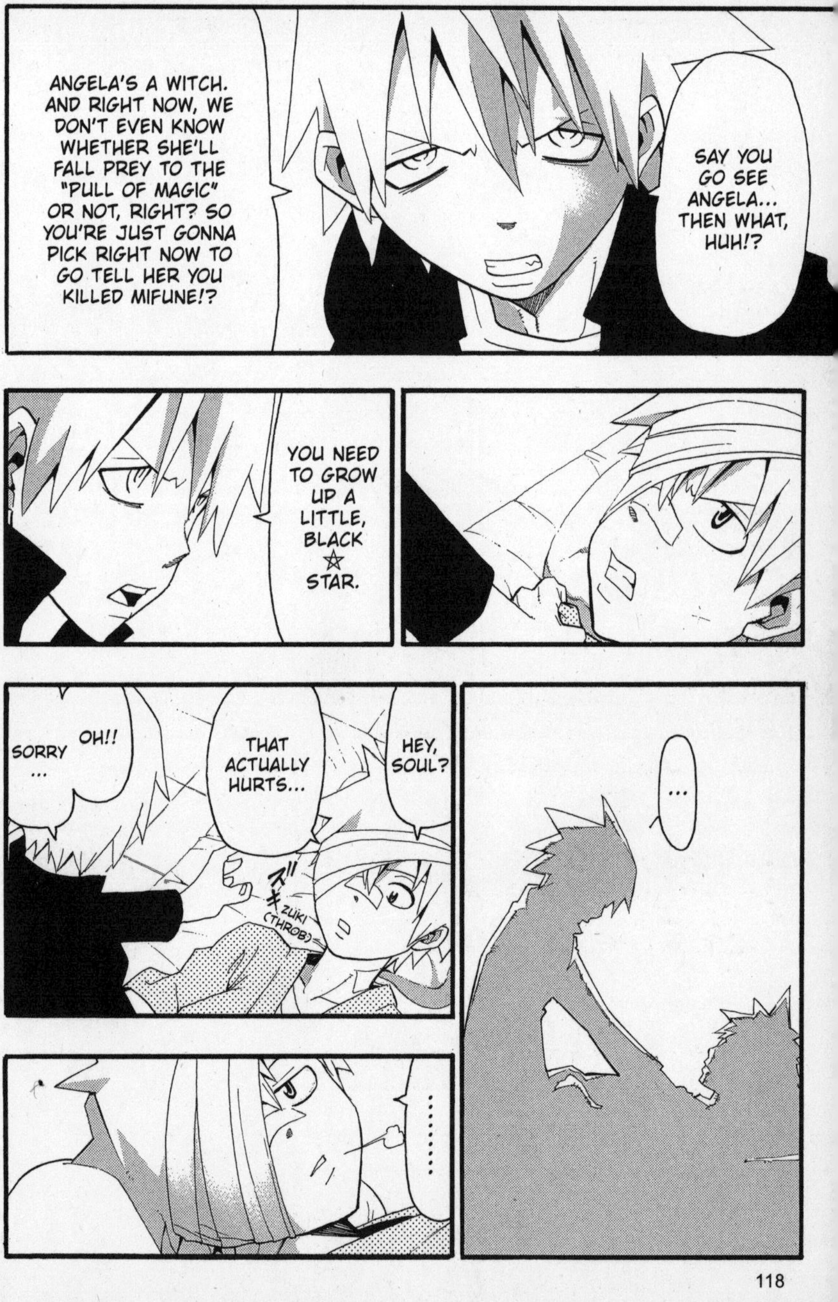
SAY YOU GO SEE ANGELA... THEN WHAT, HUH!?
ANGELA'S A WITCH. AND RIGHT NOW, WE DON'T EVEN KNOW WHETHER SHE'LL FALL PREY TO THE "PULL OF MAGIC" OR NOT, RIGHT? SO YOU'RE JUST GONNA PICK RIGHT NOW TO GO TELL HER YOU KILLED MIFUNE!?
YOU NEED TO GROW UP A LITTLE, BLACK☆STAR.
...
HEY, SOUL?
THAT ACTUALLY HURTS...
ZUKI (THROB)
OH!!
SORRY ...
....

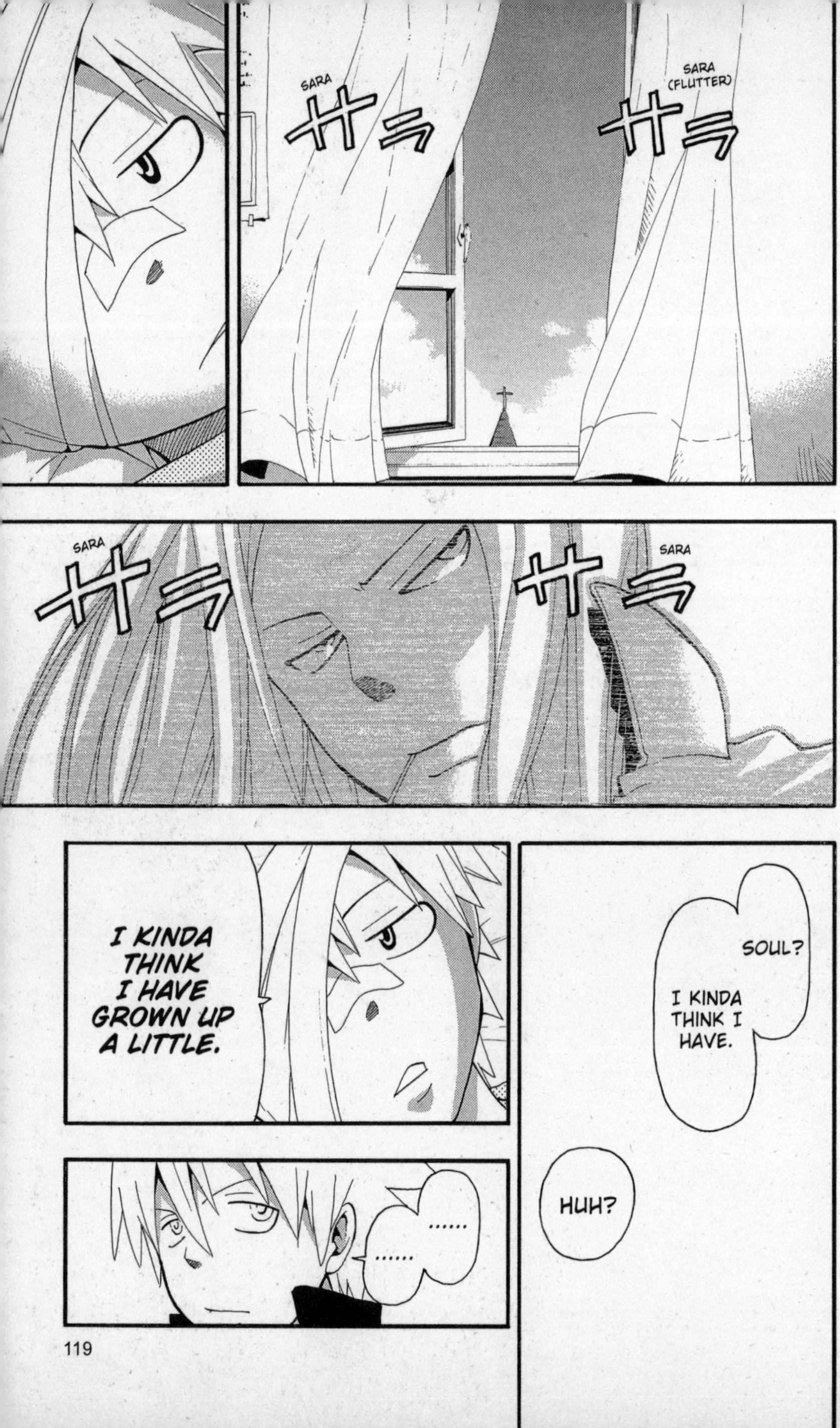
サラ
SARA (FLUTTER)
サラ
SARA
サラ
SARA
サラ
SARA
SOUL?
I KINDA THINK I HAVE.
HUH?
I KINDA THINK I HAVE GROWN UP A LITTLE.
......
......

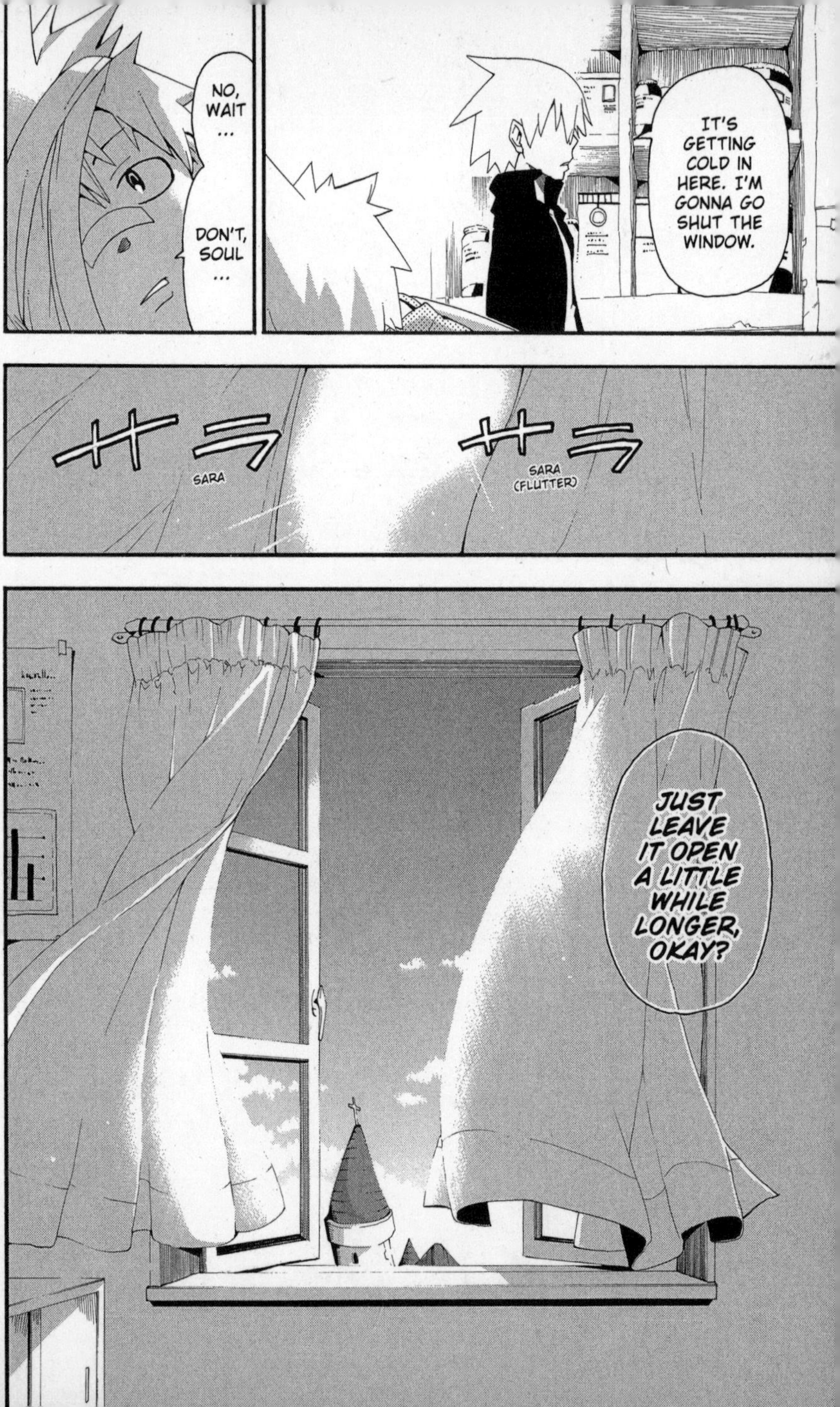

IT'S GETTING COLD IN HERE. I'M GONNA GO SHUT THE WINDOW.
NO, WAIT...
DON'T, SOUL...
サラ
SARA (FLUTTER)
サラ
SARA
JUST LEAVE IT OPEN A LITTLE WHILE LONGER, OKAY?

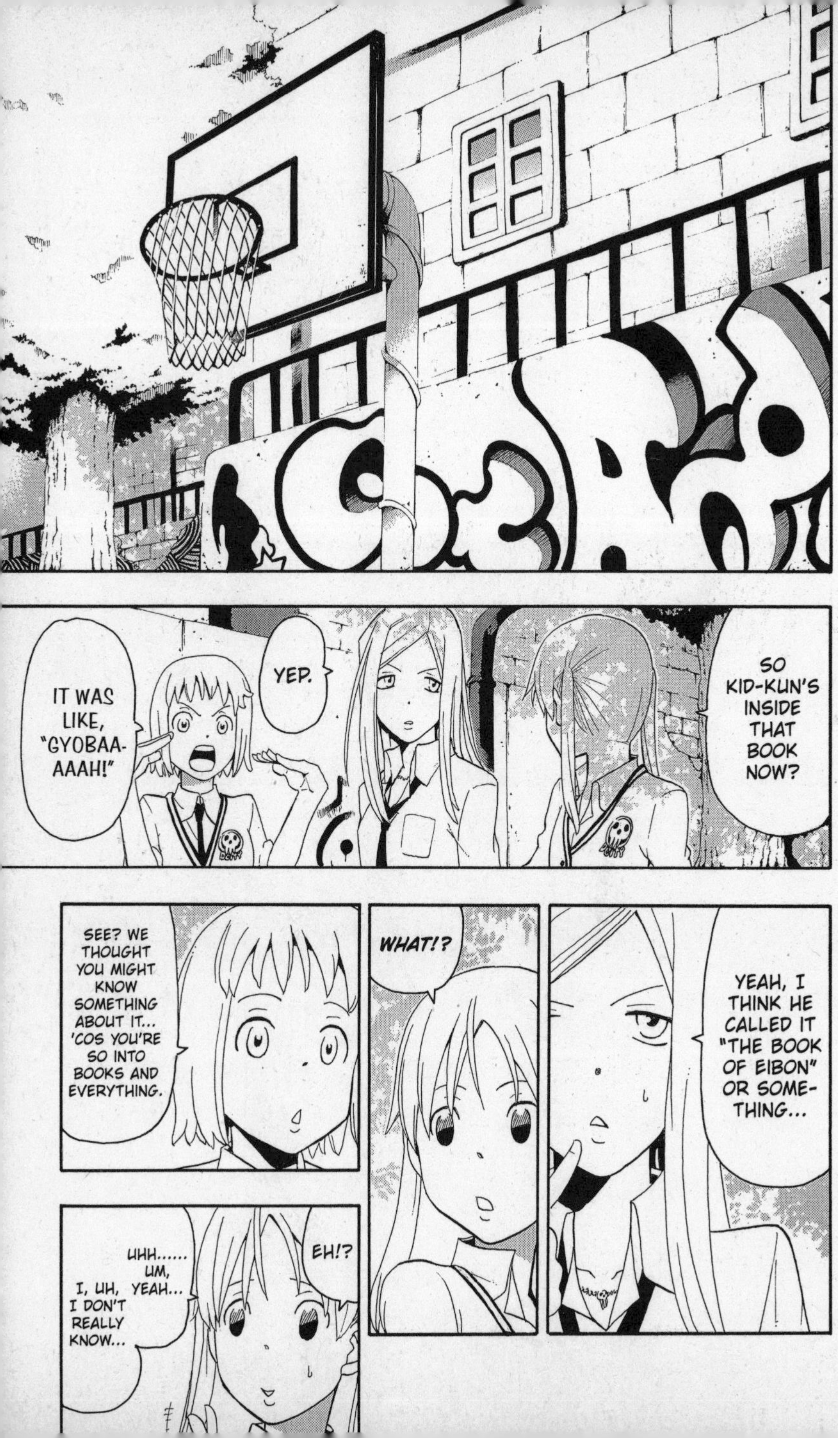
SO KID-KUN'S INSIDE THAT BOOK NOW?
YEP.
IT WAS LIKE, "GYOBAA-AAAH!"
YEAH, I THINK HE CALLED IT "THE BOOK OF EIBON" OR SOME-THING...
WHAT!?
SEE? WE THOUGHT YOU MIGHT KNOW SOMETHING ABOUT IT... 'COS YOU'RE SO INTO BOOKS AND EVERYTHING.
EH!?
UHH...... UM, YEAH...
I, UH, I DON'T REALLY KNOW...

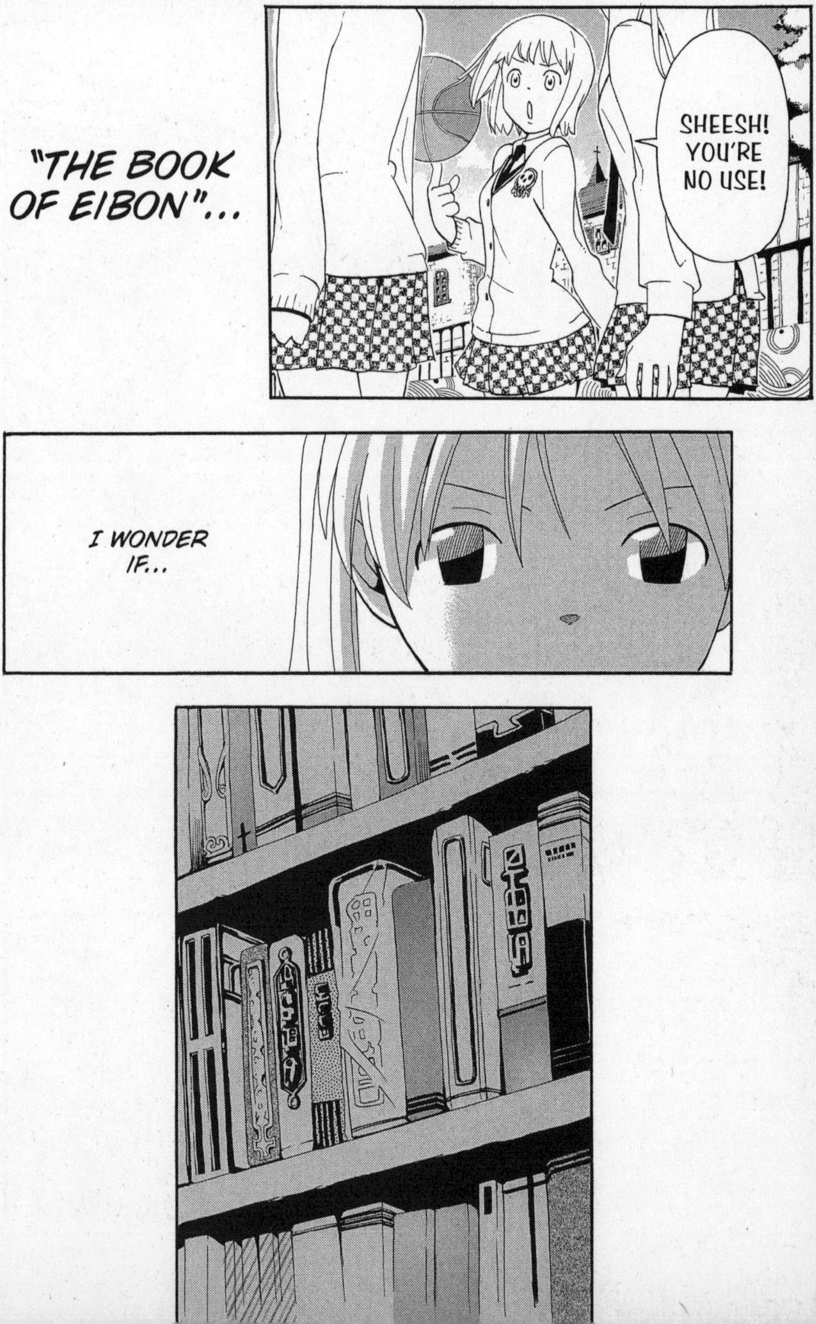
SHEESH! YOU'RE NO USE!
"THE BOOK OF EIBON"...
I WONDER IF...

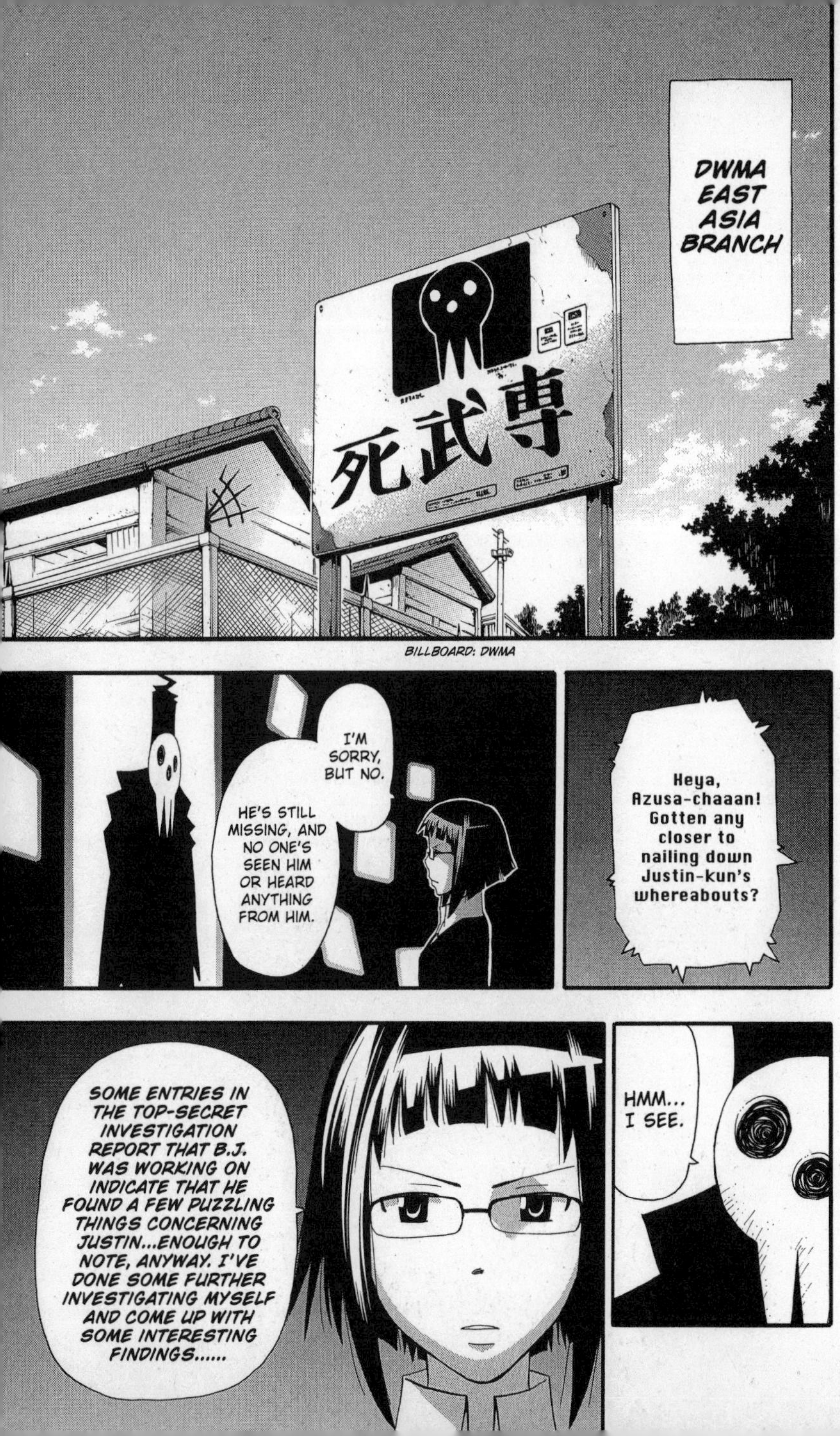
DWMA EAST ASIA BRANCH
死武専
BILLBOARD: DWMA
Heya, Azusa-chaaan! Gotten any closer to nailing down Justin-kun's whereabouts?
I'M SORRY, BUT NO.
HE'S STILL MISSING, AND NO ONE'S SEEN HIM OR HEARD ANYTHING FROM HIM.
HMM... I SEE.
SOME ENTRIES IN THE TOP-SECRET INVESTIGATION REPORT THAT B.J. WAS WORKING ON INDICATE THAT HE FOUND A FEW PUZZLING THINGS CONCERNING JUSTIN...ENOUGH TO NOTE, ANYWAY. I'VE DONE SOME FURTHER INVESTIGATING MYSELF AND COME UP WITH SOME INTERESTING FINDINGS......

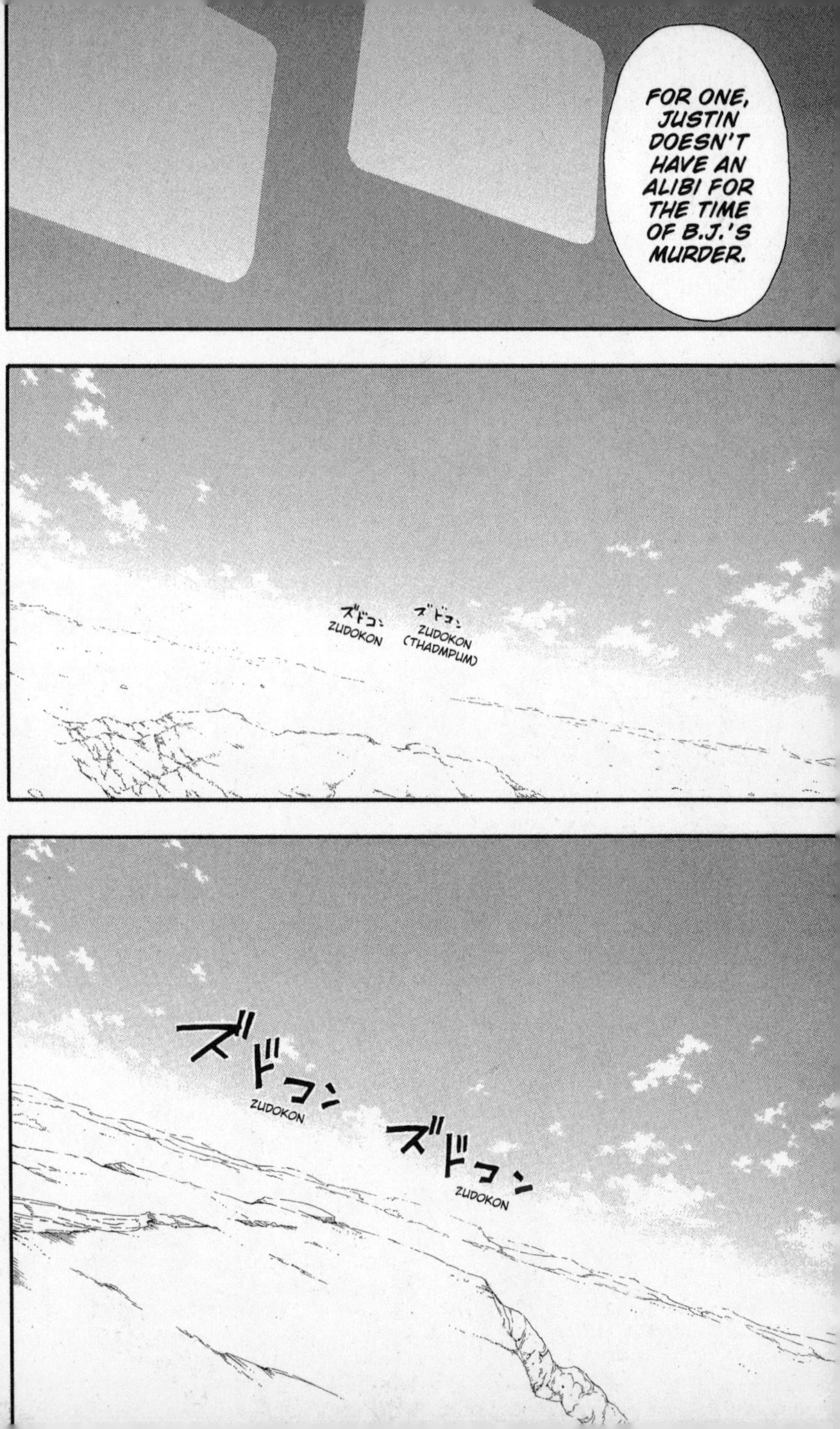
FOR ONE, JUSTIN DOESN'T HAVE AN ALIBI FOR THE TIME OF B.J.'S MURDER.
ズドコン
ZUDOKON (THADMPUM)
ズドコン
ZUDOKON
ズドコン
ZUDOKON
ズドコン
ZUDOKON

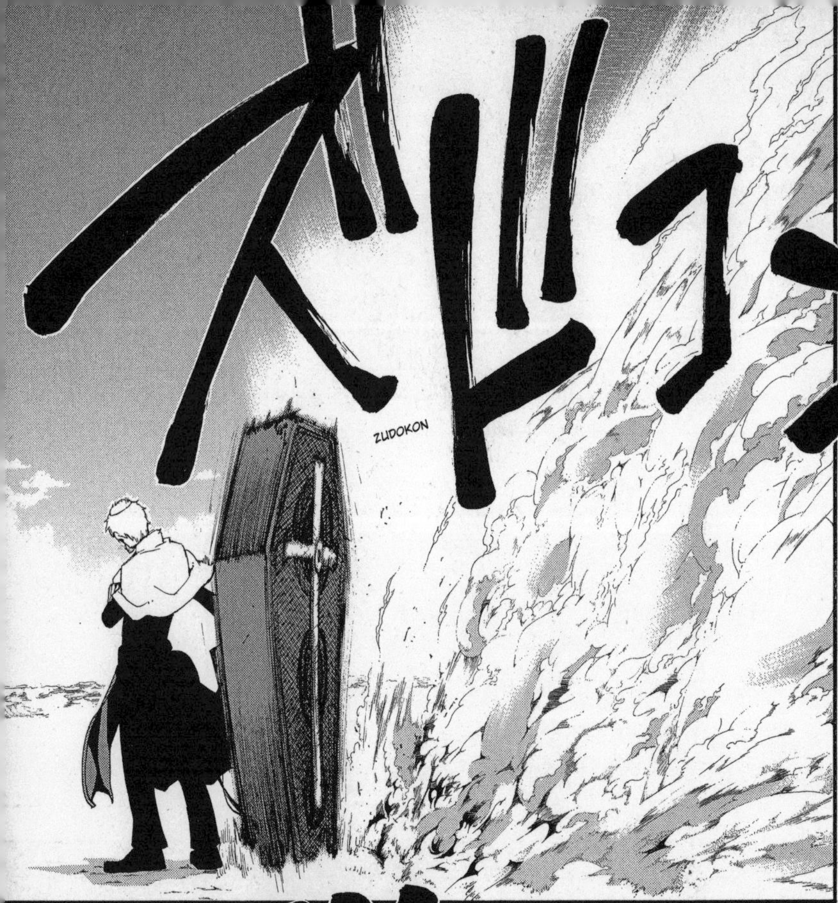
ZUDOKON
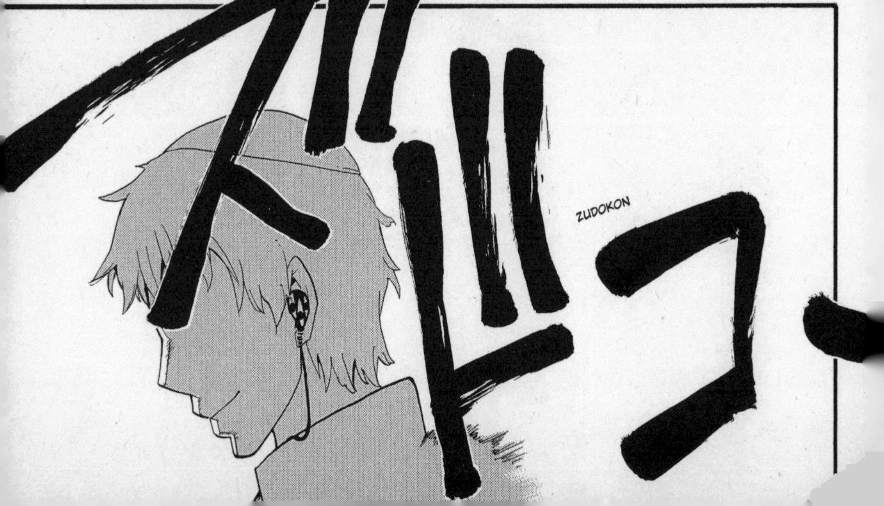
ZUDOKON

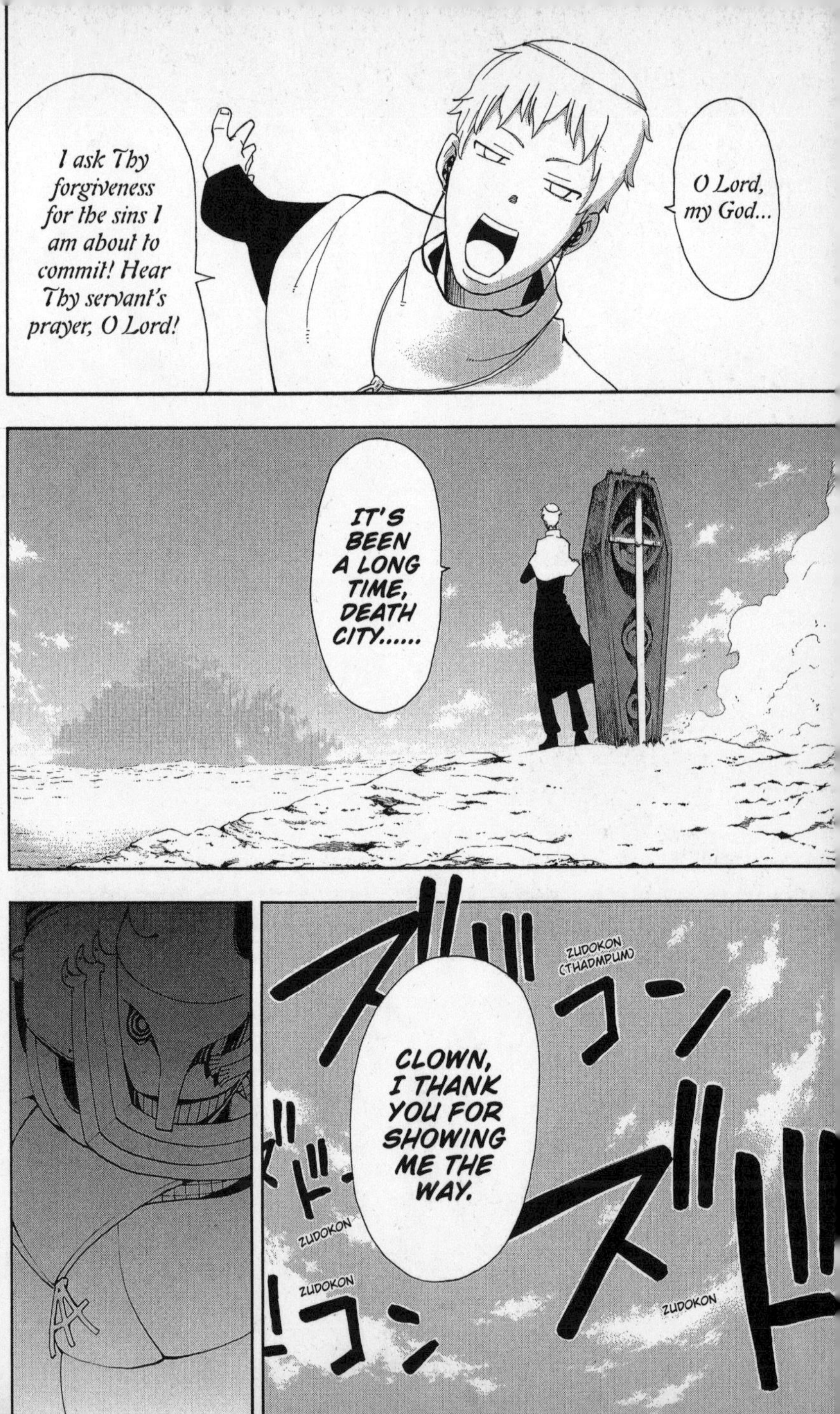
O Lord, my God...
I ask Thy forgiveness for the sins I am about to commit! Hear Thy servant's prayer, O Lord!
IT'S BEEN A LONG TIME, DEATH CITY......
ZUDOKON (THADMPUM)
CLOWN, I THANK YOU FOR SHOWING ME THE WAY.
ZUDOKON
ZUDOKON
ZUDOKON

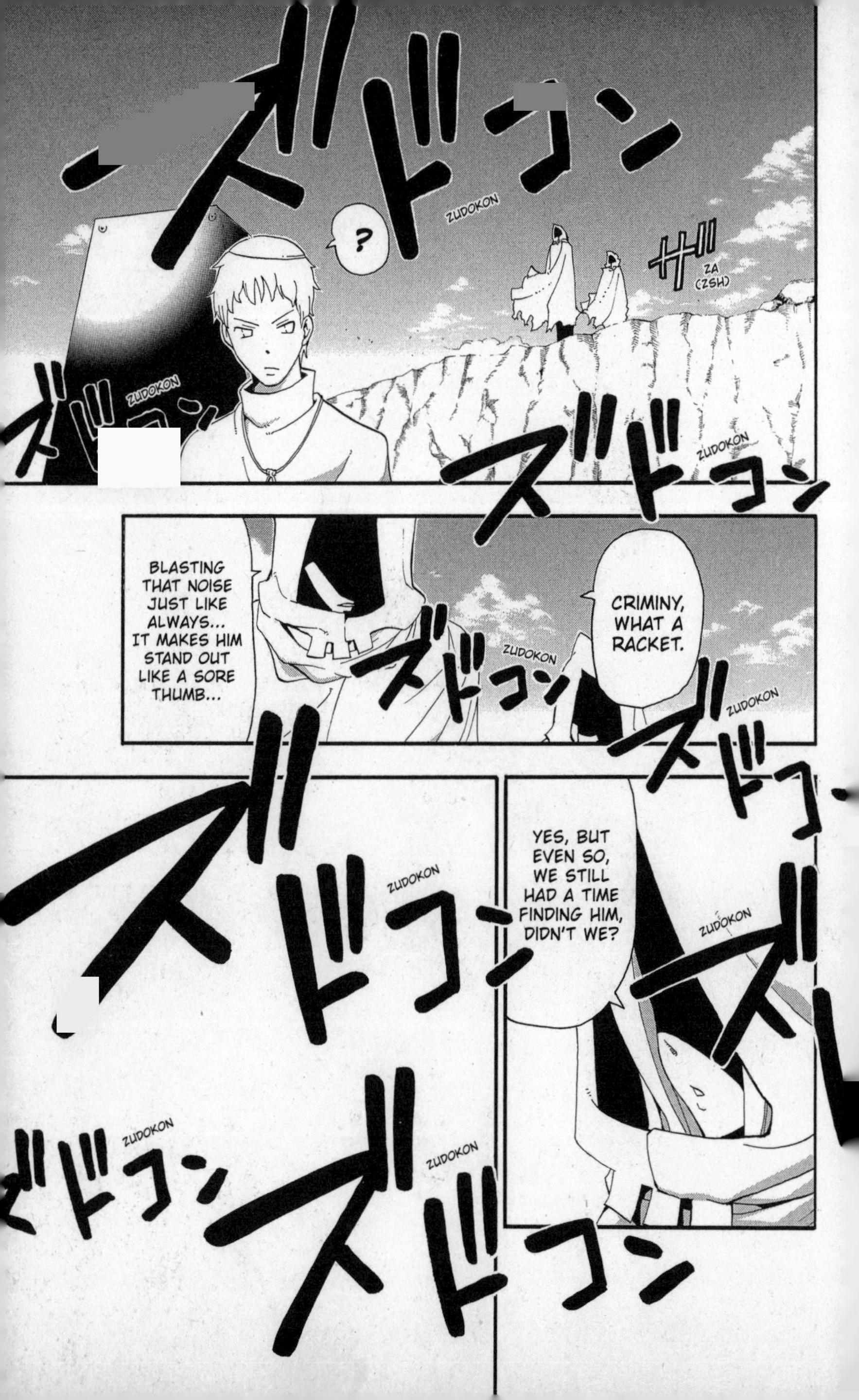
ZUDOKON
?
ZA (ZSH)
ZUDOKON
ZUDOKON
CRIMINY, WHAT A RACKET.
ZUDOKON
BLASTING THAT NOISE JUST LIKE ALWAYS... IT MAKES HIM STAND OUT LIKE A SORE THUMB...
ZUDOKON
YES, BUT EVEN SO, WE STILL HAD A TIME FINDING HIM, DIDN'T WE?
ZUDOKON
ZUDOKON
ZUDOKON
ZUDOKON

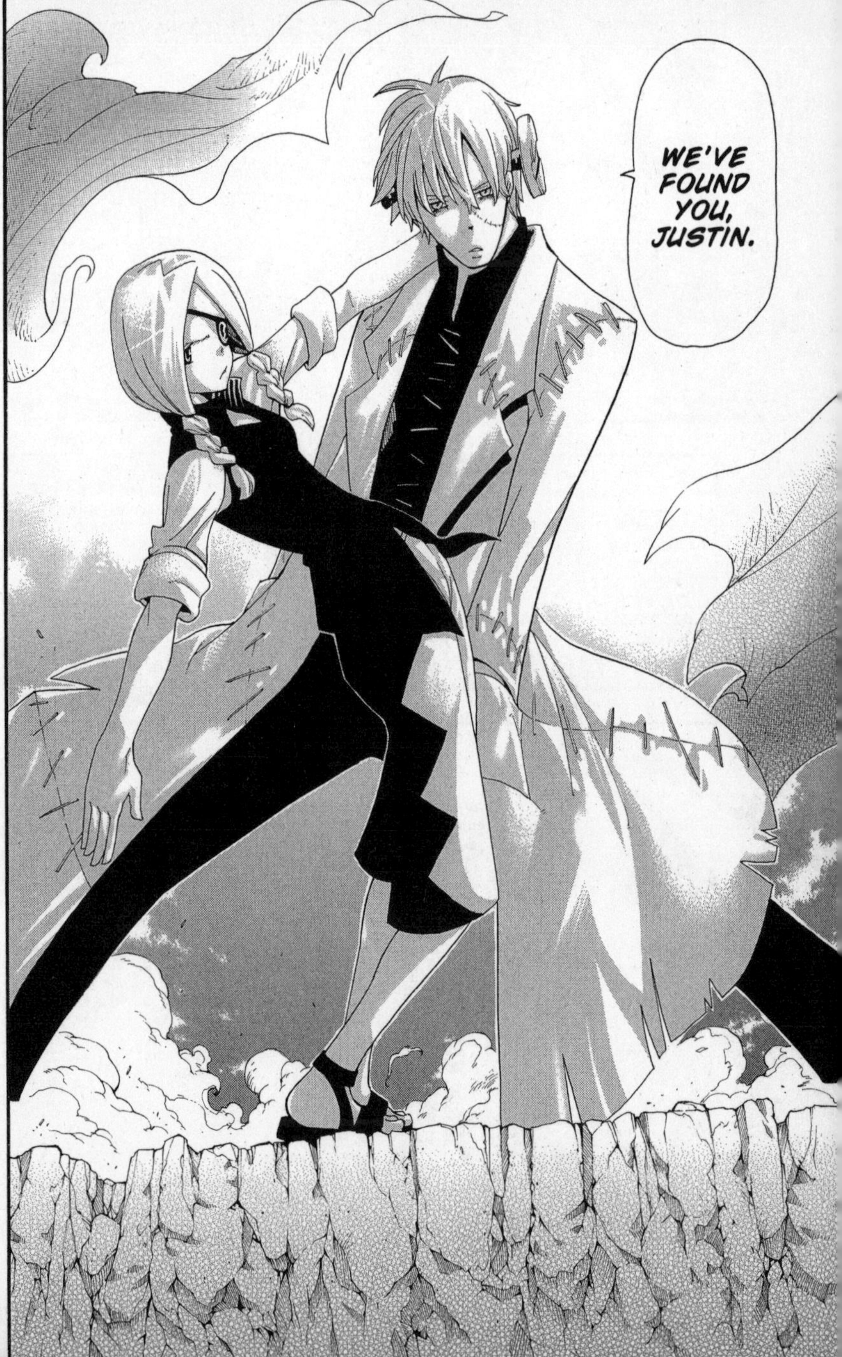
WE'VE FOUND YOU, JUSTIN.

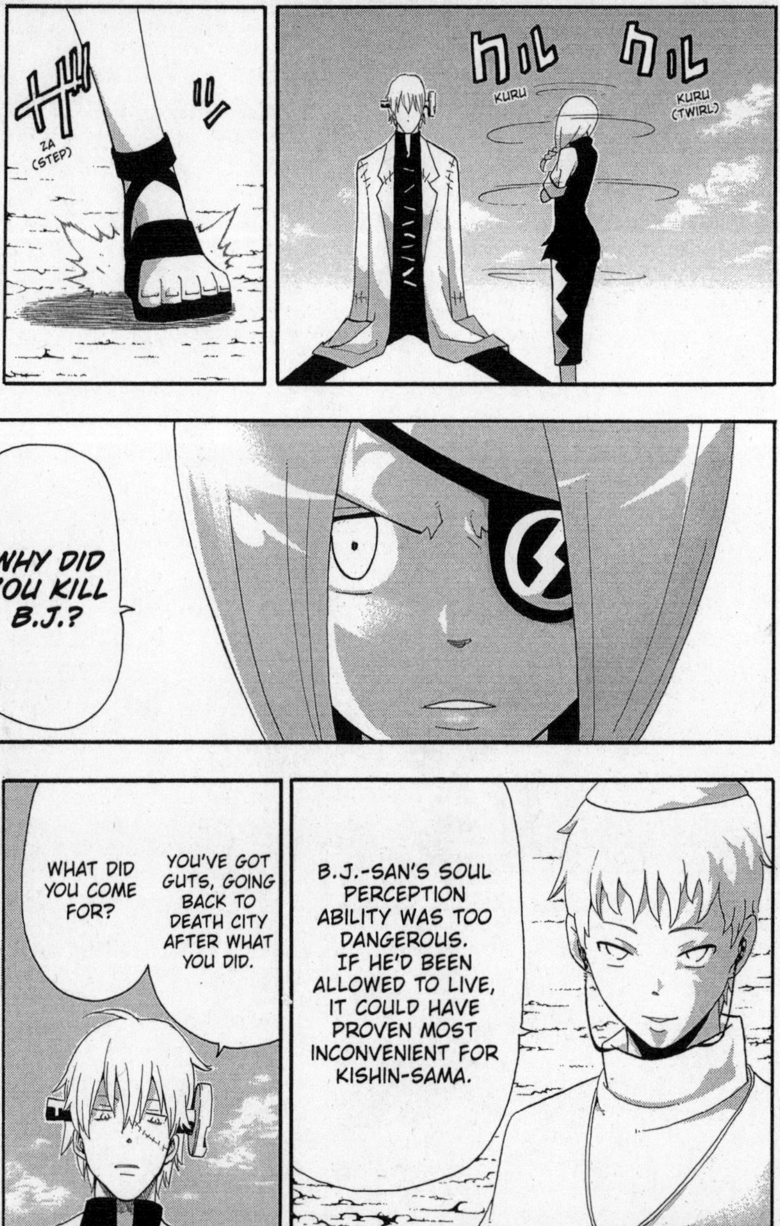
KURU
KURU (TWIRL)
ZA (STEP)
WHY DID YOU KILL B.J.?
B.J.-SAN'S SOUL PERCEPTION ABILITY WAS TOO DANGEROUS. IF HE'D BEEN ALLOWED TO LIVE, IT COULD HAVE PROVEN MOST INCONVENIENT FOR KISHIN-SAMA.
YOU'VE GOT GUTS, GOING BACK TO DEATH CITY AFTER WHAT YOU DID.
WHAT DID YOU COME FOR?

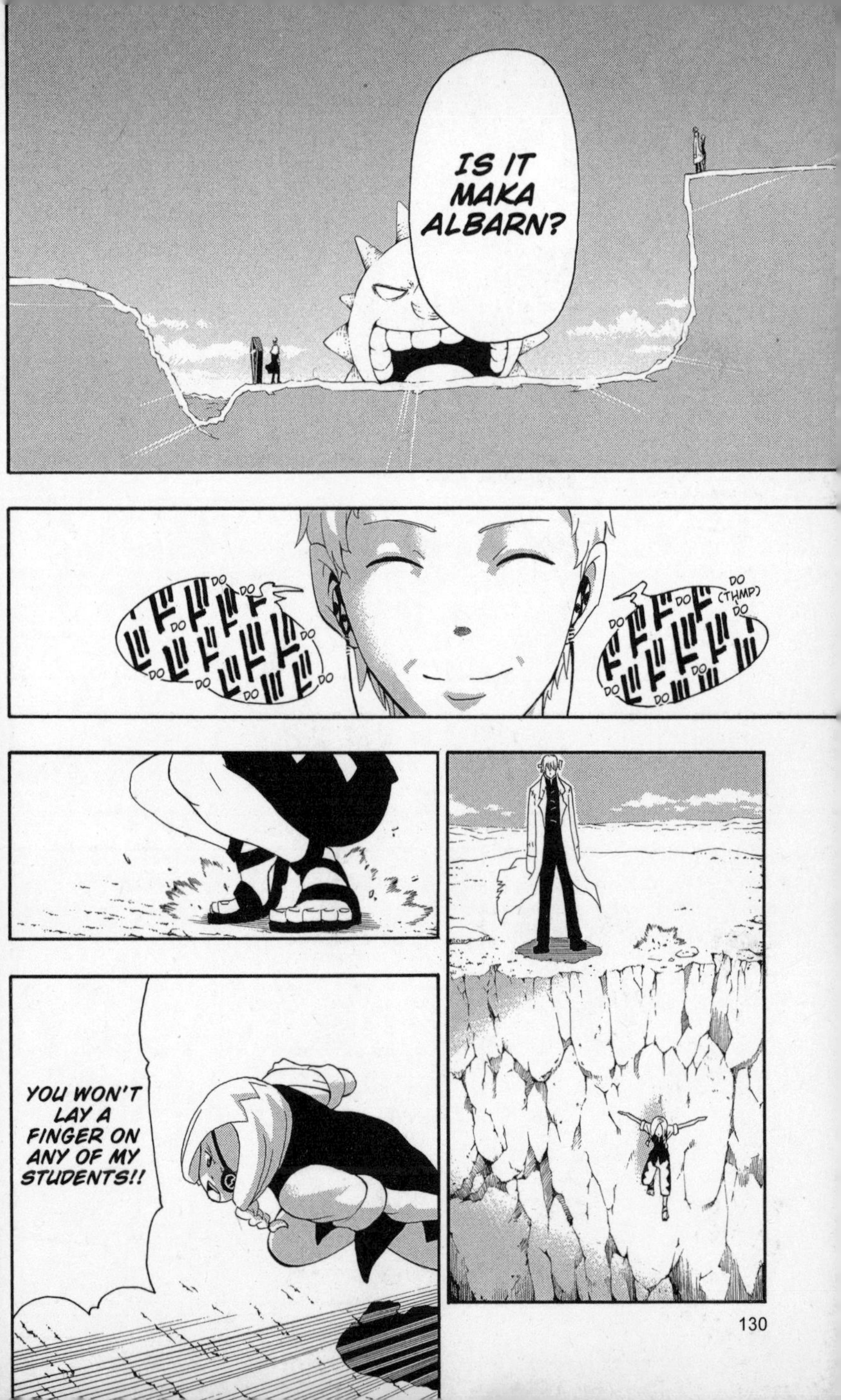
IS IT MAKA ALBARN?
DO (THMP) DO
YOU WON'T LAY A FINGER ON ANY OF MY STUDENTS!!

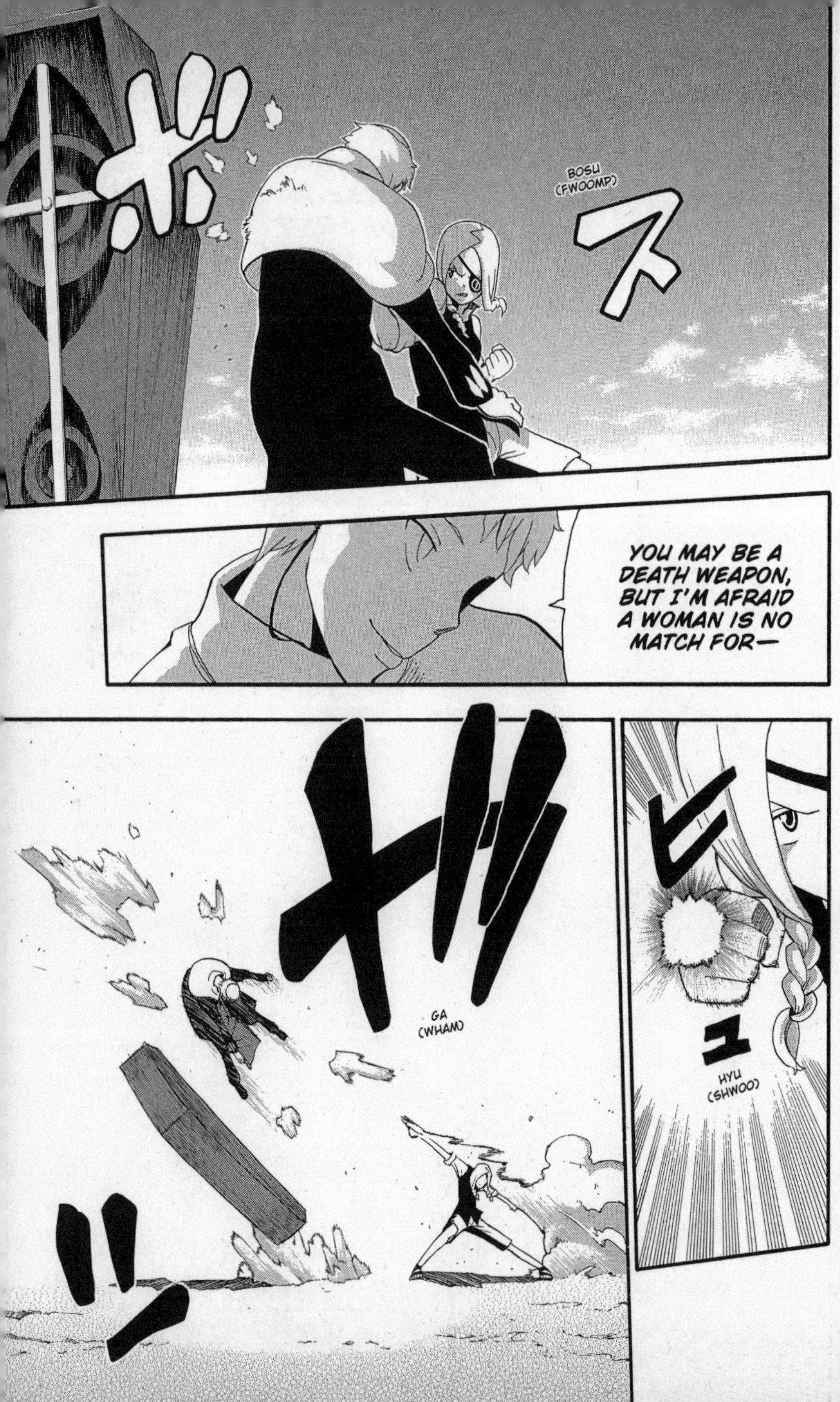
BOSU
(FWOOMP)
YOU MAY BE A DEATH WEAPON, BUT I'M AFRAID A WOMAN IS NO MATCH FOR—
HYU
(SHWOO)
GA
(WHAM)

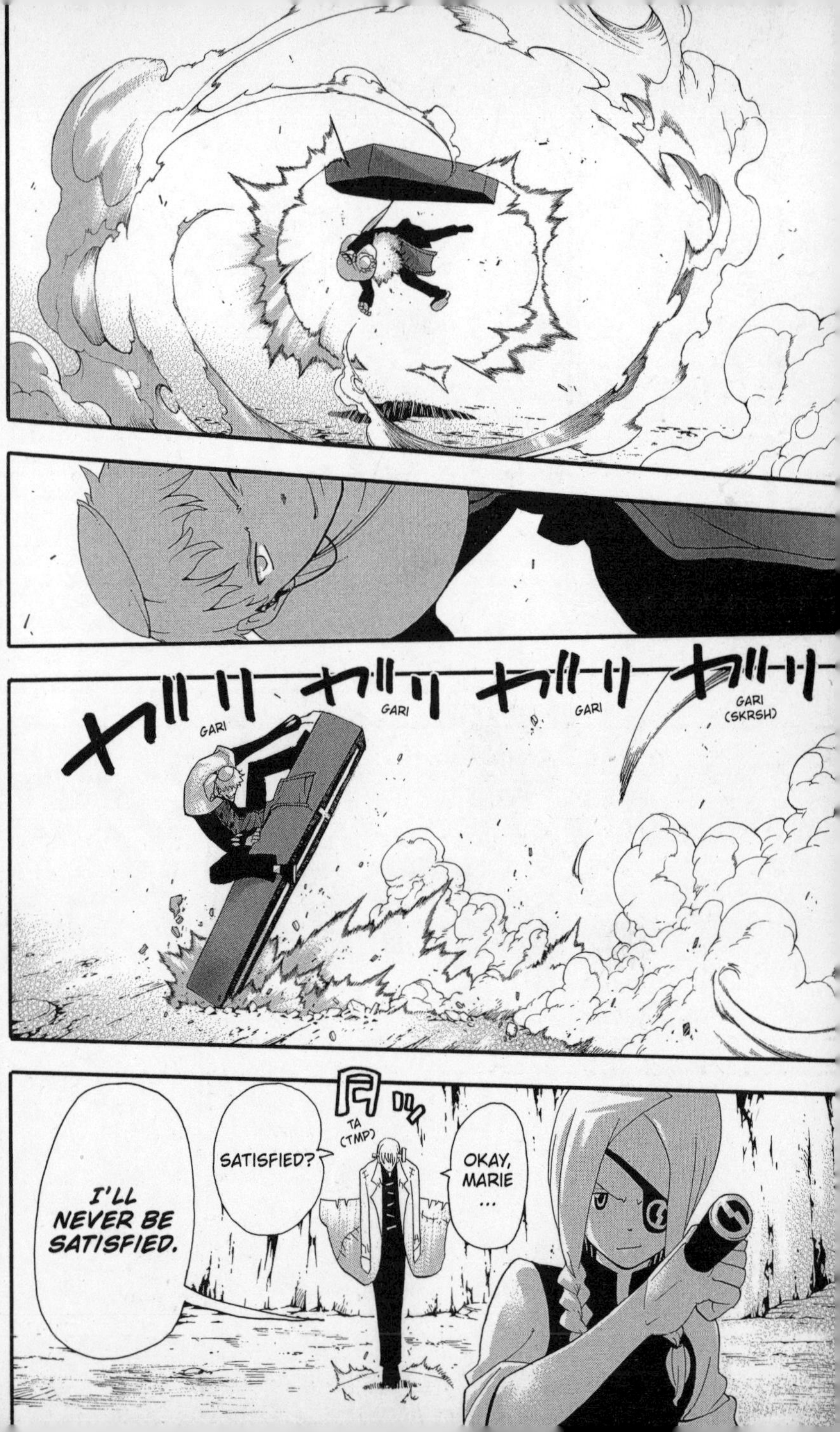
ガリ
GARI (SKRSH)
ガリ
GARI
ガリ
GARI
ガリ
GARI
OKAY, MARIE ...
タ
TA (TMP)
SATISFIED?
I'LL NEVER BE SATISFIED.

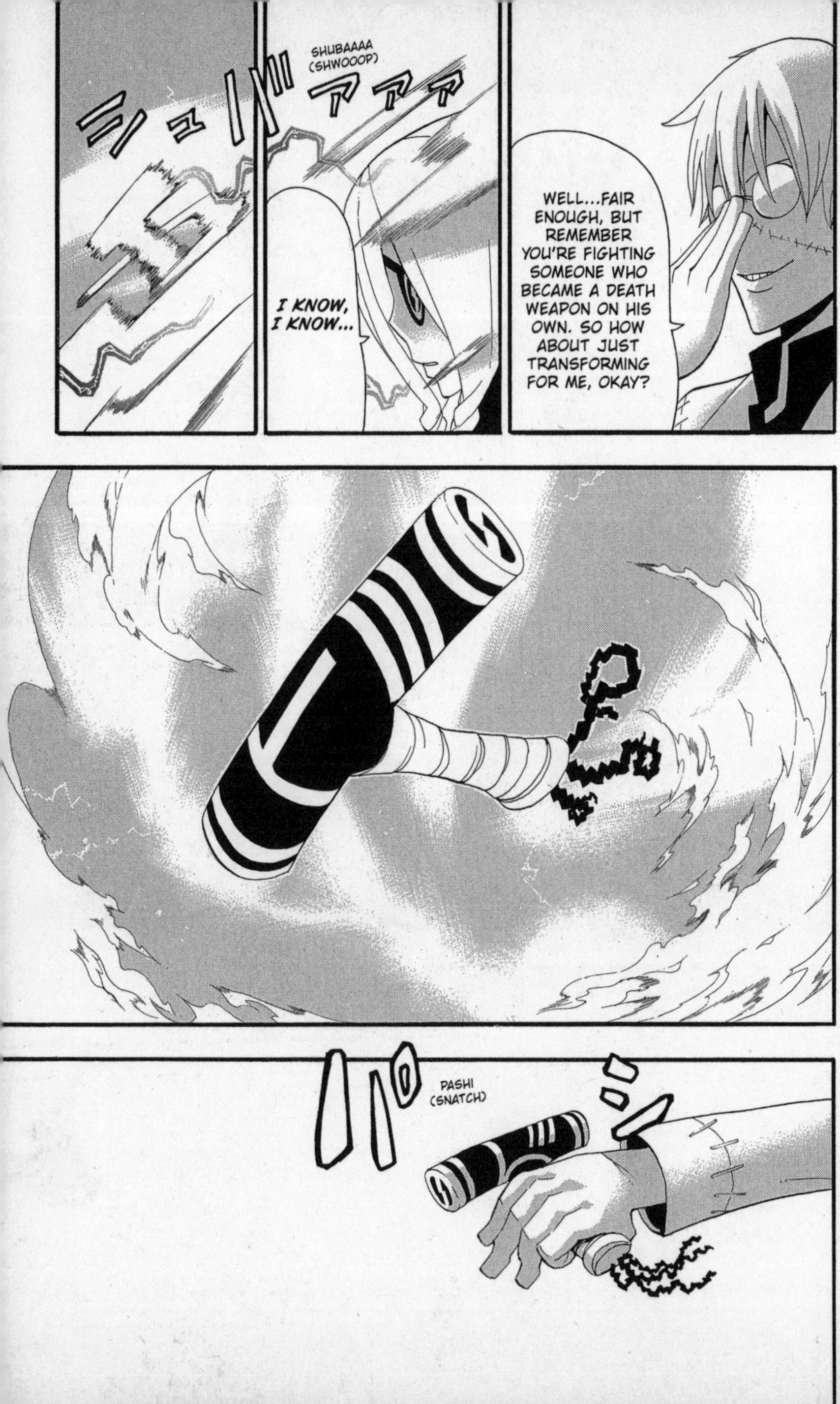
WELL...FAIR ENOUGH, BUT REMEMBER YOU'RE FIGHTING SOMEONE WHO BECAME A DEATH WEAPON ON HIS OWN. SO HOW ABOUT JUST TRANSFORMING FOR ME, OKAY?
I KNOW, I KNOW...
SHUBAAAA (SHWOOOP)
PASHI (SNATCH)

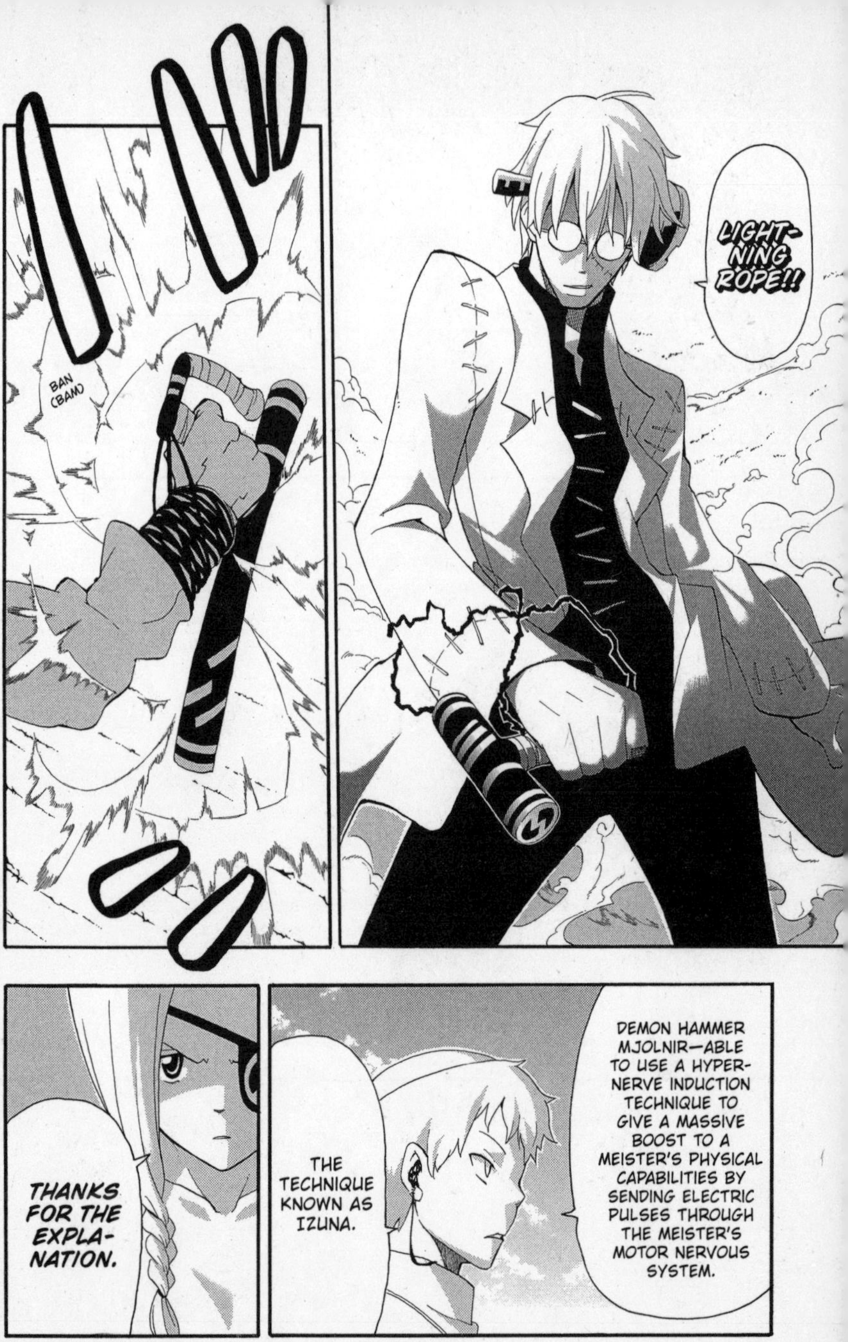
LIGHT-NING ROPE!!
BAN (BAM)
DEMON HAMMER MJOLNIR—ABLE TO USE A HYPER-NERVE INDUCTION TECHNIQUE TO GIVE A MASSIVE BOOST TO A MEISTER'S PHYSICAL CAPABILITIES BY SENDING ELECTRIC PULSES THROUGH THE MEISTER'S MOTOR NERVOUS SYSTEM.
THE TECHNIQUE KNOWN AS IZUNA.
THANKS FOR THE EXPLA-NATION.

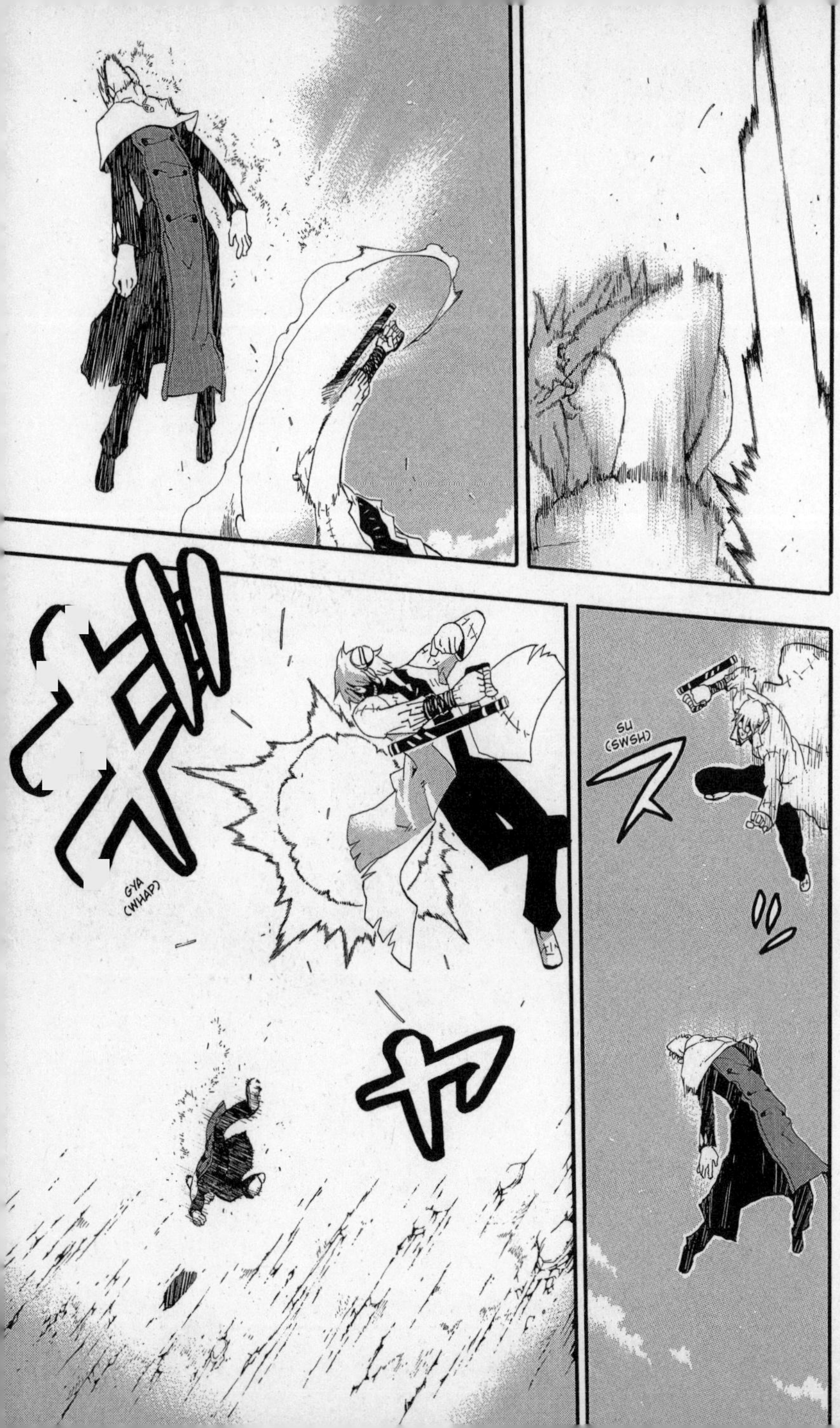
SU
(SWSH)
GYA
(WHAP)

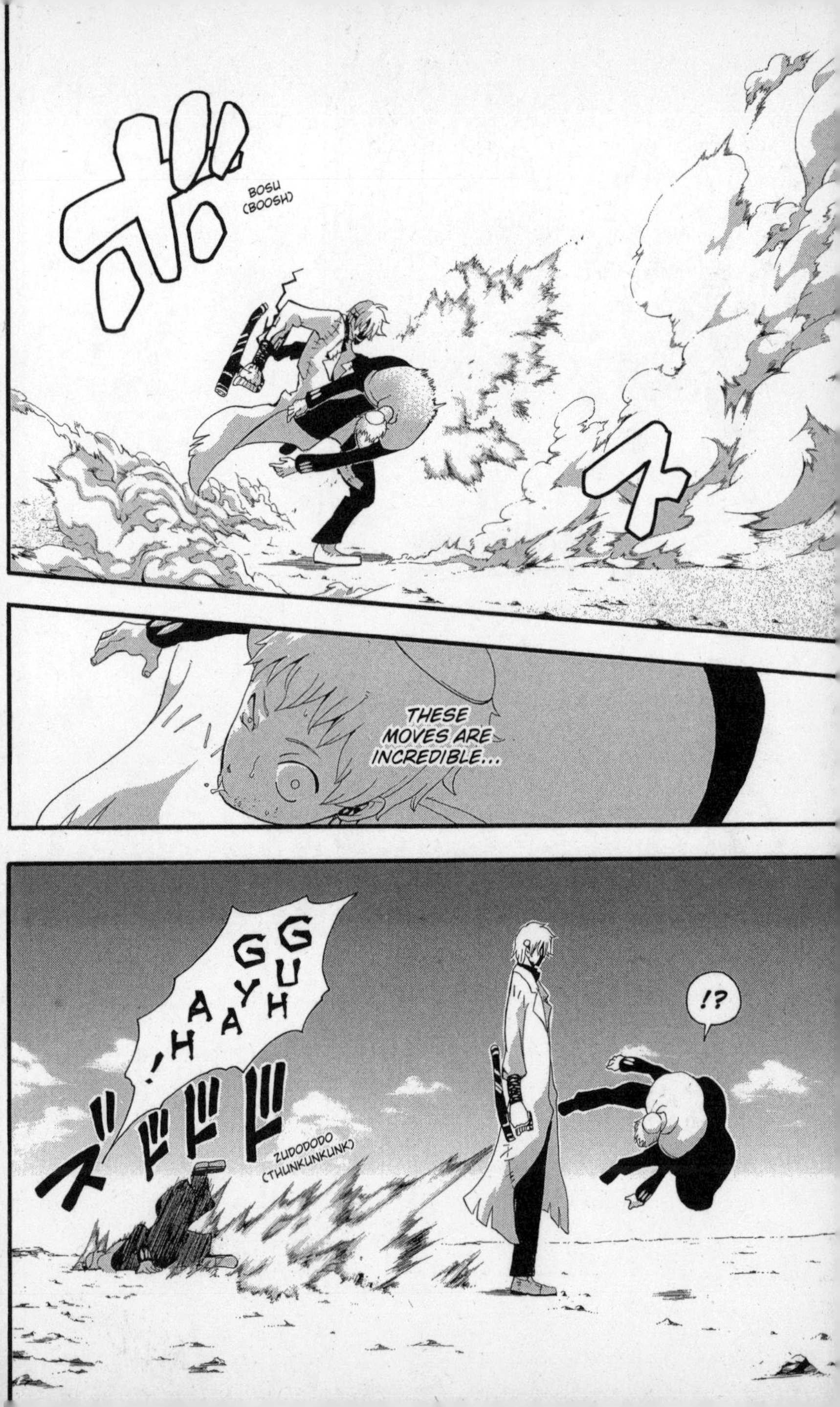
BOSU (BOOSH)
THESE MOVES ARE INCREDIBLE...
!?
GGUHHAYAH!
ZUDODODO (THUNKUNKUNK)

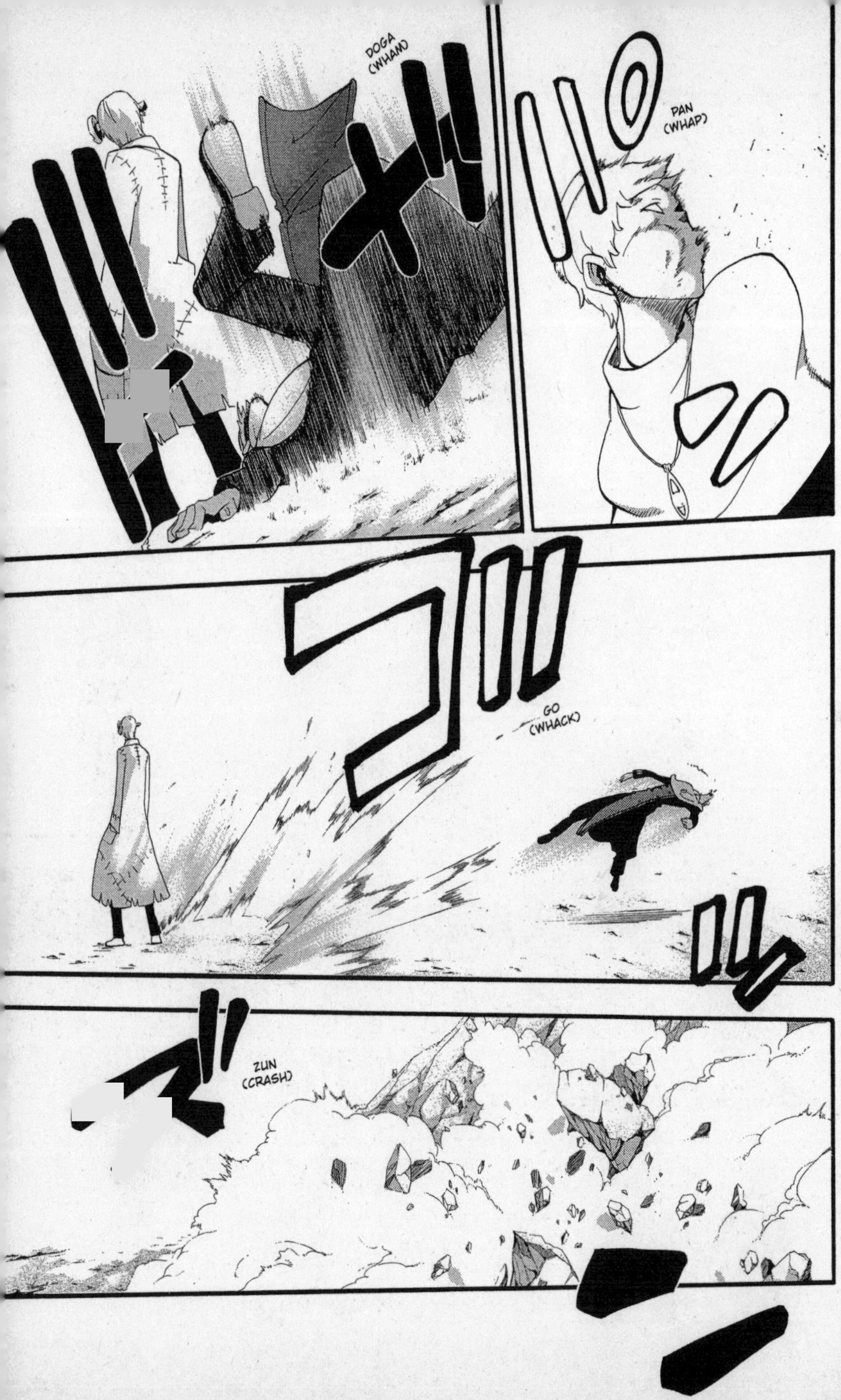
PAN
(WHAP)
DOGA
(WHAM)
GO
(WHACK)
ZUN
(CRASH)

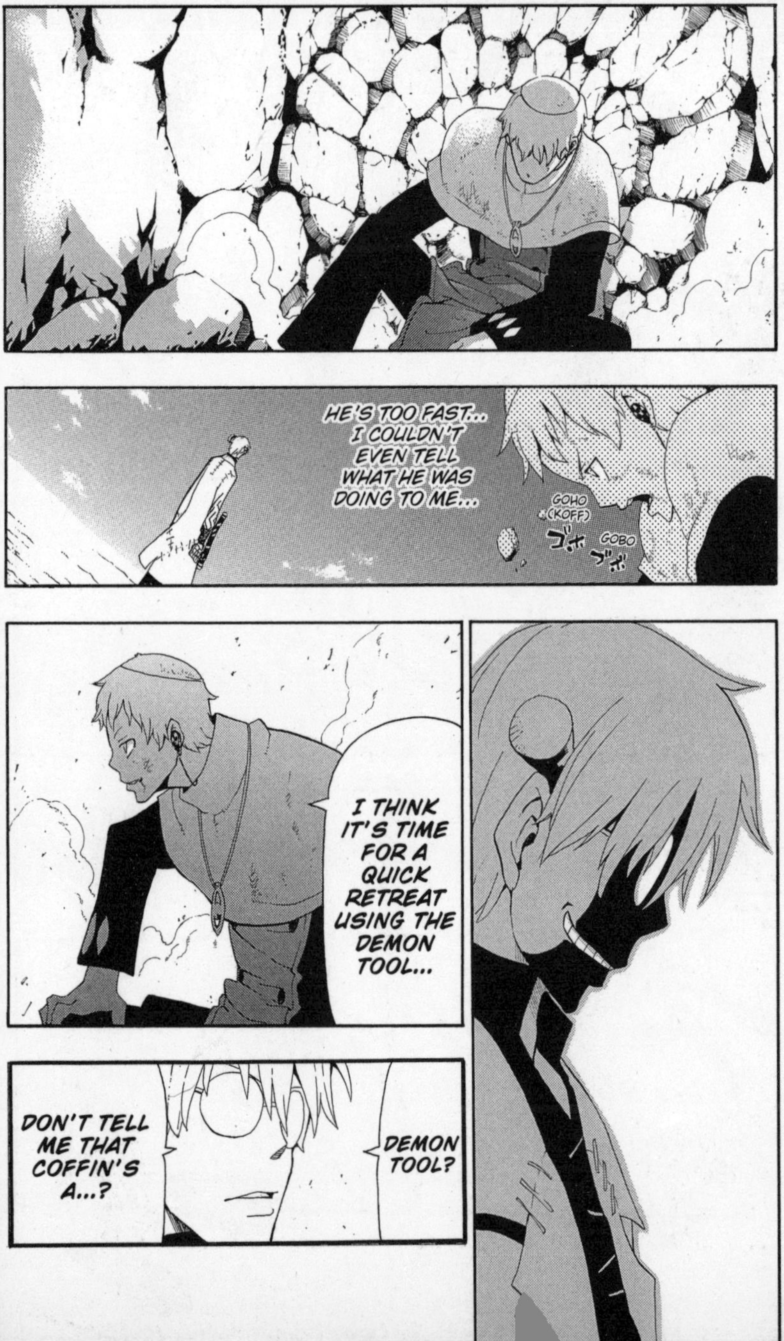
HE'S TOO FAST... I COULDN'T EVEN TELL WHAT HE WAS DOING TO ME...
GOHO (KOFF)
ゴホ
GOBO
ゴボ
I THINK IT'S TIME FOR A QUICK RETREAT USING THE DEMON TOOL...
DEMON TOOL?
DON'T TELL ME THAT COFFIN'S A...?

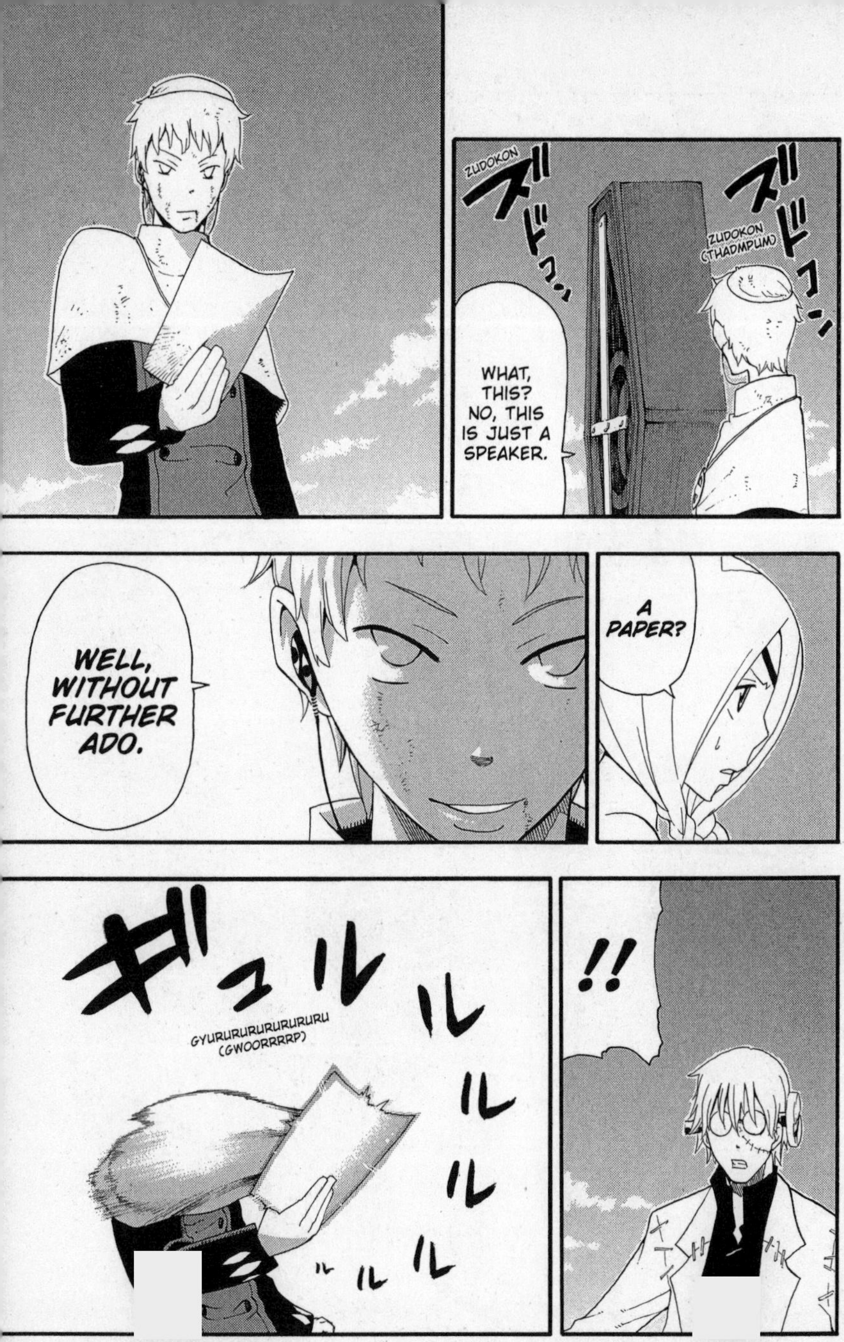
ZUDOKON
ZUDOKON (THADMPUM)
WHAT, THIS? NO, THIS IS JUST A SPEAKER.
A PAPER?
WELL, WITHOUT FURTHER ADO.
!!
GYURURURURURURURU (GWOORRRRP)

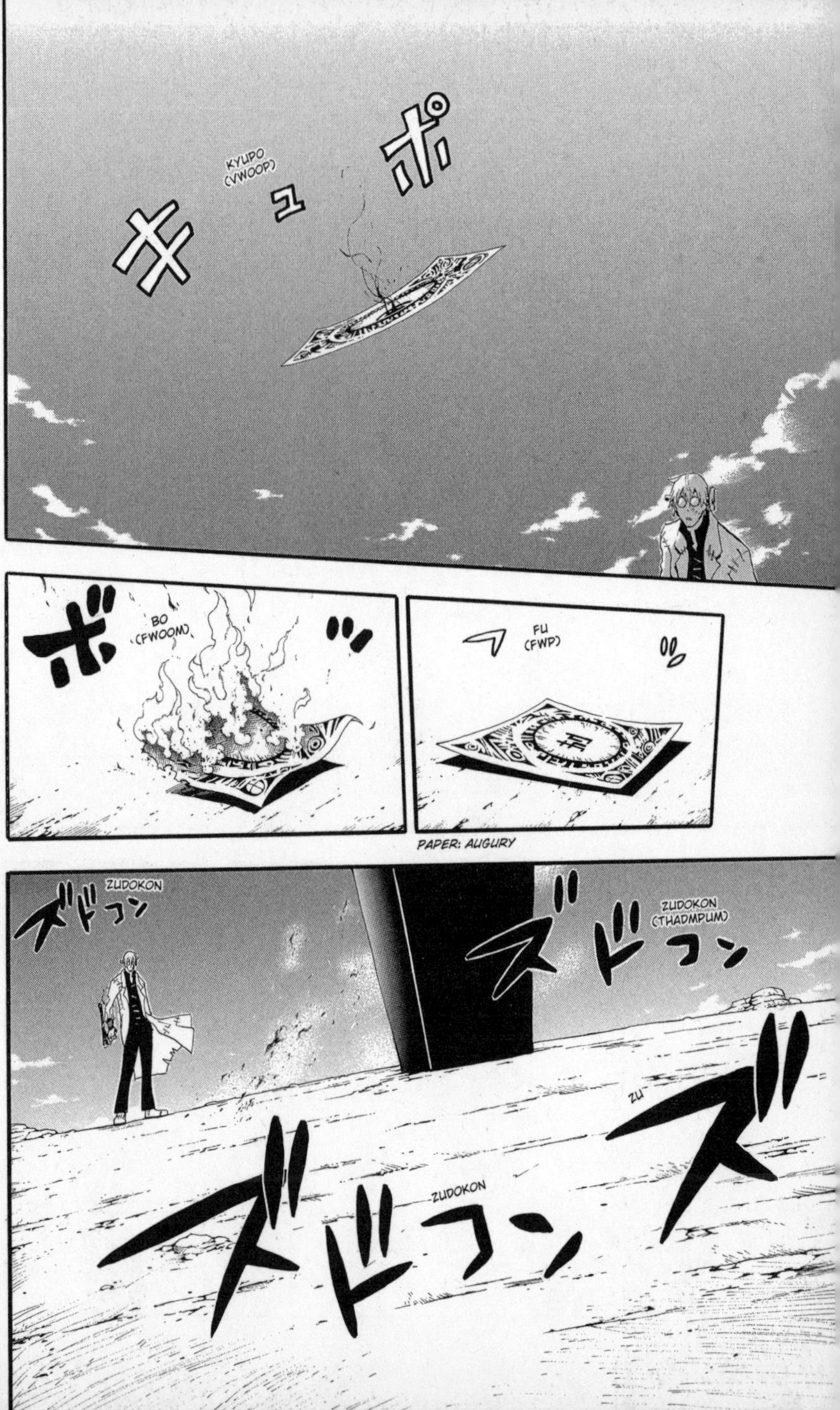
KYUPO
(VWOOP)
FU
(FWP)
BO
(FWOOM)
PAPER: AUGURY
ZUDOKON
(THADMPUM)
ZUDOKON
ZU
ZUDOKON

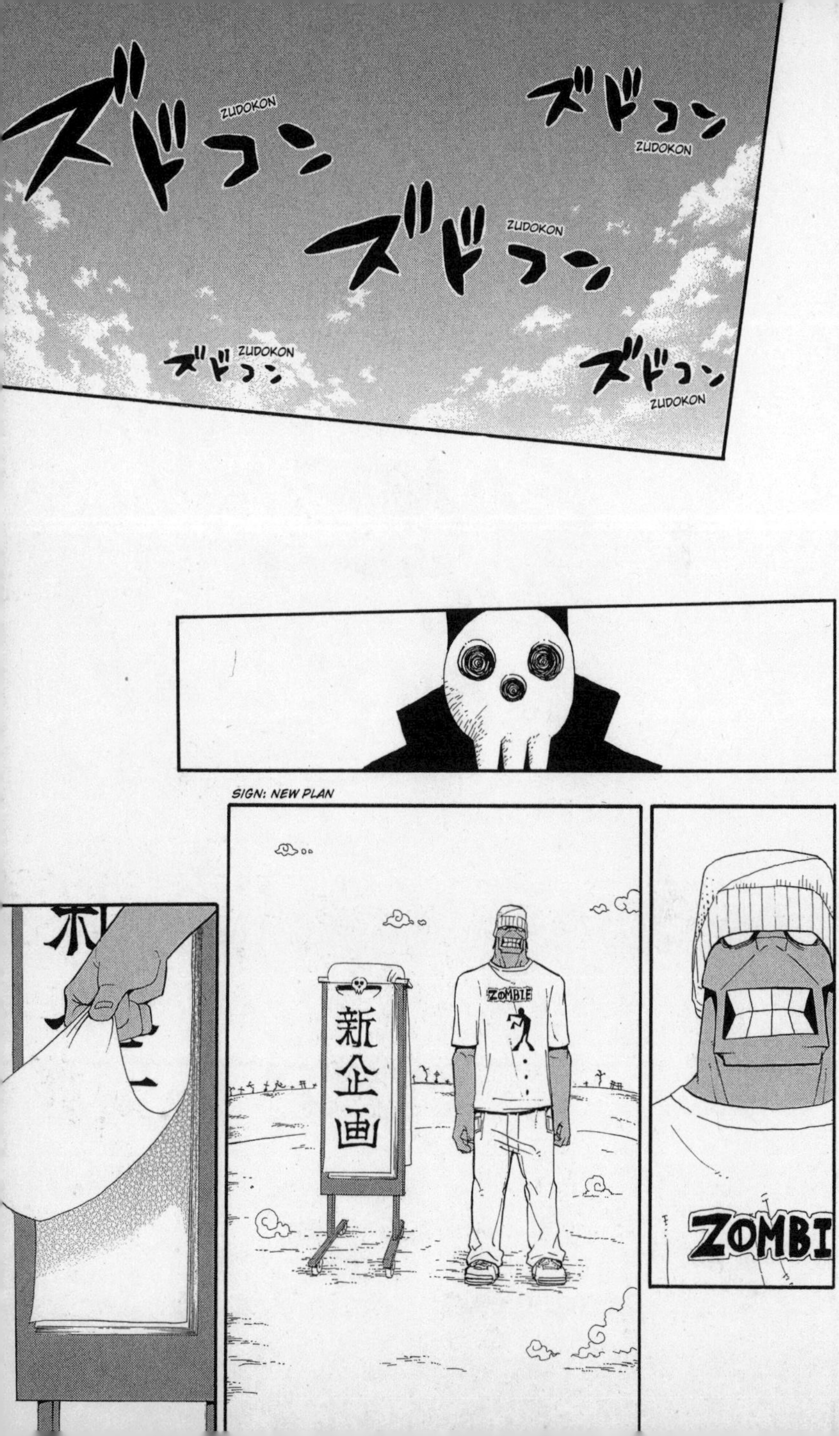
ズドコン
ZUDOKON
ズドコン
ZUDOKON
ズドコン
ZUDOKON
ズドコン
ZUDOKON
ズドコン
ZUDOKON
ZOMBI
SIGN: NEW PLAN
新企画
ZOMBIE

DWMA ELITE YOUTH UNIT

SOOO... LET'S JUST CALL IT THE "DWMA KID SQUAD" FOR SHORT!

SOUL EATER

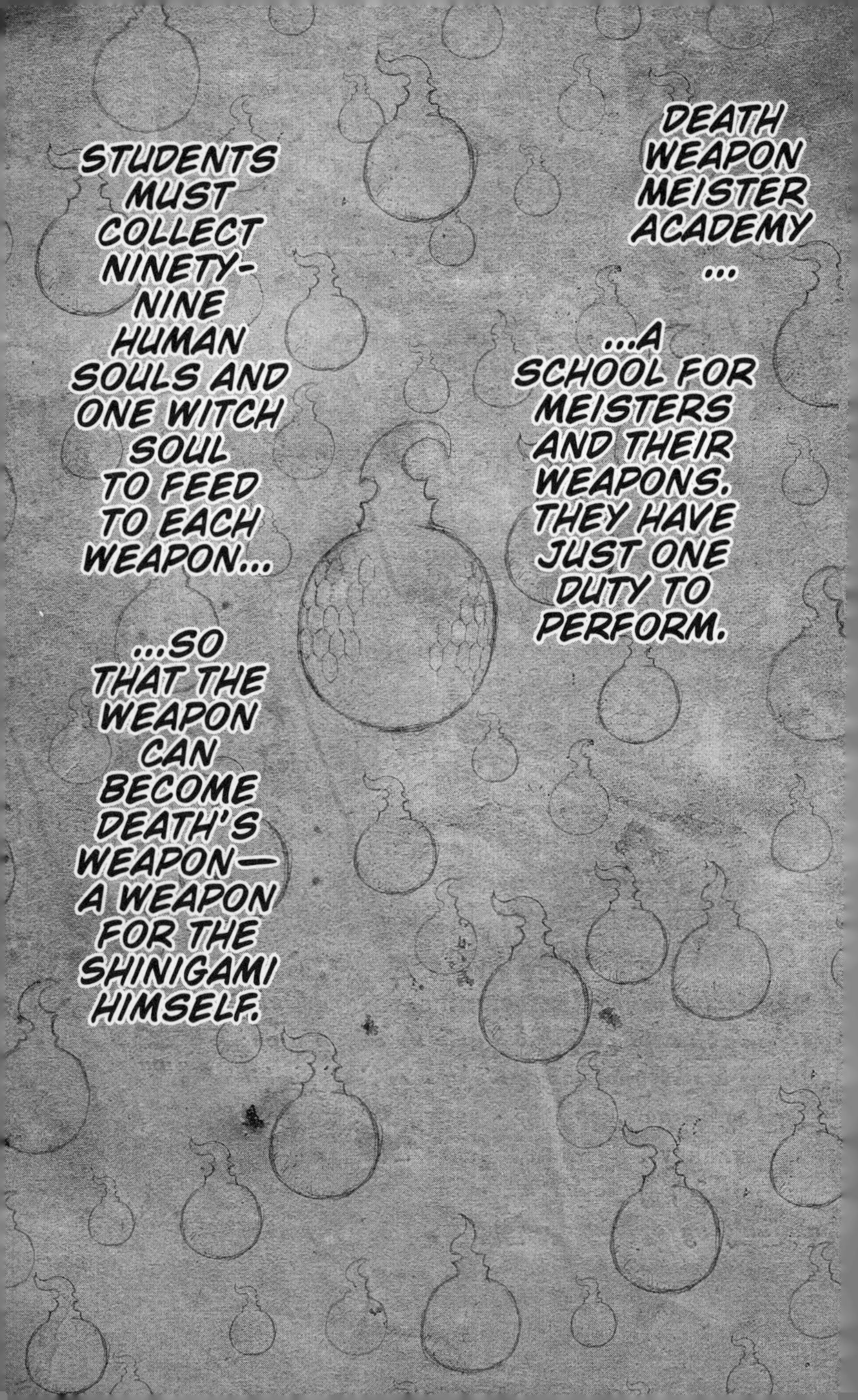
DEATH WEAPON MEISTER ACADEMY...
...A SCHOOL FOR MEISTERS AND THEIR WEAPONS. THEY HAVE JUST ONE DUTY TO PERFORM.
STUDENTS MUST COLLECT NINETY-NINE HUMAN SOULS AND ONE WITCH SOUL TO FEED TO EACH WEAPON...
...SO THAT THE WEAPON CAN BECOME DEATH'S WEAPON—A WEAPON FOR THE SHINIGAMI HIMSELF.

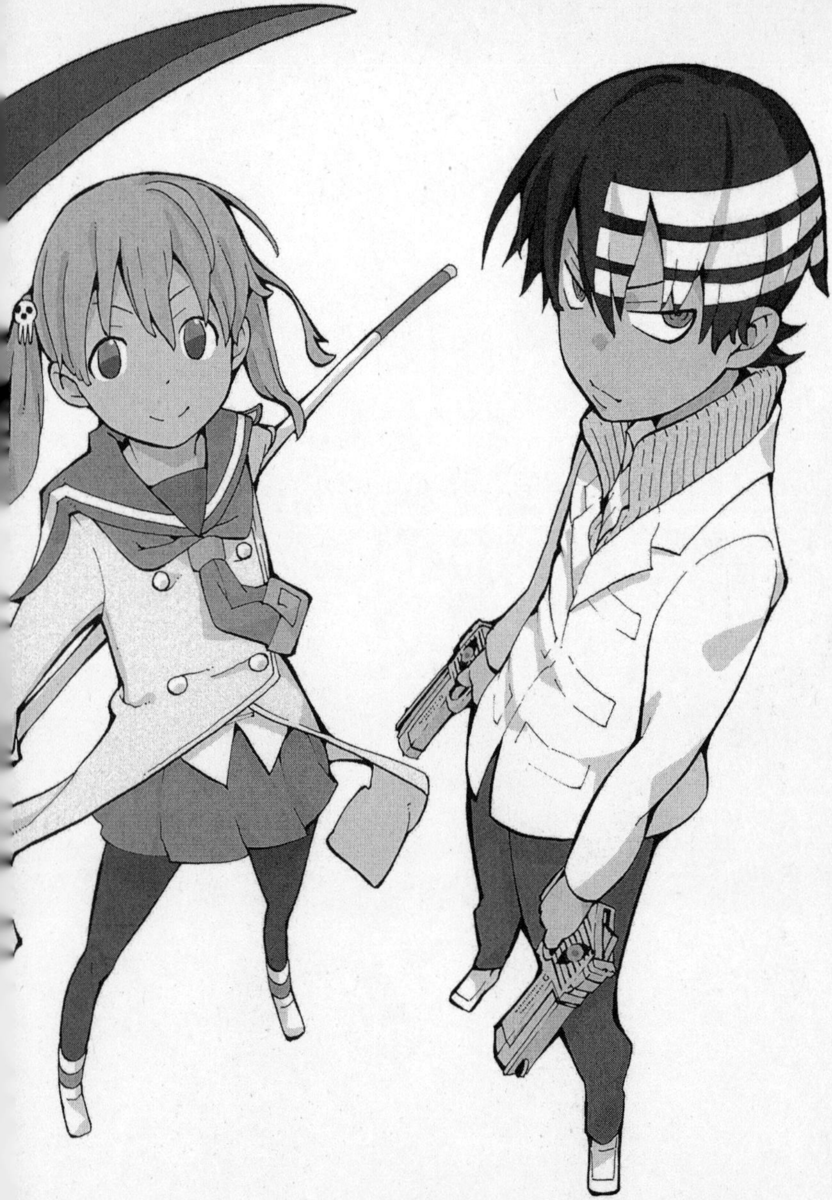

CHAPTER 62: STARTUP

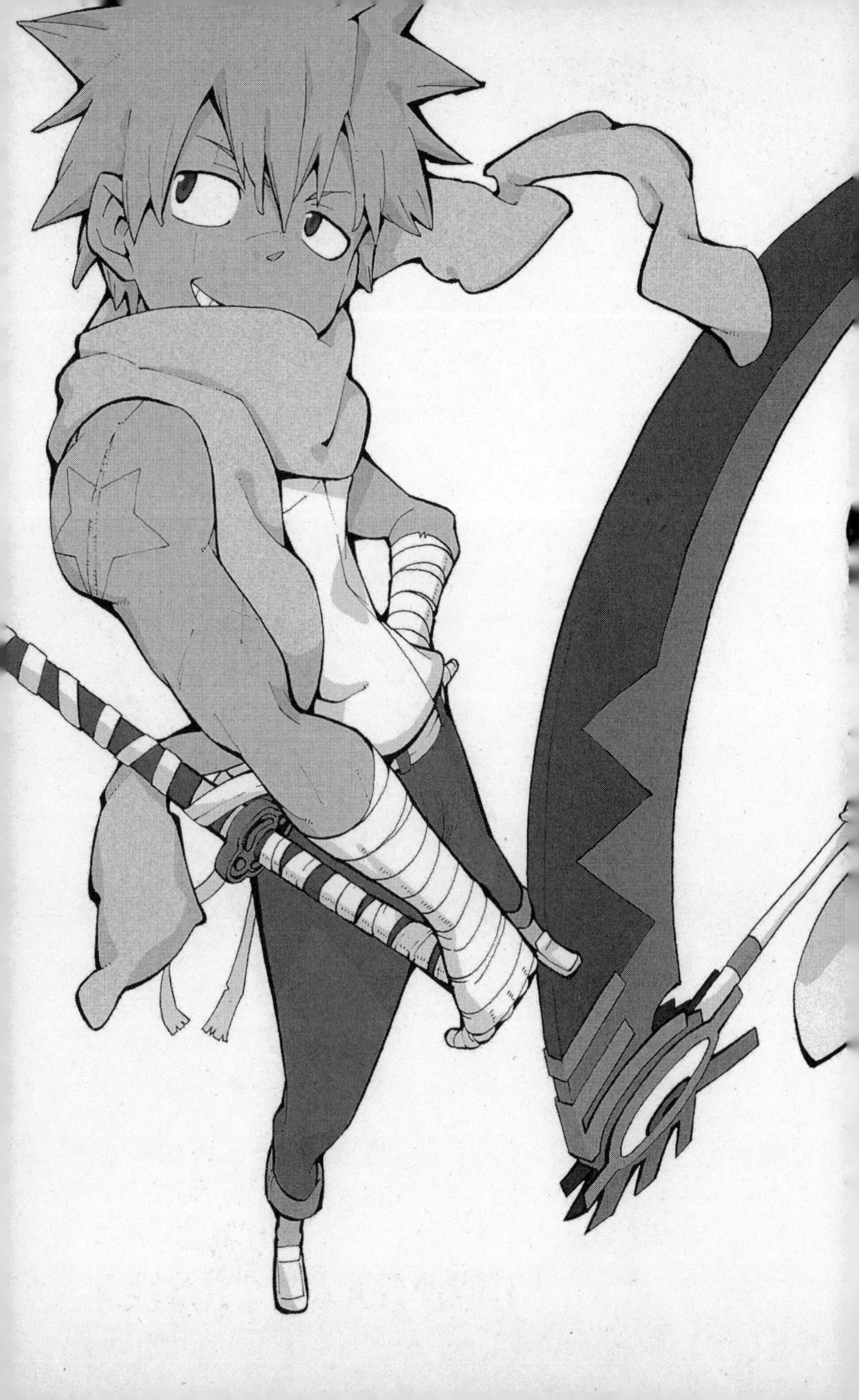

SOUL EATER

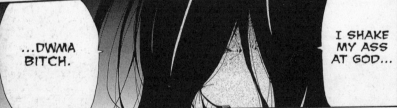

...DWMA BITCH.

I SHAKE MY ASS AT GOD...

SERIAL KILLER FREY D. SADOKO.

YOU FORCE PEOPLE TO LISTEN TO A CURSED RECORDING...

...AND THEN KILL THEM INSIDE THEIR NIGHT-MARES.

BUT NOW... YOUR SOUL IS OURS.

HEY, MAKA...

...YOU KNOW WHAT THIS MEANS FOR US, RIGHT?

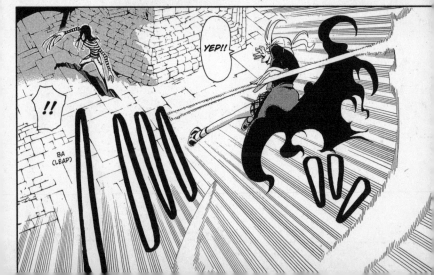

YEP!!

!!

BA
(LEAP)

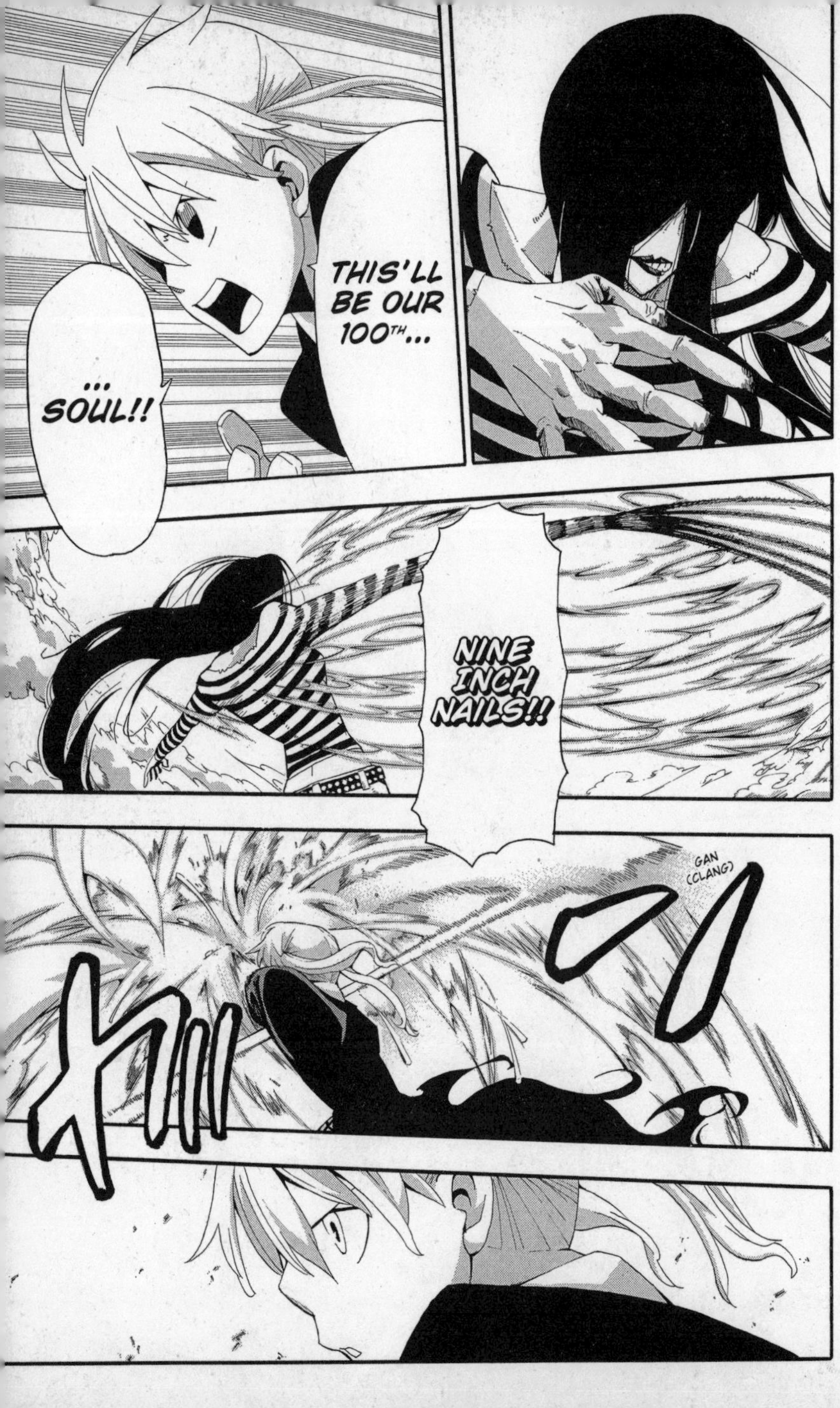
THIS'LL BE OUR 100TH...
... SOÜL!!
NINE INCH NAILS!!
GAN (CLANG)

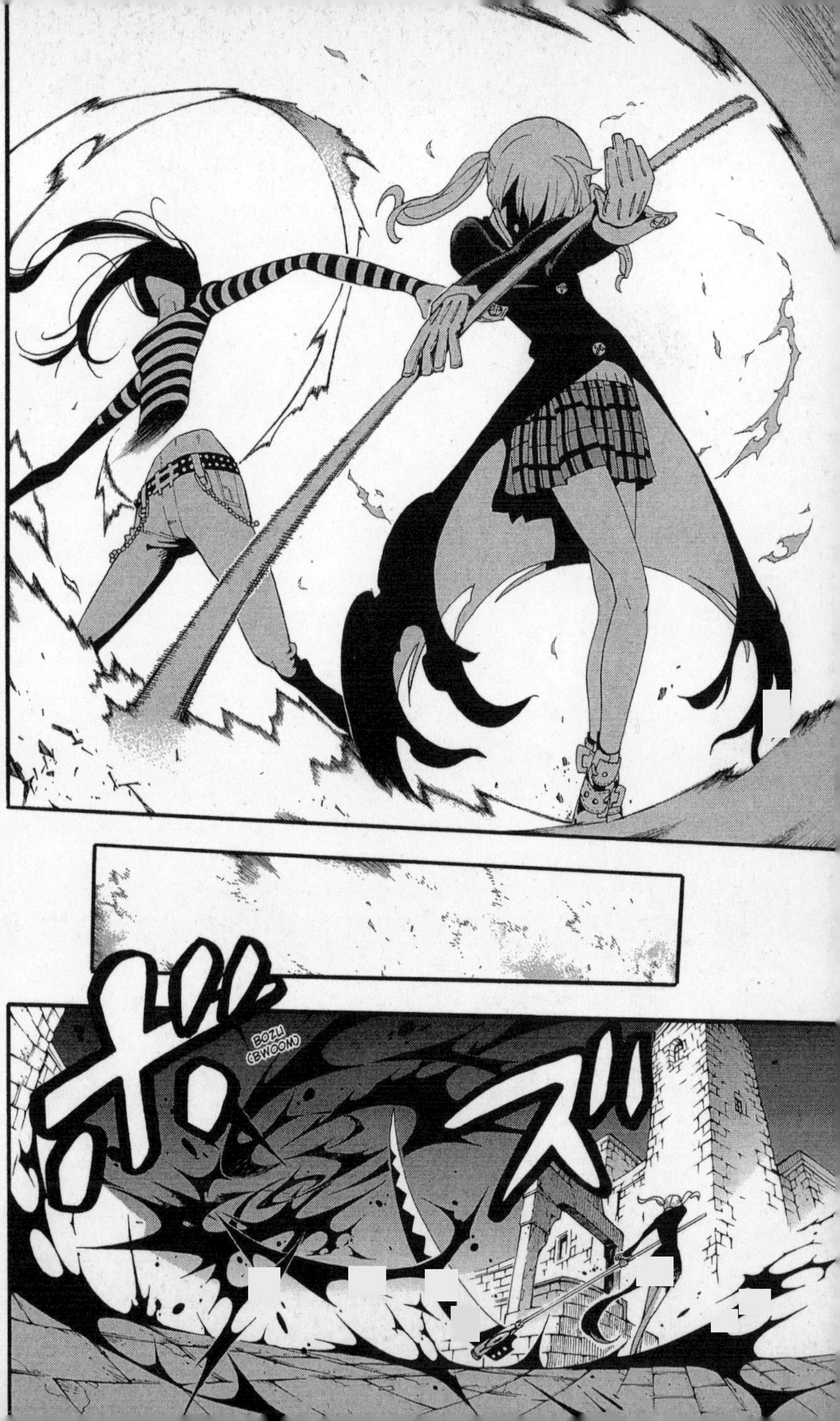
BOZU
(BWOON)

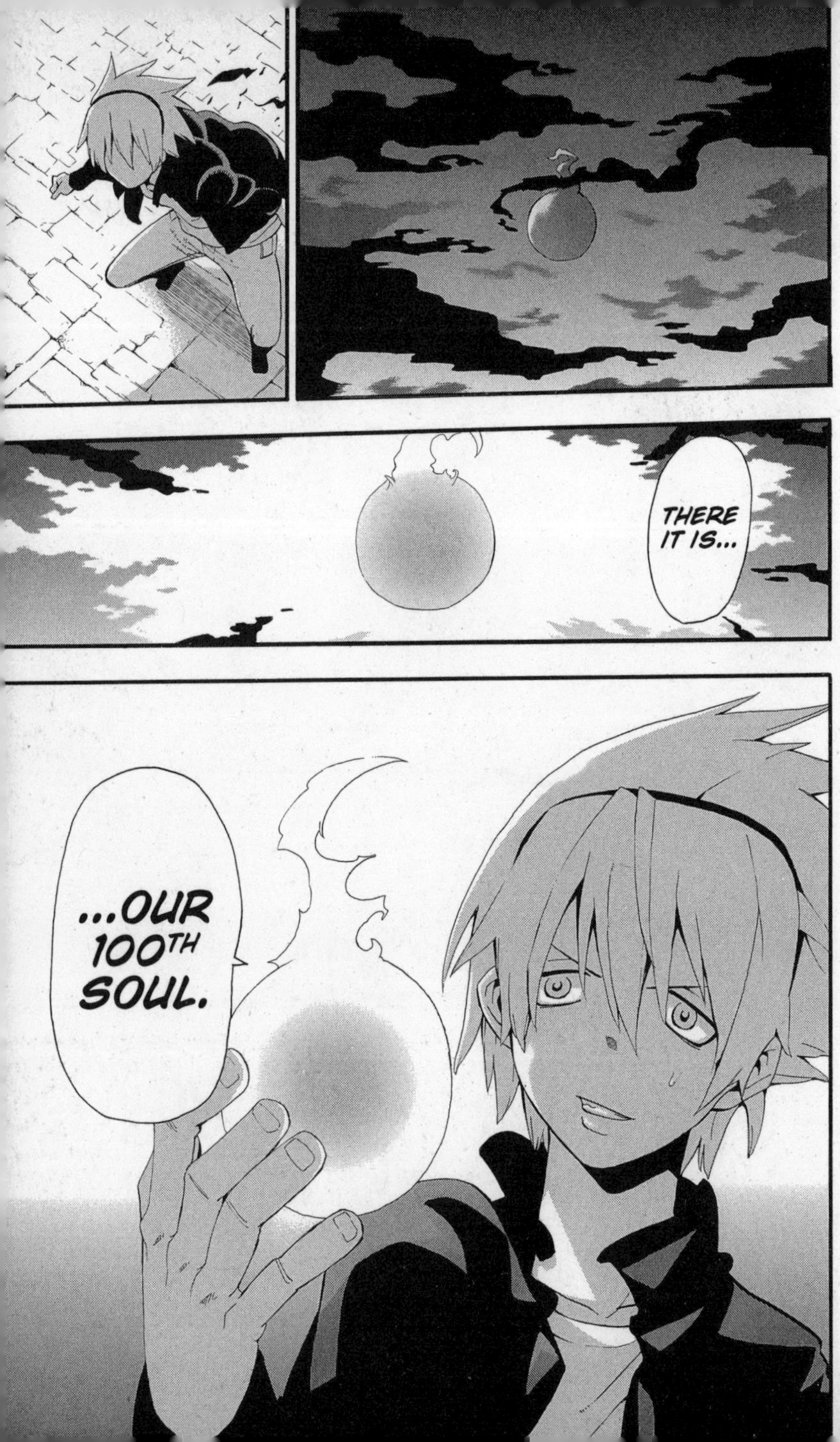
THERE IT IS...
...OUR 100TH SOUL.

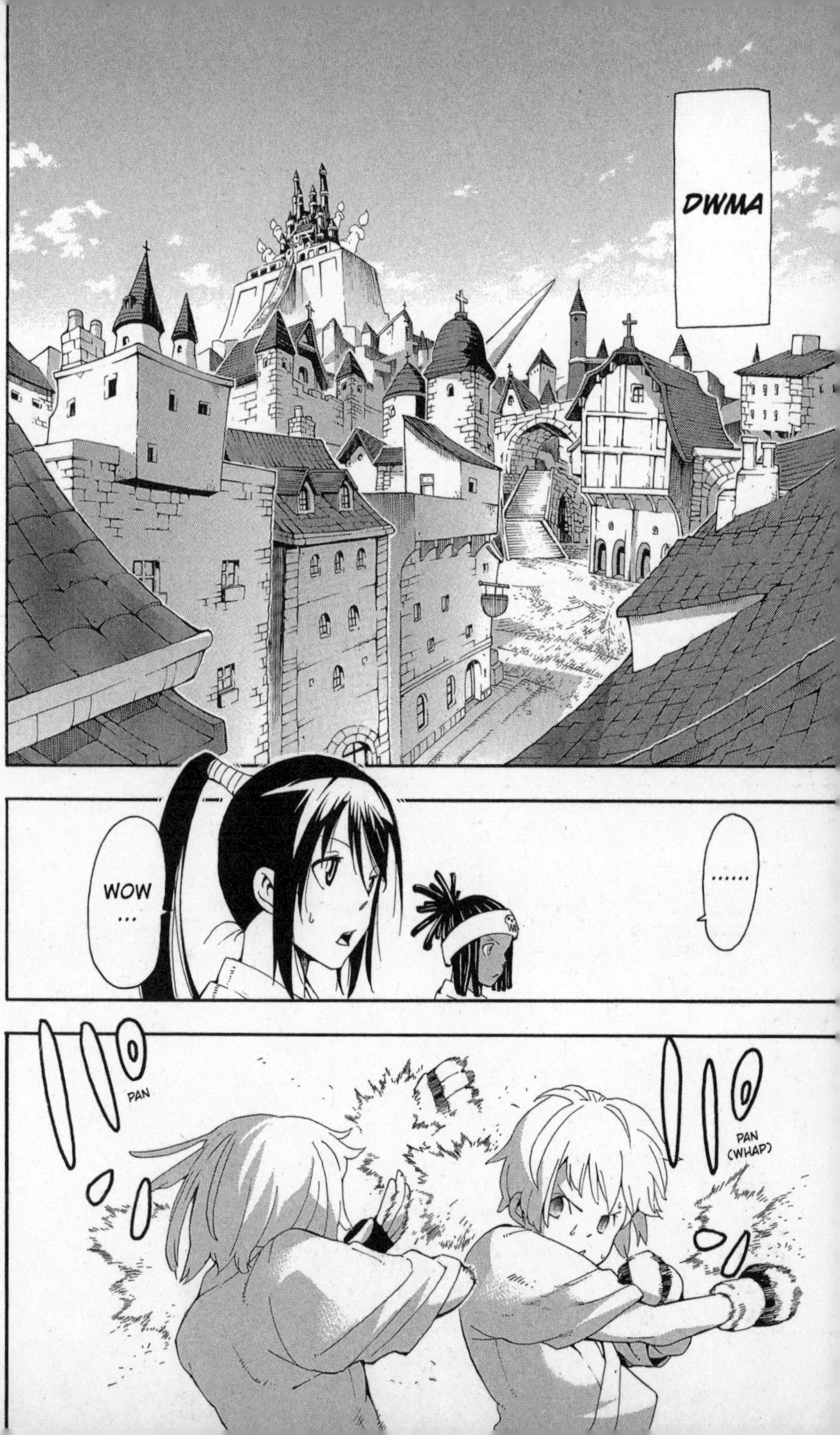
DWMA
......
WOW ...
PAN (WHAP)
PAN

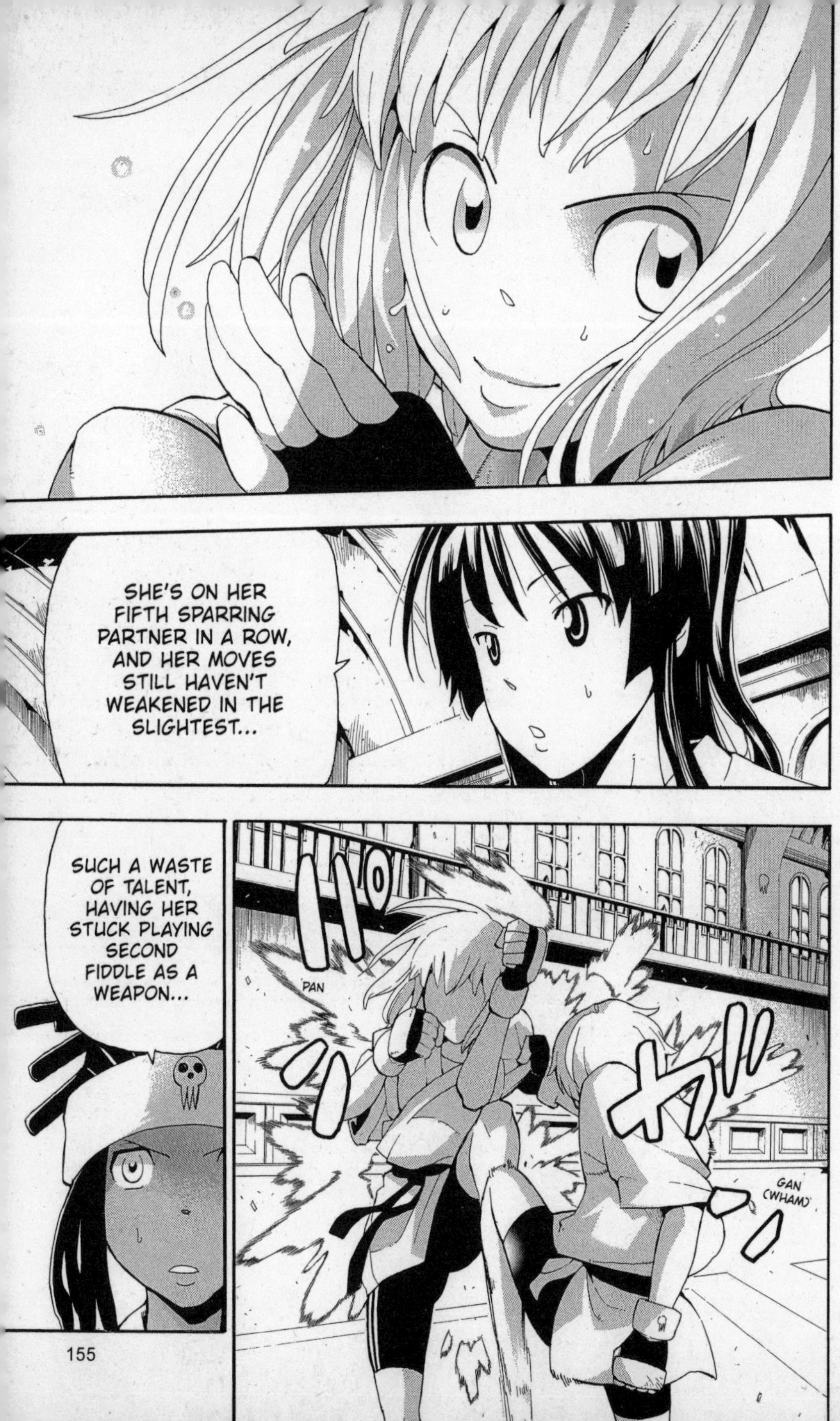
SHE'S ON HER FIFTH SPARRING PARTNER IN A ROW, AND HER MOVES STILL HAVEN'T WEAKENED IN THE SLIGHTEST...
PAN
GAN (WHAM)
SUCH A WASTE OF TALENT, HAVING HER STUCK PLAYING SECOND FIDDLE AS A WEAPON...

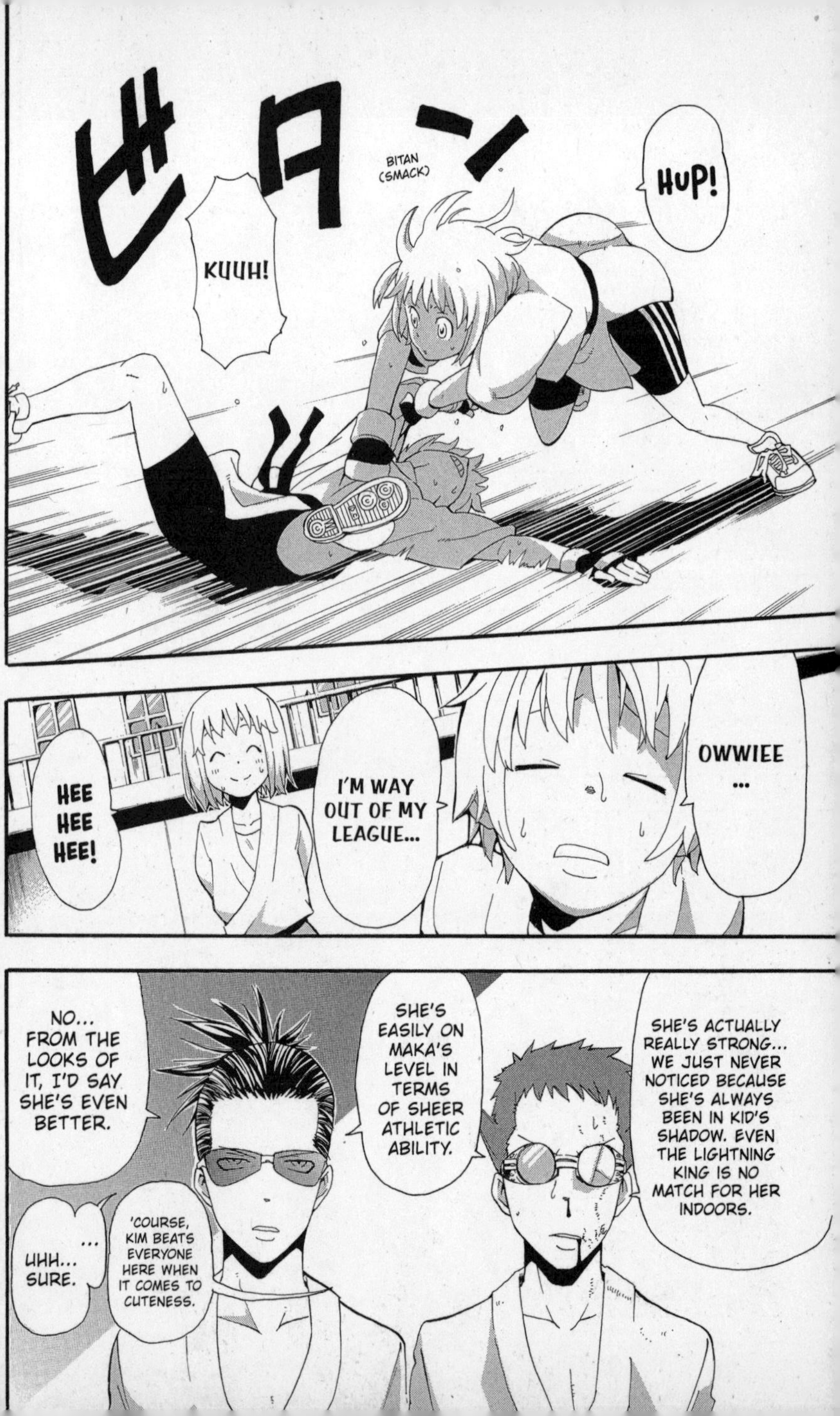
HUP!
ビターン
BITAN (SMACK)
KUUH!
OWWIEE ...
I'M WAY OUT OF MY LEAGUE...
HEE HEE HEE!
SHE'S ACTUALLY REALLY STRONG... WE JUST NEVER NOTICED BECAUSE SHE'S ALWAYS BEEN IN KID'S SHADOW. EVEN THE LIGHTNING KING IS NO MATCH FOR HER INDOORS.
SHE'S EASILY ON MAKA'S LEVEL IN TERMS OF SHEER ATHLETIC ABILITY.
NO... FROM THE LOOKS OF IT, I'D SAY SHE'S EVEN BETTER.
'COURSE, KIM BEATS EVERYONE HERE WHEN IT COMES TO CUTENESS.
... UHH... SURE.

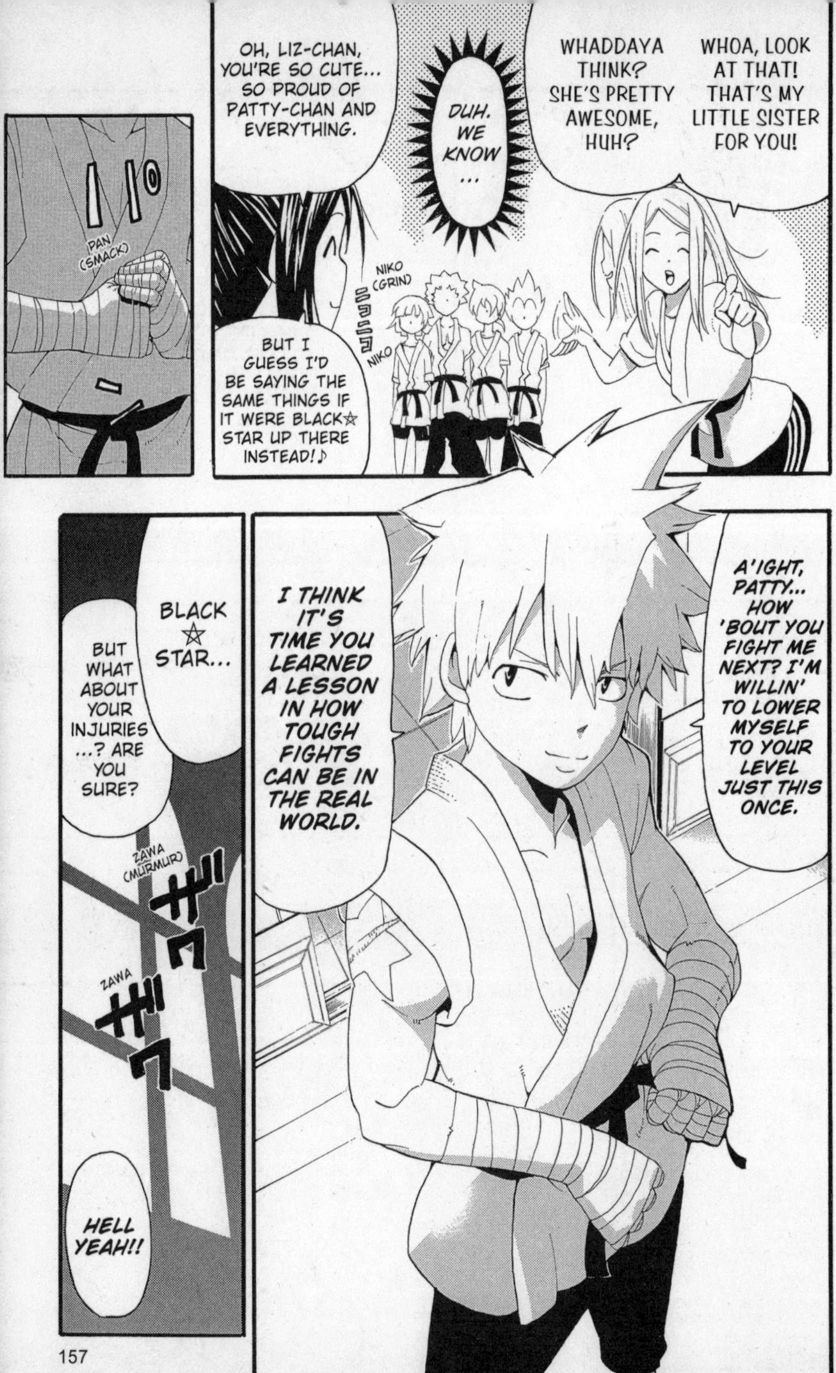
WHOA, LOOK AT THAT! THAT'S MY LITTLE SISTER FOR YOU!
WHADDAYA THINK? SHE'S PRETTY AWESOME, HUH?
DUH. WE KNOW ...
OH, LIZ-CHAN, YOU'RE SO CUTE... SO PROUD OF PATTY-CHAN AND EVERYTHING.
NIKO (GRIN)
NIKO
BUT I GUESS I'D BE SAYING THE SAME THINGS IF IT WERE BLACK☆STAR UP THERE INSTEAD!♪
PAN (SMACK)
A'IGHT, PATTY... HOW 'BOUT YOU FIGHT ME NEXT? I'M WILLIN' TO LOWER MYSELF TO YOUR LEVEL JUST THIS ONCE.
I THINK IT'S TIME YOU LEARNED A LESSON IN HOW TOUGH FIGHTS CAN BE IN THE REAL WORLD.
BLACK☆STAR...
BUT WHAT ABOUT YOUR INJURIES ...? ARE YOU SURE?
ZAWA (MURMUR)
ZAWA
HELL YEAH!!

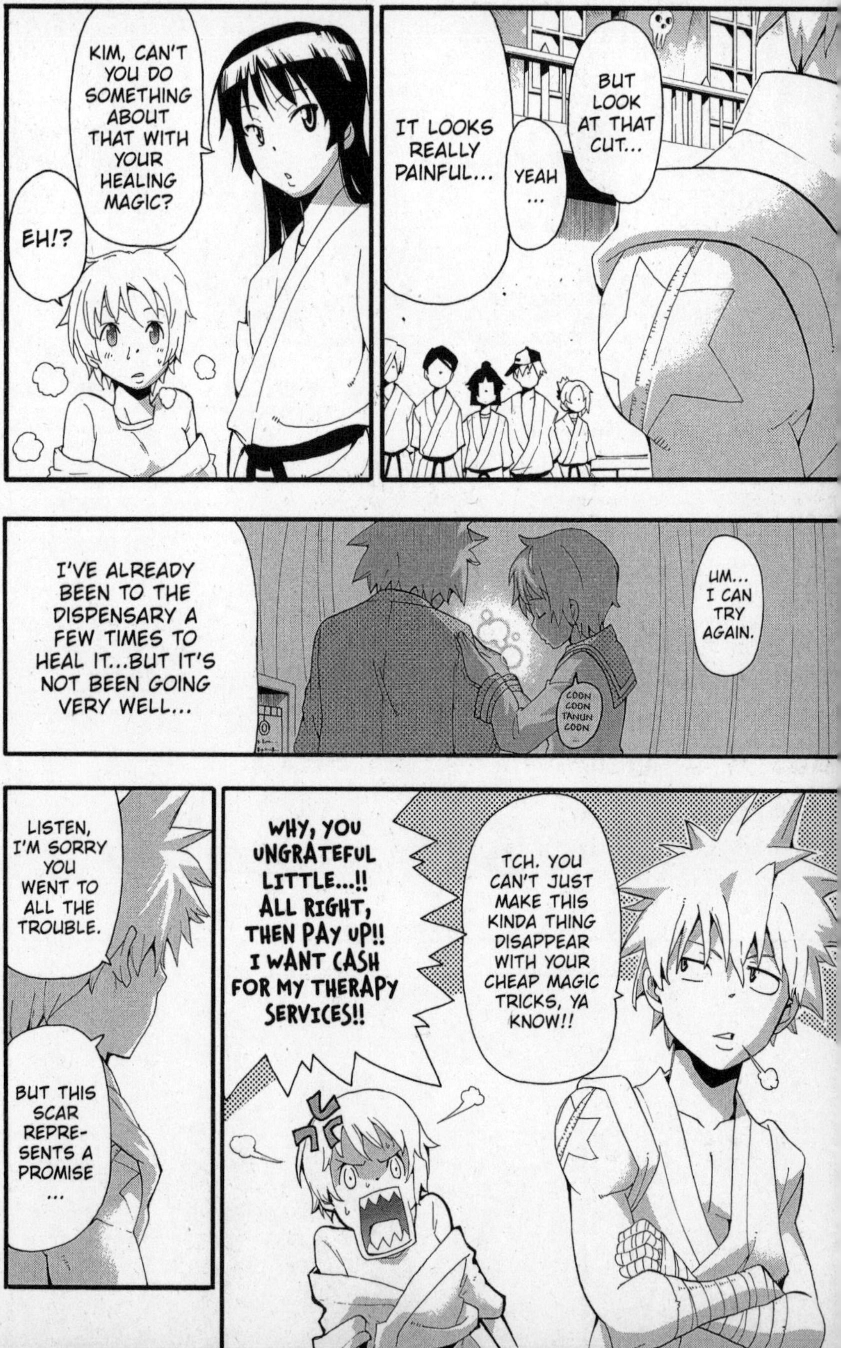
BUT LOOK AT THAT CUT...
YEAH...
IT LOOKS REALLY PAINFUL...
KIM, CAN'T YOU DO SOMETHING ABOUT THAT WITH YOUR HEALING MAGIC?
EH!?
UM... I CAN TRY AGAIN.
COON COON TANUN COON ...
I'VE ALREADY BEEN TO THE DISPENSARY A FEW TIMES TO HEAL IT...BUT IT'S NOT BEEN GOING VERY WELL...
TCH. YOU CAN'T JUST MAKE THIS KINDA THING DISAPPEAR WITH YOUR CHEAP MAGIC TRICKS, YA KNOW!!
WHY, YOU UNGRATEFUL LITTLE...!! ALL RIGHT, THEN PAY UP!! I WANT CASH FOR MY THERAPY SERVICES!!
LISTEN, I'M SORRY YOU WENT TO ALL THE TROUBLE.
BUT THIS SCAR REPRESENTS A PROMISE...

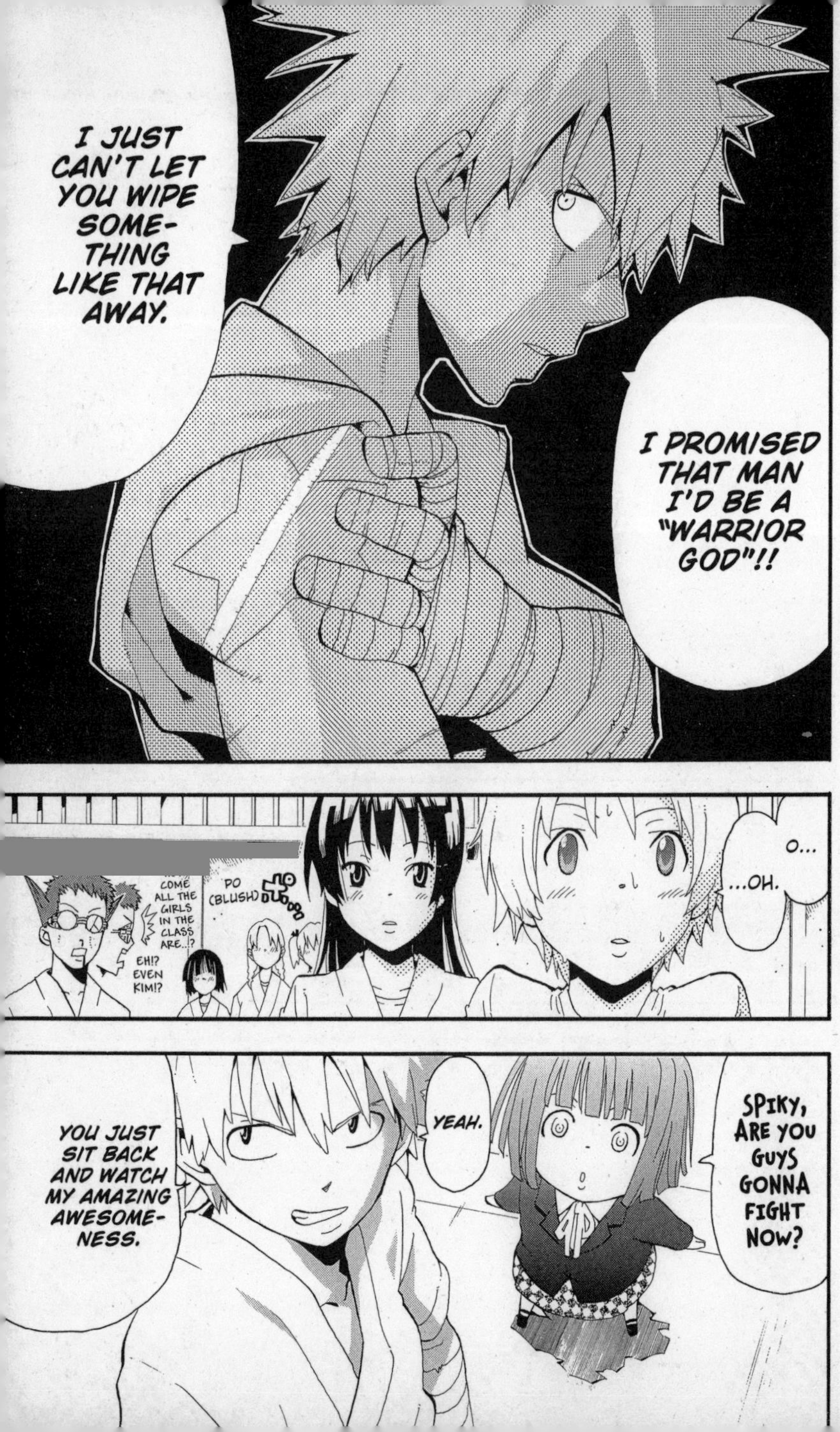

I JUST CAN'T LET YOU WIPE SOME-THING LIKE THAT AWAY.
I PROMISED THAT MAN I'D BE A "WARRIOR GOD"!!
O...
...OH.
PO (BLUSH)
COME ALL THE GIRLS IN THE CLASS ARE...?
EH!? EVEN KIMI!?
SPIKY, ARE YOU GUYS GONNA FIGHT NOW?
YEAH.
YOU JUST SIT BACK AND WATCH MY AMAZING AWESOME-NESS.

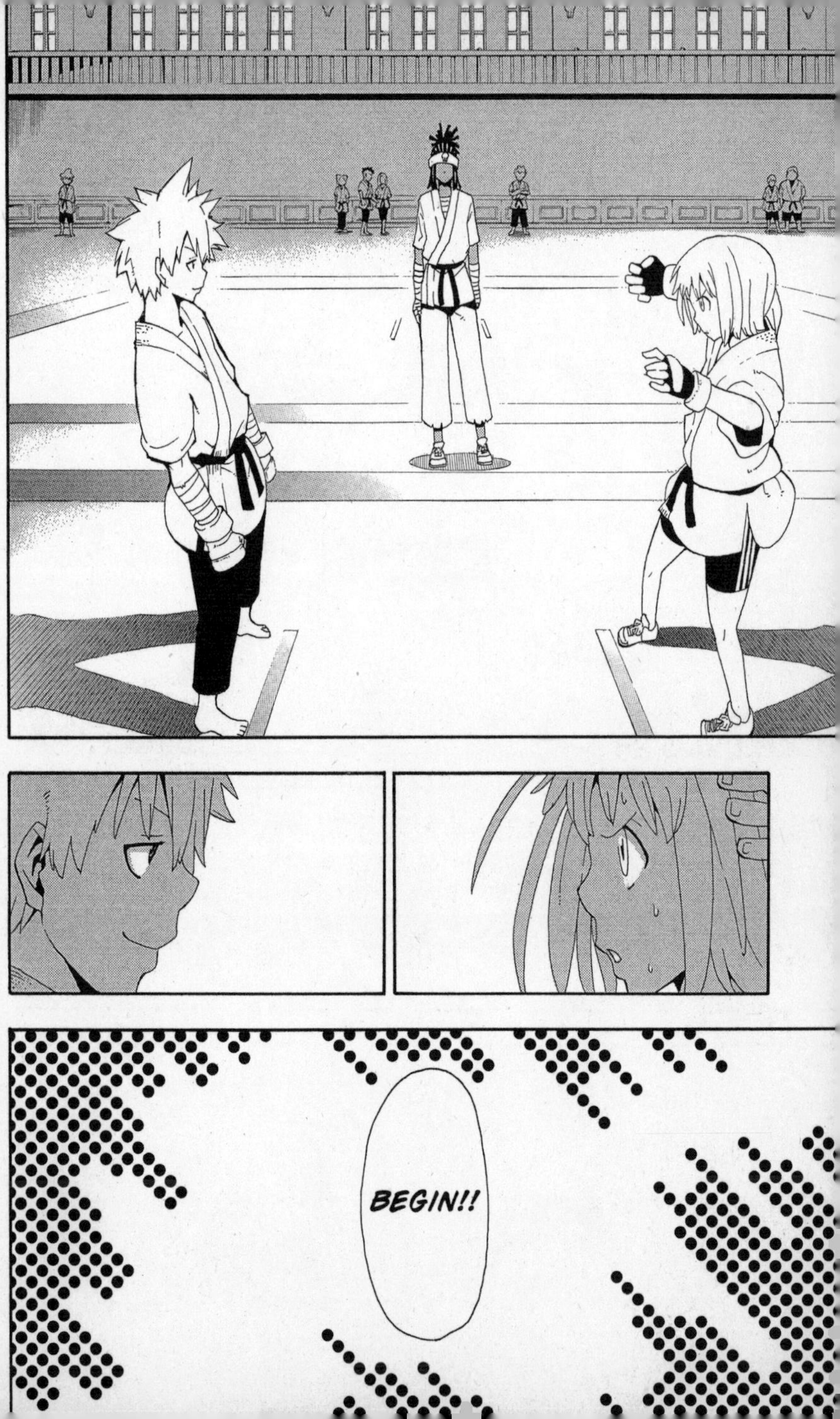
BEGIN!!

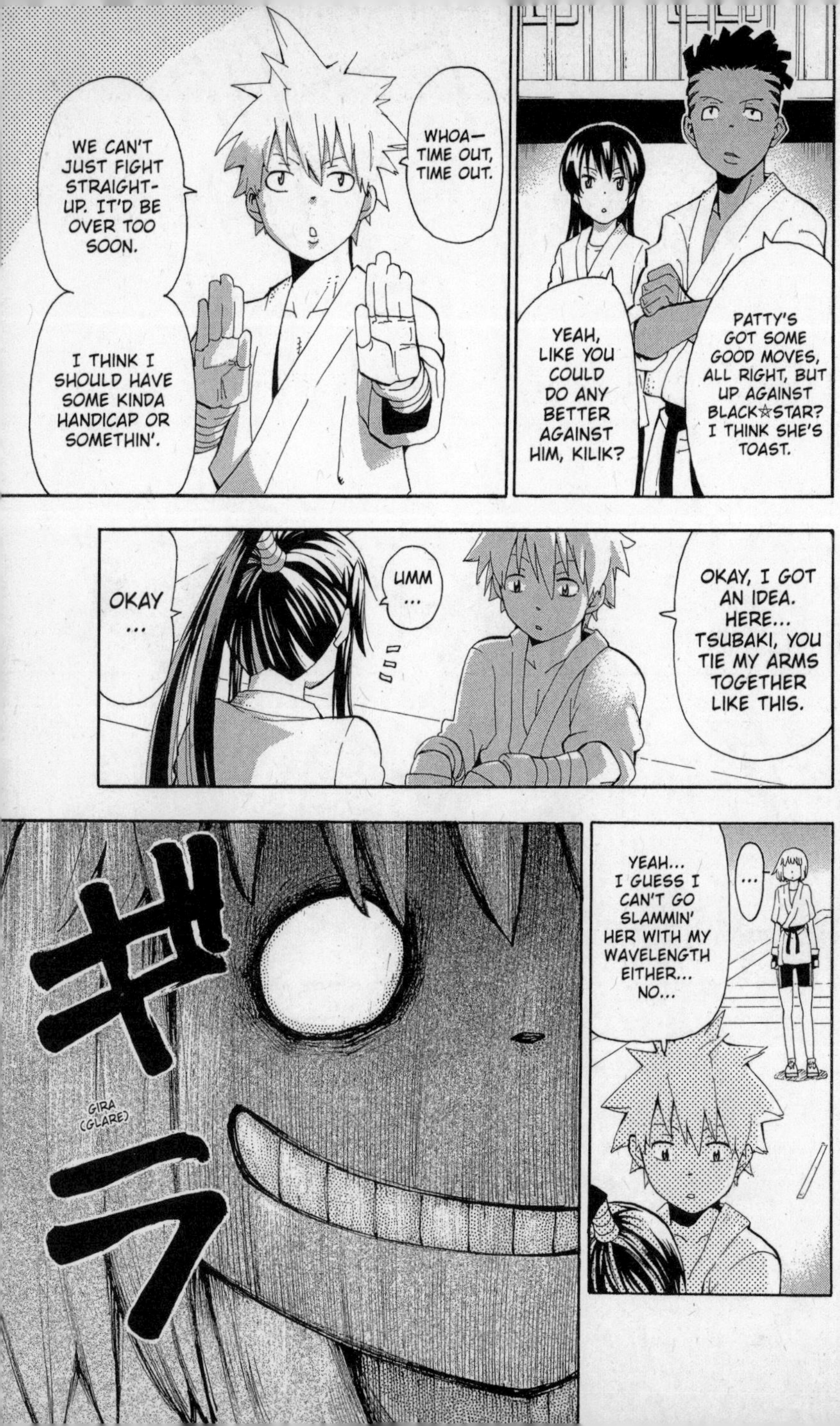

PATTY'S GOT SOME GOOD MOVES, ALL RIGHT, BUT UP AGAINST BLACK☆STAR? I THINK SHE'S TOAST.
YEAH, LIKE YOU COULD DO ANY BETTER AGAINST HIM, KILIK?
WHOA— TIME OUT, TIME OUT.
WE CAN'T JUST FIGHT STRAIGHT-UP. IT'D BE OVER TOO SOON.
I THINK I SHOULD HAVE SOME KINDA HANDICAP OR SOMETHIN'.
OKAY, I GOT AN IDEA. HERE... TSUBAKI, YOU TIE MY ARMS TOGETHER LIKE THIS.
UMM ...
OKAY ...
...
YEAH... I GUESS I CAN'T GO SLAMMIN' HER WITH MY WAVELENGTH EITHER... NO...
ギラ
GIRA (GLARE)

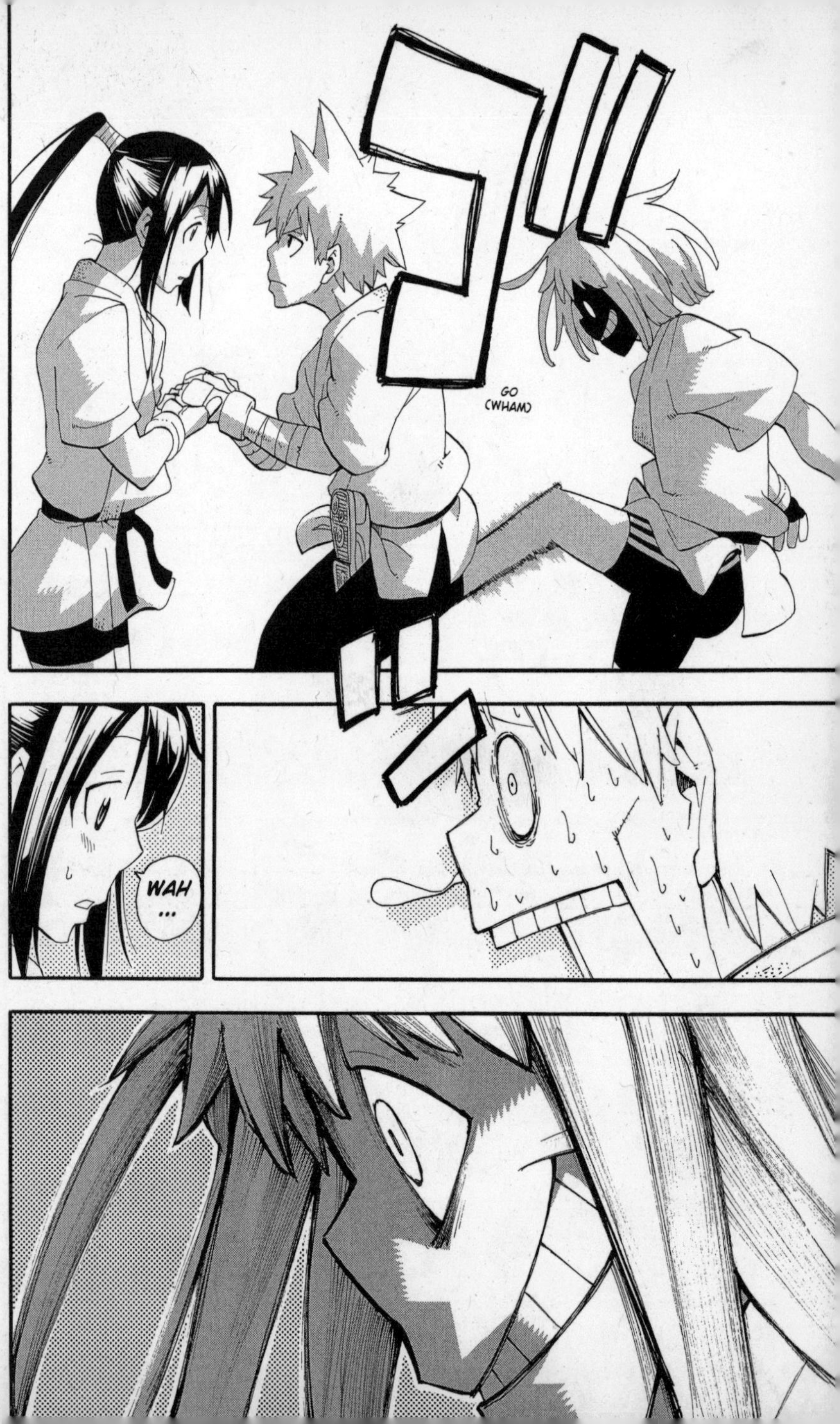
GO
(WHAM)
WAH
...

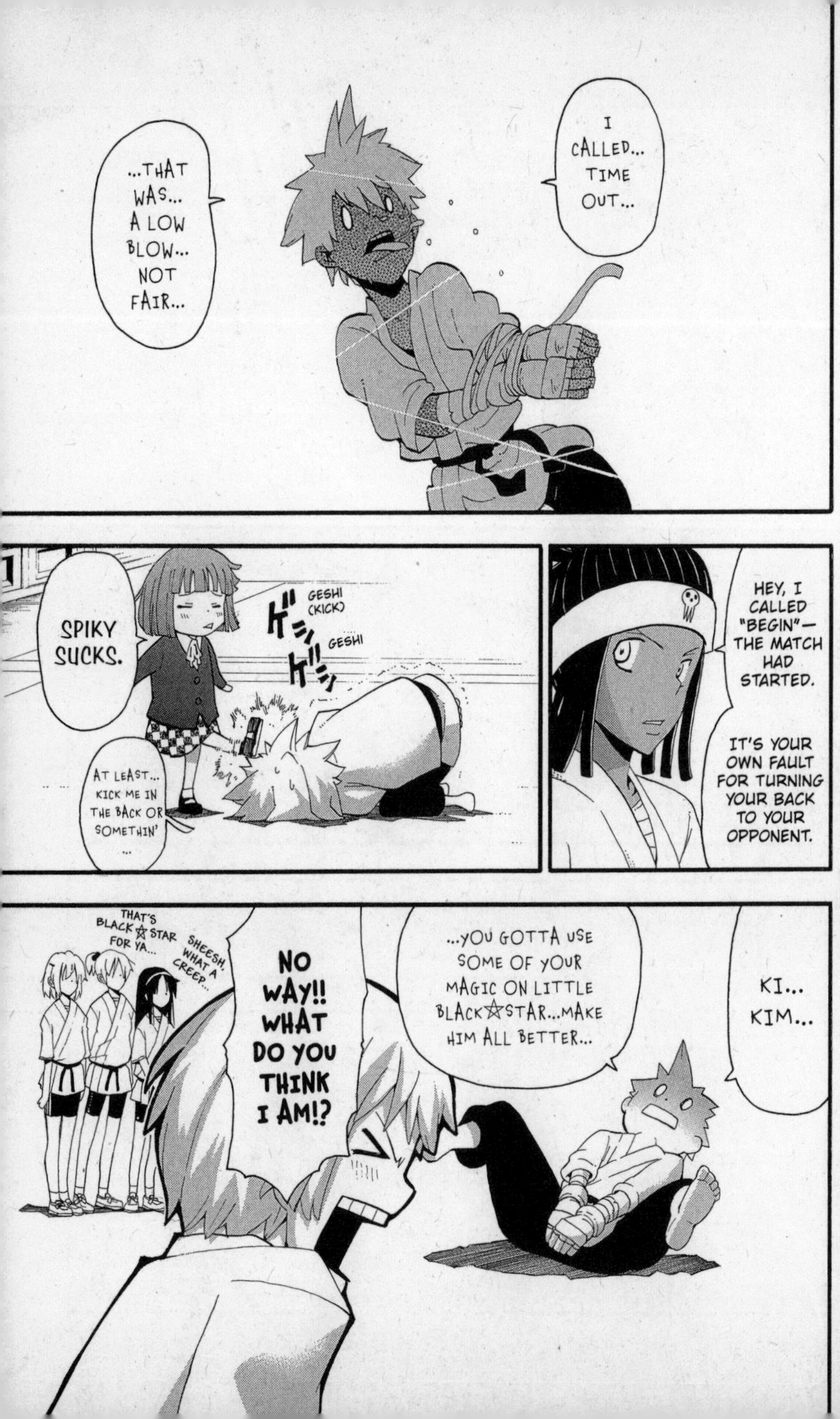
I CALLED... TIME OUT...
...THAT WAS... A LOW BLOW... NOT FAIR...
HEY, I CALLED "BEGIN"—THE MATCH HAD STARTED.
IT'S YOUR OWN FAULT FOR TURNING YOUR BACK TO YOUR OPPONENT.
GESHI (KICK)
... GESHI
SPIKY SUCKS.
AT LEAST... KICK ME IN THE BACK OR SOMETHIN' ...
KI... KIM...
...YOU GOTTA USE SOME OF YOUR MAGIC ON LITTLE BLACK☆STAR...MAKE HIM ALL BETTER...
NO WAY!! WHAT DO YOU THINK I AM!?
SHEESH. WHAT A CREEP...
THAT'S BLACK☆STAR FOR YA...

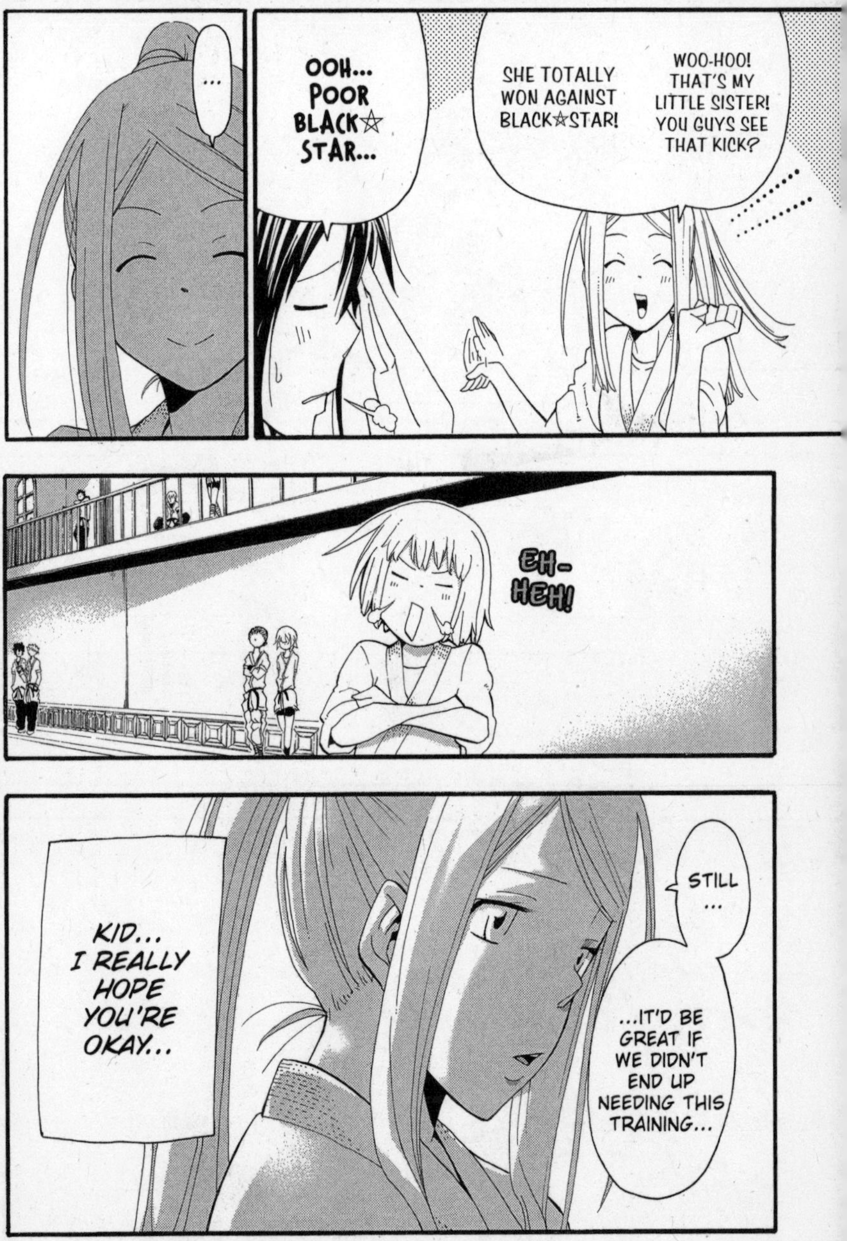
WOO-HOO! THAT'S MY LITTLE SISTER! YOU GUYS SEE THAT KICK?
SHE TOTALLY WON AGAINST BLACK☆STAR!
OOH... POOR BLACK☆STAR...
...
EH-HEH!
STILL...
...IT'D BE GREAT IF WE DIDN'T END UP NEEDING THIS TRAINING...
KID... I REALLY HOPE YOU'RE OKAY...

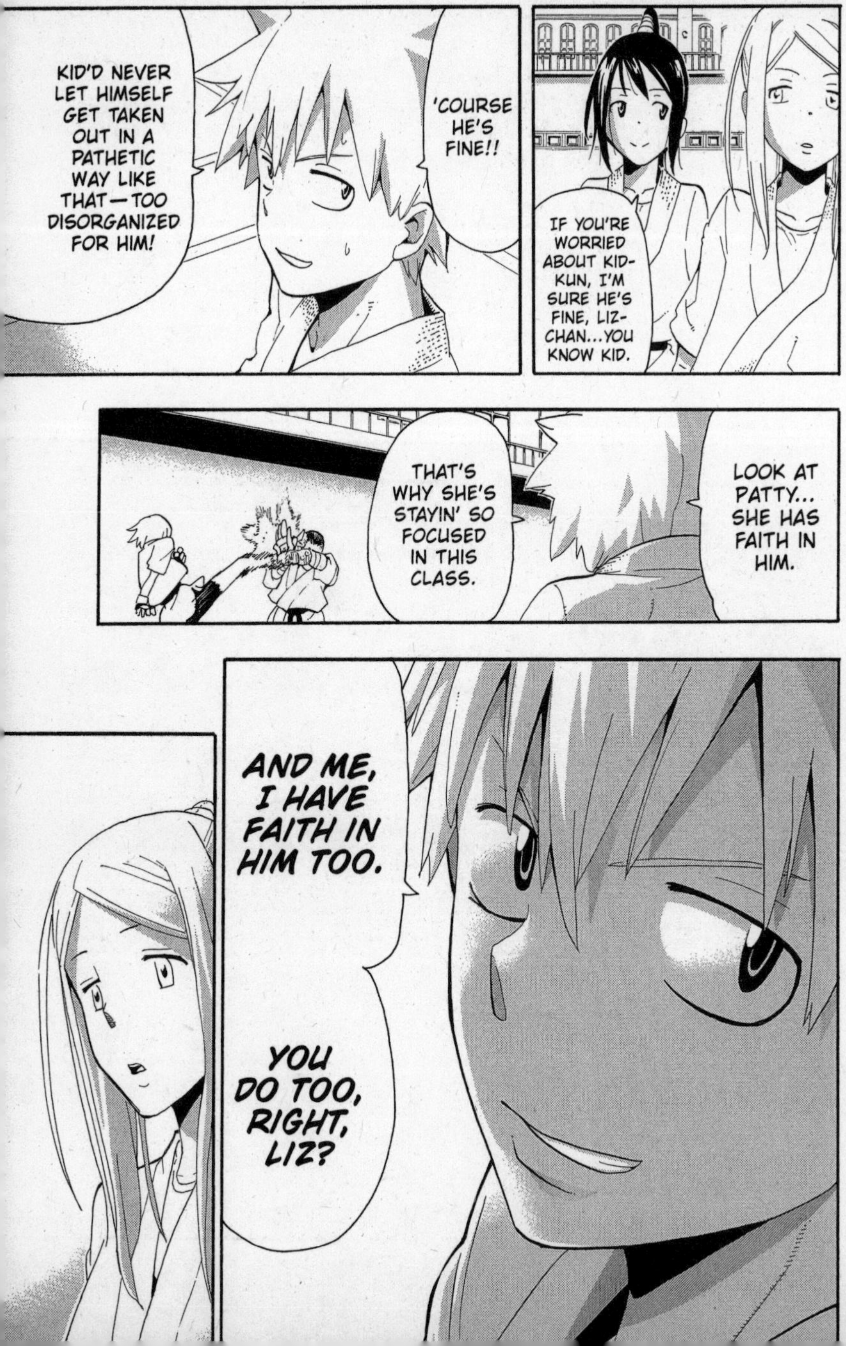
IF YOU'RE WORRIED ABOUT KID-KUN, I'M SURE HE'S FINE, LIZ-CHAN...YOU KNOW KID.
'COURSE HE'S FINE!!
KID'D NEVER LET HIMSELF GET TAKEN OUT IN A PATHETIC WAY LIKE THAT—TOO DISORGANIZED FOR HIM!
LOOK AT PATTY... SHE HAS FAITH IN HIM.
THAT'S WHY SHE'S STAYIN' SO FOCUSED IN THIS CLASS.
AND ME, I HAVE FAITH IN HIM TOO.
YOU DO TOO, RIGHT, LIZ?

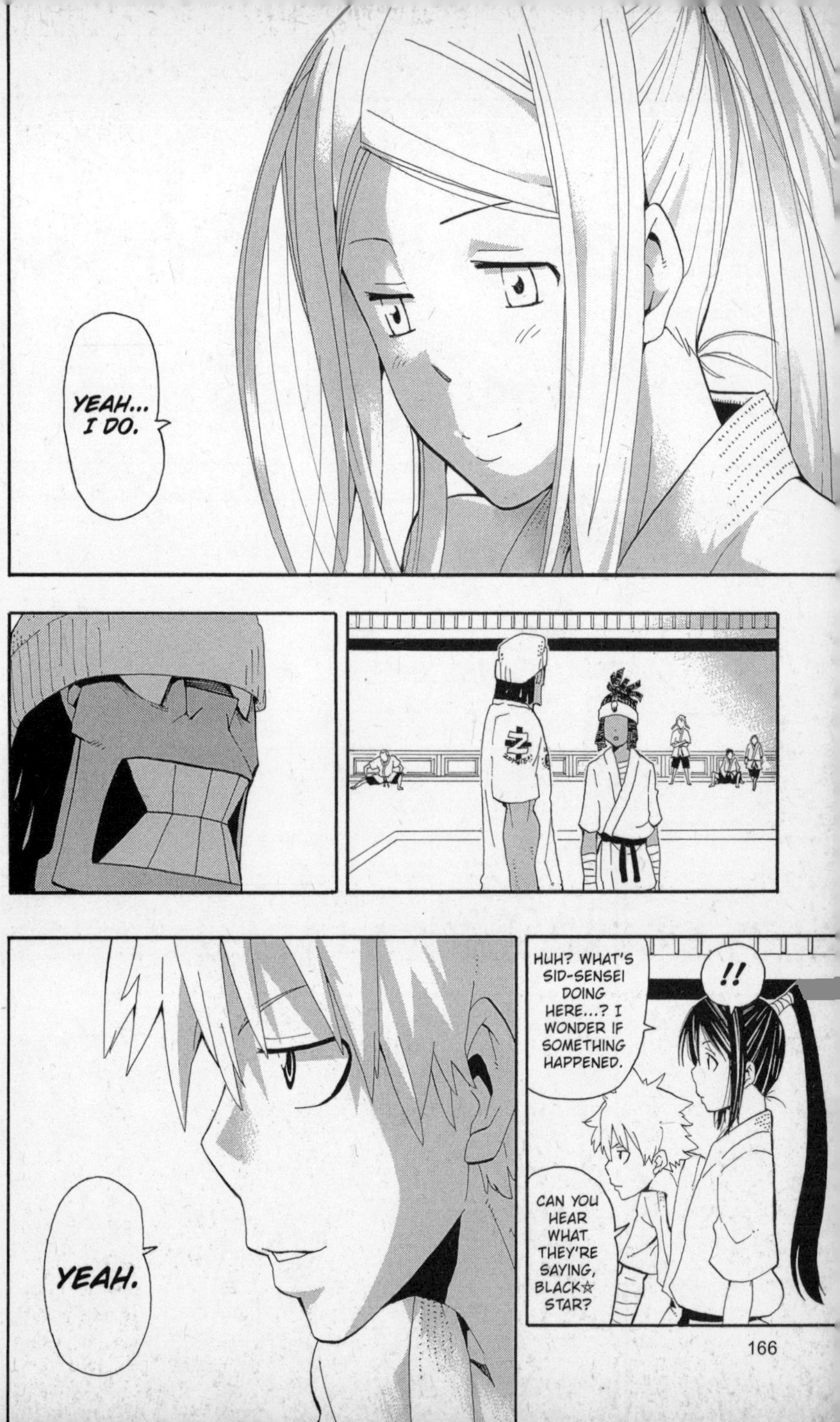
YEAH... I DO.
!!
HUH? WHAT'S SID-SENSEI DOING HERE...? I WONDER IF SOMETHING HAPPENED.
CAN YOU HEAR WHAT THEY'RE SAYING, BLACK☆STAR?
YEAH.

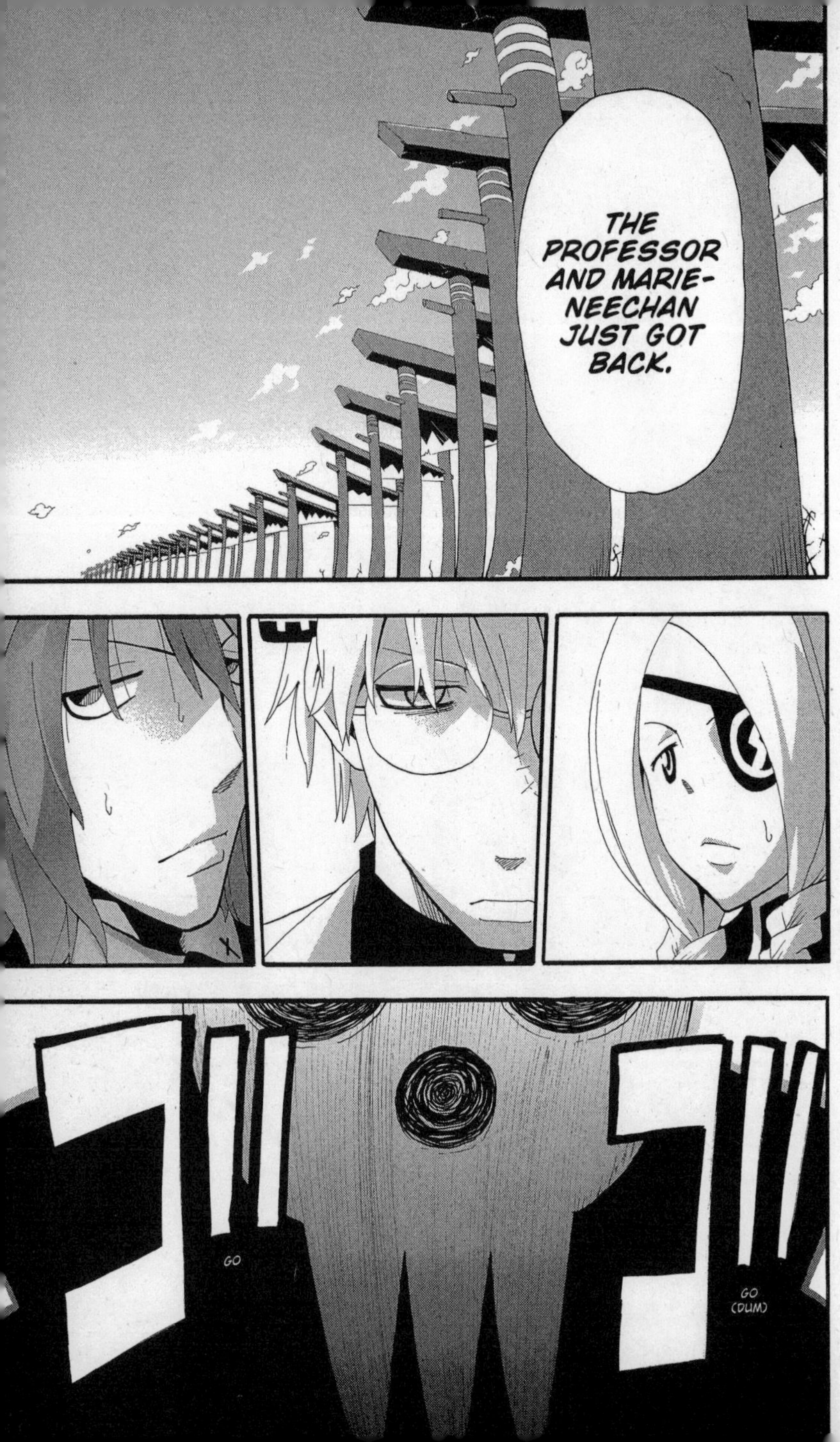
THE PROFESSOR AND MARIE-NEECHAN JUST GOT BACK.
GO
GO (DUM)

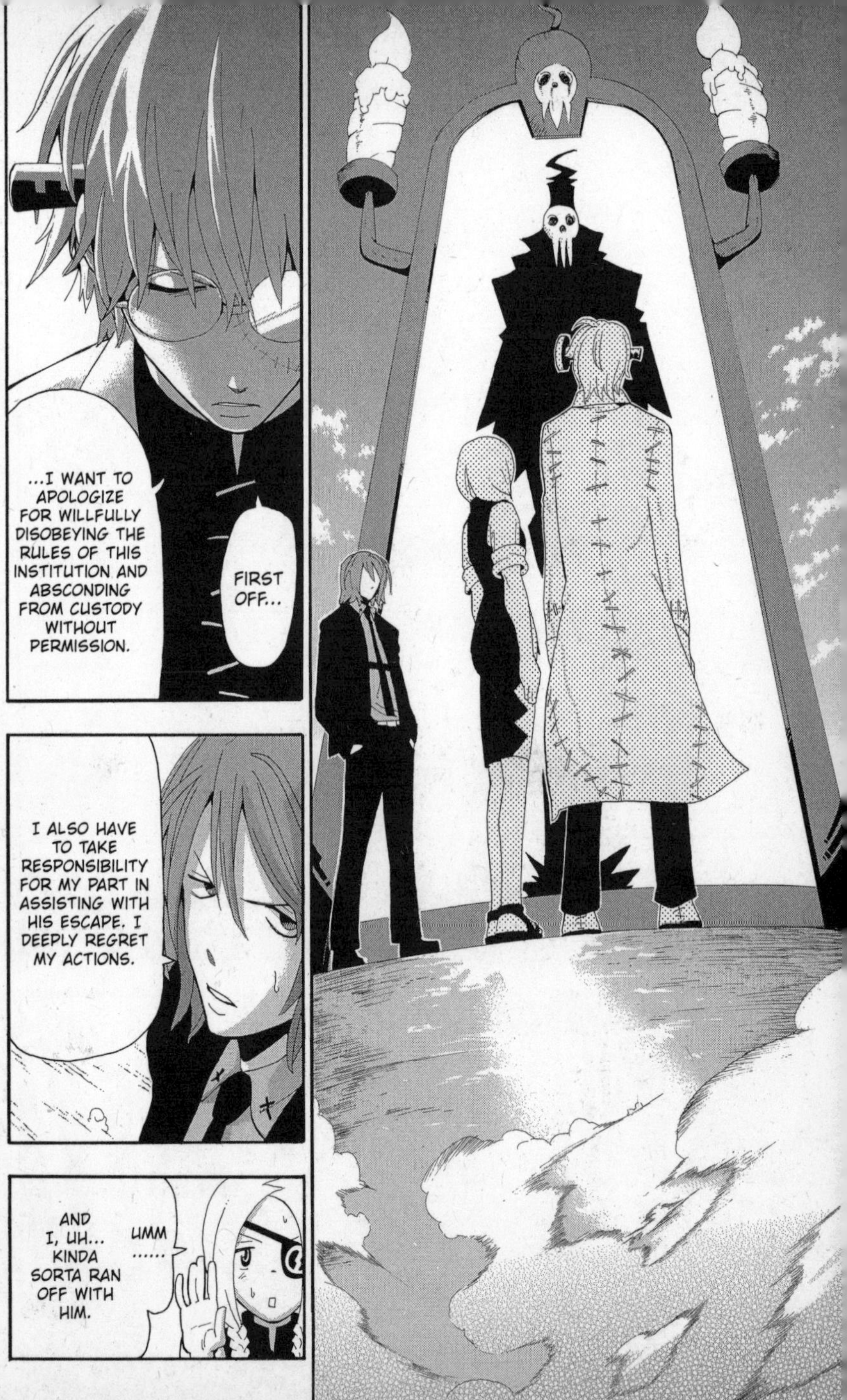
FIRST OFF...
...I WANT TO APOLOGIZE FOR WILLFULLY DISOBEYING THE RULES OF THIS INSTITUTION AND ABSCONDING FROM CUSTODY WITHOUT PERMISSION.
I ALSO HAVE TO TAKE RESPONSIBILITY FOR MY PART IN ASSISTING WITH HIS ESCAPE. I DEEPLY REGRET MY ACTIONS.
UMM ......
AND I, UH... KINDA SORTA RAN OFF WITH HIM.

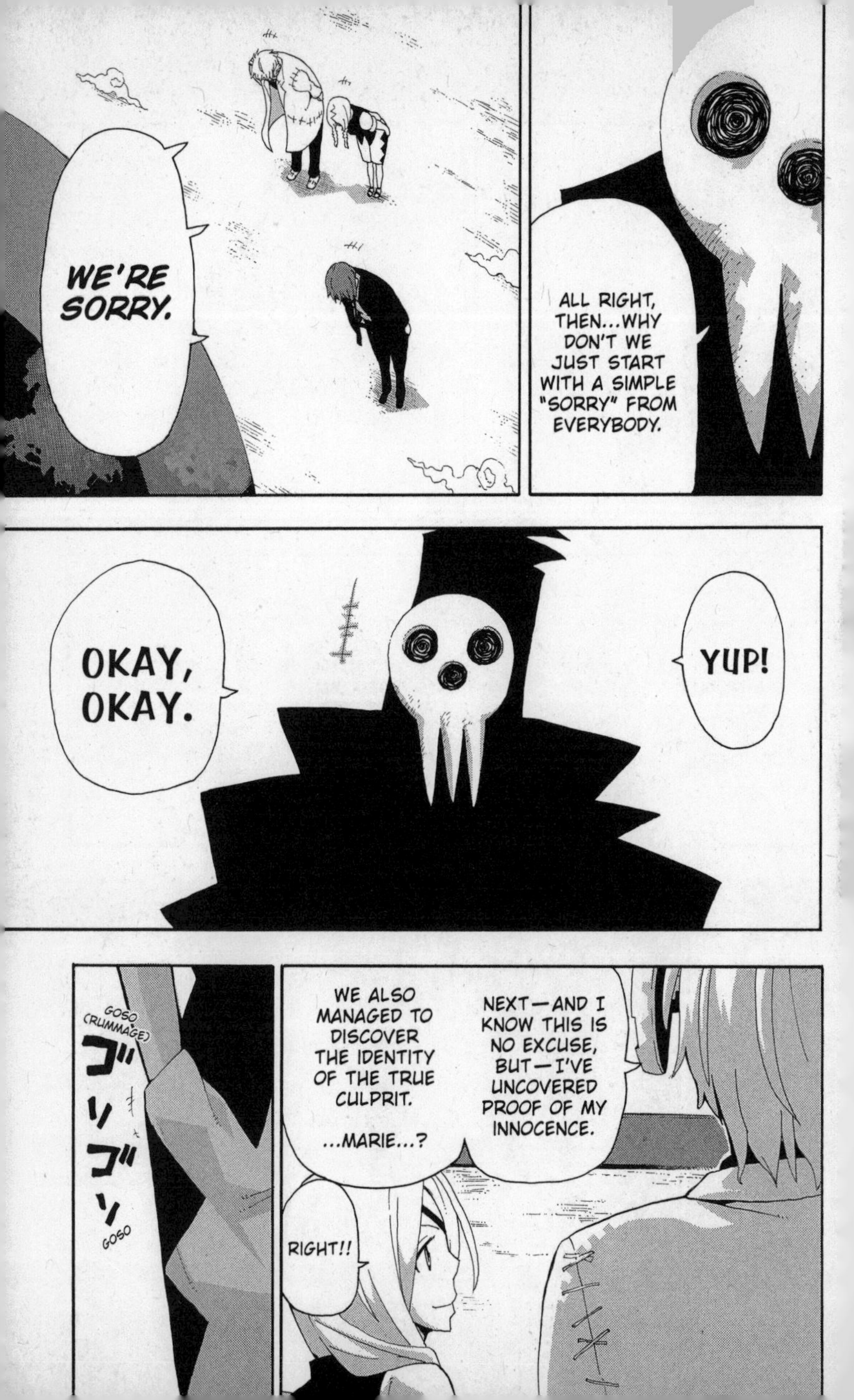
ALL RIGHT, THEN...WHY DON'T WE JUST START WITH A SIMPLE "SORRY" FROM EVERYBODY.
WE'RE SORRY.
YUP!
OKAY, OKAY.
NEXT—AND I KNOW THIS IS NO EXCUSE, BUT—I'VE UNCOVERED PROOF OF MY INNOCENCE.
WE ALSO MANAGED TO DISCOVER THE IDENTITY OF THE TRUE CULPRIT.
...MARIE...?
RIGHT!!
GOSO (RUMMAGE)
ゴソゴソ
GOSO

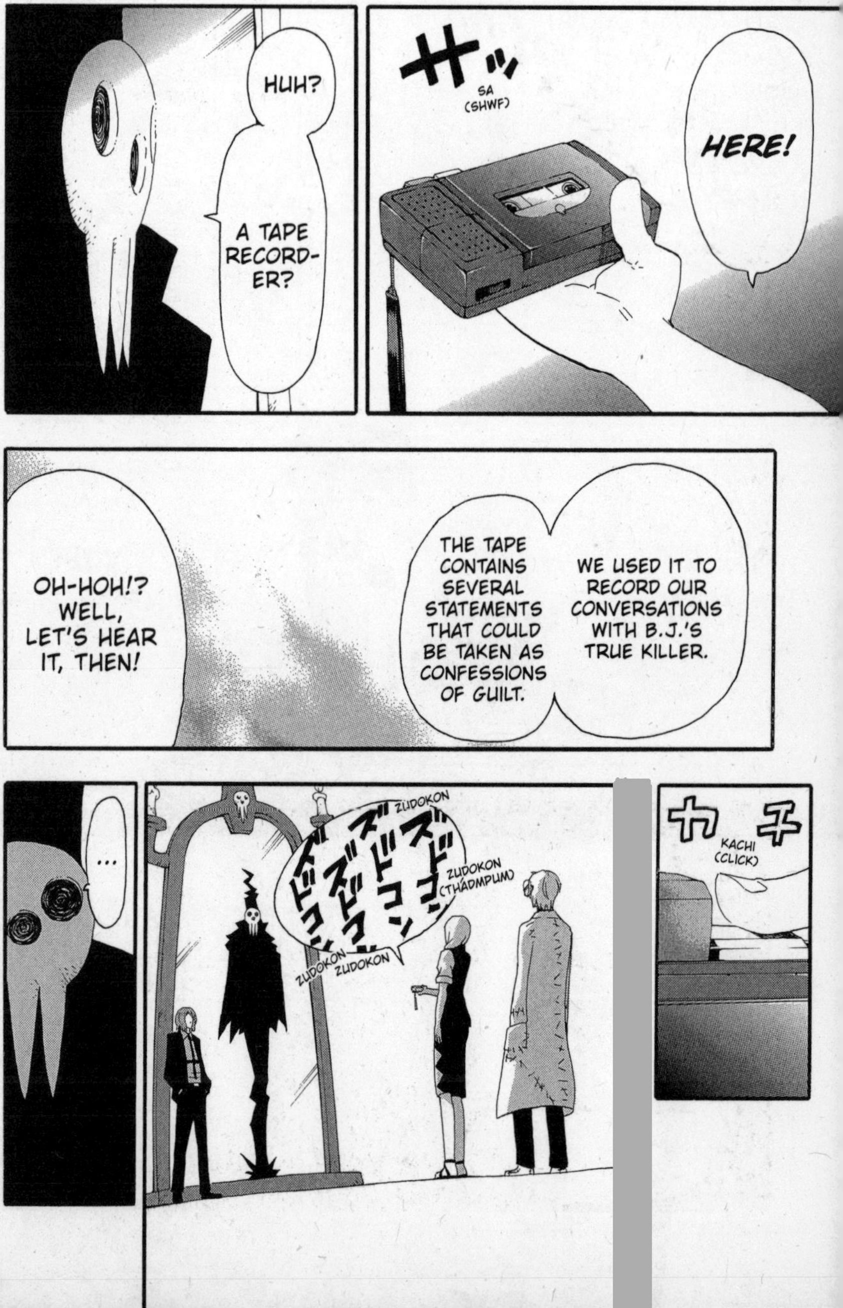

サッ
SA (SHWF)
HERE!
HUH?
A TAPE RECORDER?
WE USED IT TO RECORD OUR CONVERSATIONS WITH B.J.'S TRUE KILLER.
THE TAPE CONTAINS SEVERAL STATEMENTS THAT COULD BE TAKEN AS CONFESSIONS OF GUILT.
OH-HOH!? WELL, LET'S HEAR IT, THEN!
カチ
KACHI (CLICK)
ズドコン ズドコン ズドコン ズドコン
ZUDOKON
ZUDOKON (THADMPUM)
ZUDOKON
ZUDOKON
...

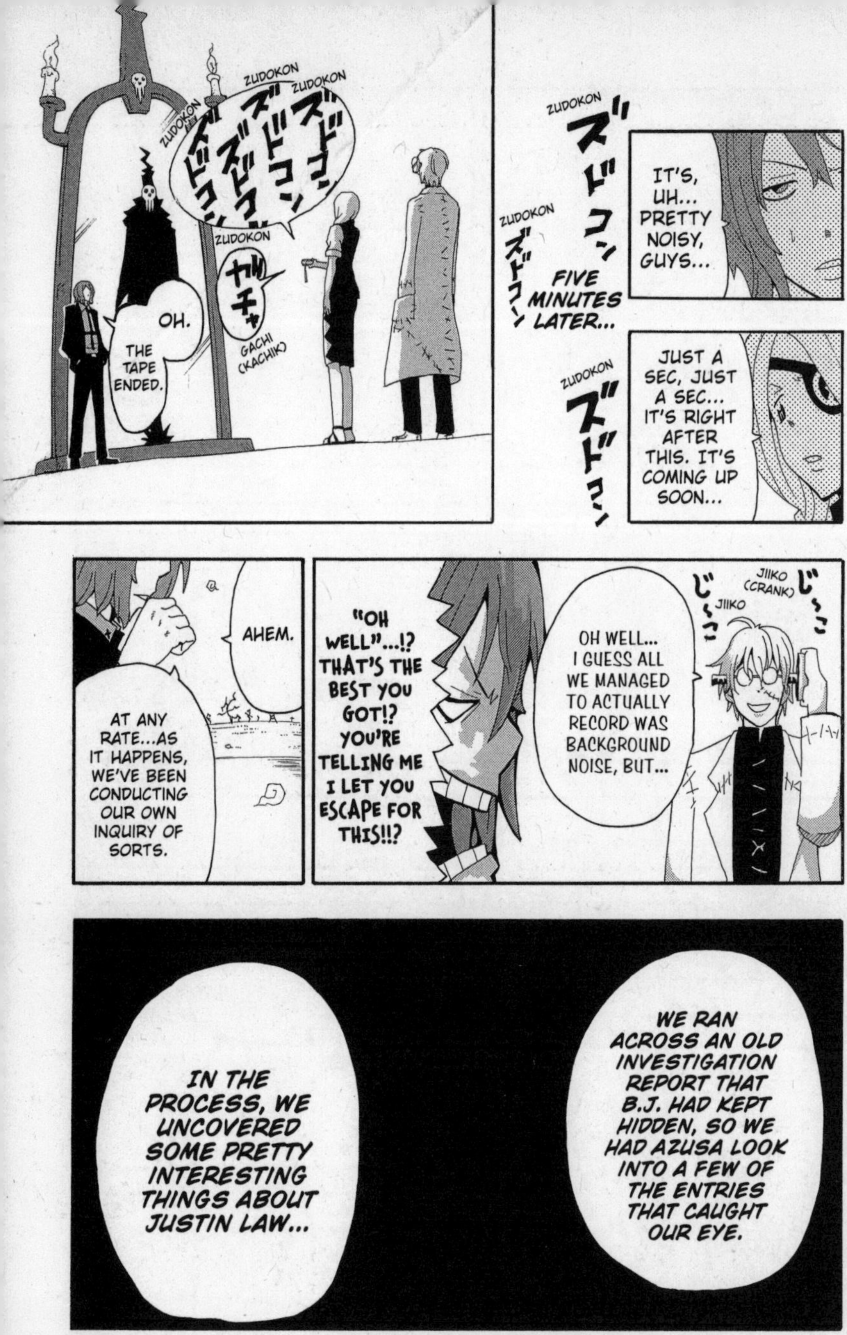
ZUDOKON
IT'S, UH... PRETTY NOISY, GUYS...
ZUDOKON
FIVE MINUTES LATER...
ZUDOKON
JUST A SEC, JUST A SEC... IT'S RIGHT AFTER THIS. IT'S COMING UP SOON...
ZUDOKON
ZUDOKON
ZUDOKON
ZUDOKON
GACHI (KACHIK)
OH.
THE TAPE ENDED.
JIIKO (CRANK)
JIIKO
OH WELL... I GUESS ALL WE MANAGED TO ACTUALLY RECORD WAS BACKGROUND NOISE, BUT...
"OH WELL"...!? THAT'S THE BEST YOU GOT!? YOU'RE TELLING ME I LET YOU ESCAPE FOR THIS!!?
AHEM.
AT ANY RATE...AS IT HAPPENS, WE'VE BEEN CONDUCTING OUR OWN INQUIRY OF SORTS.
WE RAN ACROSS AN OLD INVESTIGATION REPORT THAT B.J. HAD KEPT HIDDEN, SO WE HAD AZUSA LOOK INTO A FEW OF THE ENTRIES THAT CAUGHT OUR EYE.
IN THE PROCESS, WE UNCOVERED SOME PRETTY INTERESTING THINGS ABOUT JUSTIN LAW...

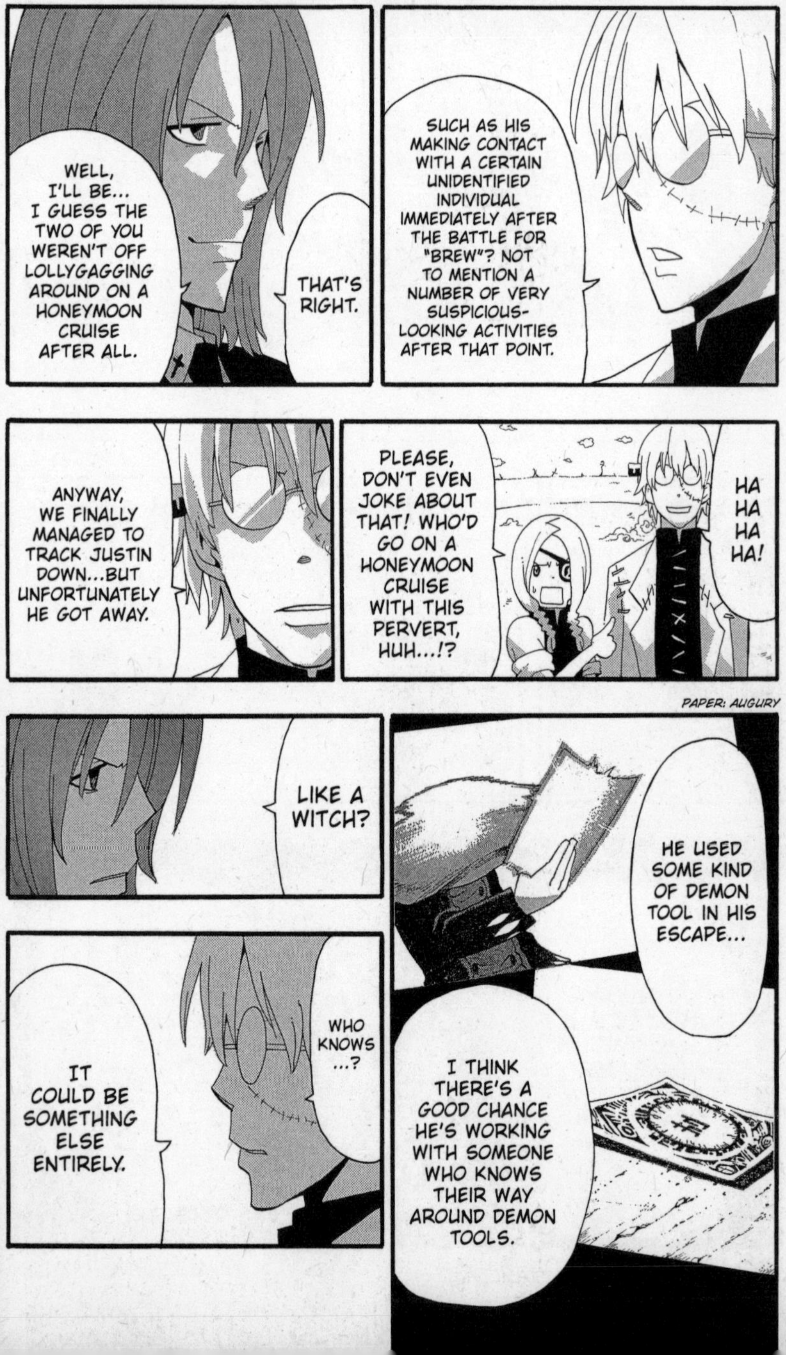

SUCH AS HIS MAKING CONTACT WITH A CERTAIN UNIDENTIFIED INDIVIDUAL IMMEDIATELY AFTER THE BATTLE FOR "BREW"? NOT TO MENTION A NUMBER OF VERY SUSPICIOUS-LOOKING ACTIVITIES AFTER THAT POINT.
THAT'S RIGHT.
WELL, I'LL BE... I GUESS THE TWO OF YOU WEREN'T OFF LOLLYGAGGING AROUND ON A HONEYMOON CRUISE AFTER ALL.
HA HA HA HA!
PLEASE, DON'T EVEN JOKE ABOUT THAT! WHO'D GO ON A HONEYMOON CRUISE WITH THIS PERVERT, HUH...!?
ANYWAY, WE FINALLY MANAGED TO TRACK JUSTIN DOWN...BUT UNFORTUNATELY HE GOT AWAY.
PAPER: AUGURY
HE USED SOME KIND OF DEMON TOOL IN HIS ESCAPE...
I THINK THERE'S A GOOD CHANCE HE'S WORKING WITH SOMEONE WHO KNOWS THEIR WAY AROUND DEMON TOOLS.
LIKE A WITCH?
WHO KNOWS ...?
IT COULD BE SOMETHING ELSE ENTIRELY.

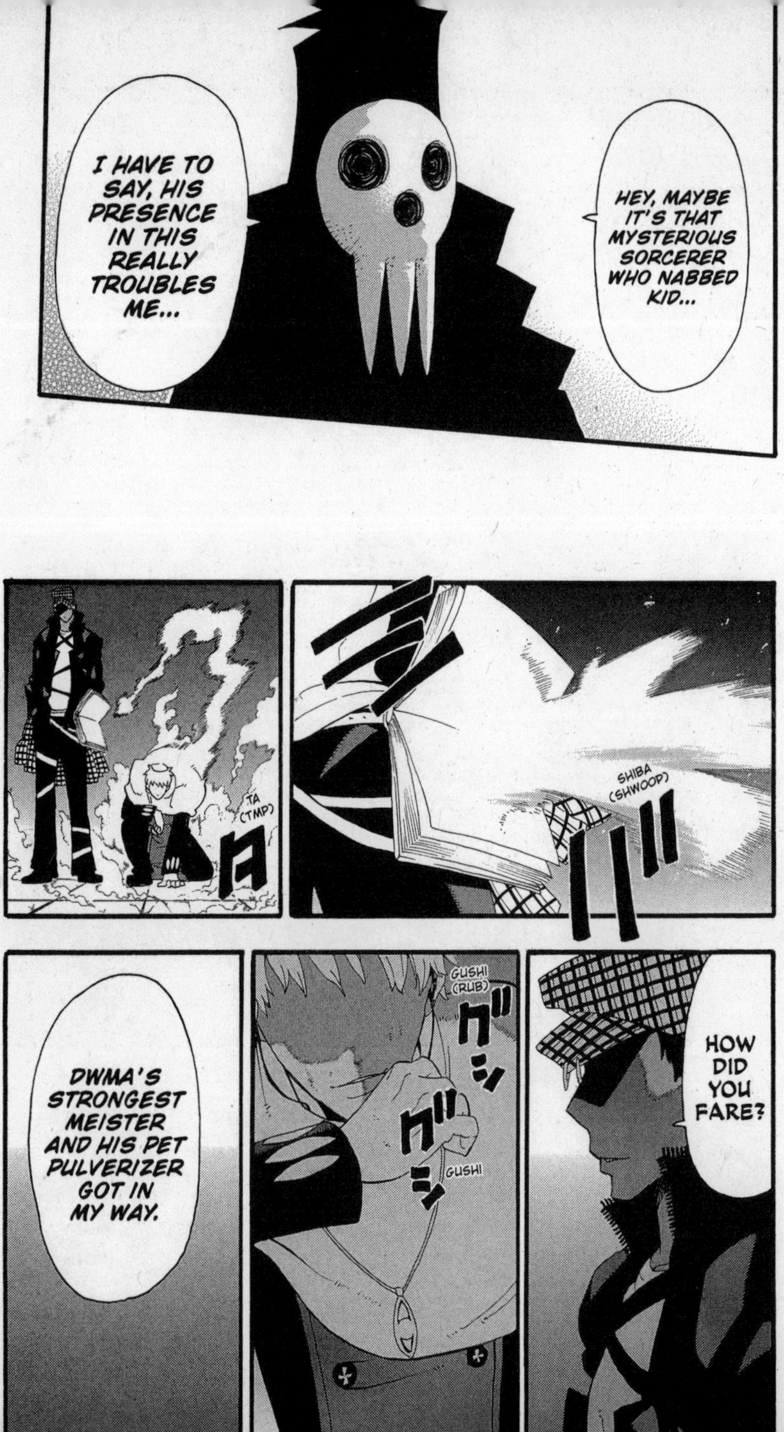
HEY, MAYBE IT'S THAT MYSTERIOUS SORCERER WHO NABBED KID...
I HAVE TO SAY, HIS PRESENCE IN THIS REALLY TROUBLES ME...
SHIBA (SHWOOP)
TA (TMP)
HOW DID YOU FARE?
GUSHI (RUB)
GUSHI
DWMA'S STRONGEST MEISTER AND HIS PET PULVERIZER GOT IN MY WAY.

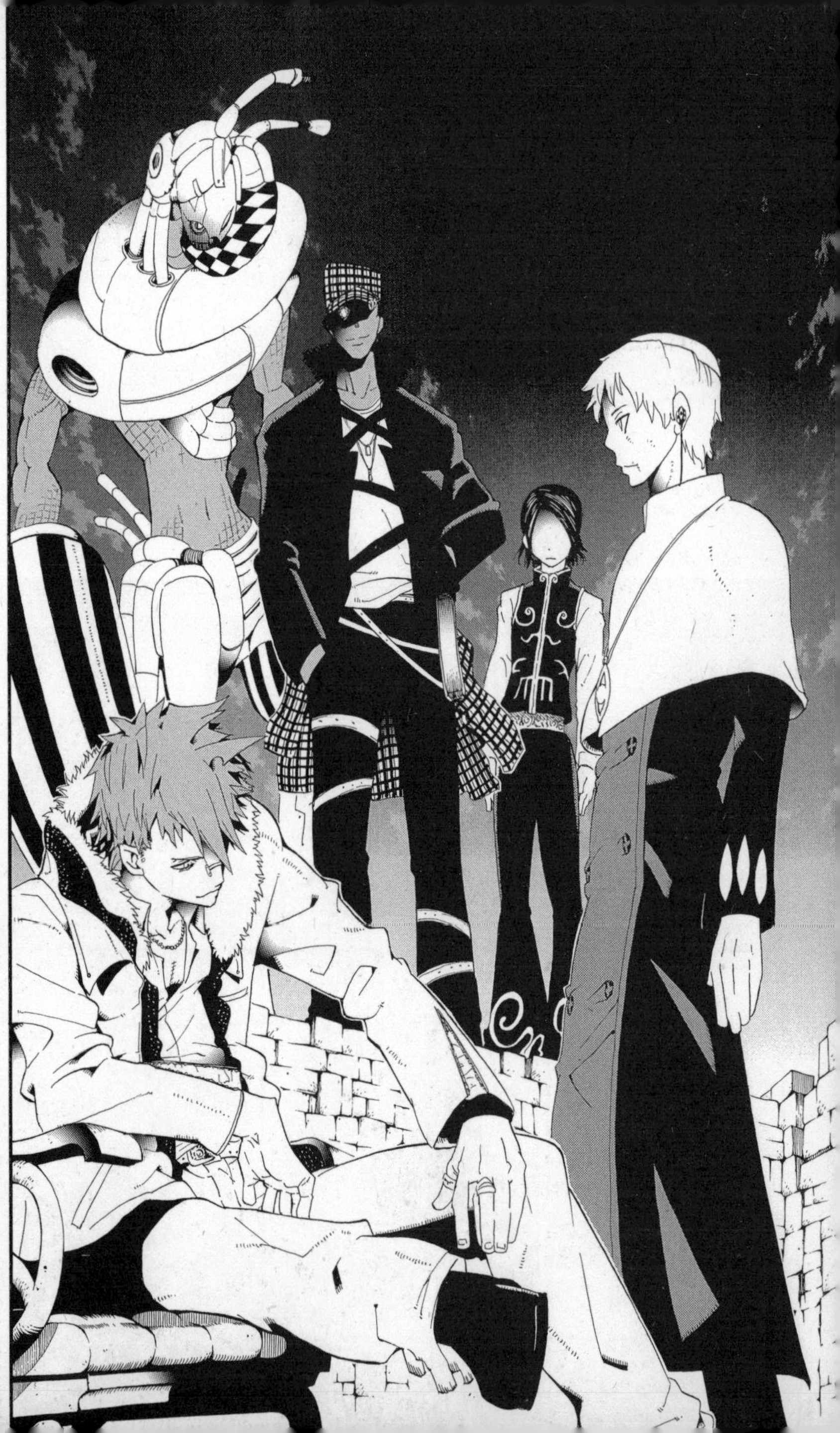

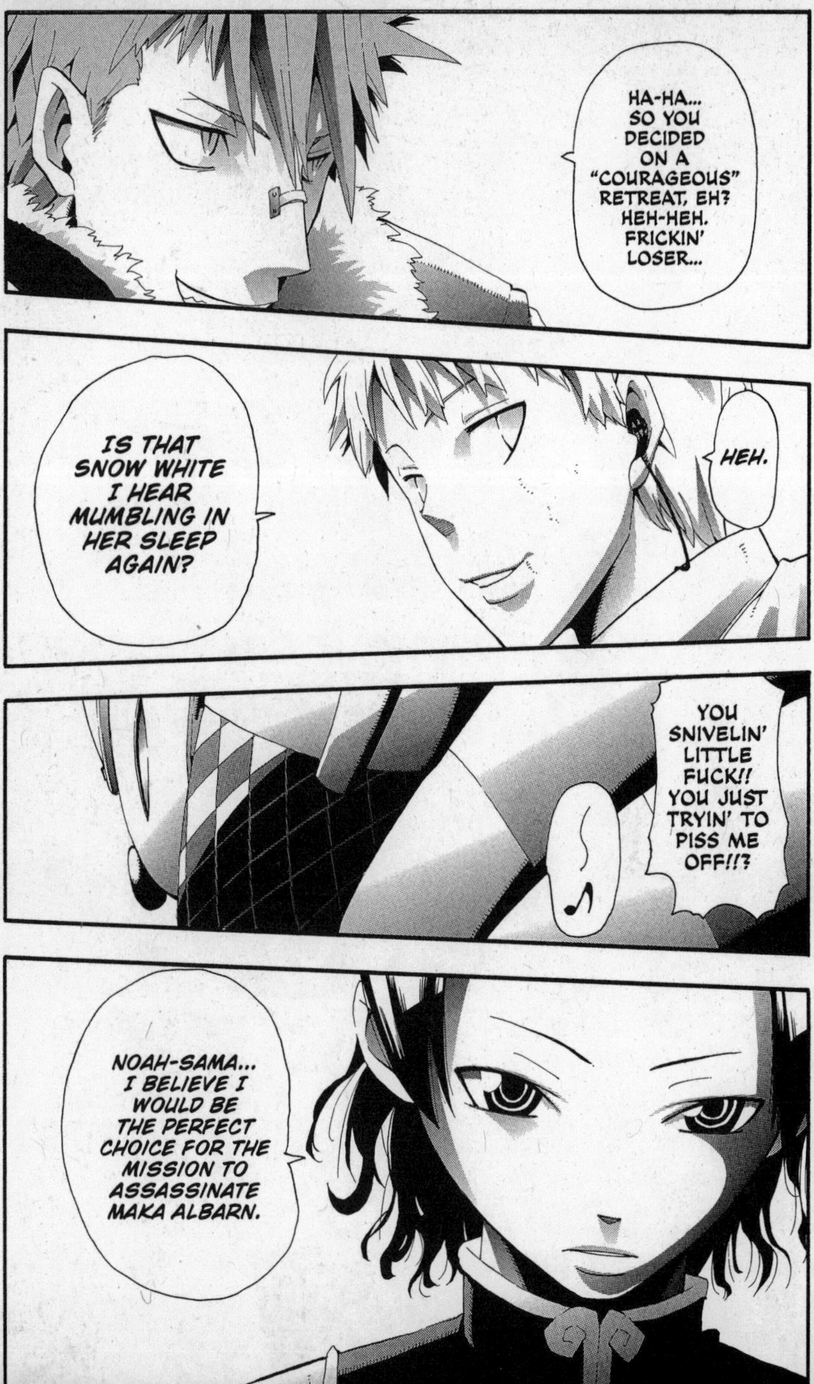
HA-HA... SO YOU DECIDED ON A "COURAGEOUS" RETREAT, EH? HEH-HEH. FRICKIN' LOSER...
HEH.
IS THAT SNOW WHITE I HEAR MUMBLING IN HER SLEEP AGAIN?
YOU SNIVELIN' LITTLE FUCK!! YOU JUST TRYIN' TO PISS ME OFF!!?
NOAH-SAMA... I BELIEVE I WOULD BE THE PERFECT CHOICE FOR THE MISSION TO ASSASSINATE MAKA ALBARN.

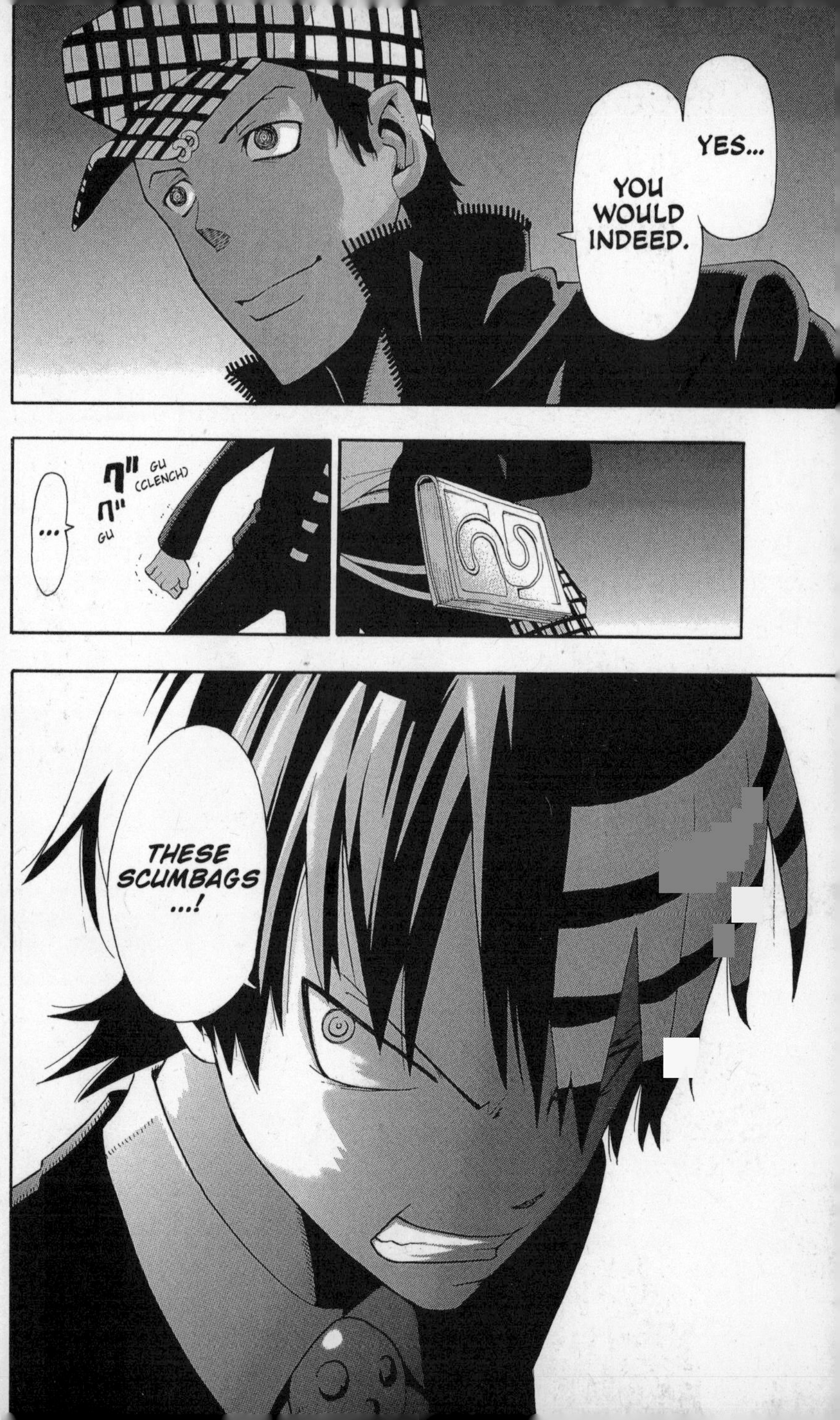
YES...
YOU WOULD INDEED.
グ GU (CLENCH)
グ GU
...
THESE SCUMBAGS ...!

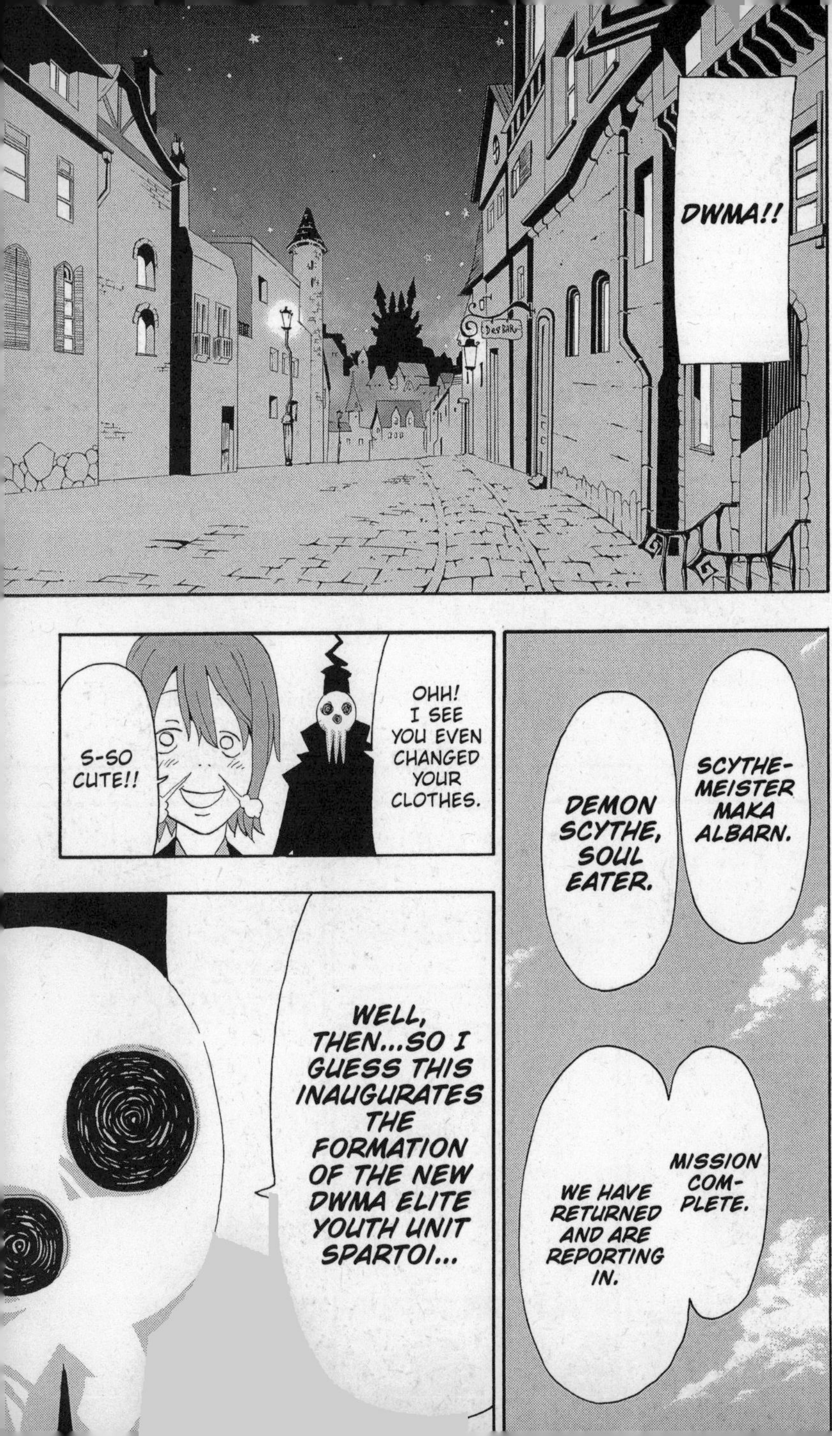
DWMA!!
SCYTHE-MEISTER MAKA ALBARN.
DEMON SCYTHE, SOUL EATER.
MISSION COMPLETE.
WE HAVE RETURNED AND ARE REPORTING IN.
OHH! I SEE YOU EVEN CHANGED YOUR CLOTHES.
S-SO CUTE!!
WELL, THEN...SO I GUESS THIS INAUGURATES THE FORMATION OF THE NEW DWMA ELITE YOUTH UNIT SPARTOI...

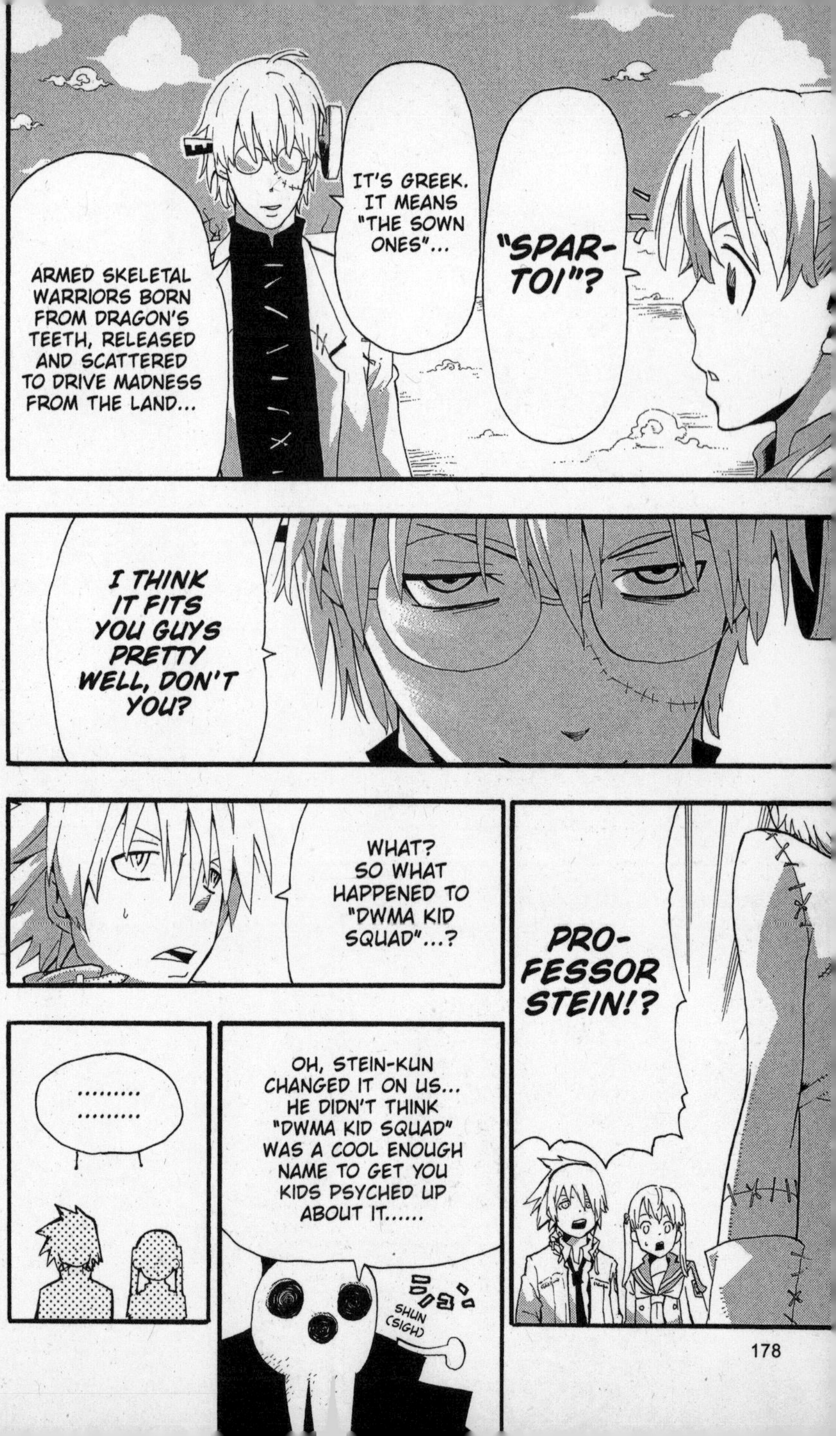
"SPAR-TOI"?
IT'S GREEK. IT MEANS "THE SOWN ONES"...
ARMED SKELETAL WARRIORS BORN FROM DRAGON'S TEETH, RELEASED AND SCATTERED TO DRIVE MADNESS FROM THE LAND...
I THINK IT FITS YOU GUYS PRETTY WELL, DON'T YOU?
PRO-FESSOR STEIN!?
WHAT? SO WHAT HAPPENED TO "DWMA KID SQUAD"...?
OH, STEIN-KUN CHANGED IT ON US... HE DIDN'T THINK "DWMA KID SQUAD" WAS A COOL ENOUGH NAME TO GET YOU KIDS PSYCHED UP ABOUT IT......
SHUN (SIGH)
....
....

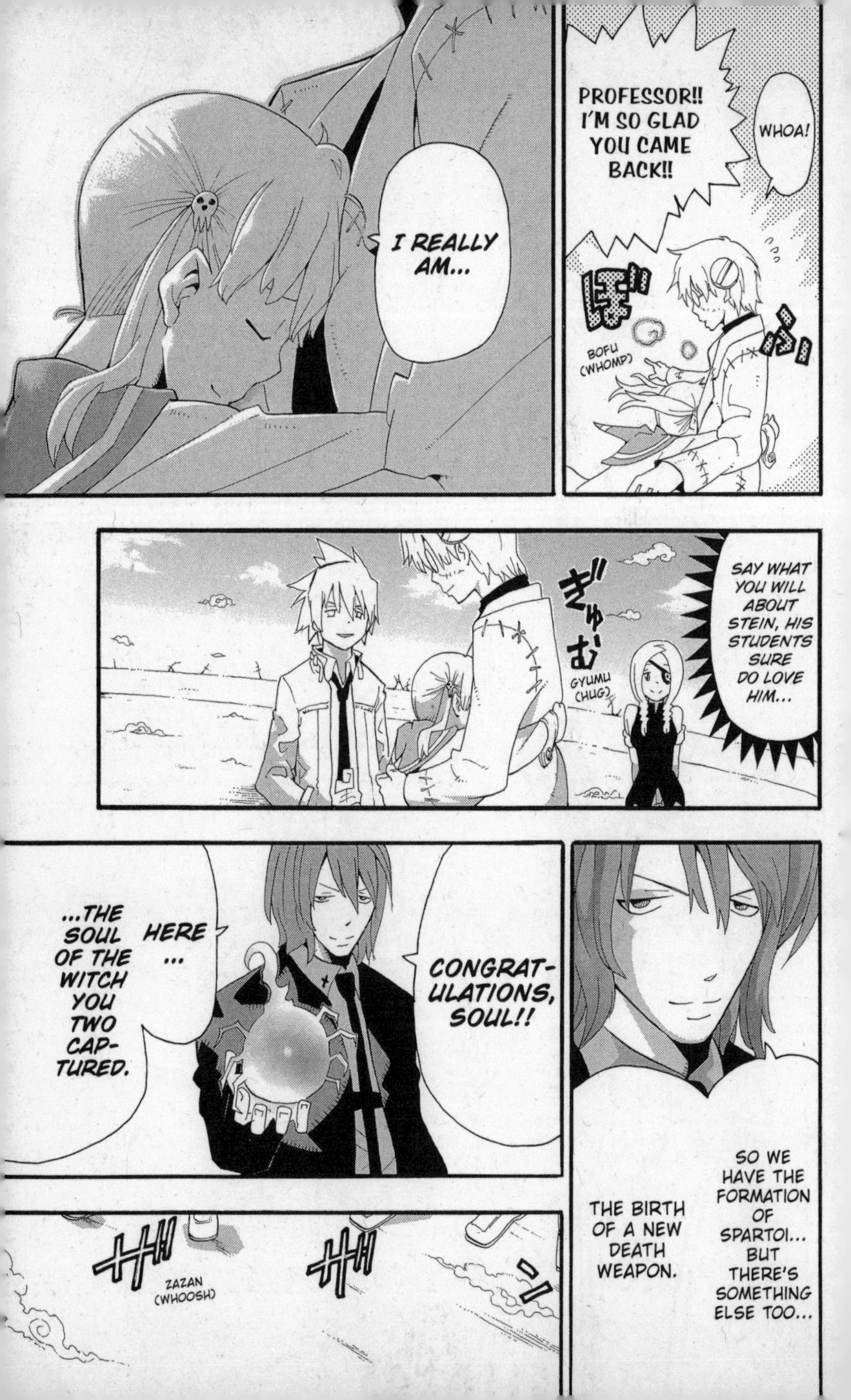
PROFESSOR!! I'M SO GLAD YOU CAME BACK!!
WHOA!
ぼふ
BOFU (WHOMP)
I REALLY AM...
SAY WHAT YOU WILL ABOUT STEIN, HIS STUDENTS SURE DO LOVE HIM...
ぎゅむ
GYUMU (HUG)
SO WE HAVE THE FORMATION OF SPARTOI... BUT THERE'S SOMETHING ELSE TOO...
THE BIRTH OF A NEW DEATH WEAPON.
CONGRAT-ULATIONS, SOUL!!
HERE...
...THE SOUL OF THE WITCH YOU TWO CAP-TURED.
ZAZAN (WHOOSH)

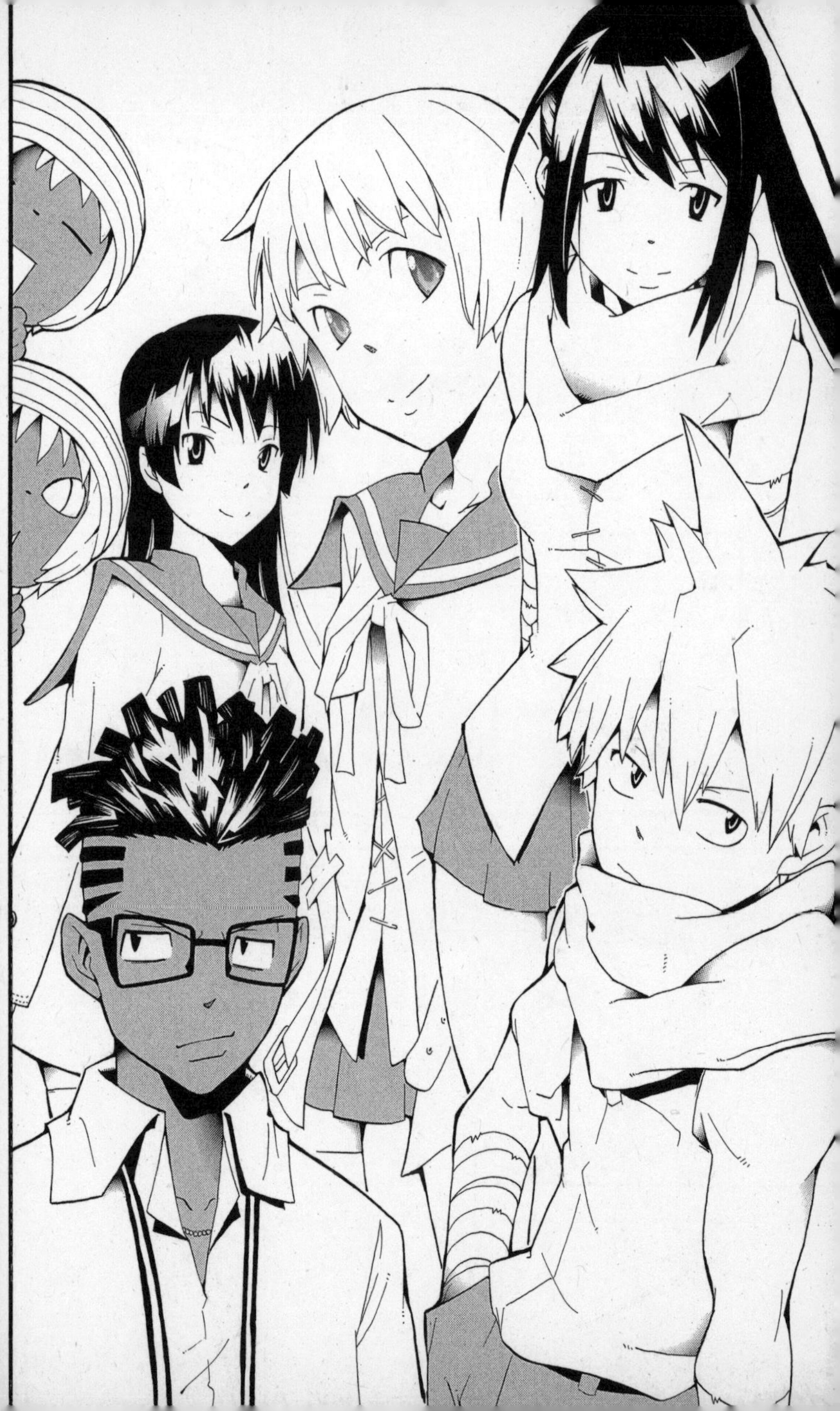

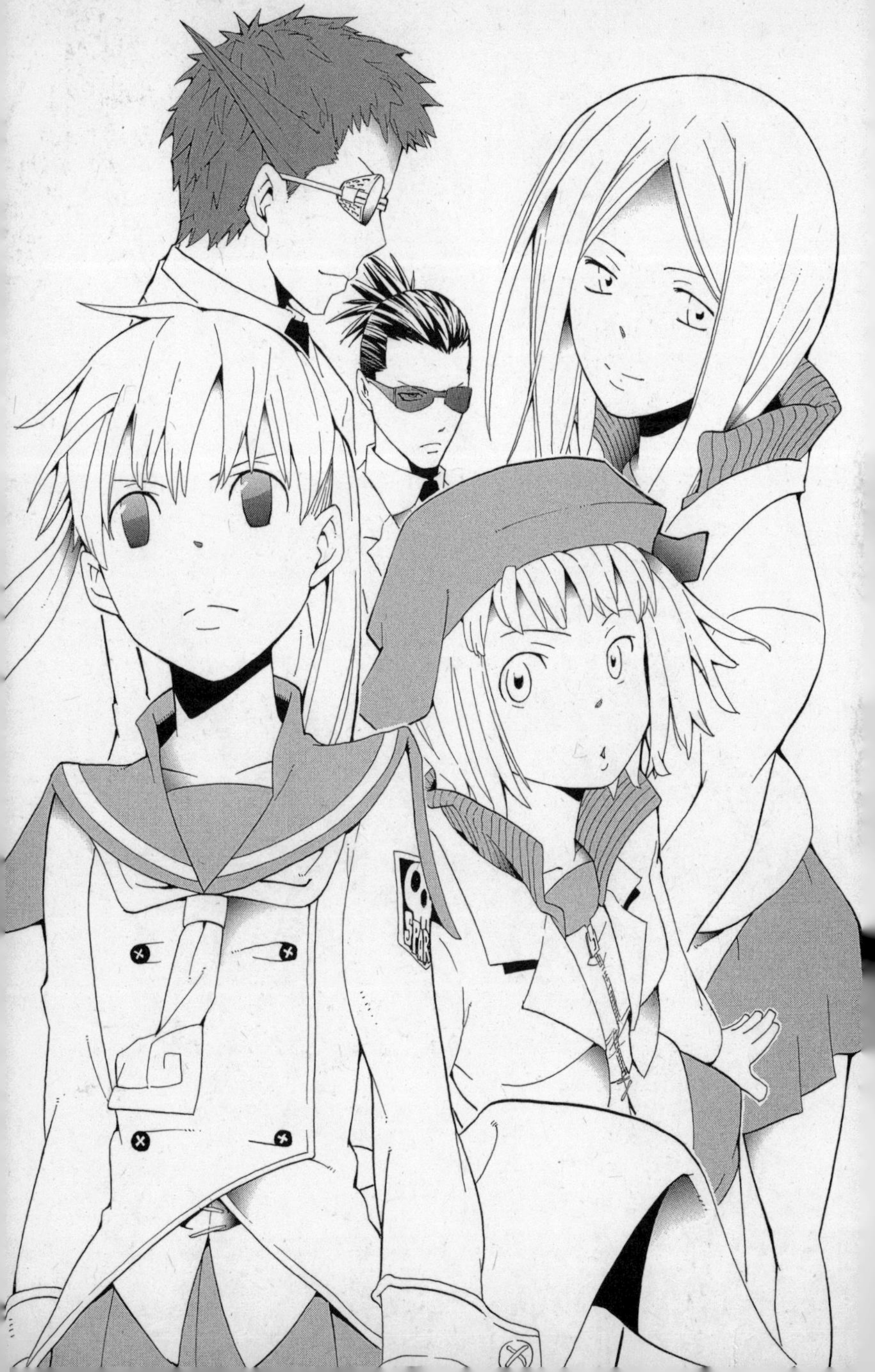

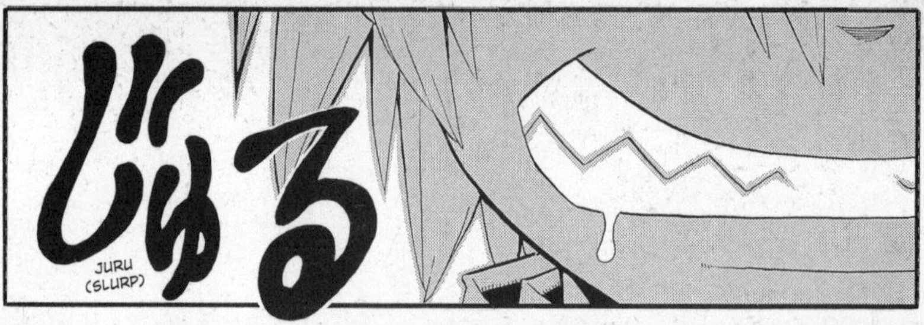
じゅる
JURU (SLURP)

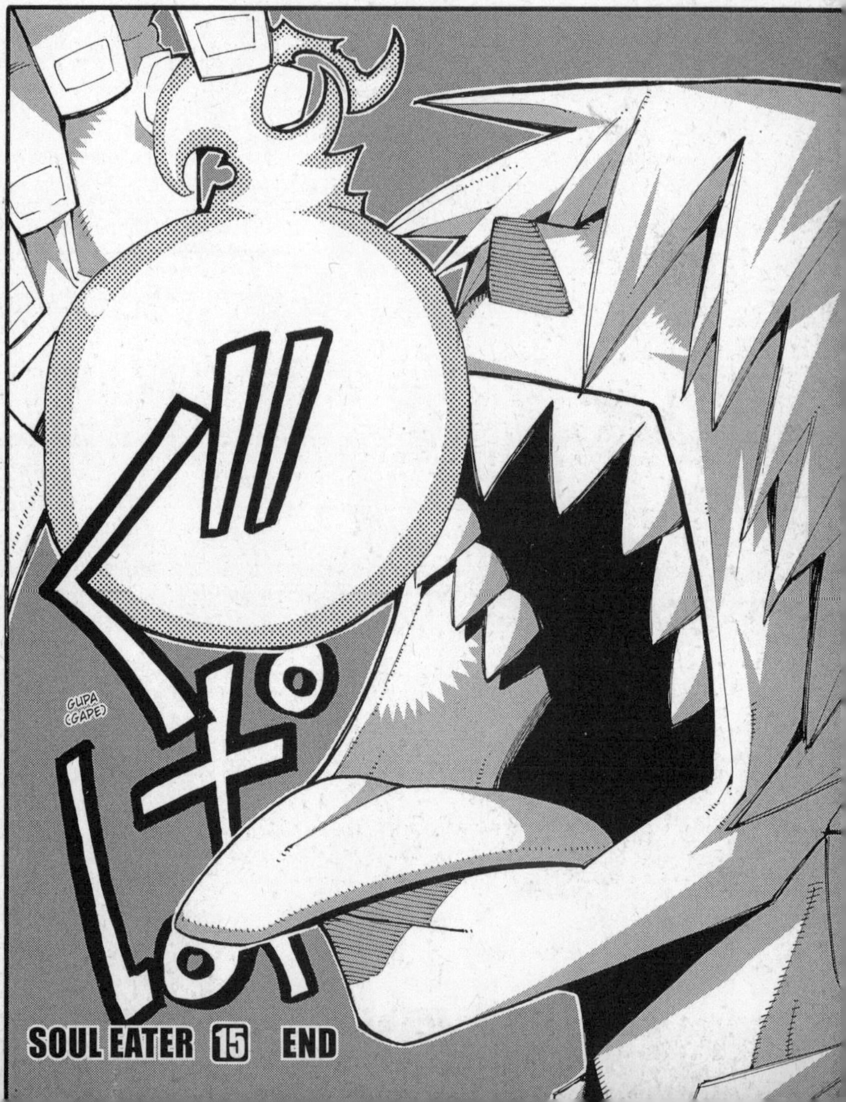
ぐぱ
GUPA (GAPE)
SOUL EATER 15 END

SOUL EATER

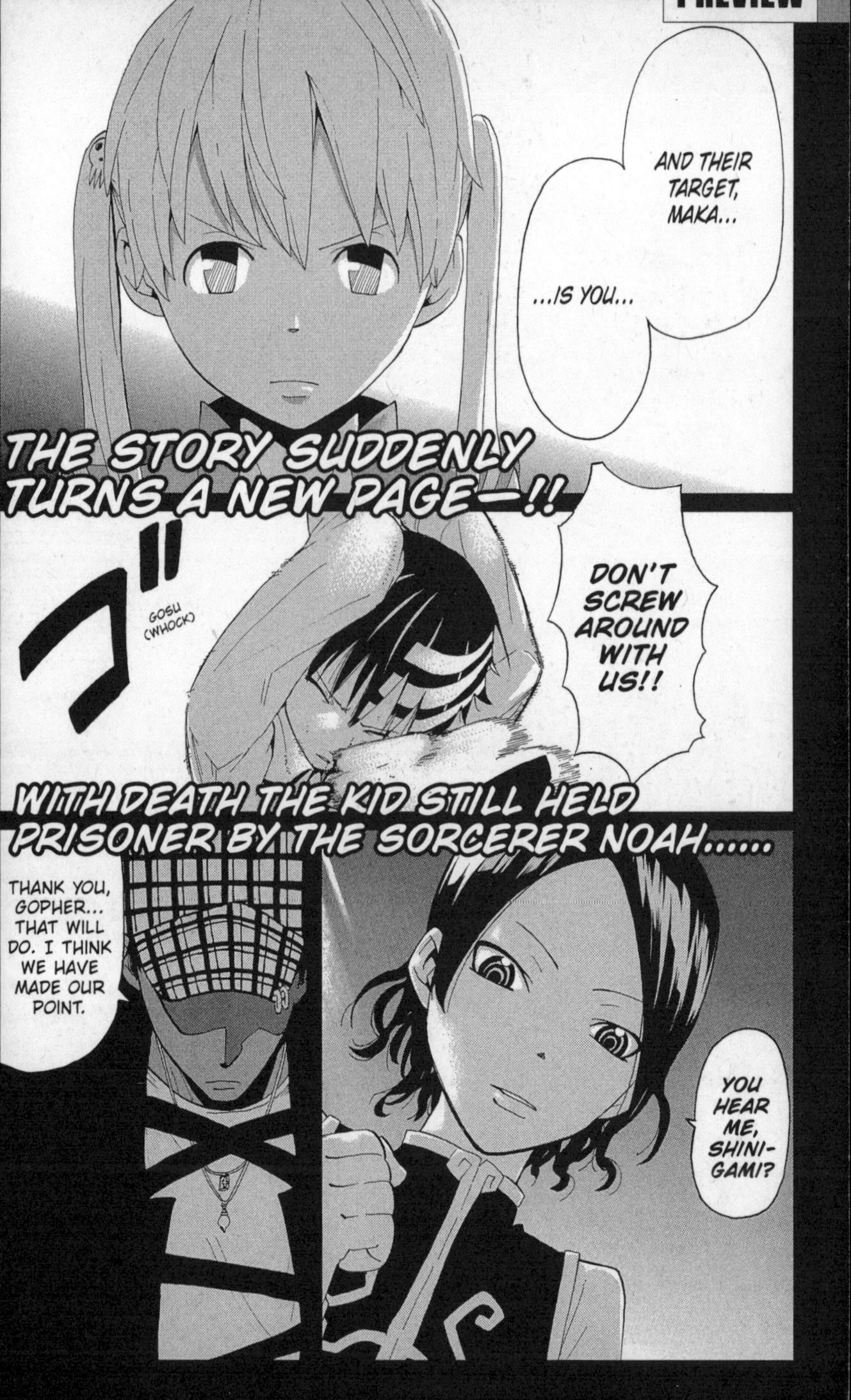
AND THEIR TARGET, MAKA...
...IS YOU...
THE STORY SUDDENLY TURNS A NEW PAGE—!!
DON'T SCREW AROUND WITH US!!
GOSU (WHOCK)
WITH DEATH THE KID STILL HELD PRISONER BY THE SORCERER NOAH......
YOU HEAR ME, SHINIGAMI?
THANK YOU, GOPHER... THAT WILL DO. I THINK WE HAVE MADE OUR POINT.

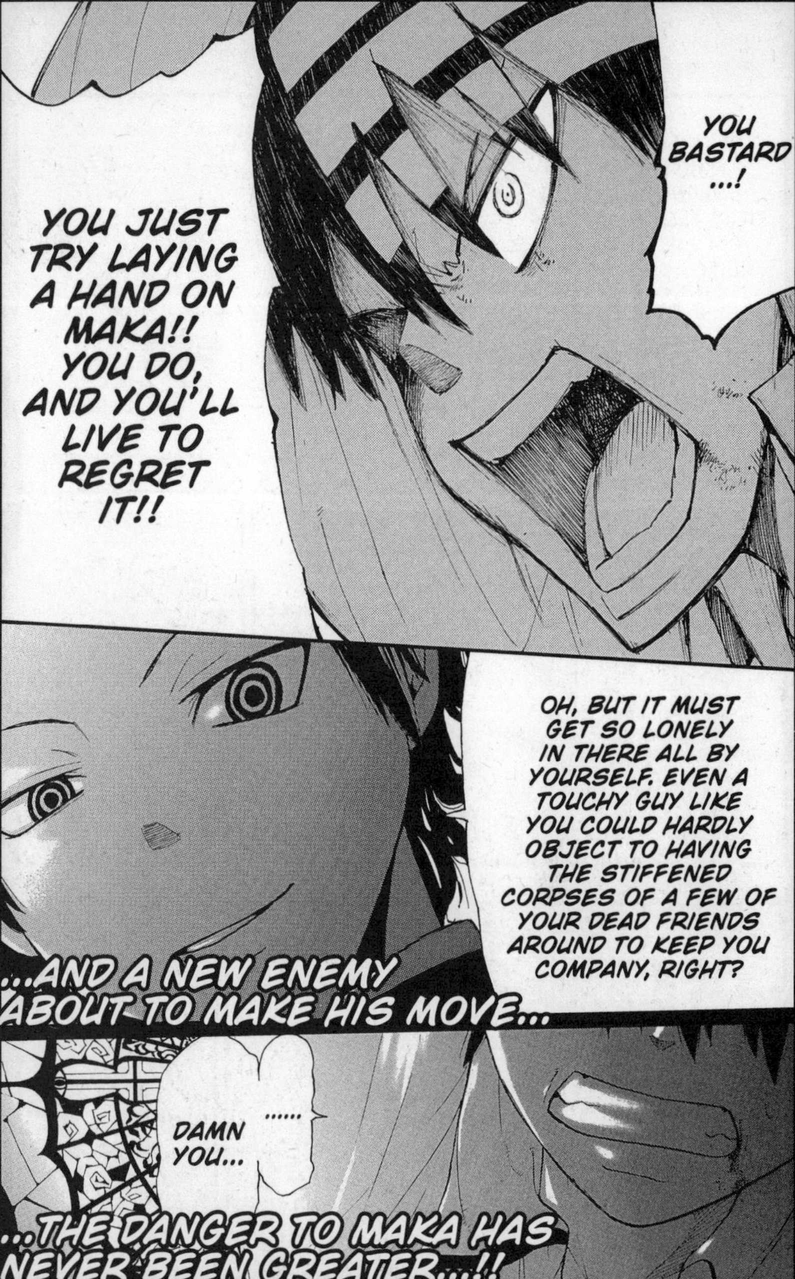
YOU BASTARD ...!
YOU JUST TRY LAYING A HAND ON MAKA!! YOU DO, AND YOU'LL LIVE TO REGRET IT!!
OH, BUT IT MUST GET SO LONELY IN THERE ALL BY YOURSELF. EVEN A TOUCHY GUY LIKE YOU COULD HARDLY OBJECT TO HAVING THE STIFFENED CORPSES OF A FEW OF YOUR DEAD FRIENDS AROUND TO KEEP YOU COMPANY, RIGHT?
...AND A NEW ENEMY ABOUT TO MAKE HIS MOVE...
......
DAMN YOU...
...THE DANGER TO MAKA HAS NEVER BEEN GREATER...!!

Continued in Soul Eater Volume 16!!

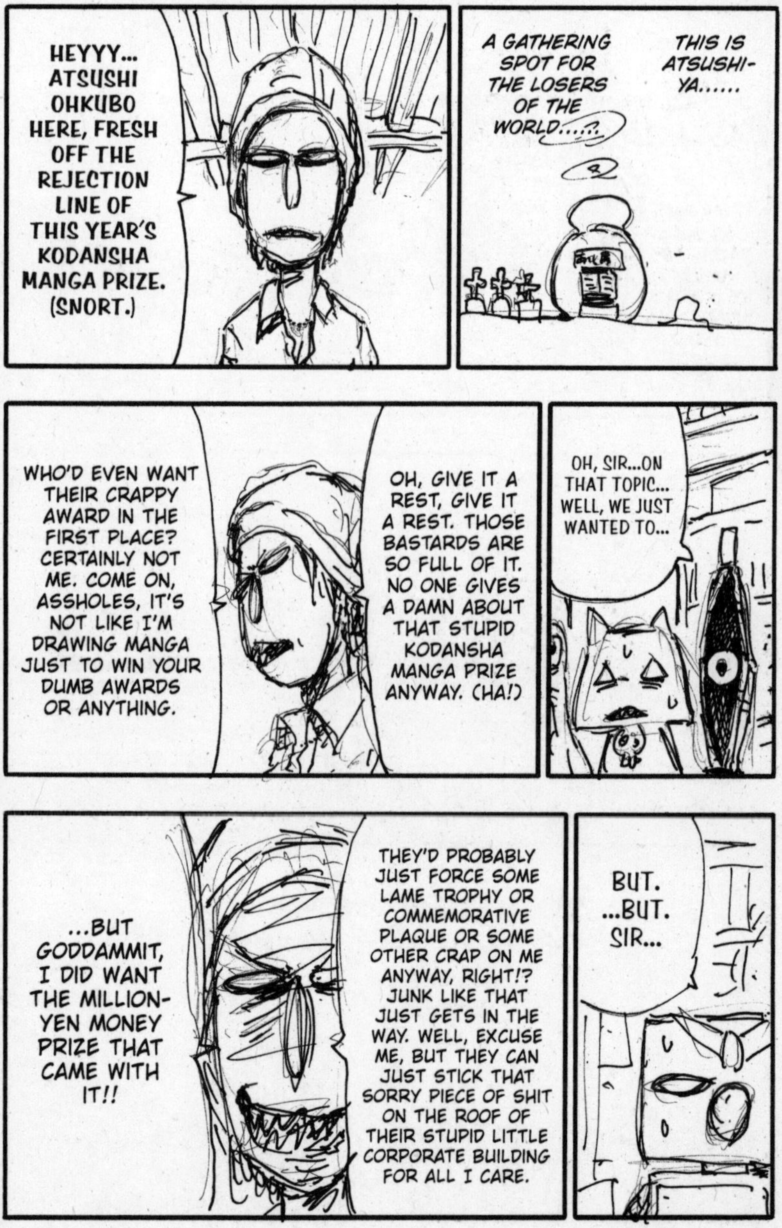
THIS IS ATSUSHI-YA......
A GATHERING SPOT FOR THE LOSERS OF THE WORLD......
HEYYY... ATSUSHI OHKUBO HERE, FRESH OFF THE REJECTION LINE OF THIS YEAR'S KODANSHA MANGA PRIZE. (SNORT.)
OH, SIR...ON THAT TOPIC... WELL, WE JUST WANTED TO...
OH, GIVE IT A REST, GIVE IT A REST. THOSE BASTARDS ARE SO FULL OF IT. NO ONE GIVES A DAMN ABOUT THAT STUPID KODANSHA MANGA PRIZE ANYWAY. (HA!)
WHO'D EVEN WANT THEIR CRAPPY AWARD IN THE FIRST PLACE? CERTAINLY NOT ME. COME ON, ASSHOLES, IT'S NOT LIKE I'M DRAWING MANGA JUST TO WIN YOUR DUMB AWARDS OR ANYTHING.
BUT. ...BUT. SIR...
THEY'D PROBABLY JUST FORCE SOME LAME TROPHY OR COMMEMORATIVE PLAQUE OR SOME OTHER CRAP ON ME ANYWAY, RIGHT!? JUNK LIKE THAT JUST GETS IN THE WAY. WELL, EXCUSE ME, BUT THEY CAN JUST STICK THAT SORRY PIECE OF SHIT ON THE ROOF OF THEIR STUPID LITTLE CORPORATE BUILDING FOR ALL I CARE.
...BUT GODDAMMIT, I DID WANT THE MILLION-YEN MONEY PRIZE THAT CAME WITH IT!!

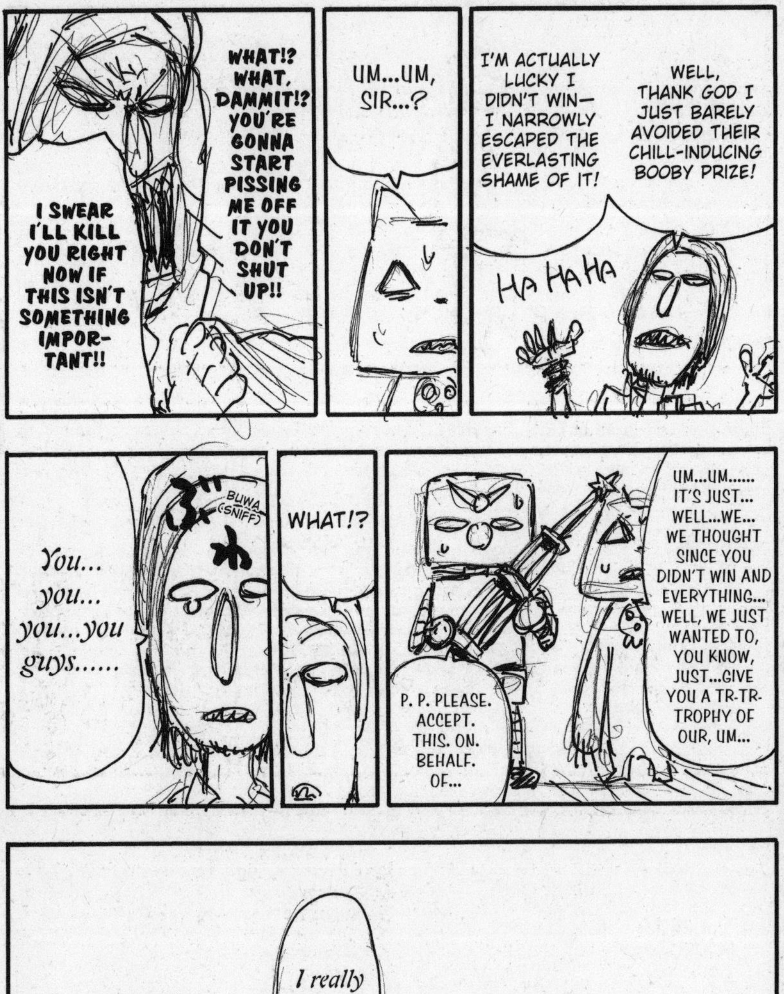
WELL, THANK GOD I JUST BARELY AVOIDED THEIR CHILL-INDUCING BOOBY PRIZE!
I'M ACTUALLY LUCKY I DIDN'T WIN— I NARROWLY ESCAPED THE EVERLASTING SHAME OF IT!
HA HA HA
UM...UM, SIR...?
WHAT!? WHAT, DAMMIT!? YOU'RE GONNA START PISSING ME OFF IT YOU DON'T SHUT UP!!
I SWEAR I'LL KILL YOU RIGHT NOW IF THIS ISN'T SOMETHING IMPOR-TANT!!
UM...UM...... IT'S JUST... WELL...WE... WE THOUGHT SINCE YOU DIDN'T WIN AND EVERYTHING... WELL, WE JUST WANTED TO, YOU KNOW, JUST...GIVE YOU A TR-TR-TROPHY OF OUR, UM...
P. P. PLEASE. ACCEPT. THIS. ON. BEHALF. OF...
WHAT!?
BUWA (SNIFF)
You... you... you...you guys......
I really hate you guys......

Translation Notes

Common Honorifics

no honorific: Indicates familiarity or closeness; if used without permission or reason, addressing someone in this manner would constitute an insult.

-san: The Japanese equivalent of Mr./Mrs./Miss. If a situation calls for politeness, this is the fail-safe honorific.

-sama: Conveys great respect; may also indicate that the social status of the speaker is lower than that of the addressee.

-kun: Used most often when referring to boys, this indicates affection or familiarity. Occasionally used by older men among their peers, but it may also be used by anyone referring to a person of lower standing.

-chan: An affectionate honorific indicating familiarity used mostly in reference to girls; also used in reference to cute persons or animals of either gender.

-senpai: A suffix used to address upperclassmen or more experienced coworkers.

-sensei: A respectful term for teachers, artists, or high-level professionals.

Page 17
Eibon and **The Book of Eibon** are direct references to Lovecraft's Cthulhu Mythos. They were originally conceived by Clark Ashton Smith (an early member of Lovecraft's circle of fellow writers and correspondents) and appeared first in his stories of Hyperborea, but were also referenced numerous times in Lovecraft's own stories.

Page 99
Tezca Tlipoca's name comes from the Aztec god Tezcatlipoca, a deity associated with the night, storm winds, and other dark and destructive forces, as well as with temptation and sorcery. He is often depicted in Aztec sources with a black stripe across his face and wearing a smoking obsidian mirror around his neck (according to myth, the mirror's smoke had the power to kill). The name itself has a disputed etymology, but it is generally agreed among Aztec linguists and historians that the *tezcatl* element is the Nahuatl word for "mirror" and the *poca* element is related to *popoca* ("to emit smoke"). Hence, something like "The Smoking Mirror" is usually given as the translation of the god's name.

Page 140
The character (扐) on the **demon tool paper** that Justin uses to escape is a rare Chinese character meaning "divination"—specifically, using the *Yi Jing* (*Book of Changes*) to interpret yarrow straw sticks. I chose the uncommon word "augury" in order to retain some of the mystical flavor.

Page 150
Frey D. Sadoko is a combination of "Freddy" (for Freddy Krueger from the *Nightmare on Elm Street* movies) and "Sadoko" (for Sadoko Yamamura from the *Ring* movies). Note that she has the ghostly skin and hair of Sadoko paired with the long nails of Freddy Krueger, and she kills her victims by forcing them to listen to a cursed recording (à la Sadoko) and then killing them inside their nightmares (à la Freddy Krueger).

Page 151
In addition to being an obvious nod to the US music group and a reference to the length of this character's deadly nails, the **Nine Inch Nails** attack is written with characters meaning "Well-Rudeness-Pain" (as in pain coming rudely from a water well) and is also readable in Japanese as "Id Break" (a fighting technique from the SaGa game series...a spinoff of Final Fantasy originally produced by Square Enix).

Page 159
The phrase Black☆Star actually uses for **Warrior God** is *bushin* ("war god"), which is a direct contrast to *kishin* ("demon god"). He first used the term when asserting his refusal to walk "the path of the demon"—which leads to becoming a Kishin—and instead reiterating his pledge to walk "the path of the warrior"—which presumably leads to a similar godlike state, hence the parallelism of terms.

Page 178
According to Greek myth, the legendary **Spartoi** were so named because they sprang from the earth after Kadmos, the founder of Grecian Thebes, sowed the teeth of a dragon (on the advice of Athena) that he had slain. He did so in order to replace his men who were killed fighting the dragon in the first place. The Spartoi were very unruly, however, so Kadmos tossed some rocks into their midst (also on the advice of Athena), and the confused Spartoi, each thinking one of the others was throwing rocks, fought amongst themselves until only five remained. Some of the unsown dragon teeth were later given to Jason (of Argonauts fame) by King Aeetes, who offered to hand over the Golden Fleece if Jason could kill all the Spartoi that sprouted from the ground after scattering the teeth. Interestingly (and in contrast to the version presented here by Stein), it was a witch named Medea who helped Jason get the Spartoi to kill each other instead of him.

AVAILABLE NOW!

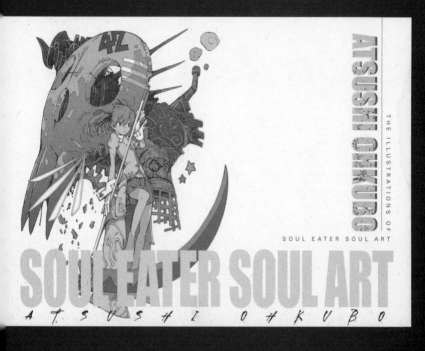

Over 200 full-color illustrations from the bestselling creator of *Soul Eater* and *B. Ichi*! This handsome hardcover edition includes cover art and color pages from the original magazine publications, promotional artwork, designs from the *Soul Eater* video games, and much more!

SIMULTANEOUS SERIALIZATION!
READ THE LATEST CHAPTER NOW IN *YEN PLUS* ONLINE! WWW.YENPLUS.COM

DING-DONG! DEAD-DONG!

DON'T BE LATE FOR THE "NOT" CLASS AT DEATH WEAPON MEISTER ACADEMY!

OLDER TEEN OT

Yen Press

SOUL EATER NOT!

ATSUSHI OHKUBO

SOUL EATER ⑮

ATSUSHI OHKUBO

Translation: Jack Wiedrick

Lettering: Alexis Eckerman

SOUL EATER Vol. 15 © 2009 Atsushi Ohkubo / SQUARE ENIX. All rights reserved. First published in Japan in 2009 by SQUARE ENIX CO., LTD. English translation rights arranged with SQUARE ENIX CO., LTD. and Hachette Book Group through Tuttle-Mori Agency, Inc.

Translation © 2013 by SQUARE ENIX CO., LTD.

Yen Press
Hachette Book Group
237 Park Avenue, New York, NY 10017

HachetteBookGroup.com
YenPress.com

Yen Press is an imprint of Hachette Book Group, Inc. The Yen Press name and logo are trademarks of Hachette Book Group, Inc.

First Yen Press Edition: July 2013

ISBN: 978-0-316-23490-0

10 9 8 7 6 5 4 3

BVG

Printed in the United States of America